A Survey of Guyanese History

A Collection Of Historical Essays And Articles By A Guyanese Scholar

Dr. Winston Mc Gowan

Copyright © 2018 by Dr. Winston Mc Gowan
All rights reserved. No part of this publication may be reproduced, distributed, or transmitted in any form or by any means, including photocopying, recording, or other electronic or mechanical methods, without the prior written permission of the publisher, except in the case of brief quotations embodied in critical reviews and certain other noncommercial uses permitted by copyright law. For permission requests, write to the publisher, at the address below.

Publisher
Guyenterprise
234 Lance Gibbs and Irving Streets,
Queenstown, Georgetown,
Guyana
guyenterprise.ltd@gmail.com

Production Editor: Danielle Swain
Design and Layout: Maria Lopes

First printed in Georgetown, Guyana, 2018
by F&H Printing

ISBN 978-976-96182-0-6

Contents

Foreword	A Historical Exploration..X
Preface	A Survey of Guyanese History............................XV
	Abbreviations...XVIII

Part One	General Historical Descriptions	1
Chapter 1	Guyana, 200 years ago...2	
Chapter 2	Guyana, 100 years ago...6	

Part Two	Demography	22
Chapter 3	Guyana: past and present: A Historical Demographic Outline...23	
Chapter 4	Demographic change in nineteenth century Guyana, 1800 - 1850.................................28	

Part Three	The slave trade, slavery and abolition	36
Chapter 5	The coming of Africans to Guyana................37	
Chapter 6	The resistance of captive Africans to the Atlantic Slave Trade in West Africa...............45	
Chapter 7	Slave rebellions at sea..56	
Chapter 8	Some features of the Slavery system in Guyana..63	
Chapter 9	The origins of the 1763 Berbice Slave Rebellion..67	
Chapter 10	The Causes of the 1823 Demerara Slave rebellion...72	
Chapter 11	John Smith and the origins of the 1823 Demerara Slave Rebellion..........................76	

CHAPTER 12	QUAMINA AND THE 1823 DEMERARA SLAVE REBELLION..80
CHAPTER 13	THE COURSE OF THE 1823 DEMERARA SLAVE REBELLION..86
CHAPTER 14	THE CONSEQUENCES OF THE 1823 DEMERARA SLAVE REBELLION........................91
CHAPTER 15	THE DISTINCTIVE FEATURES AND SIGNIFICANCE OF THE 1823 DEMERARA SLAVE REBELLION..97
CHAPTER 16	THE 1763 AND 1823 SLAVE REBELLIONS: A COMPARATIVE PERSPECTIVE....................101
CHAPTER 17	THE IMPACT OF THE RESTRICTION AND ABOLITION OF THE TRANS-ATLANTIC SLAVE TRADE IN DEMERARA - ESSEQUIBO, 1805 - 1831..105
CHAPTER 18	SLAVERY, ABOLITION AND EMANCIPATION............113
CHAPTER 19	SLAVERY AND APPRENTICESHIP IN GUYANA........116
CHAPTER 20	SLAVERY AND INDENTURESHIP IN GUYANA: A COMPARATIVE PERSPECTIVE....................120

PART FOUR	ECONOMIC HISTORY	124
CHAPTER 21	THE BEGINNING OF THE SUGAR INDUSTRY IN GUYANA..125
CHAPTER 22	THE BRITISH GUIANA SUGAR INDUSTRY IN 1900..128
CHAPTER 23	THE BEGINNINGS OF RICE CULTIVATION IN GUYANA..132
CHAPTER 24	THE BEGINNING OF THE GOLD MINING INDUSTRY IN GUYANA..141
CHAPTER 25	THE ORIGINS OF THE FISHING INDUSTRY IN GUYANA..147
CHAPTER 26	BRITISH GUIANA'S FISHING INDUSTRY: PROGRESS AND PROBLEMS 1894-1960....................153
CHAPTER 27	GUYANA'S PURSUIT OF A DIVERSIFIED EXPORT ECONOMY..161

PART FIVE	CHURCH HISTORY	168
CHAPTER 28	THE BEGINNINGS OF THE CONGREGATIONAL CHURCH IN GUYANA	169
CHAPTER 29	CHRISTIANITY AND SLAVERY: REACTIONS TO THE WORK OF THE LONDON MISSIONARY SOCIETY IN DEMERARA, 1808 - 1813	179
CHAPTER 30	THE ORIGINS OF THE PRESBYTERIAN CHURCH IN GUYANA	193
CHAPTER 31	100 YEARS OF THE SALVATION ARMY IN GUYANA, 1895 - 1995	198
CHAPTER 32	FROM OBSCURITY TO PROMINENCE: THE STORY OF THE FULL GOSPEL FELLOWSHIP, 1964 - 2014	209
CHAPTER 33	THE EVANGELICAL WITNESS IN GUYANA: A HISTORICAL OUTLINE	213

PART SIX	EDUCATION	219
CHAPTER 34	THE BEGINNINGS OF ELEMENTARY EDUCATION, 1800 - 1840	220
CHAPTER 35	PRIMARY EDUCATION IN GUYANA 100 YEARS AGO	224
CHAPTER 36	THE STORY OF QUEEN'S COLLEGE: ITS FIRST 150 YEARS, 1844 - 1994	229
CHAPTER 37	LANDMARKS IN THE HISTORY OF QUEEN'S COLLEGE, 1844 - 1994	237
CHAPTER 38	UNIVERSITY OF GUYANA: FORTY YEARS LATER, 2003	242
CHAPTER 39	WALTER RODNEY AND THE UNIVERSITY OF GUYANA	246
CHAPTER 40	WALTER RODNEY, THE HISTORIAN	255
CHAPTER 41	GRADUATE STUDIES IN HISTORY AT THE UNIVERSITY OF GUYANA	261
CHAPTER 42	THE UNIVERSITY OF GUYANA HISTORY SOCIETY	265

Part Seven	Cricket	276
Chapter 43	Some major developments and landmarks in the history of Guyanese cricket	277
Chapter 44	Robert Christiani: Guyanas first Test Centurion	288
Chapter 45	The Bourda Cricket Ground and its Heroes	293
Chapter 46	Profiles of two successful Test cricketers: John Trim and Clive Lloyd	301
Chapter 47	Lance Gibbs, Bowler Par Excellence	306
Chapter 48	Famous Indo - Guyanese Cricketers	312
Chapter 49	Shivnarine Chanderpaul: From Unity to the top of the world	321
Chapter 50	More truth about Carl Hooper	325
Chapter 51	History at Bourda, 2005	328
Chapter 52	Remembering the glory days of West Indies cricket	331

Part Eight	Labour and Trade Unionism	337
Chapter 53	Hubert Nathaniel Critchlow and the beginning of Trade Unionism in Guyana	338
Chapter 54	Obstacles to the early trade union movement in Guyana, 1919-1930	346

Part Nine	Biography	350
Chapter 55	UWI Honours Sister Mary Noel Menezes	351
Chapter 56	Pryor Jonas: Mentor, Educator, Sportsman and Sports Commentator	355
Chapter 57	UWI Honours Outstanding Guyanese Academic: Gordon Rohlehr	359

| PART TEN | NATIONALISM AND THE MOVEMENT TOWARDS INDEPENDENCE | 363 |

CHAPTER 58	THE ORIGINS AND GROWTH OF NATIONALISM IN BRITISH GUIANA, 1880-1961	364
CHAPTER 59	BRITISH PERCEPTIONS OF GUYANESE POLITICIANS IN 1953: CHEDDI JAGAN	382
CHAPTER 60	TURNING BACK THE CLOCK: THE SUSPENSION OF THE BRITISH GUIANA CONSTITUTION IN 1953	387
CHAPTER 61	THE UNITED STATES OF AMERICA AND THE BEGINNING OF THE DELAYED POLITICAL INDEPENDENCE OF BRITISH GUIANA	394

| PART ELEVEN | MISCELLANY | 402 |

CHAPTER 62	THE BRITISH OCCUPATION OF GUYANA IN 1796	403
CHAPTER 63	CHRISTMAS IN GUYANA 200 YEARS AGO	408
CHAPTER 64	THE EFFECTS OF THE HAITIAN REVOLUTION ON GUYANA	414
CHAPTER 65	VILLAGE PROBLEMS AT THE END OF THE NINETEENTH CENTURY	417
CHAPTER 66	MILESTONES IN GUYANESE HISTORY	422
	END NOTES	442
	A SELECT BIBLIOGRAPHY	455
	INDEX	462

Foreword

A Historical Exploration

This collection of essays is perhaps the sum total of the historical exploration of a Guyanese scholar, who over the span of a fruitful academic career, applied historical methodology and passion to a wide range of issues, topics and subject areas germane to a proper understanding of aspects of the society in which he lived and worked. The collection is presented in eleven sections, each containing a number of essays, some more than others, shedding scholarly insights on aspects of the subtitled section.

This collection has been devised to offer an overview of current topics in the field of history, education, nationalism, labour, biographies and cricket. Thus, it is neither a complete text on any one topic or subject, nor a conference proceedings but simply a compilation of high quality research papers, many of which have been published in first-class, international journals. Instead, it is here presented as a collection of fifty plus high-quality essays, which together provide an overview of the frontline research of a committed Guyanese, erudite scholar and respected university academic.

Prof. Emeritus, Winston McGowan, BA Hons (UWI, 1965), PhD (London, 1979), gave distinguished service to the University of Guyana from 1970 to 2008. He was promoted to Senior Lecturer in 1980, and for the great volume and exceptional quality of his work as a Lecturer, his outstanding research, publications and administration, made Professor of Guyanese and West Indian History in 2000. He served as Head of the Department of History (1985-1996), Assistant Dean of the Faculty of Arts (1975-1976), Coordinator of the MA Programme in Guyanese and West Indian History (1990-2008), and Chairman of the Board for Graduate Studies (1992-1996).

In addition to the excellence of his scholarly and academic output, Prof. McGowan enhanced the University of Guyana's international reputation through his service as External Examiner for Doctoral Dissertations at the

University of Waterloo; Chairman of the Nominating Committee and Secretary-Treasurer of the Association of Caribbean Historians and an Examiner for the Caribbean Secondary Examination Certificate in History.

McGowan specialized in African history, Transatlantic Slavery and World Revolutions. He subsequently broadened his academic interest to include World Civilization and as a diversion, the history of Guyanese and Caribbean Cricket. As an academic he was highly thought of by both his students and his peers and for several years occupied the Walter Rodney Chair. He was a prolific researcher and respected presenter at the annual Association of Caribbean Historians conferences. As the Walter Rodney Professor, he was required to undertake research in Guyanese history, an obligation he honoured faithfully and with considerable distinction.

This collection is subdivided into eleven sections and much of what is found in these sections are original works, many in areas previously unattended.

The first section of the book is of special character. It deals with the early history of the Guyana society. The two essays in this section, titled, **Guyana, 200 years ago and Guyana, 100 years ago,** respond to a long-felt need. In view of the deficiencies of the existing research, such an overview is valuable in and by itself. Further, it is much needed to provide some contextual background for some of the subsequent sections. The second section comprises two essays, whose common denominator is the demographic formation of the society. **Guyana, Past and Present: A Historical Demographic Outline and Demographic Change in nineteenth - century Guyana, 1800 - 1850** are perhaps the first focal population studies on early Guyana. Using primary source material, the author provides interesting insights into the early population growth and settlement patterns of Guyana.

Section 3 focuses on African enslavement, resistance, abolition, emancipation and Indian Indentureship. As an academic teaching at the University of Guyana, McGowan specialized in the experience of the enslaved African in Guyana and the Caribbean and while the historiography on enslavement per se is far from sparse, McGowan's primary focus is the African's resistance and self-liberating activities.

This is the largest section consisting of sixteen essays and includes several original discourses dealing with the traffic in captive persons and the enslavement phenomenon. Here McGowan is in his element. He is the unrivalled scholar in the field, having researched the area for most of his life as a scholar. His essays on resistance on the African slave coast and during the transatlantic passage fractured the veil of silence on self-liberating activities of enslaved peoples outside of the Americas, while his comparative studies offered enabling insights, helping both students and scholars to better appreciate the consistent tenor of resistance throughout the period.

Section 4 focuses on the economic history of Guyana starting with the dominance of the cane sugar industry followed by the emergence of the rice, gold mining, and fishing industries and the pursuit of a diversified export economy. Here his Walter Rodney Chair essays on the fishing industry stand out as the single most focused scholarly examination of this economic activity in Guyana.

This is followed by a section on church history, including the beginning of the Congregational Church in Guyana, Christianity and Slavery: Reactions to the work of the London Missionary Society in Demerara, 1808 - 1813, The origins of the Presbyterian Church in Guyana, One Hundred years of the Salvation Army in Guyana, 1895 - 1995, From obscurity to prominence: The Story of the Full Gospel Fellowship, 1964 - 2014 and the Evangelical Witness in Guyana: A Historical Outline. McGowan is a robust religious leader with a large denominational congregation in the capital city Georgetown. His focus on church history therefore comes as no surprise and sheds much light on another of the grey areas of local history.

In the next section McGowan explores the history of education in Guyana. In this section McGowan presents the Beginnings of Elementary Education, 1800 - 1840 and Primary education in Guyana 100 years ago; but his real focus is on Queen's College and the University of Guyana to which he adds two vignettes on the celebrated Guyanese historian, Walter Rodney, and an interesting piece on the University of Guyana History Society.

McGowan is a faithful follower of Cricket in general but more particularly of West Indian Cricket and while he features some major developments and landmarks in the history of cricket in Guyana, he is primarily taken with the notables of Guyanese Cricket, Robert Christiani, John Trim, Clive Lloyd, Lance Gibbs, Shivnarine Chanderpaul and Carl Hooper. A lover of Caribbean cricket would find each a very special gem. There is next a brief exploration into the early trade union movement in Guyana. Here there are two essays, one a semi-biographical piece on Hubert Nathaniel Critchlow, the father of the local trade union movement, and the beginning of Trade Unionism in Guyana and the other examining the obstacles to the early trade union movement in Guyana, 1919-1930.

Another tour, essentially biographical, treats with three significant personalities who have, in various ways, exercised some influence on McGowan's life. These include, Distinguished Emeritus History Professor, Mary Noel Menezes, Pryor Jonas, teacher and cricket commentator, and Gordon Rohlehr, Caribbean scholar and critic of West Indian literature.

The penultimate section treats with Nationalism and the Movement towards Independence and includes such works as the origins and growth of nationalism in British Guiana, 1880 -1961, British perceptions of Guiana politicians in 1953: Cheddi Jagan, Turning back the clock: the Suspension of the British Guiana constitution in 1953, and the United States of America and the beginning of the delayed political independence of British Guiana.

McGowan uses these essays to shed further light on a vexing period of local history, the anti-colonial movement and the frustration of the liberation struggle by the Anglo-American alliance fearful that Jagan was intent on turning Guyana into a communist state. This collection comes after the release of British and American documents which together shed interesting light on the conspiracy.

The final section aptly titled, Miscellany, consists of such varied explorations as the British Occupation of Guyana in 1796, Christmas in Guyana 200 years ago, The effects of the Haitian Revolution on Guyana, Village problems at the end of the nineteenth century and Milestones in Guyana History. While each marks an important elaboration of our understanding of the event, the impact of the Haitian Revolution and the effects of the British occupation are without a doubt the pieces most sought after by the researcher and student of Guyanese history.

The process of historical writing involves investigation and analysis of competing ideas, facts and purported facts to create coherent narratives that explain "what happened" and "why or how it happened" and modern historical writing is not shy on drawing upon the social sciences, including economics, sociology and politics, to explain historical events. An important part of the contribution of many modern historians is the verification or dismissal of earlier historical interpretations and accounts through reviewing newly discovered sources, interrogating recent scholarship or through parallel disciplines like sociology.

In this collection, McGowan, the historian, has drawn on a number of parallel disciplines and in the end, has done great service to his profession and his society. Though pitched at an undergraduate audience for popular access and appreciation, there is nothing condescending about the tone of his writing, nor the complexity of his reasoning. He treats all the topics examined in order to convey both breadth and depth and provides more than enough to satisfy the appetite of the voracious reader and the committed student of history.

For readers seeking an accessible introduction to an academic text on many of the silent aspects of the historical development of the Guyana society this is a great collection of essays. But for a variety of other excellent reasons, this is a wonderful addition to your collection as well as an enjoyable and informative read.

James Rose

Preface

A Survey of Guyanese History

This publication is not a General History of Guyana. Regrettably the lack of an authoritative modern general text still remains a major deficiency in the growing historiography of our country. A Survey of Guyanese History is a collection of historical essays or articles about Guyana which I wrote during my thirty odd years as a member of the teaching staff of the Department or Division of History of the University of Guyana, where I served from my initial appointment in 1970 to my retirement in 2008.

The Survey covers a wide range of subjects and is arranged under eleven sections or themes in which the collection is divided. The length of the essays or articles varies considerably, depending on the forum for which they were originally prepared. The majority of them were prepared as newspaper articles, while others, especially a few of the longer ones, were papers presented at conferences or articles published in scholarly journals or books. The other lengthy ones are either the text of hitherto unpublished public lectures or multipart newspaper articles. The shorter essays are for the most part one or two-part newspaper articles or articles presented in little-known, sometimes non-professional, magazines which required brevity. Many of the essays in the collection have been published before, especially in the daily or weekly column entitled "History Today" or "History This Week" which the History Society and the Department or Division of History of the University of Guyana maintained from the early 1990s in two of our country's daily newspapers, at first the **Guyana Chronicle** and later the **Stabroek News**. This was a major component of the Society's and Department's/Division's public education programme designed to inform Guyanese of their country's history. Several of the essays, however, have never been published before, including some that were written especially for inclusion in this collection. Many of the essays in the collection have benefited from the work of other scholars. None of them, however, is merely a synthesis of previously available information. Each one is partly a result of my own independent research, enhancing knowledge on the particular subject. Several of them, such as those on the history of fishing and some on the history of cricket, for example, are completely the product of original research on a hitherto unaddressed subject.

The collection reflects the special focus of much of my research about Guyanese History over the years. This focus included a concentration on a few subjects, notably African resistance to the Transatlantic Slave Trade and slavery in the territory that now constitutes Guyana, in particular the 1823 East Coast Demerara slave rebellion. Other areas of focus were church history, the life and work of Walter Rodney and the history of Guyanese and West Indies cricket. In general, the focus of my research, and as a result of this collection of essays, has been the political, economic and social history of Guyana, with little attention to cultural history and the history of ideas. Most of the essays in the collection, however lengthy, should be regarded, at best, as an introduction to the subject. To facilitate further exploration of the subject a short list of published books and articles is attached to most essays under the heading "For Further Reading". In the rare cases where such a list is not included, it is simply because I am not aware of any helpful accessible other publication on the subject. To assist readers further, a bibliography of major works on Guyanese History is included.

It is hoped that this collection of essays will be of benefit not only to the general public, but also especially to teachers and students of Guyanese and Caribbean History. If that hope is realized, the collection will be a useful addition to the existing body of knowledge on this subject.

I cannot conclude this introduction without acknowledging the persons and institutions who have greatly facilitated the production of this book. Notable among them are past and contemporary professional historians and the staff of the Guyana National [now the Walter Rodney] Archives and the Caribbean Research Library of the University of Guyana, where I conducted much of my research. A special debt of gratitude is also owed to the University's History Society and Department/Division of History for providing the stimulus for research and writing and to the **Guyana Chronicle** and **Stabroek News** for willingly providing the outlet for the original appearance of many of the essays.

I thank my friend and former colleague, Dr. James Rose, for his generous foreword. I have always valued his knowledge of Guyanese History, viewing him as the leading authority especially of the post – Emancipation period of the subject.

Sincere thanks also to my immediate family for allowing me the time necessary to produce the collection.

My greatest human debt, however, is to my former classmate and long-standing friend, Victor Insanally, for agreeing to undertake the publication of the book, including the raising of funds to make that possible. The staff of his agency, Guyenterprise, has been extremely helpful throughout, in particular Danielle Swain who, among other things, typed the lengthy manuscript. I thank them for their collaboration.

Above all, I am deeply grateful to the God whom I serve for His wonderful grace which has permitted and sustained my long professional career as a teacher, researcher and writer of history.

Winston Mc Gowan

ABBREVIATIONS

AFC	Alliance for Change
APNU	A Partnership for National Unity
B.G.L.U.	British Guiana Labour Union
CJRC	Cheddi Jagan Research Centre
C.M.S.	Church Missionary Society
C.O.	Colonial Office records, Public Record Office, London, England.
Encl.	Enclosed/enclosure.
F.O.	Foreign Office records, Public Record Office, London, England.
G.C.C.	Georgetown Cricket Club
G.I.W.U.	Guiana Industrial Workers Union.
Ibid.	Latin Ibidem, in the same book, article or place.
L.C.P.	League of Coloured Peoples
L.M.S.	London Missionary Society (Records), England.
M.C.P.	Minutes of the Court of Policy, in the Walter Rodney Archives, Georgetown.
M.P.C.A.	Man Power Citizens' Association.
n.d.	Not dated.
N.L.F.	National Labour Front.
op.cit.	Abbreviation for Latin opera citate, in the work already cited.
P.A.C.	Political Affairs Committee.
P.N.C.	People's National Congress.
P.P.P.	People's Progressive Party.
P.R.O.	Public Record Office, London, England.
Q.C.	Queen's College, Georgetown.
S.P.A.	Sugar Producers Association.
U.C.W.I.	University College of the West Indies.

U.D.P.	United Democratic Party.
U.F.	United Force.
U.G.	University of Guyana.
U.W.I.	University of the West Indies.
WIC	The Dutch West India Company .
W.P.A.	Working People's Alliance.
WRA	Walter Rodney Archives, Georgetown, formerly N.A.G., (National Archives of Guyana).

Part One

General Historical Descriptions

New Amsterdam in the late 18th century

Members of the Arbitral Tribunal of 1899

Stabroek and New Town about 1800

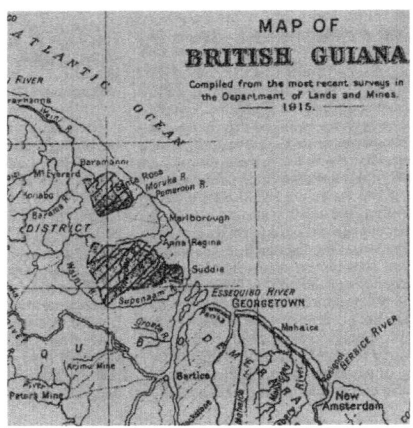

A Map of British Guiana in 1915

Chapter 1

Guyana, 200 Years Ago

This chapter focuses on certain aspects of the history of Guyana 200 years ago. An analysis and evaluation of the situation then will permit an appreciation or understanding of the momentous changes which have taken place over these two centuries.

Perhaps the most obvious structural difference between Guyana of the late eighteenth century and modern Guyana is that in the late 1790s the area was not unified politically. Rather it consisted of two entities, namely, the colony of Berbice and the United Colony of Demerara-Essequibo, of which Demerara was the more progressive part. Until 1789 Berbice, Demerara and Essequibo were, in fact, three separate colonies. It was only in 1831 that they were finally united into a single entity, British Guiana, the name which the country bore until it was changed to Guyana on the achievement of political independence from Britain on 26 May, 1966.

In 1797 Berbice and Demerara-Essequibo had just begun what proved to be a long and virtually uninterrupted period of British rule which lasted 170 years, for in April 1796 Britain had taken advantage of the existence of international warfare to occupy these Dutch colonies[1]. In 1797 the two colonies were still in political transition. Their civilian administration still remained in the hands of the Dutch governor and other Dutch officials, but the British held military control by means of an occupying garrison. Literacy in Dutch was necessary for residents in both colonies to qualify for election or appointment to the Council of Policy and the Court of Justice, the two dominant political institutions in both colonies, where deliberations were conducted in Dutch.

The transition from Dutch to British colonies was also evident in other areas. For example, there was a growing influx of British settlers, many of whom purchased estates from Dutch proprietors who returned to the Netherlands permanently. The growing strength of the British population in

Berbice and Demerara-Essequibo was being reflected in a marked increase of British influence. The use of the English language gained ground, dominating the local press. Moreover, for the first time government proclamations began to appear in Dutch as well as in English, owing to the appointment of a special Dutch-English translator.

The growth of British influence in the two colonies in the late 1790s was also reflected in the establishment of the Anglican Church, which for the first time was able to hold regular services. These services were conducted on Sundays in Demerara-Essequibo by the chaplain of the British garrison in a small room in the Court House in the capital, Stabroek, for as yet no building had been constructed for worship. Like the other churches, namely, the Lutherans in Berbice and the Dutch Reformed Church in both colonies, the Anglicans catered exclusively for the minority white population. They prohibited slaves from attending services, for fear that exposure to Christianity would make them more discontented and rebellious.

Nevertheless, the white population of both colonies was notorious for its lack of religiosity and piety. As a resident British physician, George Pinckard, noted,

> "the total neglect of sacred ordinances...prevails in these colonies. All the ceremonies of the Sabbath are utterly disregarded. No church or temple is to be found in the settlements...Sunday, it is true, has been set apart as a day of rest, but no solemn ceremony marks it as the Sabbath. Idleness and merriment alone distinguish it from the other days of the week." [2]

At that time Berbice and Demerara-Essequibo were populated by three races, namely, Amerindians, Europeans and Africans. The Blacks, who were mostly slaves and constituted the bulk of the labour force of the two colonies, were more numerous than either of the other two races. Their only hope of gaining freedom was by flight or rebellion, for manumission was extremely rare. Amerindians, on the other hand, were free for the Dutch government had outlawed enslavement of Amerindians in 1793. They were employed to maintain the slave system. As Thomas Pierronet, an American visitor, noted in 1798, Amerindians "are under the protection of the Dutch government who find them the only barrier against the desertion of their Negroes, who are frequently apprehended by the Bucks." [3]

In 1797 Berbice and Demerara were witnessing the early phase of significant urban development which would eventually transform the capitals of these two colonies into the most important towns in the area. New Amsterdam, the new capital of Berbice, was in its infancy. Yet Pinckard was impressed with Government House there, declaring it "beyond all comparison, the handsomest and most spacious edifice I have yet seen in South America."[4] Stabroek (renamed Georgetown in 1812), the capital of Demerara-Essequibo, was in 1797, after sixteen years of existence, still in its early phase of development. It was virtually identical with the present Georgetown ward, Stabroek. It consisted of one main street, Brickdam, and less than 200 houses built in two rows on either side of this road, with two canals at the back of the houses. One canal was the present Croal Street/South Road canal, while the other existed where Hadfield Street is now located.

In the opinion of most English residents, the most significant feature of Berbice and Demerara-Essequibo in 1797 was the economic growth which these colonies were enjoying. Since their establishment as European colonies-Essequibo by 1616, Berbice in 1627 and Demerara in 1746-they had been distinguished by underdevelopment, owing to the low esteem in which they were held by the Netherlands. As a result, they suffered from limited investment and an inadequate supply of slave labour.

The British occupation of these colonies in 1796 brought immediate change to this situation. Englishmen were impressed by the fertility and potential of the comparatively virgin soil of Berbice and Demerara-Essequibo, especially when compared with the growing soil exhaustion and declining profitability of older British colonies in the Caribbean, such as Barbados and Antigua. The traders used their dominance of the transatlantic traffic in captive Africans to supply Berbice and Demerara-Essequibo with slaves without restrictions over an extended period for the first time in the colonies' history. Thus Pinckard noted, "great numbers of slaves have been imported, since our arrival."[5] Within two and a half years of British occupation an estimated 13,300 slaves were imported into the two colonies.

With this improved labour supply new plantations were established, the area under cultivation on existing estates was extended and a remarkable increase in agricultural production occurred. There was such a remarkable transformation that by 1800 Berbice and Demerara-Essequibo, whose economic growth had long been stifled, had become the second largest producer of sugar in the British West Indies, the largest producer of coffee in the British Empire and the greatest producer of raw cotton in the entire world. This proved to be arguably the most buoyant period in the entire economic history of Guyana. Admittedly, the beneficiaries of the wealth generated were not the black slaves who provided the labour, but their white masters who exploited them. Many planters also gained additional wealth by cultivating plantains for local consumption, mainly by slaves.

In short, 200 years ago Guyana was in the process of experiencing very significant changes which have permanently affected the country's history.[6] Though in some areas considerable progress has since been made, in others the country may have retrogressed. This seems certainly to have been the case with the agricultural economy which has lost its highly diversified character with three main staples. Today in terms of income generation from exports, Guyana possesses only two major agricultural commodities, namely, sugar and rice, neither of which currently enjoys the status which cotton, coffee and sugar all possessed in the international market in 1797.

For Further Reading

Bolingbroke, Henry	**A Voyage to Demerary, Containing a Statistical Account of the Settlements There and Those of the Essequibo, the Berbice, and other Contiguous Rivers of Guiana** (orig. pub. 1808). Reprint Georgetown, Daily Chronicle Ltd, 1942).
McGowan, Winston	"The French Revolutionary Period in Demerara-Essequibo, 1793-1802", **History Gazette,** No.55, April 1993.
Pinckard, George	**Letters from Guiana, 1796-97** (extracted from **Notes on the West Indies** (Georgetown: Daily Chronicle Ltd., 1942).
St. Clair, Thomas	**A Soldier's Soujourn in British Guiana, 1806-1808** (Georgetown: Daily Chronicle Ltd., 1947).
Thompson, Alvin	**Colonialism and Underdevelopment in Guyana, 1580-1803** (Bridgetown: Carib Research and Publications, Inc.,1987) .

Chapter 2

Guyana, 100 Years Ago

Introduction

One hundred years ago Guyana was in many ways markedly different from what it is today. Where its political status is concerned, today it is an independent republic within the British Commonwealth, whereas in 1900 it was a colony of Great Britain named British Guiana, which had been subjected to uninterrupted British rule since 1803.

In 1900 the country had just experienced the trauma of having its boundaries with its western neighbour, Venezuela, submitted to international arbitrators. It was anticipated that the decision of the arbitrators in Paris, France in 1899 would bring an end to Venezuelan claims to territory in the county of Essequibo. This expectation, however, proved eventually to be false, for before the colony gained its political independence from Britain in 1966 Venezuela challenged the validity of the arbitrators' award and renewed its spurious claim to a sizeable portion of Essequibo. This claim was reaffirmed in 1999 by Venezuela who used the centenary of the award to repudiate it vigorously.

At the time when the boundary arbitrators met in Paris in 1899, British Guiana was in many ways in transition. One significant area of change was the country's politics.

Politics

Since at least the eighteenth century the country's political system had been dominated by white planters who enjoyed a virtual monopoly of political power under an archaic constitution which they consistently refused to modify so as to retain their privileges. Eventually, however, modest changes were made to the constitution in 1891 in response to a vigorous campaign for constitutional reform led by middle-class Coloureds and Blacks, supported by Portuguese businessmen. Among the changes were a reduction in the property or income qualifications to sit in the country's legislature to individuals other than owners of a large quantity of land.

As a result of these changes and the introduction in 1896 of secret ballot at national elections, by 1900 a few Coloureds and Blacks had won seats in the legislature, breaking the monopoly of the old planter oligarchy. This was the beginning of a significant shift in the colony's political balance of power in the next twenty-five years, which witnessed the progressive displacement of the white sugar planters from the legislature and their replacement mostly by representatives of the black and coloured sections of the population. This increasing ascendancy of non-white elements in the society which occurred between 1900 and 1925 and the progressive transfer to them of much of the political power formerly possessed by the planters greatly disturbed both the planters and the colonial authorities.

Whereas by 1900 black and coloured residents had begun to experience a measure of political power, no Amerindian, Chinese, East Indian or Portuguese had as yet tried to gain a seat in the legislature. It was not until the following year, 1901, that the Portuguese made such a move, but all three Portuguese candidates who contested the elections lost. Five years later, however, Francis Dias, a barrister and businessman, became the first Portuguese to enter the colonial legislature, ten years before, the first East Indian became a member in 1916.

In short, in 1900 the colony was in the early stage of an important process of political change which would eventually result in the active participation of all its ethnic groups in national politics. The working class, however, was still completely unrepresented in national politics for its members were unable to satisfy the criteria for either the franchise or for candidature for a seat in the legislature. Unlike modern elections, which are conducted on the principle of universal adult suffrage introduced in 1953, in 1900 there were high property qualifications as well as a literacy test for the franchise which greatly restricted the size of the electorate. Thus, under this narrow franchise only 3000 persons out of a total population of about 320,000 qualified to vote at general elections. This electorate was extremely small when compared with that of the other main British Caribbean territories.

Furthermore, in 1900 the structure of government was very different from what exists today. British Guiana was governed then by three main bodies, the Court of Policy, the Combined Court and the Executive Council. The most important of these bodies was the 16-man Court of Policy, which consisted of seven appointed government officials and eight elected non-official members (five from rural constituencies and three from the urban constituencies of Georgetown and New Amsterdam) and was presided over by the colony's governor, who had both a deliberative and a casting vote. The Court of Policy was responsible for all matters with the exception of those related to finance and taxation which were dealt with by the Combined Court.

The Combined Court, which had the power especially to impose taxes and to control the appropriation of public revenue, was a body comprising the entire Court of Policy and six elected individuals known as the Financial Representatives. The Executive Council, in striking contrast, was a completely non-elected body. It consisted of the Governor, who since December 1897 was Sir Walter Joseph Sendall, the Attorney General, the Government Secretary, and two other officials and three members of the planting and business community, all five nominated by the Crown. Its duty was to perform the executive and administrative functions of the Court of Policy, but it was not accountable to that body. In 1900 all its members were white, unlike the mixed racial composition of the Court of Policy and the Combined Court. The non-official members of the Court of Policy and the Financial Representatives were elected every five years. Like the other members of these bodies and the Executive Council, they were all males, for women were not yet eligible to vote or to enter the legislature. While in 1900 British Guiana was experiencing the results of the important constitutional reforms of 1891, equally striking changes were being witnessed in its economic life. These economic changes were mainly as a result of grave difficulties encountered by the colony's sugar industry.

THE ECONOMY

In 1900 the sugar industry, the pillar of the economy since the 1820s, was experiencing a prolonged crisis dating back to 1884. This crisis was due mainly to the effective competition which British Guianese sugar was encountering in its traditional market in the United Kingdom from government-subsidised beet sugar from Germany, France, Austria and other European countries. The great impact of this crisis on the sugar industry and the colonial economy as a whole is examined in detail below as well as the expedients employed by the Guianese planters to survive it.[7]

In short, in 1900 one of British Guiana's greatest needs was the restoration of the ailing sugar industry, which was the main concern of the second West

Indian Agricultural Conference held in Barbados in January of that year. The planters soon secured a measure of relief by a decision of the Canadian government to purchase Guianese and other British imperial sugar at preferential rates. Their main hope of recovery, however, was the abolition of the beet sugar subsidies by the continental European governments which was finally achieved in 1903 largely as a result of continuous pressure exerted by the British government on the governments of the beet-producing countries.

While the crisis in the sugar industry continued in 1900, British Guiana was experiencing an unexpected significant effect of the crisis, namely, the diversification of its export economy which in 1884 rested almost completely on sugar and its by-products, rum and molasses. The devastating results of the crisis forced the local colonial authorities and the metropolitan government in London to recognise the danger of having such a narrowly-based economy and the urgent need to support and develop other economic initiatives to counterbalance sugar monoculture. Such initiatives had been consistently and successfully opposed by the sugar plantocracy since the end of slavery in 1838 for fear that they would divert much-needed labour from the sugar industry. Owing, however, to the chronic depression in the sugar industry after 1884, the planters, many of whom were forced to retrench workers, could no longer gain support from the local and metropolitan governments for their traditional policy of opposition to peasant agriculture and the development of the interior of the country.

By 1900 two new industries, gold mining and rice cultivation, had begun to flourish.[8] Gold began to be exported regularly on a small scale in 1885 when new sources were discovered in the Essequibo, Mazaruni and Cuyuni Rivers. Its production increased substantially from 1889 as a minor gold rush developed and reached its peak in 1893-94 when an estimated 138,528 ounces worth over half a million pounds sterling were exported. Thereafter there was a disconcerting decline in both the quantity and quality of gold produced, owing partly to the exhaustion of the larger and richer claims and the non-discovery of new ones and the drying up of capital which initially came from local sources. Nevertheless in 1900 about 112,000 ounces of gold were exported, contributing about 20 per cent of the total value of the colony's exports. The gold mining industry was providing employment for about 5000 individuals, principally persons of African descent from the coast. The seasonal withdrawal of these miners from the villages to the goldfields weakened agriculture there and frequently caused a shortage of vegetables and ground provisions on the coast.

In 1900 the area under rice cultivation was about 18,000 acres compared to 4000 acres in 1890. Production, though increasing, was still insufficient to satisfy local demand, thus necessitating the continued importation of rice especially from India. However, rice imports, which in 1900 were about 11,300 tons compared to about 22,000 tons in 1895, were declining as local production rose. The colony continued to import rice until 1922, but began to export it regularly from 1903 when a small quantity of five tons was sent to other territories in the British Caribbean. Its rice industry grew in spite of major problems such as the lack of efficient water control, especially the absence of unfavourable weather conditions, particularly prolonged drought.

While by 1900 rice cultivation and gold mining could be said to be fairly well-established in British Guiana, the mining of diamonds was just beginning. It was in that year that diamonds first appeared in the colony's exports with a small quantity of 996 carats. A company, the British Guiana Diamond Company, was registered and organised operations had begun in the Upper Mazaruni area.

Unlike today, in 1900 fishing was not yet an important economic or industrial pursuit, although the colony's waters, then as now, contained an abundance of fish. Admittedly, however, there was some deep-sea fishing, as a result of which the colonial market, especially in Georgetown, was often well-supplied with fish such as grouper, dolphin and red snapper.[9]

In addition to diamonds, other minor exports in 1900 included cocoa, coffee, corn, cassava, coconuts, balata, starch, gums, fish glue, poultry, cattle, sheep, firewood, shingles, charcoal and timber, especially greenheart, mora and bulletwood. While the colony's major exports, sugar, rum, molasses and gold, were destined mainly for markets in the United Kingdom, the United States, and Canada, most of the minor exports were sent to the British West Indies, but some also to Suriname and the French and Danish West Indies.

Notwithstanding the growing diversification of the colony's economy, sugar and its by-products, rum and molasses, continued to be its pillar. They, however, had lost a significant degree of the dominance they had enjoyed before the depression commenced in 1884. Thus whereas in every year between 1838 and 1883 these three commodities together had contributed at least 88 per cent of the value of the exports of British Guiana, in 1900 they contributed about 70 per cent, with gold and diamonds supplying about 21 per cent. Gold, the colony's second main export in 1900, provided about 87 per cent of the total value of the colony's exports apart from sugar, rum and molasses.

While most of the sugar cane was cultivated on the estates, a small but increasing amount was being produced by black peasants who sold it to neighbouring estates. These and other small farmers, who produced coconuts, vegetables and ground provisions, faced a variety of problems. Prominent among these problems were insufficient capital, the high incidence of praedial larceny, the inadequacy of drainage, irrigation and other infrastructure necessary to cope with flood and drought, diseases which affected their crops, the high cost of transportation of produce, the small size of their landholdings, and the sale of their land because of their inability or unwillingness to pay road and village taxes. The plight of the villagers was partly a reflection of deeper problems of prejudice and discrimination which they were encountering in a plural society where colour, class and race played a significant role.

Social Organisation

In 1900 British Guiana was a multi-ethnic society with distinct classes based on race, colour, and wealth. At the top of the social pyramid were Whites who were senior government officials, plantation owners, attorneys or managers of absentee proprietors and agents of the sugar companies. They were almost invariably British by nationality and did not usually mix with the upper classes of other races. They had their exclusive social clubs, in particular the Georgetown Club founded in 1858, dressed elegantly, lived in luxurious houses often with gorgeous flower gardens and were prominent at high society balls and private dinner parties. Many of them sent their children to Britain for education.

Below this aristocracy was a class of persons consisting mainly of English, Portuguese and Chinese businessmen, black, coloured, Portuguese and East Indian professionals and white doctors and plantation overseers and bookkeepers. They could not afford the luxury of the elite, but they regarded themselves as superior to the working class. Like the elite, they were eligible to vote at national elections and to sit in the Court of Policy and Combined Court. Some of them also sent their children to Britain for schooling.

The next class consisted mostly of small farmers, woodcutters, shopkeepers and others who, like them, were self-employed and possessed modest financial resources. Finally, at the bottom of the social pyramid were the masses, consisting mainly of poor urban and rural workers involved in manual labour and the unemployed. They were principally Blacks, East

Indians and Amerindians. These class divisions were closely related to the demography of the colony.

Demography

In 1900 as today, Guyana was a plural society consisting of five races, namely, Amerindians, Europeans, People of African Descent, East Indians and Chinese. The Europeans comprised two main groups, Britons and Portuguese, who were regarded by the Britons as second-class Whites.

The colony's population in 1900, excluding the Amerindians who lived mainly in the interior and whose numbers were difficult to estimate, was about 280,000. The largest centre of population was the capital, Georgetown, which had a rapidly growing population of about 53,000 residents, while the most populated village and sugar estate were respectively Plaisance and Plantation Lusignan, both on the East Coast of Demerara.

The colony's population was growing slowly mainly through immigration, not natural reproduction, for high mortality rates hindered growth by natural means. Since the early 1880s regular Chinese and Portuguese immigration had ceased and British West Indian, especially Barbadian, immigration, which was substantial in the 1870s and early 1880s, had by 1900 declined to a trickle. However, significant East Indian immigration from India continued annually, as the sugar planters sought not only to make up for the loss of labourers to the goldfields, but also continue their long-standing policy of maintaining an oversupply of labourers so as to depress wages on the estates. Owing, however, to financial difficulties and other problems caused by the depression in the sugar industry, the planters could not afford and did not have any compelling reason or need to bring in as many immigrants as before. Thus whereas in the decade from 1885 to 1894 there was an average annual arrival of 3803 immigrants from India, in the following decade this figure dropped significantly to 2744. In 1900, however, seven ships arrived, bringing a total of 4301 East Indian immigrants.

This immigration served to increase the East Indian population in British Guiana. Another cause of its growth was that fewer indentured labourers were claiming the return passage to India to which they were entitled after ten years of residence in the colony. Admittedly, the depressed conditions of the sugar estates did make some of them seek repatriation. Many of them, however, were choosing instead to remain in the colony because of the increased opportunity after 1898 of obtaining land especially to plant rice. The planters, eager to retain an adequate labour force on their estates and unwilling to pay the high cost of the return passage, induced some East Indians to remain there by offering them incentives, particularly the provision of rice beds or small residential lots on the front lands of the estate for rent or purchase. They also encouraged them to accept land in new land settlement and housing schemes in places such as Whim in the Corentyne, Maria's Pleasure in Wakenaam and Bush Lot in West Coast Berbice which were developing into Indian villages.

Owing to these and other factors, in 1900 two striking developments were occurring in the colony's East Indian population. Firstly, partly because of the crisis in the sugar industry, a significant but growing minority of them were moving off the estates to live in East Indian and African villages and, to a lesser extent, in the towns. Thus while in 1891, 28,477 or 32 per cent of the colony's East Indians were estimated to be living off the sugar estates, by 1911 these figures had risen to 58,500 or 51.9 per cent. By 1900 also a comparatively small but increasing number of them, estimated at about 6,000, were settled in Georgetown and its environs, where they were involved in occupations such as watchmen, grooms, grass cutters, dairying, goldsimths, barbers, gardeners, fishermen and domestics.

The second development was that the ethnic balance in the colony's population, which was dominated numerically by Blacks and East Indians, was changing. At the time of the arrival of the first batch of East Indians in British Guiana in 1838, Blacks, numbering more than 90,000, had comprised more than 70 per cent of the colony's population. In 1890, however, they enjoyed only a small numerical advantage over the Indians who by 1900 had begun to outnumber them. Thus whereas in 1891 the colony contained an estimated 115,588 Blacks and 105,463 East Indians, by 1911 the respective figures were 115,486 Blacks and 126,513 East Indians.

This change was due mainly to more intensive East Indian immigration, about 203,000 Indian indentured workers coming between 1838 and 1900, and the limited slow growth of the black population because of comparatively low birth and high mortality rates and miscegenation. The mixed population, which stemmed mainly from the sexual unions Blacks had with all other ethnic groups, grew from an estimated 14,750 in 1851 to about 30,000 in 1891 largely at the expense of the black element in the population.

The East Indian numerical ascendancy over Blacks, evident in 1900, continued and increased during the remainder of the twentieth century. The numerical strength of these two ethnic groups enabled them to play very influential roles in the social life of the colony.

SOCIAL LIFE

One prominent feature of social life in British Guiana in 1900 was the considerable racial consciousness of all the country's ethnic groups. There was even tension within some groups, particularly among the Europeans. The Portuguese were held in contempt by the British residents who did not regard them as fellow Whites and did not invite them to their social activities. Even the colony's decennial censuses differentiated between Portuguese and "English Whites" or "Europeans". Britons could not forget that the Portuguese from Madeira were not "Anglo-Saxon" or from Europe, were Roman Catholics not Protestants, and had originally come to British Guiana to do humble manual labour as workers contracted by British planters.

The strongest racial animosity and friction in the colony, however, existed between the Portuguese and the black working class. Blacks were victims of high prices and unfair business practices at the hands of the Portuguese shopkeepers who had established a virtual monopoly of the huckster and retail trades after pushing Blacks out of these occupations. No violent confrontation between the two groups, however, had occurred since a major incident in 1889 known as the "Cent Bread Riots".

There was much less tension and friction then between Blacks and East Indians than between Blacks and Portuguese. Friction between Blacks and East Indians stemmed partly from differences in religion and culture, but, above all, from economic rivalry for Blacks saw Indians as persons who were robbing them of employment and land and were responsible for the depression of wages. There was, however, little open conflict between the two groups. Such conflict was brief and usually subsided without violence and fatalities.

The most common racial feeling in the colony in 1900 was probably the contempt showed by all races to the Amerindians. Apart from the work of Christian Churches, especially the Anglicans and Roman Catholics, no serious attempt was being made in 1900 to improve the welfare of Amerindians and to integrate them into the rest of the society.

Apart from racism, perhaps the most disturbing feature of social life in British Guiana in 1900 was the problems which resulted from the great paucity of women among the East Indians and Chinese. This situation stemmed from the great sexual imbalance which characterised East Indian and Chinese immigration in which males far outnumbered females. It enabled Indian women to have unusual freedom to choose and change male partners, to be unfaithful and to dissolve their marriages. Such behaviour angered Indian men who often resorted to physical abuse to ensure the fidelity of their wives or punish them for their callous behaviour. There were numerous instances of the brutal murder of wives and lovers by jealous or peeved husbands or ex-paramours, 34 between 1859 and 1870 and 79 between 1872 and 1890. In 1900 such crime, committed mainly by indentured men, was still occurring, but seemed to be declining in frequency.

Another important feature of social life in 1900 was the existence, especially among Blacks, of friendly and burial societies, other benevolent societies and lodges. Many of these organisations had as their main purposes the provision of social interaction and financial assistance and other benefits in times of sickness and death. They grew in number in the 1880s and 1890s as residents, especially the working class, sought desperately to deal with the challenging socio-economic conditions which they were facing.

Socio-Economic Conditions

One of the most obvious features of these conditions in 1900 was the grim plight of workers, who for the most part were recipients of low stationary or declining wages at a time when the cost of living was increasing. There was also endemic unemployment and underemployment, both in the towns and on the rural plantations, and everywhere workers were complaining about the inconsiderate behaviour and treatment of employers.

In spite of the gravity of these problems, however, there were as yet no trade unions in British Guiana. Admittedly, there was some evidence of the beginning of attempts by workers to organise themselves. These attempts were partly in the form of friendly societies among black shop assistants and artisans in Georgetown, a union of printers and compositors, a mechanics' union which aimed at providing employment for its members, and a Bakers' Association consisting of employees of bakeries. There were also in all three counties some Farmers' associations designed partly to fight for financial and technical assistance from the government. Finally, there was a Teachers' Association, founded in 1884, teachers being in 1900 the best organised category of workers.

None of these bodies, however, united a wide range of workers or was a modern labour organisation. There were, in fact, major obstacles to the formation of trade unions. Among them was the illegality of such bodies, the absence of able leadership, and the division of the labour force created by ethnicity, caste, geography, type of work, the intrigue of employers and cultural differences. Workers, in fact, had to work nearly twenty years more for the establishment of the country's first trade union, the British Guiana Labour Union, founded by Hubert Nathaniel Critchlow in January 1919, and until July 1922 for the introduction of legislation legalising the formation of trade unions in the country.[10]

In spite of the absence of trade unions in British Guiana in 1900, sugar estate workers were particularly militant, resorting regularly to desertion and sometimes deserters' strikes. In 1900 warrants were issued for the apprehension of 397 deserters and in 1901 there were 25 strikes on the sugar estates, the largest number in any year since 1889, when 42 such strikes occurred. Most strikes were minor protests which were settled quietly, but a few of them, like those at Blairmont and Peter's Hall in 1899, posed serious difficulties in finding a solution. In striking contrast, in 1900 there was little visible protest by urban workers. It was not until 1905 that urban workers staged a major protest.

Like wages and working conditions, in 1900 health and sanitation left much to be desired. The two most urgent needs in the area of sanitation were an adequate pure water supply for drinking purposes throughout the colony and an efficient method for the disposal of faecal matter, especially in the villages.

Poor sanitation was one contributory cause of the widespread disease in the colony. Three types of diseases were prominent - firstly, those conveyed by impure water, including dysentery, diarrhoea, and enteric fever; secondly, those transacted by insects, especially malaria, yellow fever and filariasis; and thirdly, those like tuberculosis, and ankylostomiasis, resulting from insanitary habits. Victims could secure free medical attention at the colony's five public hospitals, located in Georgetown, New Amsterdam, Suddie, Morawhanna and Bartica. The main causes of death of patients at the two urban public hospitals were phthisis, kidney diseases, dysentery and pneumonia. Other government medical institutions included a leper asylum at Mahaica, a lunatic asylum in New Amsterdam, and an Alms House in Georgetown with 600 inmates which provided for the disabled and elderly.

Health conditions in the villages were particularly unsatisfactory. This situation was partly the result of the fact that the Central Board of Health, influenced by the poor collection of rates in most villages, did little or no work there. Thus though malaria was being tackled through the use of quinine, there were very little anti-malarial measures being undertaken in the villages.

Another area of concern in 1900 was the high incidence of crime. Particularly common were offences against the person and against property, including praedial larceny which was a major disincentive to the practice of small farming. The problem of crime across the colony's boundaries was beginning to gain more attention. Thus at the end of 1899 a port was established at Springlands on the Corentyne primarily with a view to reducing the smuggling of opium and ganja.

One area where progress was slow was that of education, which in 1900 was dominated by the activity of Christian denominational schools which received small financial grants from the government. The education system, though improving, had many deficiencies. Firstly, in spite of the existence since 1876 of legislation making primary education compulsory, there was a high incidence of absenteeism, especially among East Indian children whose parents often kept them at home for economic pursuits as well as out of fear that they would be converted to Christianity at the denominational institutions. Thus, out of a total number of 27561 students on roll in the colony's schools in 1900, the average attendance was only 16397 or 59 per cent. It was a major achievement for a child to complete primary school. Furthermore, education was handicapped by the deficiencies of the teachers, most of whom were not trained. The performance of the teachers was also affected by grievances which they had, especially low wages, the payment by results system, and the lack of job security.

Admittedly, the inadequately small number of secondary schools had a more competent staff. The curriculum there, however, was limited, with very little scientific or vocational training. This was the situation even at the top secondary institution, Queen's College, which in 1900 was an elitist school with 72 privileged students of wealthy parents, mostly locally-born Britons, Portuguese and a few members of the coloured middle class. There was as yet no secondary school catering for children from low-income homes. There was also little tertiary education.

The uneven geographical distribution of the schools made access to education more difficult in Essequibo and Berbice where there were respectively 45 and 56 schools, than in Demerara where 111 schools were located. Unlike today, the educational system did not benefit from the existence of a public library service, which was not introduced until 1909. The few libraries existing in 1900 were private institutions. There was a

Reading Society in Berbice which had a library of 4000 volumes, while the Royal Agricultural and Commercial Society in Georgetown had a more richly endowed one with 23000 volumes.

Above all, however, the system of education in British Guiana in 1900 suffered from the inadequate support given by the government, which left too much responsibility in the hands of the churches. Even the government's financial contribution to the churches to assist in their work in education was very small. In 1899, for example, only $104,000 was voted for grants to primary schools, an average of just over $500 per school.

The existence of such major deficiencies ensured that the quality of education given in most schools left much to be desired. Not surprisingly, wealthy residents, especially expatriate Englishmen and some Portuguese, sent their children to England to be educated.

Apart from that possessed by the sugar interests, most of the colony's wealth was in the hands of the Portuguese who dominated business and owned a considerable amount of property all over the country. In 1900 their involvement in business was growing in scale and variety and included shopkeeping, wood and charcoal production, cattle rearing, the manufacture of cocoa and chocolate, market gardening and pawnbroking. The leading Portuguese merchants traded with Madeira, importing large quantities of garlic, potatoes, onions, wine and other commodities for which there was a considerable consumer demand in the colony.

The purchasing power of the Guianese masses, however, was restricted by the poor wages which they were receiving. After being virtually stationary for decades, wages in the sugar imdustry had been reduced substantially in 1884 and 1885 and again in 1894-95 when sugar prices fell drastically. Urban workers were also suffering from low wages and the attendant poverty.

In 1900, with the exception of the slum areas of Georgetown, it was the African villages on the coast which were most deeply affected by this poverty. Most of them were in a depressed state and their residents were experiencing a significant deterioration in the quality of life. The villages were suffering from a wide range of serious problems, especially their inability to cope effectively with the formidable challenges of sea and river defence, drainage and irrigation. Other major problems which they faced included a lack of capital, the relative paucity of good land, damage to crops and livestock by flooding and drought, the low price of ground provisions, poor sanitation and the inefficiency and lack of integrity of many of the village overseers. They were also severely handicapped by the virtual lack of financial support, apart from small loans, from the government, which devoted most of the colony's revenue to buttress the sugar industry. This factor and the widespread unsatisfactory collection of village rates prevented the execution of many urgently needed projects to enhance village life.

In these circumstances most villages were unable to develop a viable economy. By 1900 many villagers were so discouraged that they had begun to neglect agriculture. As the report of the Inspector of Villages for 1899 noted.

&

"cultivation of the ground provisions in the villages is not satisfactory; large amounts of land are left absolutely untilled, and the cultivation of the rest is, as a rule kept up in a very perfunctory manner, some beds being tilled and others not. Nearly all the coffee and fruit trees in most of the Villages have been allowed to die for want of attention."[11]

&

One of the few areas where the villages were not suffering unduly was that of pastimes.

Leisure and Pastimes

In 1900 residents of British Guiana had a variety of pastimes. One increasingly common pastime was participation in the activities of clubs established to satisfy the recreational and other needs of their members. This practice was very pronounced especially among the landowning elite and the Portuguese. Some of the clubs were exclusive organisations designed to emphasise class, race and gender concerns. For example, the famous Georgetown Club, which was founded in 1858, had a membership restricted to the white male elite of leading planters, merchants and senior government officials. The Portuguese had active dramatic and musical societies in Georgetown, which staged well-attended plays and concerts where Portuguese actors and bands were the main performers.

Recreation was provided by a wide range of mostly outdoor sports, including cricket, football, cycling, lawn tennis, golf, athletics, boxing, hockey, horse-racing, rifle-shooting, boat racing and cockfighting. Some of them, for example, boat racing, lawn tennis, golf and rifle shooting, were virtually restricted to Whites, while others like cricket were played by inhabitants of every class and colour in most parts of the country.

The most popular spectator sports were horse-racing and cricket. Horse-racing, with which gambling and heavy drinking were associated much to the displeasure of the churches, was held not only at the famous D'Urban Race Course in Georgetown, but also at other venues such as Belfield and Golden Grove on the East Coast of Demerara and at Suddie and Wakenaam in Essequibo.

Cricket, which was introduced by Englishmen in the mid-eighteenth century, was the outdoor game which had the greatest male participation. In 1900, it was spreading rapidly especially among Blacks, East Indians, Portuguese and people of mixed race. The headquarters of the game was the Georgetown Cricket Club, located since 1885 at the now famous Bourda Ground. The periodic intercolonial matches against Barbados and Trinidad evoked considerable interest. In 1900 British Guiana was seeking to regain ascendancy it had achieved in 1895 for the first time when it won the biennial regional tournament started in 1891 owing mainly to the brilliant batting of its two star players, Edward Wright and Clement King. In 1897, however, the team suffered a 10-wicket defeat at the hands of Barbados at Kensington Oval in Bridgetown. In 1900 it lost again to the Barbadians by seven wickets at the Queen's Park Oval, but defeated the hosts, Trinidad, by 46 runs.

In 1900, there were several indoor games, including checkers, cards, billiards, darts and chess. Of these card playing and billiards were the most popular and were played at virtually all the hotels and social clubs. Chess had a much smaller number of participants from the upper classes. It was promoted by a club in Berbice and by the Demerara Chess Club which in 1900 organised an intercolonial tournament by telegram with Barbados. Chess, like cricket, was one of the few sports in which British Guiana was involved in foreign competition.

Conclusion

Guyana has undergone considerable change during the past one hundred years. Many of the prominent features of modern Guyana were in their formative stage in 1900 which was an important period of transition for the country. The current diversified export economy based on two agricultural staples, sugar and rice, supplemented by mining (gold and diamonds, but not yet bauxite) was just emerging in 1900. Other outstanding traits of

Guyana today such as the dominance of non-Whites in national politics, migration from the countryside to the towns, labour organisations, the numerical ascendancy of East Indians and racial conflict between them and Blacks, all had their real beginnings in the period around 1900. Thus, modern Guyana is in many ways a development of new trends which began to emerge around 1900. In short, much of Guyana in 2000 was in miniature one hundred years ago.

For Further Reading

Adamson, Alan	**Sugar Without Slaves: The Political Economy of British Guiana, 1838-1904** (New Haven: Yale University Press, 1972).
Bayley, George (ed.)	**Handbook of British Guiana** (Georgetown, 1909).
Harrison, J.	**British Guiana and Its Resources** (London, 1907).
Lutchman, Harold	"The British Guiana Constitutional Change of 1891", **History Gazette**, No.40, January 1992.
Moohr, Michael	"The Discovery of Gold and the Development of Peasant Industries in Guyana, 1884 – 1914: A Study in the Political Economy of Change", **Caribbean Studies**, Vol.15, No.2, July 1975.
Moore, Brian	**Race, Power and Social Segmentation in Colonial Society: Guyana After Slavery 1839-1891** (New York: Gordon and Breach, 1987).
Moore, Brian	**Cultural Power, Resistance and Pluralism. Colonial Guyana, 1838-1900** (Kingston: The Press University of the West Indies, 1995).
Rodney, Walter	**A History of the Guyanese Working People, 1881-1905** (Baltimore: The Johns Hopkins University Press, 1981).

Part Two

Demography

A group of Amerindians

Portuguese Dancers

Francis Dias, the first Portuguese Legislator

East Indian Indentured Immigrants

A mixed group of residents

CHAPTER 3

GUYANA, PAST AND PRESENT: A HISTORICAL DEMOGRAPHIC OUTLINE

Guyana today is the most cosmopolitan country in the English-speaking Caribbean where the ethnic composition of its population is concerned. The earliest Guyanese are the Amerindians, who recently have begun to insist that they should be referred to as the indigenous peoples. They were the first of the immigrant groups who today constitute the population of Guyana.

It is believed that the Amerindians came to the area that is now Guyana from Asia about eleven thousand years ago during an era which historians call the last Ice Age because much of the earth's surface was then covered with ice. A hunting people, they are said to have left their homeland to follow herds of animals which were their principal source of food and to have crossed the land bridge now covered by the Bering Strait from East Asia into North America. It is believed that from there they moved southwards gradually and some of them reached and settled in modern Guyana about 9,000 B.C., apparently entering the country first in the area known today as the North-West District.

In the following millennia the Amerindians were able to adjust to a variety of challenging environments. They seem to have spent a lot of time and energy trying to secure food. Initially and for a long time they lived from hunting wild animals and gathering fruits and nuts from trees. Eventually, however, they learnt to cultivate the land, to domesticate animals and to fish. The increased food supplies enabled them to sustain a more sizable population, though it was never large. They tended to live in small, scattered, essentially nomadic groups, with settlements of relatively short duration.

While their culture was not as advanced as that of some other Amerindian groups in the Americas, such as the Aztecs of Mexico, the Incas of Peru and the Maya of Central America, the Guyanese Amerindians had some notable achievements. Among these were their skill in the manufacture of pots and baskets, impressive carvings and paintings called petroglyphs on boulders and on the walls of caves, and canoe construction which revolutionized transport.

The Amerindians remained the sole inhabitants of what is today Guyana until about six hundred years ago when they were joined by Europeans. The first Europeans to reach Guyana were the Spaniards who discovered the area in 1498 and later began to make periodic visits there. The Spaniards never made a serious attempt to establish major or permanent settlements in Guyana. Their main interest there was restricted by their failure to discover the fabled wealth of El Dorado and the hostility which they encountered from the Caribs.

The first Europeans to make permanent settlements in Guyana were the Dutch from the Netherlands. They began to settle in Essequibo by 1616, in Berbice in 1627 and in Demerara in 1746, forming separate Dutch colonies in the three areas. The Dutch were responsible for at least four major developments in Guyana, namely, the introduction of captive Africans from West Africa, Christianity and a measure of western education, plantation agriculture (initially sugar, and later coffee and cotton, cultivation) and critical infrastructure. This infrastructure, provided by the Dutch engineering skills and African slave labour, enabled settlement of the usually flooded low coastal plain through the creation of a network of dams, canals, sluices and sea defences, including the famous concrete sea walls still extant today.

Captive Africans brought across the Atlantic not only provided most of the manual labour initially for the infrastructure and plantation agriculture, but also they introduced African culture, including the religions of animism, ancestral worship and Islam and their languages, dances and musical instruments, especially the drum. Much of this culture, however, did not survive partly because the white slave masters often sought to suppress it for fear that it would be used in mounting resistance to slavery.

Slavery was a cruel, inhumane institution which was legally abolished by the British on 1st August, 1834, with the captives becoming completely free on 1st August, 1838. The British who had begun to settle in significant numbers in Essequibo, Berbice and Demerara in the 1740s, took possession of these three Dutch colonies in 1796 during a period of international warfare. In 1831 they unified the three areas into a new entity called British Guiana, the name which it bore until the grant of political independence from Britain on 26th May, 1966, when it was changed to Guyana.

The British maintained and extended many of the Dutch initiatives, especially plantation agriculture and Christianity and western education. They also initiated some new developments, including the entrenchment of the English language and the introduction of cricket. As a result of these two developments, today Guyana is unique in being the only country in South America that is English-speaking and has cricket as its principal national game.

It was during the period of British colonial rule that the population of the country was increased and diversified by the arrival of three new immigrant groups, namely the Portuguese, East Indians and Chinese. These immigrants came at least initially as indentured workers to replace Africans, many of whom, as expected, abandoned the plantations in 1838 when they became completely free, creating a labour crisis.

About 30,000 Portuguese arrived in British Guiana between 1835 and 1880 mostly from the Atlantic island of Madeira, a Portuguese colony. They were allowed quite early to abandon agricultural labour and were able to establish themselves as successful businessmen, especially through the ownership of spirit, retail and wholesale shops. They also made an important contribution to the colony's cultural and religious life especially in music, drama, sport and the establishment of Roman Catholicism. They also added new delicacies to the local diet, especially garlic pork, which is still a favourite among many Guyanese today.

East Indians from India were by far the largest of the three new immigrant groups, about 238,000 arriving between 1838 and 1919. By 1900 they had become the largest ethnic group in the colony, surpassing Africans. Their most important contribution especially initially was to the survival and growth of the sugar industry through their labour in the fields and gradually and increasingly in the factory. By 1900 they also had begun to embark seriously on rice cultivation and dairy farming as profitable enterprises. They were also responsible for the significant growth of Islam in the colony and the introduction there of Hinduism, their music and art forms and new foods such as roti and curry and dhal.

The Chinese were the smallest of the three new immigrant groups. About 14,000 of them arrived in British Guiana between 1853 and 1880 when immigration from China virtually ceased. Because of this relatively small immigration, the paucity of females among them and their low birth rate, the Chinese population in Guyana never exceeded more than 3.5 per cent of the country's population. Like the Portuguese, the Chinese were allowed to abandon manual labour on the plantation quite early. They also made a useful contribution to the country's economic life, especially through the development of small farming and expansion of the commercial sector, particularly through the establishment of laundries, jewellery shops and pharmacies. They too diversified the country's diet by the introduction of their cuisine, especially chowmein.

The coming of the Portuguese, Indians and Chinese changed the ethnic composition of the country substantially, transforming it into what many people call "the land of six peoples", namely, Amerindians, Europeans, Africans, Portuguese, East Indians and Chinese. Strictly speaking, however, it is five peoples for the Portuguese are, in fact, Europeans. The classification of the Portuguese as a separate race was due to Anglo-Saxon prejudice which viewed them as second-class or inferior largely because of their initial involvement in despised manual labour.

The transformation of British Guiana into a plural or multiracial society was accompanied by stresses and strains between the various groups. In the nineteenth century, the major friction was between the Portuguese and Africans, who resented the fact that the Portuguese had ousted them from their positions in huckstering and small shop-keeping and used their dominance in these areas to increase prices for basic consumer goods. In the twentieth century, the main contention was between the two largest groups, Indians and Africans, who were rivals in the pursuit of political power.

The demographic structure of the country did not change substantially in the first half of the twentieth century. Admittedly, the numerical preponderance of Indians over other racial groups increased progressively. Furthermore, there was a growing number of persons of mixed race as the earlier prejudice against interracial marriage and other liaisons lost some of its potency.

Significant changes, however, have occurred in the population since the country gained political independence in 1966. Most visible among them has been the marked decrease in the Chinese and Portuguese population. Many Chinese and Portuguese have migrated especially to Canada because of their dissatisfaction with post-independence political and economic developments. The most striking feature, however, of Guyana's population today, especially when compared to that of most countries in the Caribbean and elsewhere in the hemisphere, is the existence of a sizable minority of Amerindians. About seven per cent of Guyana's current population of about 750,000 are Amerindians. They exist in nine tribal groups-Arawaks, Caribs, Warraus, Akawaios, Wapisianas, Macusi, Arekuna, Wai-Wais and

Patemonas. In spite of their comparatively unsophisticated culture, the Amerindians have made a significant contribution to modern Guyana. In the area of food, pepperpot is a highly esteemed national dish and cassava bread is widely consumed. The indigenous people have also given the country hammocks for resting, boats and canoes for travel, numerous place names and knowledge of the hinterland and the medicinal properties of wild plants.

The Amerindians for the most part still live in the interior of the country, their traditional home. Since 1946, and especially after 1966, efforts have been made to integrate them into the rest of the country's population, but only with limited success. This limitation and friction between Africans and Indians are major barriers to the realization of the country's motto of "One People, One Nation, One Destiny".

For Further Reading

Cumpston, I.	**Indians Overseas in British Territories, 1834-1854** (London: Oxford University Press, 1953).
Laurence, Keith	**Immigration into the West Indies in the 19th Century** (Barbados: Carib University Press, 1971).
Laurence, Keith	**A Question of Labour - Indentured Immigration into Trinidad and British Guiana, 1875-1917** (Kingston: Ian Randle Publishers, 1994).
Look Lai, Walton	**Indentured Labour, Caribbean Sugar: Chinese and Indian Migrants to the British West Indies** (1838-1918) (Baltimore: The Johns Hopkins University Press, 1993).
Mangru, Basdeo	**Benevolent Neutrality: Indian Government Policy and Labour Migration to British Guiana, 1854 – 1884** (London: Hansib Publishing, 1987).
Menezes, Mary	**Scenes from the History of the Portuguese in Guyana** (London: The Author, 1986).
Moore, Brian	"The Settlement of Chinese in Guyana in the Nineteenth Century", **Immigrants and Minorities**, Vol 7, No.1, 1988.
Potter, Lesley	"The Amerindians of Guyana and their Environment", **History Gazette**, No.52, January 1993.
Roberts, G	"Immigration of Africans into the British Caribbean", **Population Studies**, Vol.8, No.3, March 1958.
Roberts, G. and Johnson, M.	"Factors involved in immigration and movements in the working force of British Guiana in the nineteenth century.", **Social and Economic Studies**, Vol.23, No.1, 1974.
Roth, Walter	**An Introductory study of the arts, crafts and customs of the Guiana Indians** (Washington: US Government Printing Office, 1924).
Williams, Denis	**Prehistoric Guiana** (Kingston: Ian Randle Publishers, 2003).

Chapter 4

Demographic Change in Nineteenth Century Guyana, 1800-1850

One of the distinguishing features of the history of Guyana in the nineteenth century was significant change in the population of the area. These changes were particularly evident in three aspects of the population, namely, its size, ethnic composition and spatial distribution. These developments were first witnessed in the earlier decades of the century, which are the focus here, and became more pronounced in the latter half of the century.

In 1800 the area occupied by the modern Republic of Guyana consisted of two Dutch colonies named Berbice and the United Colony of Demerara-Essequibo, occupied by the British since April 1796. The two colonies were populated by three distinct racial groups, Africans, Amerindians and Europeans, as well as people of mixed race, predominantly a European and African mixture. The Blacks, of whom the overwhelming majority were slaves, were numerically by far the largest group, their numbers being maintained and increased mainly by continuous importation of slaves from Africa.

In 1800 the population of Berbice and Demerara-Essequibo was growing rapidly, owing to the large number of slaves brought there since the British occupation in 1796 by British traders who were dominating the transatlantic slave traffic. Many of these slaves were purchased by new British settlers who had bought land and were seeking to establish or extend coffee, cotton and sugar plantations. The high prices being offered in Britain for these three commodities were an inducement to these settlers to seek to maximize production and profits through the acquisition of African slave labour. Between 1800 and 1802 an annual average of about 8000 slaves was supplied to Demerara-Essequibo.

The rapid growth of the population of Berbice and Demerara-Essequibo continued until 1805, when the British government imposed a severe limitation on the slave traffic to these two colonies, before abolishing the trade completely in 1807 throughout the British empire. At the time of abolition, the two colonies had a combined slave population of about 109,000. After 1808 this population, no longer replenished from Africa, stagnated and then began to decline steadily owing to a low birth rate and a high mortality rate caused mainly by overwork, underfeeding, disease, physical brutality and poor medical care.

In short, after 1808 the slave population of Berbice and Demerara-Essequibo proved incapable of maintaining itself by natural reproduction. In Berbice it declined from about 22,000 in 1812 to about 16,000 in 1822, while in Demerara-Essequibo it dropped progressively from about 77,000 in 1820, to 74,000 in 1823, to 71,000 in 1826, to 69,000 in 1829, to 65,000 in 1832. The combined slave population of the two colonies fell from about 101,000 in 1817 to about 83,000 in 1834. This decline was due largely to the fact that among the slaves deaths exceeded births. In Demerara-Essequibo, for example, it was estimated that there were 18,558 slave births and 27,693 slave deaths between 1817 and 1829. The decline in the slave population was due in only very small measure to manumission, which was rare in the two colonies.

As a result of the low incidence of manumission, Berbice and Demerara-Essequibo had a very small free coloured population which was often even more negligible than the tiny white population. For example, in 1798 in Essequibo there were an estimated 361 free coloured (68 men, 123 women and 170 children) compared to 701 Whites and 12,360 slaves. By 1830 the situation had not changed significantly. In that year in Demerara-Essequibo the percentage of free Coloureds and Whites in the population of about 85,000 was 3.5% and 2.7% respectively, while in Berbice with a population of about 28,000 the corresponding statistics were 3.5% and 1.7%.

The composition of the slave population changed significantly in two ways after 1807. Firstly, the African-born element, numerically dominant then, declined mainly as a result of deaths. In Demerara-Essequibo it fell from about 42,000 in 1817 to 34,000 in 1823, to 30,500 in 1826, to 26,000 in 1829 to 22,000 in 1832. By 1832 the creole or locally born slaves there, who in 1817 were much less than the African-born, almost doubled the latter, increasing from about 34,900 in 1817 to nearly 43,000 in 1832.

Secondly, the proportion of women, who before 1807 constituted a smaller part of slave cargoes than males, now rose in the slave population which became increasingly dependent on natural reproduction. In Demerara-

Essequibo the female element remained virtually stationary numerically between 1817 and 1829 but during these years increased proportionally from 43% to 47%. In 1817 the slave population of 77,163 there consisted of an estimated 43,771 males and 33,392 females compared with 37,141 males and 32,326 females in 1829 when there were 69,467 slaves.

The trend of declining population in Berbice and Demerara-Essequibo began to be reversed after the legal abolition of slavery in 1834 and especially after the full Emancipation of the slaves in 1838 when they completed four years of a modified form of slavery euphemistically called apprenticeship. The planters rightly anticipated that there would be a mass exodus of the apprentices from the estates after Emancipation, creating a serious labour crisis. To prepare for this unwelcome prospect, the planters began in 1834 to make efforts to secure an alternative labour force by inviting immigrants from the Caribbean and more remote areas of the world. Initially they secured Blacks from the British West Indian islands and Portuguese from Madeira and later immigrants from India, West Africa and China. A total of about 55,000 immigrants arrived in British Guiana between 1834 and 1850. This immigration had an immense impact on the demographic and other aspects of the history of the country.

Owing to this immigration, the decline in the size of the black element in the population, witnessed especially between 1817 and 1834 as a result of the abolition of the slave trade from Africa, was checked. The number of Blacks in British Guiana increased between 1834 and 1850 from two sources. One factor was the arrival of thousands of residents of British Caribbean islands who were attracted to the mainland colony by the prospect of better wages. An estimated 12,898 West Indians came to British Guiana between 1834 and 1850, about 8,000 or three fifths of them between 1834 and 1840. In 1850 the colony had about 9,200 such immigrants, of whom about 4,900 or 53 per cent came from Barbados, where there was a surplus of labour and very low wages. Many of the West Indian immigrants were seasonal visitors, not permanent settlers.

The black population of British Guiana received a second impetus from 1841 from immigrants from West Africa, particularly from Sierra Leone. These immigrants were mostly Liberated Africans, that is, former captives who had been rescued mainly by British warships from slave vessels involved in the illegal trade across the Atlantic in defiance of their country's abolition laws. They were highly esteemed by the plantocracy in British Guiana because of their ability as workers and the fact that it was cheaper to transport them there than immigrants from India and their death rate was lower than that of other immigrant groups.

In the first year, 1841, 1,102 Liberated Africans arrived in the colony and 10,528 in the decade between 1841 and 1850. Their immigration reached its peak between 1847 and 1850 when the British metropolitan government decided to bear the total cost of transporting them to the colony. In those years, 3,027 of them came to the colony. Their migration was regarded by the planters as particularly valuable during the period of suspension of East Indian immigration in the early 1840s when African immigration was the largest source of labour, with 5,829 African immigrants arriving in the colony between 1841 and 1845 compared with 5,601 Portuguese and 4,379 West Indians. Many of the African immigrants returned to West Africa, claiming their contractual right of a return passage and thus minimizing their effect on the population growth in the colony. In 1850 there were about 7,160 African immigrants in British Guiana, constituting about six per cent of the colony's non-Amerindian population. In spite of their presence, however, because of the large number who had returned to Africa and the high mortality among the colony's ex-slaves, the African-born element in the population declined from about 30,500 in 1826, to about 15,800 in 1841, to about 14,200 in 1850.

As a result of the arrival of West Indians and Liberated Africans, notwithstanding the fact that deaths exceeded births, the black population of the colony grew, reaching about 91,710 by 1851. The white component in the population, which for many years had been small and virtually stationary, also increased between 1834 and 1850 owing partly to some additions of British, Germans and Maltese, but above all of Portuguese immigrants from the Atlantic island of Madeira, a Portuguese possession.

The first batch of Portuguese immigrants arrived in British Guiana in May 1835. Between that year and 1850 about 17,365 of them came to the colony. However, owing to the high mortality among them and the fact that many of them returned to Madeira, by 1850 there were only about 7,900 Portuguese in British Guiana. Nevertheless, mainly due to their presence the white population of Demerara, Essequibo and Berbice, which numbered only about 3,500 in 1829, had by 1850 increased significantly to about 11,500, of whom about 7,500 were Portuguese born in Madeira. The remaining 4,000 Whites consisted of other Europeans, especially Englishmen, Scots, Irish, Dutchmen and Germans, a few Americans and Portuguese born in the colony. The number of Whites there apart from Portuguese, however, was actually declining owing to the collapse of coffee and cotton plantations and difficulties being experienced in the sugar industry.

Although the Portuguese immigrants were Europeans, they were regarded as distinct by the British residents who viewed them as second-class Whites mainly because they were brought to the colony as indentured labourers to do despised manual labour. In addition, the Portuguese, who were Roman Catholics and not Protestants, were different in religion and also spoke a different language. Thus, in censuses and other official records, the Portuguese were not considered "Europeans". This was the origin of the practice that still persists of considering Guyana as the land of six, not five peoples (Amerindians, Africans, Europeans, Portuguese, East Indians and Chinese).

The most significant development in the colony's population between 1834 and 1850 was the coming of immigrants from India who first arrived in May 1838 and eventually became the main replacement for Blacks on the plantations. About 12,770 of them came between 1838 and 1850, notwithstanding the fact that Indian immigration was suspended for several years between 1841 and 1845. By 1850, this important development was still in its early phase, with the Indian population then numbering about 7,600.

In the period between 1834 and 1850 there was also a growing population of mixed race which, in 1851, was estimated at 14,754. As before, this group consisted largely of a mixture of European and African descent. By 1850, the population of the colony (excluding Amerindians) had grown to about 125,000. This increase was due to immigration, not natural increase, for the mortality rate continued to exceed the birth rate. In 1848 a medical report showed a death rate of 84.8 per 1000 among the indentured immigrants, with the rate among the Portuguese being almost double that of the other groups. This high mortality rate was due to many factors, including extremely inadequate sanitation, swampy and flooded areas of residence, polluted water, poor housing, malnutrition and epidemics.

In 1850 Blacks, numbering about 91,000, were still a sizable majority in the population, but not as dominant numerically as in 1834, owing to Portuguese and Indian immigration. By 1850, however, new trends were appearing among immigrants with an increase of Indians and a decline in the number of West Indians and Africans. Of the 24,848 immigrants who arrived in the colony during the years, 1846, 1847 and 1848, 11,025 were from India and 10,036 from Madeira. This meant that only a maximum of

3,787 were West Indians and Africans. In short, by 1850 changes were taking place that would result later in the erosion of the numerical ascendancy of Blacks in the population.

According to the 1851 census, the population of British Guiana (excluding Amerindians) was 125,692. This figure included 91,710 Blacks, 14,754 persons of mixed race, 11,558 Whites and 7,682 East Indians. In short, about 72 per cent of the population was black, with about 86,000 or two-thirds among them Creole, that is, born in the colony.

Between 1834 and 1850 the population of British Guiana changed not only in size and composition but also in spatial distribution. For example, the colony's urban population, especially the people of Georgetown, increased. This growth was due not to natural increase, but to migration from the countryside especially of former slaves and indentured immigrants who had completed their contracts. Both of these two groups were seeking jobs away from agriculture.

The population of Georgetown grew from 9,097 in 1820 to 10,514 in 1824, to 12,604 in 1829, to 18,585 in 1841, to 25,508 in 1851-an average annual increase of about eight per cent. In 1851 it consisted of 3,370 Whites, 14,133 Blacks, 6,774 persons of mixed race and 871 East Indians. The population of the second town, New Amsterdam, where job opportunities were fewer, grew much more slowly, numbering only 4,633 in 1851. In short, in 1851 the colony's total urban population was 30,151, compared to a rural population (excluding Amerindians) of about 95,000.

Between 1834 and 1850 two other important changes occurred in the spatial distribution of the population. Firstly, a growing proportion of the population began to reside in Demerara. In 1851 it was estimated that 75,767 or 60 per cent of the colony's total non-Amerindian population of about 125,000 resided in Demerara, while 22,722 lived in Essequibo and 27,003 in Berbice. Secondly, by 1851, 43,995 persons, mostly Blacks, were residing in the villages which the former slaves had established since Emancipation. These persons constituted about 35 per cent of the country's non-Amerindian population. The villages with the largest population were all located on the East Coast of Demerara, namely Buxton, Plaisance, Victoria, Friendship and Beterverwagting.

In examining the demographic changes which occurred in Guyana in the nineteenth century, little can be said about the Amerindians. This is partly because the majority of them lived in the somewhat remote interior and consequently were not usually included in the censuses. Occasionally, however, some of "those located in or near the cultivated portions of the colony"[12] featured in the periodic censuses. For example, the 1851 census included 2003 Amerindians residing in the Pomeroon area of Essequibo. Typical of the comments in the censuses was the following made in that census: "In consequence of the wandering habits of the Indians (Amerindians) and the difficulty in reaching them, no exact account has been attempted of the different Tribes throughout the Province."[13]

The first half of the nineteenth century witnessed very important changes in the population of Guyana. Slavery was abolished and replaced by indentured or free labour. Two new groups, namely, Portuguese and East Indians, were added to the country's multiethnic and multicultural population. The immigration of these and other groups enabled the population that had declined in the wake of the restriction and abolition of the slave trade to increase, though somewhat slowly because of the high mortality rate. Thus the non-Amerindian population of the colony grew from about 98,000 in 1841 to about 125,000 in 1851. Males continued to outnumber females except in Georgetown, where many females were attracted especially by the prospect of securing jobs as domestics. The African-born element in the population declined from about 42,000 or 35 per cent of the non-Amerindian population in 1817 to an estimated 14,251 or 12 per cent in 1851. In 1851, 7,083 or about half of the African-born residents were former slaves, while the others (7,168) were new immigrants who had arrived in the colony since Emancipation in 1838. By 1850, the black numerical ascendancy, though still substantial, was beginning to be eroded by the increasing volume of immigrants from Madeira and India.

Many of these important developments would continue and become more pronounced in the latter half of the century. For example, by the mid-1890s, East Indians had replaced Blacks as the largest ethnic group in the country's population.

For Further Reading

Eltis, David	"The Traffic in Slaves between the British West Indian Colonies, 1807 – 1833", **Economic History Review**, 2nd series, VOL XXV, No .1, 1972.
Higman, Barry	**Slave Populations of the British Caribbean, 1807-1834** (Baltimore: The Johns Hopkins University Press, 1984.).
James, Anand	"The Emigration of Liberated Africans to British Guiana,

	1841 – 1852", **History Gazette,** No.31, March 1991.
Mangru, Basdeo	**Indians in Guyana: A Concise History from their Arrival to the Present** (New York: Adams Press, 1999).
Mc Gowan Winston	"The French Revolutionary Period in Demerara-Essequibo, 1793-1802", **History Gazette,** No. 55, April 1993.
Menezes, Mary	**The Portuguese of Guyana: A Study In Culture and Conflict** (Gujarat: Anand Press, 1992).
Nath, Dwarka	**A History of Indians in Guyana** (Leeds: The Author, 1970).
Ramdeyal, Desiree	"Demographic Change In Georgetown, 1820 -1881", **History Gazette,** No.56, May 1993.
Roberts, G. and Johnson, M.	"Factors involved in immigration and movements in the working force of British Guiana in the nineteenth century", **Social and Economic Studies**, Vol.23, No.1, 1974.

Part Three

Slave Trade, Slavery and Abolition

A coffle of slaves being marched to the coast of West Africa

Monument in Georgetown commemorating the leader of the 1763 Berbice Slave Rebellion

Rev. John Smith

A Map of East Coast Demerara Plantations in 1823

CHAPTER 5

THE COMING OF AFRICANS TO GUYANA

The presence of Africans in Guyana seems to date back to the early decades of the seventeenth century, when they were brought there by the Dutch traders and settlers to work in the incipient Dutch colonies of Essequibo and Berbice. They were victims of the trans-Atlantic traffic in captive Africans, a movement which involved the forced migration of millions of Africans mostly from West and Central Africa to the Americas between the fifteenth and nineteenth centuries.

The early Afro-Guyanese were unwilling immigrants. The vast majority of them had been kidnapped, captured in raids or taken prisoner in wars by fellow Africans and sold to the Dutch slave traders on the African coast. Not only initially, but also at least until the second half of the eighteenth century, the Dutch were the main suppliers of slaves to Essequibo and Berbice. Until 1730 this supply was provided almost exclusively by the Dutch West India Company, a state-chartered body which was founded in 1621 to challenge Portuguese influence in West Africa and Spanish ascendancy in the Caribbean and South America. The Company enjoyed an official monopoly of Dutch trade in West Africa and the Americas.

Partly because of the Company's inability to supply enough African slaves, its monopoly was withdrawn in 1730. The Dutch trade in captive Africans was then opened to individual Dutch citizens, who thereafter became the principal suppliers of Africans to Essequibo, Berbice and, after 1746, Demerara until April 1796 when Britain captured these colonies from the Dutch.

The most striking feature of the Dutch slave trade to these three colonies was its relatively small volume, compared to the size of the territories, their manpower needs and the scale of the traffic to other Caribbean countries, especially Barbados, Cuba, Jamaica, Saint Domingue and Suriname. It was not until the late eighteenth century that the Africans were brought to

Essequibo, Berbice and Demerara in significant numbers. Thus, as late as 1770 the slave population of these colonies was very small, about 14,000, while that of Barbados was about 68,000, Suriname 74,000 and Jamaica nearly 200,000.

The comparatively small number of African slaves brought to Essequibo, Berbice and Demerara was due to a variety of factors. One of them was the basic commercial policy of the Dutch West India Company. The Company's preoccupation with the maximisation of profits and other considerations made it decide to supply many, if not most, of its slaves to the colonies of other European Powers, particularly Barbados and the Spanish mainland territories, where prices were higher and the markets larger, rather than to Dutch possessions like Essequibo and Berbice. For example, the Company played a crucial role in the establishment of the Barbados sugar industry. It was the principal supplier of slaves there, providing about 46,000 of them to the island between 1640 and 1663.

Another aspect of the Company's commercial policy which helped to minimise its supply of African slaves to Essequibo and Berbice was the low esteem and priority which its Directors accorded to these colonies, especially when compared to other Dutch possessions. For example, between 1630 and 1654 the Company supplied a colony which it had in north-eastern Brazil with more than 26,000 African slaves, in striking contrast to the few hundred captives which it sent to Essequibo and Berbice. Similarly, after 1667, when the Netherlands secured Suriname from Britain, the Company regarded this new Dutch possession with its already flourishing and rapidly expanding plantation system as having much more value and potential than the small colonies in Essequibo and Berbice, from which the Netherlands was deriving only minimal profit. It therefore pursued a deliberate policy of supplying slaves to Suriname in preference to Essequibo and Berbice. Thus, in the 70-year period between 1668 and 1738 it provided an annual average of 924 slaves to Suriname compared with 119 to Berbice and 62 in Essequibo.

Largely because of these features of the commercial policy of the Dutch West India Company, Essequibo and Berbice were greatly undersupplied with African slaves in the latter half of the seventeenth and the early decades of the eighteenth centuries. It was not unusual then for two or more years to elapse without the arrival of a single slave ship from Africa. For instance, only one vessel with 330 slaves arrived in Essequibo from Africa between August 1699 and May 1701. The limited supply of African slaves did not satisfy the needs of the planters and other slaveholders there and in Berbice. Much to the disappointment of the administrators and planters there, shipments of Africans continued to be very irregular, resulting in stagnation or very negligible growth of the economies of these two colonies and ensuring that the settlements remained small. In 1735, for example, Essequibo consisted of four or five Company plantations, 25-30 private plantations, and a total population of 66 Europeans and only 859 slaves, including apparently some Amerindian slaves.

The continued arrival of a small number of African slaves in Essequibo and Berbice was occurring at a time when the need and demand for a more abundant supply of them had become more intense because of two important developments in the 1720s. Firstly, trade with the Amerindians, which had been the main focus of the Dutch there, dwindled almost to nothing with the result that the export economy of these two colonies began for the first time to be based almost completely on labour-intensive plantation agriculture. Secondly, the export economy, then based mainly on sugar cultivation, was diversified by the introduction of coffee cultivation in Berbice in 1719 and two years later in Essequibo.

The Dutch settlers in these two colonies hoped that their need for African labour would be better satisfied from the 1730s when the Dutch West India Company's monopoly would end and private Dutch traders would be able to participate legally in the slave trade to Dutch colonies. The Company continued to supply some slaves to the Americas until the 1750s, but it was quickly superseded by the private traders. Under these traders the Dutch slave traffic to the Americas increased by about one-third between the 1730s and 1760s, before declining in the 1770s.

In spite of this overall growth in the Dutch slave trade, initially there was no significant increase in the supply of slaves to Essequibo and Berbice. This was partly because the individual traders, somewhat like the Dutch West India Company, showed a marked preference to supply slaves to Suriname, the most prosperous and most populous Dutch colony in the Caribbean. This preoccupation with Suriname to the comparative neglect of the other Dutch Guiana colonies was occurring at a time when there was an unprecedented demand for slaves there owing to three major developments.

The first development was the decision of the Dutch metropolitan government in 1740 to open up its Essequibo colony to foreign nationals. This resulted in the immediate influx of a number of British planters, mostly from the older British West Indian islands such as Barbados and Antigua, where the soil, after almost one hundred years of intensive agriculture, was becoming increasingly exhausted and more difficult and expensive to cultivate. The second development was the establishment in 1746 of a new Dutch colony in Demerara, where sizable grants of land were made especially to British and Dutch planters, who soon embarked on sugar cane and coffee cultivation. The third factor was the introduction of cotton cultivation in Essequibo in the mid 1740s and its spread later to Berbice and Demerara.

The greatly increased demand for slaves stimulated by these three developments was not satisfactorily met. By the 1750s Essequibo, Berbice and Demerara were critically short of African slave labour, provoking complaints and appeals to the metropolitan government from the authorities and planters in the three colonies. In July 1763, Gedney Clarke Jr., the son of the most successful of the British planters in Demerara, made a special visit to the Netherlands to complain to the government about the grossly inadequate slave supplies from Africa and "to see what good he can get done for the inhabitants of that Infant and Negro Starved Colony".[14] He presented to the authorities there a plan, centred on an adequate supply of captive Africans, which he contended would make Demerara become the most prosperous and valuable Dutch possession in the Caribbean. Similarly, six years later in 1769 Laurens Storm van's Gravesande, the supreme Dutch administrator in Essequibo and Demerara, in a letter about Demerara to the metropolitan government castigated the Dutch free traders for their general inattention to the colony and for the high prices they demanded when they occasionally brought slave cargoes there. He complained that:

> The number of slaves imported here is far less than half that actually needed. Had there not been this dearth, what a Colony would this not have been! We have been twelve consecutive years without the arrival of a single slave ship; it has been irreparable and ruinous for the Colony that the slave trade devolved from the Honble Company to private merchants The Company would not have left the Colonies so denuded, especially as its own interests were involved, whilst the merchants, regarding their private concerns only, cared but little for the Colonies' progress. It

is all one to them as long as they make money.[15]

☙

The supply of captive Africans to Essequibo, Berbice and Demerara did not improve substantially until the 1770s. This improvement resulted in an unprecedented increase in the rate of growth of the slave population which more than doubled in all three colonies between 1769 and 1782. Thus in 1782 Demerara, which was by then the best supplied and most prosperous of the three territories, had an estimated 12,500 slaves, Essequibo about 8,700 and Berbice just over 8,000.

This unprecedented growth of the slave population and influx of Africans in these colonies in the 1770s was due above all to two factors. Firstly, it was partly the result of a decision made in 1770 by the Dutch metropolitan authorities to open the trade of Demerara and Essequibo to all the provinces of the Netherlands, instead of continuing to maintain it as a preserve of the province of Zealand alone. As a consequence, ships from the province of Holland began to land cargoes of captive Africans in these colonies, thus supplementing the supplies provided by Zealand traders.

Secondly, the increase in the supply of slaves to these colonies was due to a severe economic crisis which Suriname began to experience in 1773, the first major blow to its buoyant economy.[16] This depression of the Surinamese market made most Dutch traders who arrived there after 1773 refuse to sell many of their captive Africans there as in the past. Instead, they proceeded to Suriname's hitherto comparatively neglected neighbours in Berbice, Demerara and Essequibo, where they were able to dispose of their slave cargoes at higher prices than obtainable in Suriname. It is estimated that Demerara, Essequibo and Berbice were supplied with a total of 7000-8000 African slaves in this way in the 1770s, as the annual average number of slaves landed in Suriname dropped drastically from about 3600 in the early 1770s to about 1400 in 1779 and then to less than 500 in the 1780s.

Although the 7000-8000 slaves landed in Demerara, Essequibo and Berbice represented a substantial increase in the supply of slaves to these colonies, they were far short of the needs of the planters. This was the situation in April 1796 when Britain captured and occupied these colonies.[17]

British occupation in 1796 marked the virtual end of the Dutch trade in captive Africans to Demerara, Essequibo and Berbice. The most striking characteristic of this trade almost throughout its long history was its low volume and its inadequacy to meet the demands of the slaveholders. This limited supply of slaves was reflected in the relatively small slave population of the colonies in 1796 at the time of the British takeover. At that time Berbice had an estimated 8,232 slaves, while Demerara and Essequibo, which had been joined into a new single entity called the United Colony of Demerary- Essequibo, had a combined total of about 38,000 slaves.

British occupation was followed by an unprecedented growth in the number of Africans coming to these colonies.[18] Within five years about 28,000 slaves were landed in Demerary-Essequibo from Africa, while imports into Berbice were so massive that the slave population there doubled by 1802. By 1803 an average of 8000 slaves was being supplied each year from Africa to Demerary-Essequibo.

This rapidly growing African population, however, received a severe check in 1805 when the British metropolitan government issued a Prohibitory Order restricting the trade in captive Africans to these two colonies from Africa. The Order permitted the entry of slaves to work on existing cultivated land, but not to extend cultivation to new areas. The African population there received an even more telling blow in 1807, when Britain completely prohibited the Atlantic slave trade for all British subjects and possessions, including Demerary-Essequibo and Berbice although these territories were not yet officially British. At that time, the total slave population of these two territories was about 101,000, about seventy per cent of whom were African-born. By 1834, when the British government decided to abolish slavery, this population had declined to an estimated 83,000 slaves.[19] This was a relatively small number compared to Jamaica's 311,000 slaves and exactly the size of that of tiny Barbados.

During the remainder of the nineteenth century, British Guiana's African-born population was strengthened by additions from two sources, namely, immigration from both Africa and the Caribbean. This immigration was prompted by the expectation and then the reality of a substantial exodus of the former slaves from the plantations after full freedom came in 1838, driving the planters to seek an alternative labour force that was cheap, immobile and controllable.

Among the immigrants who came to British Guiana after 1834 to help provide the new labour force were inhabitants of the islands of the British West Indies, especially Barbados, who were attracted by the comparatively high wages being offered in British Guiana. It is estimated that about 48,000 such immigrants came to British Guiana between 1835 and 1893. An unknown number of them, apparently a very small minority, were born in Africa for as early as the 1790s Barbados, the main source, had a predominantly Creole slave population. Thus, West Indian immigration had only a limited lasting effect on the number of African-born residents of British Guiana for to a significant degree it was seasonal or temporary, with many of the immigrants returning home permanently or moving to and fro between their island home and the mainland colony.

The African-born element in the Guianese population probably received a greater boost after 1838 from residents from West Africa than from West Indian immigration. These West Africans were for the most part slaves who had been liberated by British warships from slave ships which were trading illegally in captive Africans and had been taken mainly to Sierra Leone. In spite of persistent efforts to encourage West Africans to emigrate to British Guiana to help provide the colony's new labour force, the volume of this immigration was comparatively small on the whole. About 14,000 African immigrants, mostly Liberated Africans, arrived between 1841 and 1865. This relatively small number was due partly to the fact that remuneration was not an effective inducement to many Africans to emigrate for wages were higher in Sierra Leone than in British Guiana. It decreased even more after the British government ruled in 1850 that the Caribbean colony, not the metropolis, should in future pay the cost of transporting the African immigrants there. Moreover, from the early 1850s the planters in the colony, unlike before when African immigration for some years was the most sizable type, showed little interest in introducing a large number of Africans, preferring instead East Indian indentured labourers who were beginning to arrive in increasing numbers from India.

Immigration from Africa into British Guiana dwindled and came to an end in the 1860s after the suppression of the Atlantic slave trade to Brazil and Cuba in the 1850s and early 1860s respectively and the abolition of slavery in the United States of America in 1863. These three events brought an end to the entire transatlantic trade in captive Africans by 1865, thus causing the source of Liberated African immigration to dry up completely. Nearly fifty per cent of the 14,000 African immigrants who came to British Guiana after 1840 claimed the return passage to Africa provided for in their contract, taking home savings they had accumulated in the colony.[20]

As a result of the relatively small volume of African-born immigrants into British Guiana after 1834 and the high proportion who returned to West Africa, this form of immigration had little effect on the growth of either the black or the total population of the colony. African immigration into the colony between 1834 and 1865, in fact, constituted only about seven per cent of East Indian immigration there in the same period. Furthermore, since 1865 very few persons born in Africa have settled in this Caribbean territory.

For Further Reading

Goslinga, Cornelis	**The Dutch in the Caribbean and on the Wild Coast 1580 – 1680** (Assen: Van Gorcum & Comp, 1971).
Goslinga, Cornelis	**The Dutch in the Caribbean and the Guianas 1680-1791** (Assen: Van Gorcum & Comp, 1985).
Higman, Barry	**Slave Populations in the British Caribbean, 1807- 1834** (Baltimore: The John Hopkins University Press, 1984).
James, Anand	"The Emigration of Liberated Africans to British Guiana, 1841-1852" **History Gazette**, No. 31, April, 1991.
Mc Gowan, Winston	"The African Slave Trade to Guyana" in McGowan, Winston, Rose, James and Granger, David (eds.), **Themes in African-Guyanese History** (Georgetown: Free Press, 1998).
Mc Gowan, Winston	**The Atlantic Slave Trade, Slavery and the Demographic History of Guyana** (Georgetown: Department of Social Studies, University of Guyana, 2006).
Postma, Johannes	**The Dutch in the Atlantic Slave Trade, 1600 – 1805** (Cambridge: Cambridge University Press, 1990).
Roberts, George	"Immigration of Africans into the British Caribbean", **Population Studies**, Vol 8, No.3, March 1958.
Schuler, Monica	**Liberated Africans in Nineteenth Century Guyana** (Kingston: Department of History, University of the West Indies, 1992).

CHAPTER 6

THE RESISTANCE OF CAPTIVE AFRICANS TO THE ATLANTIC SLAVE TRADE IN WEST AFRICA

The trade in captive Africans which supplied Essequibo, Berbice and Demerara with labour encountered resistance in West Africa. Some of this resistance came from African rulers, but this was relatively rare and in striking contrast to the frequent resistance displayed by the captives themselves. The resistance of the captives was evident in all three principal phases of the organisation of the trade in Africa, namely, at the time of enslavement, on the journey from the place of enslavement to the coastal marts and on the seaboard before the departure of the slave ships for the Guiana colonies and other destinations in the Americas.

Africans who were shipped across the Atlantic were enslaved as a result of a variety of circumstances. Some, including individuals given as tribute to rulers by subordinate states and chiefs, were already slaves in local societies. Others, such as debtors who could not fulfil their obligations and individuals who were sold by relatives to secure food in times of famine or food shortage, were victims of economic misfortune. Some captives were condemned to servitude by judicial or oracular decisions or for violation of cosmological norms, while others were kidnapped by Whites and especially by fellow Africans. The vast majority of captives, however, were prisoners of war, often taken in conflicts fought particularly to secure slaves for the Atlantic traffic, and victims of organised slave-raiding expeditions, often conducted at night or daybreak against unsuspecting neighbours. In short, most of the slaves shipped overseas were free men deprived of their liberty by fellow Africans in response to the demands of the Atlantic traffic.

Individual Africans demonstrated their basic love for freedom and their fundamental opposition to the Atlantic slave trade by the preventative measures which they adopted in an attempt to avoid enslavement. In areas where slave raids were prevalent, residents tried to make their homes more secure than was usual in West Africa. Many Africans also made preparations to facilitate and precipitate flight in the event of a slave raid. In the late eighteenth century an English slave trader noted that the people of Jakin "lived continually on the alarm. Accordingly, they always kept a number of canoes ready to assist their flight, in case of a sudden attack from the Dahomans."[21] In the Congo, the fear of raids drove some residents to vacate their homes at night and to sleep instead in canoes in waterways in readiness for flight, if necessary. Elsewhere, to avoid the possibility of enslavement, Africans abandoned their homes and territories permanently and re-established themselves in places, such as caves and dens in the hillsides, which were less visible and accessible and more secure, but less suited to agriculture. Such action, however, did not always guarantee the desired and expected security, for slave raiders sometimes smoked the fugitives out of their places of refuge and captured them.

In Iboland in modern Nigeria, where there was an extremely high incidence of kidnapping and slave raids, the fear of violent seizure made many residents stay at home, travel only in large armed groups and live in a state of military preparedness. As Olaudah Equiano, the famous Ibo slave who was kidnapped as a child, sold and shipped to Barbados in 1756, noted: "Our whole district is a kind of militia; on a certain signal given, such as the firing of a gun at night, they all rise in arms and rush upon their enemy."[22] When a slave raid was expected, special precautions were taken. The Ibo "guarded the avenue to their dwellings by driving sticks into the ground – sticks which are as sharp at one end as to pierce the foot and generally dipped in poison."[23]

Some African communities took special measures to protect their most vulnerable members, namely, women and children, from enslavement. For example, the men of Jakin, faced in the 1730s with the threat of slave raids by Dahomey,

> Sent their wives and children, together with the most valuable of their goods, to an island on the sea-coast about ten leagues to the eastward of Jaquin, under the protection of the King of Appah: whither they knew the enemy, from their fear of water and ignorance of navigation would not follow them.[24]

In Iboland farmers assembled their children in the yard of one of their number during the day for safe – keeping while they were away in the fields and instructed them to be on the look-out for kidnappers or raiders. The children often climbed trees to watch for kidnappers or raiders. These precautions, however, sometimes proved inadequate in the face of determined and daring kidnappers. Thus, Olaudah Equiano and his sister were kidnapped by two men and a woman who jumped over the wall of the premises where they were staying, seized them, stopped their mouths and ran off with them into a nearby forest before they could cry out or offer any resistance.

In circumstances where preventative measures failed to deter slave traders, Africans resorted to force and, above all, to flight to avoid enslavement. Victims of kidnapping almost invariably tried to resist, but usually they were eventually overpowered and subdued. Belligerents in war, deeply aware that capture might result in human sacrifice or sale to slave traders, often attempted to flee into woods and other places of safety to escape capture once it was evident that the battle was lost. Such attempts were sometimes defeated by the use of horsemen by the victors, who exploited the speed and terror generated by the animals to effect the capture of many fugitives. Africans who were subjected to slave-raiding expeditions also tended to resort to flight, especially if they were fortunate enough to receive a warning about the raid. The escape of fugitives from slave raids was to some extent facilitated by the restraint of raiders, who sought to take them alive and, if possible, without injury.

After initial enslavement, the next phase in the life of the captives was the journey, mostly by land but sometimes by water, from the place of enslavement to the coastal marts where the white slave traders from Europe and North America came to purchase them. This was often a long, demanding journey lasting several weeks or months, for increasingly many of the slaves were obtained from the interior rather than from coastal areas as was usually the case in the first phase of the Atlantic trade in the fifteenth century. Resistance during this coastward journey took many forms. Some slaves attempted to escape by breaking away from the coffle, in spite of the security measures taken by the captors, including tying their hands and them to each other. Others stubbornly refused to proceed on the journey, in spite of the infliction of severe corporal punishment, and so had to be dragged along. Some captives attempted to commit suicide, often by eating earth or by throwing themselves overboard from the canoes.

On their arrival at the coast, the slaves were herded together in forts belonging to European governments and commercial companies or in buildings called barracoons, owned by resident African, mulatto and white factory owners pending the conclusion of the arrangements for their sale to visiting slavers. There were four principal facets of the slaves' stay on the coast, namely, their detention in the forts and barracoons, their examination and sale, their embarkation and their presence on board the slaver until the vessel's departure from West Africa for Essequibo, Berbice, Demerara and elsewhere in the Americas. Often slaves had to remain on board for weeks, and sometimes for months in West African waters, while the vessel waited to collect its complement of slaves and to secure adequate supplies of foodstuffs, water and firewood for use during the Atlantic crossing.

The slaves showed their opposition to their enslavement by seeking to escape from the forts and barracoons. Sometimes captives, who were brought out of these buildings for fresh air, rebelled while they were being taken back there. Some slaves resisted by refusing to cooperate when they presented to prospective customers for an examination before purchase or by opposing branding with the purchaser's mark, a practice designed to prevent any substitution being made between the sale and the embarkation.

The time of embarkation was considered by many captains of slave ships as the most dangerous phase of the organisation of the trade in West Africa. Many slaves, grief-stricken and unwilling to leave their motherland, refused to board the canoes and small boats which were normally used to convey them to the slave ship, and often had to be beaten severely before they entered them. Others attempted to break away and dive overboard, sometimes into shark-infested waters, in an attempt to escape or commit suicide, preferring to face drowning than to go as captives to an unwelcome fate. Such resistance was reflected in the description given by Thomas Phillips, the captain of an English slaver, of the embarkation of a batch of slaves whom he purchased at Whydah on the Slave Coast in modern Benin in 1693. Phillips observed

> When our slaves were come to the sea-side, our canoes were ready to carry them off to the longboat, if the sea permitted, and we convey'd them aboard ship, where the men were all put in irons, two by two shackled together to prevent

their mutiny, or swimming ashore.

The negroes are so wilful and loath to leave their country that they have often leap'd out of the canoes, boat and ship, into the sea, and kept under water till they were drowned, to avoid being taken up and saved by our own boats which pursued them; they having a more dreadful apprehension of Barbadoes than we can of hell. We have likewise seen divers of them eaten by sharks, of which a prodigious number kept about the ships in this place.[25]

એર

While aboard the slave ships off the West African coast, captives resisted not only by throwing themselves overboard in an attempt to swim ashore or commit suicide, but also by staging mutinies in an effort to kill the crew, seize the ship and make their way to the nearby coast either by putting the ship ashore or swimming from it. Almost every year there were at least a few such cases of mutiny, the act of resistance most feared by white slave traders, who expected and prepared for its occurrence. Mutinies in fact seem to have been more frequent off the coast of Africa than during the Atlantic crossing. Those staged in African waters were the final, desperate expedient of captives to enable them to remain in their beloved homeland. They were deeply feared by the slave ship captains, for they resulted usually in injuries and fatalities among the crew, and especially among the slaves, and sometimes in the loss of the ship, and affected the profits of voyages considerably. They tended to occur especially at meal times, when all the slaves were brought on deck, and particularly in circumstances where the crew was small, weakened by illness and deaths, negligent, and indifferent to the welfare of the slaves.

Some mutinies were staged in response to information supplied to male slaves below by females on deck about the condition and activities of the crew. For example, the origin of the abortive mutiny led by the enslaved Baga chief, Tomba, on board an English slaver in 1721 was attributed largely to information and a weapon supplied by a "Woman-Slave, who being more at large, was to watch the proper Opportunity. She brought him word one night that there were no more than five white men upon the Deck, and they asleep, bring him a Hammer at the same time (all the Weapons that she could find) to execute the Treachery."[26]

Like this uprising, most mutinies proved unsuccessful, the slaves usually being overpowered by the superior weaponry of the crew. In several instances, however, the slaves succeeded in taking control of the ship and escaping to land. Such liberty sometimes proved to be short-lived, for Africans on the coast are known to have recaptured mutineers and sold them to another slaving vessel. On occasions where slaves managed to have retained their freedom after a successful mutiny, they sometimes stayed together and established their own community rather than disbanding and attempting to return to their respective homelands.

The final protest made by the captives in Africa against their enslavement normally occurred at the time the slave ship began to leave the African coast to undertake the Atlantic crossing to the Americas. The pandemonium which frequently took place was described by a white seaman on the first night of the voyage of the slave vessel **Zong** on a journey from the Gold Coast in modern Ghana to Jamaica in 1781:

> The slaves all night in a turmoil. They felt the ship's movement. A worse howling I never did hear, like the poor mad souls in Bedlam Hospital. The men shook their fetters which was deafening, for there are many below. The second mate says nigh on five hundred. One young woman (the females not being shackled) broke past the bosum when he lifted the hatch to quieten them, and ran screaming tearing her hair on the deck.[27]

Once, however, the ship left African waters and the final hope the captives had of remaining in Africa disappeared, their resistance tended to decline and the captain and the crew usually became less fearful and less anxious.

The resistance demonstrated by slaves in West Africa was due to several factors. The loss of personal freedom, the shame of enslavement, and the painful prospect of permanent separation from relatives, friends and the sacred and beloved motherland were fundamental causes of slave animosity. The most important reason for slave resistance, however, seems to have been the slaves' belief that a horrible destiny awaited them across the Atlantic. It was widely believed among them that they were being taken abroad to be offered as human sacrifices to deities in European religions, to be murdered to provide blood to dye cloth red, or, more commonly, to be killed and eaten by white cannibals. To many captives death in Africa was preferable to such an awesome fate. According to Thomas Phillips, the slaves had "a more dreadful apprehension of Barbadoes than we [Europeans] can have of hell."[28]

Terror in fact had contrasting effects on captives. It not only prompted desperate resistance, but also was the source of deep sorrow and depression among certain captives, which sometimes paralyzed them, prevented positive resistance to enslavement, and even caused some of them to lose their senses. Africans were so fearful of enslavement overseas that the threat of sale to visiting white slave traders was one of the most effective mechanisms of control employed by slaveholders in African societies over their slaves.

European visitors were struck by the depth of this fear. Mungo Park, the famous Scottish explorer who in 1796 travelled with a slave caravan from Manding in the Upper Niger to the mouth of the Gambia River, recorded his initial conversation with the slaves, who were destined to be sold to white traders at Gambia. According to him:

> They were all very inquisitive; but they viewed me at first with looks of horror and repeatedly asked if my countrymen were cannibals. They were very desirous to know what became of the slaves after they had crossed the salt water. I told them that they were employed in cultivating the land, but they would not believe me; and one of them, putting his hand upon the ground, said with great simplicity, "Have you really got, such ground as this to set your feet upon?" A deeply-rooted idea that the whites purchase Negroes for the purpose of devouring them or selling them to others, that they may be devoured hereafter naturally makes the slaves contemplate a journey towards the coast with great terror insomuch that the Slatees[29] are forced to keep them constantly, in irons, and watch them very closely to prevent their escape.[30]

This misunderstanding about the purpose of enslavement was particularly prevalent among Africans in the interior of the continent, for residents on the coast tended to be better informed, owing to the fact that they had more regular contact with Whites. The misconception stemmed partly from the fact that very few captives returned from the Americas to inform their countrymen that they had been taken there to work. Francis Moore, the British agent at James Island in the Gambia River, noted in the 1730s that the Fula of the inland state of Bondu "generally imagined that all who were sold for slaves were generally either eaten or murdered, since none ever returned."[31] There is evidence, however, that on a few occasions manumitted slaves who returned to Africa were able to correct this erroneous view temporarily and in a limited way.

In addition to general underlying causes like the fear of white cannibalism, slave resistance was provoked by specific circumstances affecting each phase of the slave's experience. For example, resistance during the journey to the seaboard was due partly to such aggravating factors as the long, rapid, exhausting marches which women and children in particular found extremely distressing, exposure to violent rains and excessive heat, and the need to travel through inhospitable areas. It was also a result of the inadequate provision of food and water, the discomfort of being at the bottom of leaking canoes sometimes almost covered with water, and the heaviness of the loads borne by the slaves, whom their captors often compelled to serve as beasts of burden to transport produce to the coast for sale.

Similarly, slaves were driven to seek to escape from the barracoons by unpleasant conditions such as overcrowding, close confinement, the impurity of the air, the intense heat, the lack of proper ventilation, exposure to sickness, infectious disease, bruises and other injuries, and at times the very long detention occasioned by the overstocking of the market or the absence of buyers. At the time of sale, resistance was often sparked off by the disruption of families and the branding of slaves. Furthermore, some of the mutinies which occurred on board the slave ships off the coast of Africa were due partly to the frenzy and other reactions provoked by storms or other adverse weather conditions.

Slave resistance on the coast could be attributed to at least four general factors. Firstly, it was partly a result of the fear, terror, surprise, shock and other features of the psychological, emotional, and mental impact which the first sight of the Atlantic Ocean, foreign ships and Whites with their peculiar colour and physical traits had on captives from the interior. Secondly, resistance was due to the lack of consideration and ill-treatment to which slaves were subjected by certain ship captains. Thirdly, resistance was particularly formidable on the coast because the captives realised that it was the last opportunity they had to gain their freedom and so to be able to remain in their native land. Finally, resistance was often incited by African residents at the coastal marts who deliberately encouraged slaves to escape from the barracoons and slave ships so that they could recapture them and sell them to some other factor or slaver.

Some acts of resistance to the Atlantic slave traffic were carried out by indomitable captives who demonstrated a remarkably strong determination to rebel, in spite of all the measures employed to control them. No mechanisms of control, including extreme physical brutality, proved able to subdue captives like the courageous Baga chief, Tomba, who was given a severe whipping for the defiance and lack of co-operation which he demonstrated at the time of examination and sale and was later killed in a serious mutiny which he staged on board the slaver off the African coast. This was true also of the unnamed slave who, after several unsuccessful attempts to escape and to burn down a barracoon in Galinhas country in the 1830s, was finally executed for being an incorrigible incendiary. Another slave, whom his captors also found incorrigible, was the leader of an abortive effort in 1730 to break out of Cape Coast Castle, a captive who had previously led several similar unsuccessful attempts to secure his freedom.

Resistance was provoked sometimes by the presence of a large number of slaves from a single ethnic group or country. On such occasions, the numerical strength and sense of relatedness of the captives served to provide the boldness and co-operation necessary to stage uprisings and commit other acts of resistance. Some ethnic groups acquired a reputation for resistance. The Fon, for example, were well-known for their resistance to enslavement. Even their women were said to have often committed suicide rather than to be sold into slavery. Africans from certain tribes, the Ibo for instance, were said to be more prone to resort to passive resistance like suicide than to active resistance like the staging of rebellions.

Slave dealers regarded resistance by the captives as natural and inevitable. They therefore took precautionary measures to check as well as suppress it. As John Newton, an English trader who did business on the Upper Guinea Coast in the 1750s, explained:

> When a hundred and fifty or two hundred stout men, torn from their native land, many of whom never saw the sea, much less a ship, till a short space before they had embarked, who have probably the same natural prejudice against a white man, as we have against a black, and who often bring with them an apprehension they are bought to be eaten: I say, when thus circumstanced it is not to be expected that they will tamely resign themselves to their situation. It is always taken for granted, that they will attempt to gain their liberty, if possible. Accordingly, as we dare not trust them, we receive them on board, from the first as enemies.[32]

The captains of slave ships were forewarned by their employers about the possibility of resistance from the captives and were urged to be particularly vigilant while they were on the African coast.

The resistance offered by slaves showed that they were unwilling captives who were determined to be free and were not glad to leave Africa, contrary to the assertions made by some supporters of the trade when it came under attack in Europe and the United States in the late eighteenth and early nineteenth centuries. The captives resisted their initial enslavement, their removal from the place of enslavement to the coastal marts, and their departure from the coast of Africa for Essequibo, Berbice, Demerara and elsewhere in the Americas. Their ideal was to escape with their lives, but, if necessary, many were prepared to commit suicide rather than to be exported as slaves. The suicide rate would certainly have been higher had it not been for the fact that some slaves did not have the courage to take their own lives. The pattern of resistance, begun in Africa, continued during the Atlantic crossing, and on the plantations and in the towns, cities and mines of the Americas. Ultimately, it was evidence of the determination of the human spirit to triumph over adversity.

For Further Reading

Mc Gowan, Winston — "African Resistance to the Atlantic Slave Trade in West Africa", **Slavery and Abolition,** Vol.11, No.1, May 1990.

Rathbone, Richard — "Some Thoughts on Resistance to Enslavement in West Africa", **Slavery and Abolition**, Vol 6, No.2, December 1985.

CHAPTER 7

SLAVE REBELLIONS AT SEA

No subject in Caribbean history has attracted the attention of scholars and students and captured the imagination of the public as much as slavery. In particular, the question of slave rebellions has evoked considerable interest. Not only have slave revolts been the focus of numerous postgraduate theses, but also the leaders of several major uprisings have been exalted in the post-independence period to the status of national heroes in Caribbean countries. For example, such status has been accorded to Kofi, Bussa and Sam Sharpe, the principal leaders of the most formidable slave rebellions in the history of Guyana, Barbados and Jamaica respectively.

Furthermore, monuments have been built in modern times in memory of these individuals and the uprisings which they led. Guyanese are familiar with the statue of Kofi at the Square of the Revolution in Georgetown, recalling the massive slave revolt in Berbice in 1763-64 which began well, but ended in failure. Similarly, a monument has recently been also erected in Georgetown in commemoration of Guyana's second major slave insurrection which occurred in 1823 on the East Coast of Demerara.

In striking contrast to this pronounced focus on slave uprisings on land in Guyana and elsewhere in the Caribbean, very little attention has so far been devoted to rebellions on board ship before the slaves reached the Caribbean. These uprisings occurred in two places, namely, on the coast of Africa before the slave ships sailed for the Americas, and during the Middle Passage, as the Atlantic crossing of the ships from Africa to the Americas is often called. This neglect of rebellions on board the ships which enslaved Africans is particularly striking in view of the fact that such revolts were far more frequent and more successful than slave uprisings on land in the Americas.

The greater frequency of slave rebellions on board the slave ships was due largely to two factors. Firstly, captives on such vessels did not have any other means of escaping alive from servitude than through a successful rebellion.

It was not possible for them, unlike slaves on land in the Caribbean, to escape and remain alive by running away. The only place to flee at sea was overboard in what was in reality an act of suicide. Many enslaved Africans, in fact, resorted to this expedient, plunging overboard deliberately to a watery grave rather than continuing in captivity.

The second reason for the higher incidence of revolts at sea by captive Africans was that certain favourable circumstances gave them a greater chance of success than those staged on land in the Caribbean. Notable among the advantages which rebels at sea enjoyed were the ability to plan in secret below deck without detection, especially at night, for there was no supervision of them there by Whites. In striking contrast, it was very difficult for slaves on land to meet, especially in large numbers, to plan a revolt without being detected and arousing suspicions.

More rebellions took place on board slave vessels on the coast of Africa before they sailed for the Caribbean than during this Atlantic crossing. This was because the captives believed that they could more easily capture the ship, guide it to the shore and escape, while it was on the coast than in the open sea. As the British slave trader, John Atkins, rightly observed, "there has not been wanting examples of rising and killing a Ship's Company, distant from land, tho not so often as on the coast."[33]

The principal objective of captives in staging rebellions at sea was to secure control of the ship and navigate it to land, preferably in Africa where hopefully they would gain their freedom. This was one reason why most slave rebellions during the Middle Passage occurred relatively soon after the ship left the African coast, usually within ten days' sail of the continent. Some uprisings actually occurred within sight of the African coast.

The view, however, which some individuals held that rebellions at sea by captive Africans only took place close to the African coast "while they had a shore to fly to", was not true. Many revolts occurred several weeks after the slave ship had left African waters. However, such rebellions, if successful, presented slaves with the difficult task of directing the ship back to Africa or to land in the Americas.

In some instances, successful rebels, who believed they had the ability to navigate the ship to land, killed all the officers and sailors or set them adrift and proceeded to make their way back to Africa. For example, in 1730 about 96 captives on board a ship named "Little George" slipped out of their chains and overpowered most of the crew, leaving the others who had taken refuge armed in a locked cabin, with the door guarded. They then concentrated on sailing back to Africa, accomplishing that goal in nine days. Two years later, in 1732, enslaved Africans on another vessel, the "William", killed the captain, set the crew adrift and returned to Africa. More often than not, however, successful rebels preserved the life of at least one member of the crew on condition that he or they helped to steer the vessel to land. This was particularly the case if the rebellion took place far out at sea.

The possibility of the outbreak of slave rebellions made the Middle Passage a very dangerous undertaking especially for the sponsors of the voyage and the officers and sailors on the slave ship. This risk was often emphasized in the instructions which sponsors gave to the captains of the slave vessels. For example, in 1775 an American captain was warned to be "very careful in keeping a good look out and watchful of your Negroes to prevent Insurrection."[34] Security from slave rebellions and the health of the slave cargo were, in fact, usually the two paramount concerns expressed by owners of slave ships to their captains.

The possibility of slave uprisings was the main source of fear of the captains of slave vessels, for revolts could endanger their own lives as well as those of the crew, who could not be replaced at sea. Captains and sponsors were also conscious of the financial implications of slave revolts at sea. Revolts could result in the financial failure of the voyage, if they caused the slaves to escape or many deaths among them or loss of the ship. These consequences were noted by the English captain, William Snelgrave, who observed

> I knew several voyages had proved unsuccessful by Mutinies, as they occasioned either the total loss of the ship and the white men's lives, or at least by rendering it absolutely necessary to kill or wound a great number of slaves in order to prevent a total destruction.[35]

The awareness of the danger of slave rebellions at sea made sponsors of slaving voyages employ many expedients to prevent their occurrence. For example, they provided chains, shackles and an unusually large crew to control the captives. They also equipped the vessel with special armament, especially close-range weaponry, including the deadly swivel guns mounted on the railings at strategic locations about the main deck.

The captains of the slave ships also took measures to prevent slave uprisings. They did everything to ensure that the members of the crew remained healthy so that they could play their critical role in the system of security on board through vigilance, including the use of armed sailors as guards. They also tried to ensure the ethnic diversification of the slave cargo and to exploit this and other divisions among the captives. Furthermore, they cleared the ship of anything which could be used by the slaves as weapons and made special security arrangements for captives suspected of planning rebellions, usually placing them under stricter guard.

In spite, however, of the wide range of mechanisms of slave control employed by the sponsors and captains, slave rebellions at sea continued. Rebellions and other forms of resistance, such as suicide and hunger strikes, were clear evidence that the captives resented their enslavement and yearned to be free. They were prompted by several factors.

The most fundamental cause of slave rebellions at sea was the natural human desire of the captives for freedom. This is easily understandable, especially as almost all the slaves on board the ships had been born free, but had lost that cherished freedom because of the transatlantic slave trade and wished to regain it. This desire was appreciated by many white participants in the traffic in captive Africans. For example, a member of the crew of a Liverpool slave ship described a rebellion which took place on it in 1749 as "a design of recovering their natural right, Liberty."[36] Similarly, Alexander Falconbridge, who served as a physician on several English slave vessels in the 1780s, attributed the outbreak of slave insurrections at sea to the fact that "very few of the negroes can so far brook the loss of their liberty."[37] He acknowledged that the captives had "a just sense of the value of liberty."[38]

Revolting slaves at sea were also influenced by their anger and grief over their removal from Africa. They were motivated by a strong desire to return to their beloved and sacred motherland, Africa, where their protective spirits and gods and revered ancestors resided, and to rejoin their family, other relatives and friends. Their grief struck many of the European slave traders. For example, James Arnold, a physician on a British slave ship, reported that captive women on board often sang songs tearfully about "their separation from their Friends and Country."[39] Furthermore, according to James Towne, an Englishman who was involved in two slaving voyages in the 1760s, when he inquired from the slaves why they had attempted revolts on his ship, "the reasons that were given me were, what business had we to make Slaves of them, and carry them away from their own country? That they had wives and children and wanted to be with them."[40]

Captive Africans were also prompted to rebel during the Middle Passage by their fears that they were destined ultimately for an awful fate. They did not know or did not believe that they were being taken from Africa to work on lands or in mines or homes across the Atlantic. Rather, many of them believed that a terrible destiny was awaiting them across the ocean, such as being offered as human sacrifices to the gods of their captors, being murdered to produce blood to dye red cloth which European traders sold in Africa, or more commonly, to be killed and eaten by their captors or other white cannibals.

The prevalence of these erroneous beliefs in Africa was noted by Adam Starr, a sailor on an English slave ship, while describing the frenzy among the slaves just before the vessel's departure from West Africa to Jamaica in 1781. He observed that:

> The blacks in their ignorance believed that the lands to which they are transported are filled with giant man-eating whites, and that they are carried across the sea to provide fodder for these monsters.[41]

A few years later another Englishman, Thomas King, who made nine slaving voyages from West Africa to the Caribbean between 1766 and 1780, told a British Parliamentary investigating committee that the fear of white cannibalism was one of three principal causes of slave rebellions at sea. In his evidence, he stated

> There are other Nations again in Africa who have an idea that the White People purchase them with intent to take them to their own country, to kill and eat them. The Negroes are sometimes on board the ship a considerable time before they are perfectly reconciled.[42]

Many captive Africans, however, never overcame this fear of white cannibalism. This was one of the main causes of the rebellions in the slave ships in the sight of land in the Caribbean and of the frenzy slaves demonstrated when Whites in Caribbean territories came on board to purchase them. This was emphasized by the French cleric, John Labat, who rightly observed that

> it is principally at the sight of land, whether one is still on the coast of Guinea or in the sight of the Islands that revolts must be feared because Negroes are possessed with the idea that they are being taken to the Islands only to eat them.[43]

There were several reasons for the widespread belief in West Africa that Whites were cannibals and for the Africans' misunderstanding of the purpose of the transatlantic slave trade. One of the main reasons was the fact that few enslaved Africans had returned to Africa from the Americas to inform their countrymen that they had been taken there to work. As Francis Moore, the British agent in the Gambia River in the 1730s correctly observed, residents of the inland state of Bondu "generally imagined that all who were sold for slaves were generally either eaten or murdered since none ever returned."[44]

Rebellions at sea were also a reaction to the terrible conditions to which the slaves were subjected during the Atlantic crossing. Among these widely known conditions, were overcrowding, poor ventilation and sanitation, intense heat, hunger and famishing thirst, seasickness and exposure to disease and death.

While these conditions made the Middle Passage unbearable, for many slaves its most distressing feature was the ill treatment, including sexual molestation of females, which they received from the crew of the ship. Some experienced captains of slave vessels, in fact, believed that maltreatment by the officers and crew was one of the principal causes of slave rebellions at sea. For example, according to the English captain, William Snelgrave,

> the Mutinies raised by them on board Ships are generally occasioned by the ill usage of the

> Sailors…If a ship captain is well inclined, slaves are easily governed.[45]

&

This view, of course, did not take sufficient cognizance of the other factors, such as the basic human desire for freedom and the desire to return to Africa, which helped to produce rebellions at sea.

In short, the terrible conditions of the Middle Passage, the pain of separation from country, relatives and friends, the shame and anger of enslavement and the fear of white cannibalism all combined to produce in the slaves a psychological condition of deep despair which guaranteed rebellions at sea. This and other forms of slave resistance, which began in Africa and manifested themselves during the Atlantic crossing, continued on the plantations of Essequibo, Berbice and Demerara and other Caribbean colonies.

For Further Reading

Mc Gowan, Winston	"The Origins of Slave Rebellions in the Middle Passage" in Thompson, Alvin (ed.), **In the Shadow of the Plantation. Caribbean History and Legacy** (Kingston: Ian Randle Publishers, 2002), 74-99.
Richardson, David	"Shipboard Revolts, African Authority and the Atlantic Slave Trade", **William and Mary Quartlerly**, 3rd series, 58, No.1, 2001.
Taylor, Eric	**If We Must Die. Shipboard Insurrections in the Era of the Atlantic Slave Trade** (Baton Rouge: Louisiana State University Press, 2006).
Walvin, James	**Crossings. Africa, the Americas and the Atlantic Slave Trade** (London: Reaktion Books Ltd., 2013), especially Chapter 5, entitled "Mutinies and Revolts".

Chapter 8

Some Features of the Slavery System in Guyana

As elsewhere in the Caribbean, slavery in Guyana was a cruel institution under which slaves suffered great humiliation and serious disabilities for which they usually could obtain no redress. The disabilities included poor housing, insufficient clothing, food that was deficient both in quantity and quality, long hours of hard work especially for field slaves, unsatisfactory medical attention and severe punishment, especially from Dutch masters, who were notorious for their brutality.

Slaves could escape from servitude by means of manumission either by paying their purchase price or as a reward by their master for meritorious service. Manumission, however, was extremely rare for several reasons. Firstly, the high price which slaves were required to pay to buy their freedom was a barrier. Secondly, to be manumitted they had until the late 1820s to receive the consent of their masters, who were extremely reluctant to grant this because of the scarcity of slaves in the society. Furthermore, masters were discouraged by the large financial deposit they were required to make into the colony's Poor Fund before freeing a slave so that the local government would be in a position to offer some charity to the freed slave if he proved unable to earn a livelihood after manumission. Thus as late as 1825, just before the British government made it obligatory for slaveholders in Guyana to free their slaves provided they could pay the price, only about 44 slaves were being manumitted each year in Demerara – Essequibo and about 11 annually in Berbice at a time when these two colonies had a slave population of about 72,000 and 21,000 respectively.

Slaves were valued, above all, for their labour. They were involved in a wide variety of occupations. Most of them, about 50 per cent, were field labourers, working in the cultivation of the three main agricultural staples grown for export, namely, sugar, cotton and coffee. The two other most common slave occupations were those of skilled tradesmen and domestics. Among the less common functions performed by slaves were those of fishing, transport workers (rowing boats), watchmen, drivers, sellers, nurses, stock keepers (rearing cattle, etc), traders, grooms, and carriers. One of the most important contributions of the slaves was in the establishment of basic infrastructure. It was they who built the sea defences, roads and the drainage and irrigation works vital for agriculture on the coast and in riverain areas.

Some slave occupations were influenced by considerations of gender and colour. For example, while there was no distinction in the employment of males and females as field labourers and as domestics, jobs such as those of drivers, fishing, stock keeping, watchmen and transport workers tended to be reserved for males, while occupations such as selling tended to be monopolised by females.

Discrimination on the basis of colour was exercised in favour of mulatto slaves who tended on the whole to be given a high percentage of the less demanding or more privileged jobs. A far smaller proportion of mulattoes than blacks served as field labourers, while a disproportionately high percentage of mulattoes were employed as domestics and skilled tradesmen.

The overwhelming majority of slaves never accepted the system of slavery with equanimity. They accommodated it or adjusted to it when they felt they had to and resisted it when they had opportunities to do so. Their responses can be categorised in three ways: firstly, adjustment or accommodation, which some masters misinterpreted to mean acceptance of slavery; secondly, escape – either by resorting to suicide or flight; and thirdly, resistance.

Flight was a common reaction of slaves to servitude. Runaway slaves who were making a bid for permanent (not temporary) freedom tended either to join or establish a village in the forest or to flee to a neighbouring country. Many runaways from Essequibo and Demerara went to the Orinoco region in modern Venezuela, while some fugitives from Berbice went to Suriname. There was a much higher incidence of flight in Essequibo and Demerara than in Berbice.

Where resistance was concerned, there were two basic types, passive and active resistance. Passive slave resistance included pretence at misunderstanding the orders of Whites, satire or ridicule of Whites, malingering, deliberately doing poor work, doing damage to the master's property, theft and feigning illness. Active resistance, on the other hand, included acts such as homicide (murder of Whites), physical attacks on Whites, and open rebellion.

One well-known example of homicide occurred in Essequibo in September 1744 when William Simpson, a British planter who had recently arrived from Barbados with his slaves, was murdered by two of them, after, apparently threatening to sell them to a Dutch planter if they did not work better. The slaves, it seems, were opposed to the strenuous work (of cutting down the forest trees to establish a new plantation) required of them, being unaccustomed to such hard work in Barbados.

Rebellions were the response from slaves most feared by Whites. They, however, were rare for they were difficult to organise, likely to fail and participants were severely punished by Whites as a deterrent to other prospective rebels. There were only two massive slave uprisings in Guyanese history – one in 1763 in Berbice and the other in 1823 in Demerara. There were, however, several small uprisings (restricted to a single plantation or a few plantations). Several intended revolts were discovered while in the process of being planned – often betrayed by some slave – and so were nipped in the bud by effective preventative action by the Whites. The best known of these aborted slave revolts was one planned to take place in West Coast Berbice in 1814.

The slave system survived because the small minority of Whites managed to devise effective mechanisms to control the overwhelming majority of slaves. At the height of the system around 1810 in Berbice as well as in Demerara – Essequibo slaves constituted about 94 per cent of the population and Whites only 1.7 per cent in Berbice and 2.7 per cent in Demerara – Essequibo.

Among the expedients employed by the white minority to keep slaves in subordination at least six stand out. The first was the prevalence of cruel, at times, sadistic punishments. Secondly, the Whites imposed restrictions on the freedom of movement of slaves, especially at night. For example, legislation in Berbice in 1804 forbade slaves to be out at nights after seven o' clock except on their master's business; in that event they were required to carry lights and written passes from their master.

Thirdly, regulations were in force to check the numerical preponderance of slaves. In particular, the colonial government required each estate to maintain a certain ratio of white adult males to slaves. Fourthly, until the nineteenth century masters denied slaves exposure to Christianity and formal education which they felt would make them more informed and rebellious. Furthermore, Whites tried to inculcate in slaves a belief in the myth of black inferiority. Finally, they established a close friendship and alliance with Amerindians, giving them annual presents and other rewards in return for services they performed such as pursuing and recapturing runaways and suppressing slave rebellions.

This system of slavery, admittedly with some modifications made from the 1820s, continued in Demerara, Essequibo and Berbice until the British government abolished it in the 1830s. As a result on 1st August, 1838 all the slaves in the colony became completely free.

For Further Reading

Cameron, A.J. Mc R.	**The Berbice Uprising 1763** (The Caribbean Press, 2nd Edition, 2011).
O'Jon, Eirene	"Slave Society in Early Nineteenth Century, Berbice", **History Gazette,** No.45, June, 1992.
Rose, James	"Runaways and Maroons in Guyanese History", **History Gazette,** No.4, January, 1989.
Thompson, Alvin	**Maroons of Guyana: Some Problems of Slave Desertion in Guyana, c. 1750-1814** (Georgetown: Free Press, 1999).
Thompson, Alvin	**Colonialism and Underdevelopment in Guyana, 1580-1803** (Bridgetown: Carib Research and Publications, 1987).
Thompson, Alvin	**A Documentary History of Slavery in Berbice 1796-1834** (Georgetown: Free Press, 2002).

CHAPTER 9

THE ORIGINS OF THE 1763 BERBICE SLAVE REBELLION

The massive slave uprising in 1763 in what was then the Dutch colony of Berbice is being commemorated in a special way this year, 2013, its 250th anniversary. Its importance has been recognized locally by the exaltation of its original principal leader, Kofi (commonly called Cuffy), to the status of a national hero in Guyana and the erection of a statue in his honour at the Square of the Revolution in an important area in Georgetown, the capital. The significance of this revolt has also been acknowledged regionally, for it is one of only four specific slave rebellions which the Caribbean Examinations Council's Caribbean History syllabus requires candidates to study in depth.

The 1763 Berbice slave rebellion is one of only a few major revolts which distinguished the history of African slavery in Guyana. It occurred sixty years before the outbreak of the second massive slave uprising in Guyana in 1823 in what was then the united British colony of Demerara-Essequibo. Apart from a slave rebellion which broke out in the French colony of Saint-Domingue in 1791 and resulted in 1804 in the establishment of the independent state of Haiti, the 1763 Berbice uprising came nearer to overthrowing white European rule in this hemisphere than any other slave rebellion. It also involved a far greater proportion of the slaves in Berbice than almost any other rebellion in any territory in the history of slavery in the Americas.

The ultimate cause of slave rebellions in the Caribbean may be said to be the basic human desire for freedom. This was particularly the case with slaves who were born in Africa, but lost that cherished freedom because of the demands of the transatlantic slave trade and slave systems in the Americas. The vast majority of the estimated 3800 black slaves in Berbice in 1763 are believed to have been African-born, possessing a strong basic desire to be free.

Apart from this fundamental desire for freedom, many of the Berbice slaves who rebelled in 1763 were incensed by two particular features of slavery there. The first grievance, which seems to have been the most important single cause of the rebellion, was the severe physical brutality to which slaves were subjected, especially on eight privately-owned plantations located in the Head Division of the Berbice River. Most of these plantations seem to have been owned by proprietors resident in the Netherlands, but were run by attorneys, who throughout the Caribbean were notorious for their excessive cruelty to slaves. As Wolfert van Hoogenheim, the Dutch governor of Berbice at the time of the revolt, recorded in his Journal a week after its outbreak

> The two leaders of the rebels [Kofi and Akara] had ordered Ramring [a clergyman] to bring me a message in which they informed me of the cause of the revolt, namely the cruel mistreatment of slaves by a party of inhabitants, whose full names were given.[46]

It is significant that many of the slaves owned by the Berbice Association, the Dutch company responsible for the administration of the colony, did not support the rebellion for they were better treated than slaves on the privately-owned plantations.

The second main grievance of Berbice slaves in 1763 was the reduction by their masters of their normal food allowances, which were always deficient in both quality and quantity. As a result, many slaves suffered hunger, but were still required by their masters to do the same amount of arduous labour as before. Those who showed dissatisfaction with the reduced rations were dealt with severely by the increased use of the whip, thereby strengthening their sense of injustice of slavery.

This problem with rations stemmed partly from the fact that a significant part of the food given to slaves was imported from Europe. However, circumstances there, notably a severe winter in 1762, for some time made it impossible for ships to leave the ice-bound ports. Furthermore, the existence of the well-known Seven Years' War (1756-1763), involving the main European states, posed serious problems for the security of supply ships on the high seas which were infested with privateers. In these circumstances the arrival of supply ships with some of the slaves' food was prevented or delayed. Some of the ships which arrived in Berbice, in fact, brought food of inferior quality or in a state of decay, rendering it difficult or impossible for masters to continue to grant slaves the normal rations.

Slaves, incensed by cruelty and reduced rations, began to think of resorting to rebellion. Slave rebellions were a rare occurrence in Berbice and in most other slave societies in the Americas for they were difficult to organise, were most likely to fail and resulted in the severe punishment of participants, especially the leaders. The organisation of a massive slave revolt in Berbice in 1763 was difficult for the slave population was very heterogeneous in terms of diverse tribal affiliation and geographical origin in Africa and was scattered over a very wide area. The rebels, however, profited from the failure of the overconfident Dutch planters and authorities to enforce Pass Laws which had been introduced in Berbice at least as early as 1735 to check the movement of slaves off their plantations, especially at night. The leaders of the rebellion or their agents were therefore able to go from plantation to plantation to organise it without detection.

They seem to have been prompted to revolt by their awareness of certain factors which favoured the success of a rebellion. Firstly, they apparently gained a psychological boost from the signs of a decline or breakdown of Dutch authority in Berbice. In 1762 the Dutch government there, adversely affected by the cowardice and weakness of its soldiers and militia, took an inordinately long period of two months to suppress a minor rebellion by 26 slaves.

Secondly, the slaves must have been conscious of the military weakness of the Dutch, stemming from the poor state of the colony's defences, in terms of both men and fortifications. Since 1756 Berbice had been suffering from a serious epidemic which affected all races, especially the Whites, causing illness and death. By 1763 the white Berbice military forces, which normally did not number more than 100 men, were severely incapacitated and unable to check or suppress a slave rebellion. As Governor Van Hoogenheim lamented at the outset of the uprising, "I found myself in a very sad and unpleasant situation, having no more than eight soldiers in service."[47]

The military capability of the Dutch government and planters was further undermined by the unavailability of many Amerindians, who were usually employed by them to suppress slave rebellions and to recapture runaway slaves. By the beginning of 1763 many Amerindians had started to move out of Berbice to escape from the ravages of the epidemic and the detrimental effects of drought on their cassava crop. The cause of the rebels was rendered more propitious by the poor state of the main Dutch Fort, Fort Nassau, which was badly in need of repair.

The military crisis facing the Dutch authorities and slave masters was clearly reflected in the decision of Van Hoogenheim to call a special meeting of the colony's legislature to discuss this vital question, as soon as he heard of the outbreak of the revolt. As he recorded in his journal entry of 6 March, 1763

> This morning the Court held a special meeting to consider the situation of this Colony with regard to the rapid success of the rebels; the weakness of our militia; the cowardice of our burghers; the bad state of our defences with regard to our small number of troops; the faultiness and age of Fort Nassau. All these maturely considered, we agreed that our situation was lamentable and, for us, past saving.[48]

The basic human desire to be free, growing resentment over physical cruelty and the reduction of their food rations and the possibility of exploiting propitious circumstances such as the breakdown of Dutch authority and Dutch military weakness combined to make slaves on the Berbice River decide to stage a massive rebellion early in 1763. If these slaves needed any further stimulus or encouragement to revolt, they must have received it from the outbreak on February 23, 1763 of what seems to have been a separate, special, isolated slave rebellion on Plantation Magdalenenburg on the Canje River, the main tributary of the Berbice River. On February 27, four days after the commencement of that apparently independent rebellion, in which Kofi was not involved, he, Akara and other leaders staged a massive slave revolt initially on the Berbice River, centring on Plantations Hollandia, Lelienburg, Juliana, Zeelandia, Elizabeth and Alexandria.

For Further Reading

Cameron, A.J. Mc R.	**The Berbice Uprising 1763** (The Caribbean Press, 2nd edition, 2011).
Hartsinck, J.J.	"The Story of the Slave Rebellion in Berbice", **Journal of the British Guiana Museum and Zoo and Royal Agricultural Society**, Nos 2620-27, December 1958-December 1960.
Netscher, Peter	**History of the Colonies Essequibo, Demerary and Berbice,** translated from the Dutch by W.E. Roth (Georgetown, 1929), originally published in 1888.
Thompson, Alvin	**The Berbice Revolt, 1763-64** (Georgetown: Free Press, 1999).
Velzing, Ineke	"The Berbice Slave Revolt of 27th February, 1763", **History Gazette,** No. 29, February, 1991.

Chapter 10

The Causes of the 1823 Demerara Slave Rebellion

The most fundamental cause of this rebellion seems to have been the slaves' desire to be free from an increasingly severe system of bondage which had developed on the East Coast of Demerara in the years immediately prior to 1823. The system was marked, above all, by excessive overwork, apparently the most bitter specific grievance shared by the majority of the slaves. As a contemporary missionary noted

> a most immoderate quantity of work had very generally been expected of them, not excepting women far advanced in pregnancy.[49]

This excessive overwork was the result of a number of factors. It stemmed partly from the decline in the size of the labour force due to the end of importation of slaves from Africa, which had been declared illegally by the British government in 1807. The slave population could not maintain itself numerically from natural reproduction because of low birth rates, and high infant and adult mortality rates, among slaves. As numbers declined, those remaining in the system, understandably, were required to work harder. To make matters worse for the field slaves, their owners demanded more work to increase agricultural productivity in an effort to counteract a decline in profits owing to a fall in the international prices of the three major commercial staples- cotton, coffee and sugar-produced by the colony.

Overwork on the East Coast of Demerara was also a consequence of a growing switch by plantation owners from the cultivation of cotton to sugar production. This change was prompted by a marked fall in cotton prices in the British market and increasingly effective competition there which Guianese cotton suffered from cotton grown in the southern United States. Slaves who were accustomed to work on cotton estates were greatly distressed by the change to sugar, which required longer hours and harder work.

In these circumstances, slaves were subjected to a number of new abuses. On some plantations an earlier beginning of the working day was introduced and the slaves' lunch period was curtailed drastically. On many estates slaves were forced to work long hours into the night, as well as on Sundays, legally a free day and the only day of leisure they were normally allowed. Everywhere the whip was used to compel tired, slow, reluctant, resentful and recalcitrant slaves to work, resulting in a marked increase of physical brutality. As a white observer noted, "their punishments have been frequent and severe… The whip has been used with an unsparing hand."[50] These developments were understandably a source of great discontent and distress to the slaves, making them more prone to revolt.

In these circumstances, the paucity of free time to cultivate their ground provisions, to sell their produce, to fish and to be with their families became increasingly a major grievance of slaves. According to Captain Croal of the Demerara Rifle Corps which helped to suppress the rebellion, Jack Gladstone, the principal leader of the revolt, told him that "he thought it very hard to work all the week and have no time for himself."[51]

In fact, by 1823 the duration and demanding nature of slave labour in Demerara were becoming a source of concern even to some white politicians there. For example, in May 1823 John Austin, a member of the Court of Policy, told other members of the legislature that "he was very anxious to call the attention of the Court to the expediency of enacting a law limiting the working hours of the slaves"[52] and announced his intention to present soon a motion to introduce such legislation. However, he withdrew his proposed motion later on hearing that the British metropolitan government had decided to implement a policy of slave amelioration in Demerara-Essequibo and other British Caribbean colonies.

One of the distinctive features of the rebellion was the leading role played by Christianized slaves, especially deacons, class-teachers and other members of Bethel Chapel, the London Missionary Society church located at Plantation Le Resouvenir. One of the main grievances of these slaves was the imposition of restrictions on the practice of their religion as a result of their masters' erroneous interpretation and application of a 16 May 1823 circular from the governor, John Murray. The circular required slaves to have written permission from their masters to leave their estates to go to Bethel Chapel and to hold religious meetings on their respective plantations at night. Contrary to the governor's intention, however, slave owners used the circular to withhold permission from slaves who wished to attend church or conduct such meetings.

Christianity affected some slaves in other ways which prompted them to rebel. For example, some of its doctrines, especially the doctrines of the equality of man in the sight of God and Christian brotherhood, made certain slaves have an enhanced value of their self-worth which seemed to them no longer compatible with the subordination of slavery. This was reflected in the remarks made by a group of rebels at the beginning of the uprising to Governor Murray that they wanted their "right… God had made all men of the same flesh and blood. They were tired of being slaves."[53]

The immediate cause of the rebellion was the slaves' erroneous belief that the British government had granted them their freedom, but that this liberty was being illegally withheld from them by the local government and their masters. This misconception stemmed from an attempt by the British government in 1823 to improve conditions of slaves in the British West Indies to make them more humane with the introduction of several measures, including the prohibition of the presence and use of the whip in the field and the outlawing of the flogging of female slaves.

The attempt to introduce this policy of amelioration was greatly resented by slave owners in Demerara. They regarded the policy as an unjustifiable violation of their right to property, as a likely cause of greater slave resistance and as a severe blow to the authoritarian control which they exercised over their slaves and regarded as crucial for the stability of slave society. They had the sympathy of the governor. Though the matter was discussed in the Court of Policy, no public announcement was made of the ameliorative proposals. It was also discussed with intemperate language in many of the planters' houses, often indiscreetly in the hearing of house slaves. Furthermore, a few Whites shared the news with slave mistresses. Soon a rumour spread among slaves that freedom had been granted by the imperial authorities, but that the governor, the other members of the Court of Policy and the planters were acting in collusion to deprive them of liberty. Thus, at the outbreak of the revolt, some rebels told the governors that "their good King had sent out orders that they should be free, and they would not work anymore".[54]

The slaves' basic desire to be free, their hatred of the increasingly severe slave system, religious considerations and misunderstanding of the ameliorative proposals were important factors in the origin of the Demerara Revolt of 1823. There were also other causes, such as the personal grievances of the slaves, especially leaders of the rebellion. For example, Jack Gladstone, the supreme rebel leader, was influenced partly by the fact that he was peeved over the loss of one of his women, who had become the mistress of John Hamilton, the white manager of Plantation Le Resouvenir, as well as over a severe punishment he had recently received for seducing another slave's wife.

In the opinion of many slaveholders on the East Coast of Demerara, the main cause of the rebellion was the influence exercised over the slaves by Rev. John Smith, the English minister in charge of Bethel Chapel on Le Resouvenir, whom they accused and charged with inciting the slaves to revolt. They exaggerated greatly, however, the influence and role of Smith. In fact, he had tried unsuccessfully to dissuade the slaves, especially his chief deacon, Quamina, from rebelling. Smith's influence and Quamina's role are interesting controversial features of this abortive uprising.

For Further Reading

Bryant, Joshua	**An Account of the Insurrection of the Negro Slaves in the Colony of Demerara which broke out on the 18th of August, 1823** (Demerara: Guiana Chronicle Office, 1824).
Craton, Michael	**Testing the Chains: Resistance to Slavery in the British West Indies** (Ithaca: Cornell University Press, 1992).
Da Costa, Emilai	**Crowns of Glory, Tears of Blood. The Demerara Slave Rebellion of 1823** (New York: Oxford University Press, 1994).
McGowan, Winston	**The Demerara Revolt, 1823** (Georgetown: Free Press, 1998).
St. Pierre, Maurice	"The 1823 Guyana Slave Rebellion. A Collective Action Reconsideration", **The Journal of Caribbean History,** Vol. 4: 1 and 2, 2007.

Chapter 11

John Smith and the Origins of the 1823 Demerara Slave Rebellion

One of the most controversial issues in the 1823 Demerara slave uprising is the role played by Rev. John Smith, the minister of Bethel Chapel on Plantation Le Resouvenir, one of the centres of the revolt, and after whom the Congregational church in Brickdam in Georgetown is named. Smith was an Englishman who was born in June 1790 in Rothwell, a town in Northamptonshire, England. His origins were humble. His father, a soldier, died in his childhood. At the age of fourteen he was apprenticed to a baker of biscuits in London where, owing to the influence of Independent churches on his life, he offered himself to the London Missionary Society (L.M.S.) for service overseas as a clergyman.

Smith was sent to the British colony of Demerara-Essequibo where he arrived in February 1817 to assume responsibility for Bethel Chapel. This was about nine years after this church with a congregation predominantly of black slaves had been founded in 1808 by John Wray, the first L.M.S. missionary to Guyana. Wray had encountered much opposition from slave owners who feared that the evangelization of the slaves would make them more discontented and rebellious. However, by the time of Smith's arrival in Demerara as a permanent replacement for Wray who had moved to Berbice, much of this opposition had subsided, though many slaveholders on the East Coast of Demerara continued to express the view that instruction in Christianity would eventually have an adverse effect on the slaves.

The slave owners' fears seemed justified when the massive slave rebellion broke out there in August 1823. Smith was accused by them of being the main cause or instigator of the rebellion. He was arrested, charged, tried, found guilty of complicity in the revolt and sentenced to death. He died from illness in prison in Georgetown in February 1824, while a reprieve from the British government in London was on its way to Demerara.

These developments stemmed partly from the fact that several of the leaders of the slave rebellion were members of Bethel Chapel, including Quamina, the chief deacon and a personal friend of Smith. From the time of his arrival in Demerara, Smith was very conscious of the difficulties and dilemmas which he faced as clergyman serving in a slave society. He was required to proclaim a gospel of spiritual liberty within a context of servitude, without preaching anything which might offend or disturb the slaveholding class or suggest rebellious ideas to the slaves. This proved to be an extremely difficult task for Smith, a man of strong convictions who was personally opposed to slavery. He was a rare example of a white man in the colony who detested slavery and became a friend of, and sympathizer with, the slaves. He was emotionally disturbed by the cruelties of slavery of which his residence on a plantation enabled him to have first-hand experience. Thus, in March 1819 he wrote: "My heart flutters at hearing the almost incessant cracking of the whip." [55] In July 1823, a month before the outbreak of the rebellion, in response to the proposals of the British government, to ameliorate slavery, he observed: "The rigours of negro slavery, I believe, can never be mitigated. The system must be abolished."[56]

By then the relationship between Smith and the slaveholders on the East Coast of Demerara had become quite bitter. Apart from his general opposition to slavery, there were at least four major causes of conflict between the clergyman and the slaveholders. Firstly, Smith objected to the employment of slave labour on Sundays, legally the only free day which the slaves had. He was opposed to Sunday labour not merely because it affected attendance at Bethel Chapel, but more fundamentally because in his opinion it was a violation of the fourth commandment to "remember the Sabbath day, to keep it holy."[57] The planters, on the other hand, felt slaves should work on Sundays because of their failure to finish sufficient work during the normal six-day working week, as punishment for alleged transgressions, and because at harvesttime in particular the considerable amount of work to be done required continuous labour.

Smith also became embroiled with the slave owners over his refusal to cease holding evening services at Bethel Chapel, especially during the week. Slaveholders objected to such meetings partly because they wished slaves to work at night. Furthermore, they claimed that their slaves returned home very late and tired from these meetings, adversely affecting their ability to work effectively the following day. Finally, the planters feared that slaves would use the opportunity of absence from their plantation at night without white supervision to plan revolts.

A third source of conflict between Smith and the slaveholders was the question of access to members of his congregation. He was annoyed because he was often not allowed to visit them without special permission from their masters except on the plantation where he resided.

Finally, the relationship between Smith and slave owners was embittered because of their belief that he and other missionaries were spies sent by the leaders of the abolitionist movement in Britain and that his secret and ultimate objective was the emancipation of the slaves. This belief grew stronger after November 1818 when the L.M.S. in London published in one of its missionary magazines a letter from Smith attributing poor attendance at Bethel Chapel to the fact that some planters were forcing their slaves to work on Sunday.

Although Smith was a strong-willed individual who was reluctant to make compromises, he made some efforts to conciliate the slaveholders. For example, eventually by November 1822 he abandoned the practice of ringing the bell announcing the start of the week-night services which the planters detested. He also ceased singing certain hymns and reading certain passages from the Bible which he felt could be misunderstood by the slaves, especially hymns and passages which dealt with spiritual freedom.

Nevertheless, his relationship with the planters continued to deteriorate and finally he was accused of exciting the slaves to rebellion. In fact, he may be considered to be partly responsible for the occurrence of the revolt, but not anywhere near the extent which the planters believed. His detestation of slavery must have strengthened the feelings of resentment which the slaves had and encouraged their opposition to servitude. Certainly his teaching, especially the doctrine of the equality of man in the sight of God, served to reinforce the slaves' view of the injustice of slavery. It does not seem, however, that Smith deliberately promoted discontent and dissatisfaction in the minds of the slaves towards their masters, managers and overseers as he was charged. Nor did he consciously excite them to revolt or resist their masters. He also tried, admittedly without success, to convince Quamina and other slaves that they were misled in their belief that the British government had granted them freedom but that this was being illegally withheld by the local authorities and their masters. It seems, however, that Smith had some knowledge or suspicions of the impending slave rebellion shortly before it erupted, but he did not communicate this to the authorities possibly because he wanted to avoid the stigma of being an informer.

For Further Reading

Chamberlin, D.	**Smith of Demerara, Martyr-Teacher of the Slaves** (London,1923).
Wallbridge, Edwin	**The Demerara Martyr: Memoirs of the Rev. John Smith, Missionary to Demerara** (Georgetown: The Daily Chronicle, 1848).
Northcott, Cecil	**Slavery's Martyr: John Smith of Demerara and the Emancipation Movement, 1817-1824** (London: Epsworth Press, 1976).
Titus, Noel	"Reassesing John Smith's Influence on the Demerara Slave Revolt of 1823" in Thompson, Alvin (editor), **In the Shadow of the Plantation. Caribbean History and Legacy** (Kingston: Ian Randle Publishers, 2002), 222-245.

CHAPTER 12

QUAMINA AND THE 1823 DEMERARA SLAVE REBELLION

The slave Quamina and the English clergyman, John Smith, are the two figures usually associated with the 1823 Demerara slave uprising. Quamina's role in the rebellion is one of the most controversial features of the revolt both in the view of contemporaries and modern historians. He was viewed by John Murray, the governor of the colony of Demerara-Essequibo in 1823, and most of the planters there as the mastermind and supreme leader of the rebellion. According to Murray, "Quamina was undoubtedly the principal ringleader in the revolt."[58] This view prompted the government of Guyana in 1985 to honour him by renaming one of the streets of Georgetown, Quamina Street, instead of Murray Street, which until then bore the name of the governor who engineered the suppression of the uprising.

Quamina was an African –born slave who apparently was sold into slavery as a child along with his mother and at least one brother and brought to Demerara, where his mother died as a slave in 1817. He worked as a slave on Plantation Success on the East Coast of Demerara. There he was apprenticed to another slave, a master carpenter who had been brought from one of the Caribbean islands, where he had been exposed to Christianity through the work of British missionaries. Quamina profited from the training and by 1820 had become the plantation's head carpenter.

It was his mentor who was largely responsible for one of the most important developments in Quamina's life, namely, his introduction to Christianity. This occurred in 1808 when Quamina reluctantly accepted the master carpenter's invitation to attend one of the meetings being conducted by the London Missionary Society (L.M.S.) clergyman, John Wray, on the neighbouring Plantation, Le Resouvenir. Quamina, whom Wray described as "one of the first fruits of my labours in Demerary",[59] was one of the earliest and most devoted converts of Wray. He was baptised by Wray on

December, 26, 1808 and admitted into the membership of Bethel Chapel. He was among the first twenty-four slaves to be granted these two privileges.

The L.M.S. archives in England has a letter written or dictated by Quamina on February 8, 1809, detailing the circumstances around his conversion and mentioning the impact which this spiritual experience and Wray's ministry had had on him. It is the earliest surviving letter written by a slave in the colony. The following is a verbatim copy of this little-known letter, modified only by dividing it into paragraphs.

※

> I thank God dat he instruct you to send to we a Missionary here to lead we out of dis darkness, dat we have been in almost all our lives, for before he was here we did' ent know our right hand from our left.
>
> Since he came here by the blessing of God, we are able ti say a prayer, & we know dat without him we can never be saved. We was so much at a loss from hearing al nonsense, which our Father & Mother teach us, we did believe all kinds of wickedness. When the Minister first came my Massa workman [i.e. the master carpenter] persuaded me to go & hear what de Minister say. Being hearing so much nonsense I was so hard to persuade by him, for I says I was no sinner it was no need for me to go & hear him. He turned away very sorrowful and asked me to come in de house at breakfast time. When I went he told me as I was a good Prentice [apprentice], he would wish to see me wel, tell me I should do him a pleasure to take a walk with him the Sunday morning.
>
> Yet still I was very hard to persuade by him. I told yes dat I'll think more about it by dinner time & according I did & went in to him and told him I'll try to go a Sunday. Then I take & related it to another man de name of Jack de next morning. Both of us went to him again, and we both agreed date we would walk with him de Sunday following

> according we did.
> We came & de Minister was already preaching, as we heard him preach de very first word we heard we was convinced den date we are a sinner. We felt such a desire (a great desire) to love Christ & sometimes we think, he is with us.
> I then went home to my eldest Brother. I thought myself was in darkness but he was worse if possible & would not have any concern with me: but one day I was telling him he could not be saved without Christ he den came & dat very day he was convinced dat he was a sinner, & now he feels more than I do. But I feel so much that I cannot sleep without praying, date I scacch [scarce] can pray but by de help of God try to overcome it. What a great love I feel for Christ. I hope God will enable me much to pray for you, may God help you to pray for our Minister & for us, also for de good Gentleman [Hermanus Post, proprietor of Plantation Le Resouvenir] that sent for our Minister. My best respects to you all, & all de good people, & we dank them all for sending us de blessed Gospel. May they all feel the love of Jesus Christ in their hearts.
> I desire dear Friends, to remain
> Yours in Jesus Christ
> Quammina[60]

The planters were keen to attribute the supreme leadership of the rebellion to Quamina because they blamed the revolt partly on the impact which the work of Rev. John Smith had on slaves on the East Coast of Demerara. He was held in very high esteem by Wray and Smith for his "upright walk" and stable marriage, the latter observing in 1822 that "Peggy and Quamina, a very superior and loving couple, had lived together as man and wife for nearly 20 years."[61] In 1816 Quamina was elected deacon of Bethel Chapel and by 1823 he had become its chief deacon, not surprisingly for he was regarded as the most loyal, best-behaved, most trustworthy and pious deacon. The office of chief deacon was the highest position an African could occupy in Smith's congregation. Quamina was also the slave who was closest to Smith in terms of personal friendship. By 1823 he was the head carpenter of Plantation Success adjacent to Plantation Le Resouvenir and was one of the most respected members of the slave community in the eyes of both his fellow slaves and free Blacks. The high esteem in which he was held was reflected in the fact that it was said that if the slave rebels had succeeded in overthrowing white rule and establishing an African state in Demerara, Quamina would have been chosen to be king.

Quamina's role in the rebellion has been greatly exaggerated. Though he was one of the leaders, he certainly was not the supreme leader, a role that belonged to his son, Jack Gladstone. His involvement was very active in the planning or the preparatory stage of the uprising, but only minimal in its execution.

Several factors seem to have prompted Quamina to be involved in the rebellion. Like many slaves on the East Coast of Demerara, he was a victim of overwork and severe physical punishment. He also resented the fact that he was not given time to care his ailing wife, Peggy, before her death in 1822. Furthermore, he was annoyed that he was forced sometimes to miss church services on Sundays, legally a free day for the slaves, because of work ordered by his master, who, like many other slaveholders, endeavoured to place restrictions on the attendance of slaves at Bethel Chapel.

Quamina was also influenced by the rumour that the British government in London had freed the slaves, but that their liberty was being withheld illegally by their masters and the local government. Although he was told by Smith that there was no truth in the rumour, he was not initially convinced and continued to believe and spread it. As Smith recorded in an entry in his private journal dated July 25, 1823, three and a half weeks before the outbreak of the rebellion

> Quamina of Success came to inquire if I had heard the report that the King had sent out orders to the Governor to free the slaves. I told him I had not heard of it, and if such a report was in circulation, it must not be believed for it was false... I told him it was likely the Governor had some orders because the Government at home wished to make

some regulations for the benefit of the slaves, but not to make them free. This answer, however, scarcely satisfied him.[62]

☙

Quamina approached Smith on several occasions about the issue. Eventually Smith's counsel seems to have made him increasingly unsure about the alleged grant of freedom. Consequently, by the time the rebellion began on 18th August 1823, he was not strongly committed to it. In fact, on the day when it started Quamina, admittedly unsuccessfully, tried to postpone, if not prevent, its outbreak.

Quamina was not very active in the rebellion after it began. About an hour before it started, he was arrested by the manager of his plantation, John Stewart, on the order of the district military officer, Michael McTurk, who was convinced that he and his son, Jack Gladstone, were behind the rebellion. He was released, however, by some slaves.

When hostilities began, Quamina did not arm himself or take part in the fighting. This was probably in keeping with his view that the slaves should strike and not resort to force to secure their freedom. At a meeting of the leaders of the rebellion on the day before its outbreak, he is purported to have said: "Tomorrow morning you must put down your shovel, and hoe and cutlass, and sit down in the house."[63]

Quamina intervened to protect John Stewart from injury when the rebels took control of Plantation Success. Stewart later declared on oath: "I did not see Quamina do anything improper; he was keeping the rest of the people from hurting me."[64]

With the suppression of the rebellion, Quamina, still unarmed, as a runaway sought refuge in the bush behind Plantation Chateau Margot. An attractive financial reward was offered for his capture. Eventually on 16th September, 1823, he was shot and killed by an Amerindian in an expedition of militia men and Amerindians sent by the government and planters to capture fugitives. His corpse was dragged to the front of Plantation Success, bound with chains and hung between two trees as a warning of the fate awaiting prospective rebels. For months it remained there, swinging in the breeze and becoming shrivelled. According to an English resident, "a colony of wasps had actually built a nest in the cavity of the stomach, and were flying in and out of the jaws which hung frightfully open."[65]

In short, Quamina's leadership of the revolt after its initial outbreak was, if not non-existent, very limited. The supreme leader of the uprising, both before and after its outbreak, was his son, Jack Gladstone, who was the chief cooper on Plantation Success and gained some of his influence because of his relationship to him. However, Jack was viewed by Governor Murray and many planters wrongly, merely as someone who was supporting his father's scheme.

For Further Reading

Da Costa, Emilia **Crowns of Glory, Tears of Blood. The Demerara Slave Rebellion of 1823** (New York: Oxford University Press, 1994).

Chapter 13

The Course of the 1823 Demerara Slave Rebellion

The rebellion broke out at Plantation Success shortly after 5:00 pm on Monday, 18th August 1823. In the following two days, it spread up the East Coast, engulfing almost all the plantations as far as Mahaica and several in the other direction between Success and Georgetown. Slaves on some estates only joined the rebellion after they were subjected to taunts that they were cowards or threats of violence on their life from the rebels, especially the leaders.

For at least one of several reasons, slaves on about five plantations between Georgetown and Mahaica refused to join rebellion. Some of them did not believe that freedom had been granted by the British government as was alleged and if it was, they were prepared to wait until they were given it. Furthermore, some slaves felt that rebellion was not justified because they had considerate managers or masters. Some slaves were also fearful that the rebellion would fail just as the one in Barbados in April 1816 and that the rebels would suffer casualties and incur severe punishment.

One plantation where the slaves refused to join the uprising was Better Hope. In fact, they opposed the rebels by force, drove them away from the estate, but were finally overwhelmed after the rebels returned with reinforcements. The slaves of Better Hope desired freedom, but they felt that it should be obtained, not by means of African rebellion, but rather by waiting until it was granted by the Whites.

From the outbreak of the rebellion, the action of the rebels assumed a general pattern. They seized the Whites- proprietors, attorneys, managers and overseers- and placed them in the stocks without hurting them to prevent them from escaping to raise an alarm or to join the militia or as an act of revenge, giving them a taste of their own medicine. They also took possession of their arms and ammunition, burnt some estate buildings and canefields, and destroyed some bridges to hinder or prevent access by troops from Georgetown. This action was rendered quite easy because of the overwhelming numerical preponderance enjoyed by the slaves, who outnumbered the Whites by as many as 50 or 60 to one on many plantations.

On a few plantations where the rebels were opposed with firearms, they resorted to the use of guns in return. These encounters resulted in the death of two and the injury of three or four white plantation personnel in defending their estates. However, the most remarkable feature of the course of the rebellion was that the slaves hardly offered personal violence to anyone, especially where they met no resistance. They had the opportunity, especially during the initial two days of the revolt, to kill most of the white personnel on the plantations, if this had been their desire or intention. Instead, they demonstrated a remarkable degree of restraint, self-control and humaneness, for the most part merely seizing them and placing them in stocks without harming them. This virtual absence of the shedding of the blood of Whites during the uprising was attributed by the slaves to the influence exerted on them by religious instruction which they had received at Bethel Chapel. They explained: "We will take no life for our pastors have taught us not to take that which we cannot give".[66]

The responsibility for suppressing the rebellion lay in the hands of John Murray, the governor of the colony. Shortly after he received personal proof of the outbreak of the rebellion, Murray dispatched up the East Coast all the regular troops which he could muster and some of the militia. He also declared martial law and all white persons capable of bearing arms were required to enrol in the forces which were being assembled to suppress the uprising. Additional detachments of soldiers – both regular troops and civilian volunteers – were dispatched to the scene of the revolt with specific instructions. They were required to reconnoitre, to rescue Whites who were besieged in the plantation houses or placed in the stocks on the plantations, or to reinforce the colony's small military post at Mahaica. Their progress was hindered by the broken bridges and by the presence of large groups of rebels with whom they had several minor encounters.

The rebels achieved some success in these initial clashes. For example, on Monday evening they fired on a small party of regular troops and forced them into a skirmishing retreat all the way back to Georgetown. Furthermore, on Tuesday about 700 or 800 of them drove Lieutenant Brady and his small garrison of 12 soldiers from Plantation Dochfour back to Mahaica.

The decisive military engagement in the rebellion occurred on the following day, Wednesday, 20th August, 1823, at Plantation Bachelor's

Adventure. There, a large body of slaves, numbering about 3000 – 4000 according to one estimate, armed mostly with cutlasses and pikes, that is, "knives fastened on poles", met 300 well-armed regular soldiers under the command of Colonel Leahy. Leahy tried to persuade the leaders of the rebels to end the rebellion and to ask their followers to lay down their arms and return to their plantation and work. However, they refused, declaring that they would fight for freedom. Eventually, Leahy ordered his troops to open fire, much to the surprise of some of the slaves who were so misguided that they expected the British troops not to fire on them. An estimated 200 of the rebels were killed and the others, dispersed in confusion, fled.

This massacre at Bachelor's Adventure was the turning point in the uprising. Within a few days of this battle, the rebellion was suppressed and public peace was virtually restored. In short, within a week of its outbreak, the East Coast Demerara uprising, in striking contrast to the slave insurrection in Berbice in 1763, can be said to have ended, in the sense that there was no further resistance from the slaves. In the following weeks, however, the local government and the planters sent several expeditions into the forested hinterland of the plantations to capture fugitive rebels. It was during one of the expeditions on 16th September 1823 that Quamina, for whose capture an attractive financial reward had been offered, was shot and killed by an Amerindian in the bush behind Plantation Chateau Margot as a runaway.

There were many reasons for the failure, especially the quick collapse, of this massive uprising in which the slave rebels had the valuable advantage of a decisive numerical advantage over the Whites. Firstly, the rebels lacked a carefully conceived and well-concerted overall plan and strategy. This weakness was reflected in the lack of agreement among their leaders as to the method to be adopted to secure the freedom which they believed had been granted by the British government. While some leaders wished the slaves to proceed armed in a body to Georgetown to claim freedom, others were in favour of remaining on the plantations, withdrawing their labour and forcing their managers to go to Georgetown to ensure that the slaves were granted freedom. Furthermore, some leaders believed that a strike would force the managers to inform them of their supposed new rights.

The cause of the rebels also suffered from inadequate military preparation. They had made no preparation for war and as a result at the outbreak of the rebellion they had no guns, gunpowder or bullets. Their military training and experience were also inadequate. Unlike the white troops, they were not trained for military service. Many of them were Creoles who had never handled a gun and therefore were not skilful in its use. Moreover, the rebels were very deficient in military tactics. As a white soldier noted when they were decimated at Bachelor's Adventure, "they soon fell into confusion for want of method".[67]

The possibility of success in the rebellion was rendered more difficult by the failure of the slaves to extend the uprising to other areas of the colony apart from the East Coast of Demerara. Their plans and efforts to persuade slaves in Georgetown and West Demerara to join in the rebellion failed. Consequently, Governor Murray was able to focus all his attention and resources on the East Coast rather than being faced with the much more frightening prospect and demanding task of having to suppress an uprising on several fronts simultaneously.

The rebels' defeat was also a result of their lack of ruthlessness. The remarkable moderation and restraint which they demonstrated towards the Whites during the uprising could not win what ultimately was a war. The slaves' attitude was in striking contrast to the extreme ruthlessness of their white opponents, facilitating the latter's victory. As Wallbridge correctly observed:

> No mercy, however, was shown to the Negro. With regard to them, there was a tremendous slaughter- under the influence… of an ill-judged and unwarrantable severity, it was deemed necessary to make terrifying examples of not a few, by killing them on the spot. Many were wantonly shot by the Militia soldiers for mere sport.[68]

The treatment of the rebels by Colonel Leahy in particular was marked by such severe cruelty that it horrified civilian volunteers who served under his command.

Another crucial factor responsible for the defeat of the revolt was the vastly inferior armament of the rebels, most of whom were armed with cutlasses and pikes. The only firearms which they possessed were the small quantity which they seized from the planters. The tremendous advantage which the Whites had in firing power, easily compensating for their numerical inferiority, was clearly demonstrated in the decisive confrontation at Bachelor's Adventure.

There, the 300 well-armed white troops suffered only two casualties - one bugler killed and one rifleman wounded- whereas the 3,000 odd rebels, who had less than 100 muskets, experienced 200 fatalities. This crushing defeat at Bachelor's Adventure had a dramatic and permanent effect on the morale of the rebels. It struck great terror in the minds of many slaves, prompting some to flee into the bush, while the greater part returned to their respective plantations and resumed work as usual.

For Further Reading

Bryant, Joshua	**An Account of the Insurrection of the Negro Slaves in the Colony of Demerara Which Broke Out on the 18th of August 1823** (Georgetown: Guiana Chronicle Office, 1824).
Da Costa, Emilia	**Crowns of Glory, Tears of Blood. The Demerara Slave Rebelloion of 1823** (New York: Oxford University Press, 1994).
McGowan, Winston	**The Demerara Revolt, 1823** (Georgetown: Free Press, 1998).
Wallbridge, Edwin	**The Demerara Martyr: Memoirs of the Rev. John Smith, Missionary to Demerara** (Georgetown: The Daily Chronicle, 1848).

Chapter 14

The Consequences of the 1823 Demerara Slave Rebellion

This abortive slave uprising had numerous consequences, both for the rebels and the Whites. It resulted in the severe punishment of the participants, especially the leaders, though some of them, notably Jack Gladstone, were given a reprieve for cooperating with the authorities. Initially this punishment was imposed by the victorious white troops, led by their ruthless commander, Colonel Leahy. Leahy marched from plantation to plantation, conducting what he called court martials, sentencing to death leaders and other slaves who were suspected of having been involved in the uprising. Later the governor, John Murray, set up special courts which subjected the slaves to less arbitrary and less summary justice.

As a result of these two types of judicial proceedings, between August 23 and October 8, 1823 an estimated 47 slaves were hanged publicly and 25 others who had been sentenced to death were reprieved. Several slaves were decapitated and their heads mounted beside the public road on the East Coast of Demerara and in Georgetown. This action was designed partly as a punitive measure, but especially as a means of producing fear among slaves which, the Whites hoped, would serve as a deterrent against future rebellion. Among the slaves who suffered such a fate was Quamina the chief deacon of Bethel Chapel and the father of Jack Gladstone, the mastermind and principal organizer of the revolt. Quamina was shot and killed by an Amerindian as a runaway in the bush behind Plantation Chateau Margot on September 16 during the course of one of the expeditions sent by the government into the forested hinterland of the plantations to capture fugitives.

Many slaves received severe whippings, in some cases as many as 1,000 lashes, far in excess of the supposed legal maximum of 39 strokes. Others were sentenced to work in chains. Moreover, as a further and general penalty by a 16 December 1823 proclamation by the Governor and Court of Policy all the slaves on the East Coast of Demerara were forbidden to have their customary Christmas dances and other entertainment which they normally enjoyed annually during this festive season.

The consequence of the 1823 revolt which attracted most attention locally and abroad was the fate of the English clergyman, Rev. John Smith, the minister in charge of Bethel Chapel since 1817. The revolt had calamitous consequences for Smith. On its third day, Smith was arrested and later charged with four major offences, namely,

> That he did promote discontent and dissatisfaction in the minds of Negro slaves towards their lawful masters, managers and overseers, thereby intending to incite the said Negroes to break out into open revolt and against the peace of our Sovereign Lord, the King.
>
> Having advised, consulted and corresponded with a certain Negro named Quamina touching an intended revolt, and did aid and assist such a rebellion.
>
> Having come to the knowledge of a certain revolt and rebellion he did not make known the same to the proper authorities.
>
> Well knowing the said Quamina to be an insurgent he did not use his utmost endeavours to secure and detain the said Quamina as a prisoner but permitted him to go at large and depart against the peace of our sovereign Lord the King.[69]

In short, Smith was charged, admittedly somewhat unfairly, with serious complicity in the revolt by slaveholders and other Whites who were keen to attribute the cause of the uprising to the influence of Smith and Christianity on the slaves. In fact, many slave owners on the East Coast of Demerara regarded Smith as the main instigator of the rebellion.

At his trial which began on October 13, 1823 before a court martial, the prosecution made much use of quotations from his private journal, which was seized at the time of his arrest, to show that he detested slavery, believed that it was evil and should be abolished, and was in sympathy and close communication with the slaves. It also depended on the perjured evidence of slaves, including Jack Gladstone. These factors and the general prejudice and ill-will of the slaveholders influenced the Court's verdict which was delivered on November 24, 1823, the 28th day of the trial.

The Court declared that it had found Smith guilty of promoting discontent among the slaves, but not guilty of directly and deliberately inciting them to rebellion "for want of sufficient proof in support thereof."[70] He was also declared guilty of aiding and abetting Quamina and of communicating with him at the beginning of the rebellion, but not guilty of rendering him further assistance. Smith was also found guilty of not informing the authorities of the intended revolt and not of making an attempt to seize and detain Quamina when the rebel visited him after the outbreak of the uprising.

The Court sentenced Smith to death by hanging, but referred the sentence to the metropolitan government for confirmation, at the same time recommending him for mercy. In February 1824, however, Smith died in prison in Demerara from illness, while awaiting a response from London, where the Crown had decided to grant him a reprieve, but to order his deportation to England.

The clergyman was buried in Georgetown one morning at about 4.00 o'clock before dawn, without funeral procession and in the presence of only a few witnesses, mainly the officiating priest, some prison officials, a free black man, his wife, Jane, and the wife of another L.M.S. missionary. This quick, essentially secret burial was in accordance with orders received from Governor Murray who was fearful of the possibility of a public demonstration, especially by members of Smith's congregation over his death.

The government and the planters were determined that no recognition would be given to the spot of his burial. Thus when some black members of Bethel Chapel attempted to rail it in, they were stopped. The bricks were scattered and the railing was torn down. Nevertheless, Smith's memory has been preserved visibly because the Congregational Church named the chapel which it built later in Brickdam in Georgetown, Smith Church, after him.

The rebellion was detrimental to the work of the L.M.S. on the East Coast of Demerara. Because of the intense animosity of Whites there against the

Society in the wake of the uprising, its Directors in London, acting on the advice of the attorney of Plantation Le Resouvenir, decided not to appoint a missionary there to replace Smith. In any event the colonial authorities in Demerara-Essequibo sequestrated Bethel Chapel, which they regarded as the source and heart of the rebellion. Later they entrusted the building to missionaries sent out to Demerara from England by the Church Missionary Society, an Anglican body which, as an arm of an established church, they and the planters deemed more trustworthy than the nonconformist L.M.S. Bethel Chapel was never returned to the L.M.S. which, owing to planter hostility, never resumed its mission at Le Resouvenir. In 1835 the building was removed to Montrose, another plantation on the lower East Coast, where one Rev. Wyatt had begun to work on behalf of the L.M.S.

Perhaps the most immediate result of the 1823 rebellion was that it shattered the confidence of the predominantly British slaveholders in Demerara-Essequibo. The uprising was a great surprise to many of them for this colony, unlike its neighbour, Berbice, had never before experienced a major slave rebellion. British slaveowners there had long boasted that they were more humane than their Dutch predecessors, whose management of the slaves they considered extremely cruel and likely to provoke slave animosity and rebellion. They therefore did not anticipate the occurrence of any major slave insurrection. After that event, however, they began to view and treat their slaves with a degree of mistrust which they had not displayed before.

This new attitude of heightened fear and deep mistrust was reflected in many ways. For example, immediately after the suppression of the rebellion the Court of Policy, the local planter-dominated legislature, began to address special attention to what it termed "the discipline of the Negroes." It also gave special consideration to the question of security. Martial law, which had been declared as soon as the rebellion broke out in August 1823, was not lifted until January 1824, about five months after the suppression of the revolt. Furthermore, the local government took what it described as the "highly prudent"[71] step of ensuring the enforcement of the "Deficiency Law", which required the maintenance of a specific minimal ratio of Whites to slaves on each estate. The Court hoped that the enforced presence "on each estate of the full number of white persons required by the existing law"[72] would discourage the slaves from seeking to rebel again. It also toyed with the idea of strengthening the local militia by taking the unprecedented step of forming a corps of free mulattoes, who until then were not allowed to enrol in the militia or perform any other military duty. The Court, however, does not seem to have implemented this proposal. It took action, however, to strengthen the Rifle Corps of the Demerara Militia by adding another company to it.

The 1823 rebellion also served to stimulate strong local white opposition to the interference of the British metropolitan government into what white residents of Demerara-Essequibo considered the colony's internal affairs. Owing to resistance from the Court of Policy and the metropolitan government's reluctance to override the Court's decisions, two more years were to elapse before any concrete action was taken in Demerara-Essequibo for the amelioration of the conditions of the slaves.

The rebellion also had a significant impact on other countries. It caused considerable tension in many colonies in the British West Indies, stimulating unrest among slaves, fear among planters of slave revolts, and white opposition to missionaries. In October 1823 a Methodist chapel was burnt down in Barbados. Missionaries throughout the British West Indies found themselves under suspicion and felt very threatened. Some of them made serious efforts to allay the fears of slaveowners and the colonial authorities. In Trinidad and St. Lucia, for example, missionaries sought interviews with the governor to solicit his support and protection.

The rebellion had serious repercussions especially on Britain. In its wake, the British government felt compelled to have a royal proclamation, dated 10th March 1824, issued and sent to the West Indies. The proclamation was designed partly to correct the misconception about the slave amelioration proposals - that is, the erroneous belief that the Crown had freed the slaves which had helped to cause the Demerara rebellion. It expressed the King's "highest displeasure against slave insubordination in Demerara",[73] requiring slaves to render entire submission and dutiful obedience to their masters. It also urged British Caribbean governors "to enforce by all the legal means in their power, the punishment of those who may disturb the tranquillity and peace of our said colonies and possessions."[74]

Although all these effects of the 1823 Demerara rebellion were significant developments, undoubtedly the most important consequence of the uprising was its impact on the anti-slavery movement in Britain and the future of Caribbean slavery. Two hundred petitions about slavery were submitted to the British Parliament in April, May and June 1824 and there was a long acrimonious debate in Parliament about the rebellion and West Indian slavery. For some time, the rebellion proved to be a serious blow to the abolitionist cause. The cause's best-known leaders, William Wilberforce and Thomas Buxton in particular, and the abolitionist movement in general, were accused by the Demerara slaveholders and their supporters of being largely responsible for the outbreak of the rebellion by their demands for the abolition of slavery. In the face and wake of this strident criticism many supporters of the abolitionist cause left the movement, which, in the circumstances, was forced to adopt a somewhat cautious approach to abolition.

But this setback to the abolitionist cause proved to be only temporary. In the long run the 1823 Demerara rebellion helped the abolitionists to triumph, particularly after the occurrence of an even more massive slave uprising in Jamaica in 1831 which resulted in the persecution of Christian missionaries and the burning down of their chapels by slaveowners and their white supporters. Memory of the 1823 rebellion, especially the treatment and death of John Smith, a white clergyman, helped to attract attention in Britain inside and outside Parliament to the evil of slavery and the necessity of abolishing it. In short, the abortive 1823 East Coast Demerara rebellion served eventually to enable the slaves to gain their objective, liberty, although none of the rebels who survived was likely to have anticipated this in the wake of the failure of the uprising.

For Further Reading

Craton, Michael	**Testing the Chains: Resistance to Slavery in the British West Indies** (Ithaca: Cornell University Press, 1982).
Da Costa, Emilia	**Crowns of Glory, Tears of Blood. The Demerara Slave Rebellion of 1823** (New York: Oxford University Press, 1994).
McGowan, Winston	**The Demerara Revolt, 1823** (Georgetown: Free Press, 1998).
Northcott, Cecil	**Slavery's Martyr: John Smith of Demerara and the Emancipation Movement, 1817-1824** (London: Epsworth Press, 1976).

Chapter 15

The Distinctive Features and Significance of the 1823 Demerara Slave Rebellion

This uprising was the first major slave revolt in the history of the United Colony of Demerara-Essequibo. In 1763, sixty years earlier, the neighbouring colony of Berbice had experienced a massive slave rebellion. Slaveholders in Demerara-Essequibo feared the occurrence of a similar revolt there, but apart from a significant rising in 1795 on the West Coast of Demerara, in which runaway slaves joined those on the plantations, their fears had not materialised. The East Coast of Demerara in particular was free from serious slave unrest. A few minor slave "conspiracies" were discovered there in the period between 1800 and 1815, but these prospective rebellions had all either been nipped in the bud or suppressed shortly after their outbreak. This pattern was altered by the outbreak of the 1823 rebellion, a major uprising.

One distinctive feature of this 1823 Demerara revolt was that it is one the most massive rebellions in the entire history of African slavery in the Americas which dated back to the late 1490s and ended finally in 1888, when Brazil became the last country in the hemisphere to abolish slavery. It is estimated that 11,000 to 12,000 slaves from about 55 plantations on the East Coast between Liliendaal and Mahaica participated in the uprising. Slaves from only five estates in this extensive area covering about twenty miles refused to join the rebellion. The participants constituted nearly one sixth of the entire slave population of Demerara-Essequibo which in 1823 was estimated at 74,978.

The only slave revolts in the Americas which are known to have involved a greater number of slave rebels than the 1823 Demerara rebellion were the successful uprising in Saint Domingue between 1791 and 1804 and the rebellion at Christmas in Jamaica in 1831. Massive rebellions, involving thousands of slaves, in fact, were extremely rare in the Americas. This was largely because they were very difficult to organise secretly over a wide area without detection by the pervasive mechanisms of surveillance and control employed by the slaveholding class. Often, they were discovered as a result of betrayal by some member of the slave community who acted as an informer in order to secure personal benefits offered by the slave-masters pursuing a "divide and rule" strategy to control the slaves.

The largest slave rebellion in the United States had just over one hundred participants, while the most sizable revolt in Brazil, the country in the Americas with the highest incidence of slave rebellions, involved only a few thousand slaves and the other main uprisings there not more than 600-700 slaves. The participation of 11,000-12,000 slaves in the 1823 East Coast Demerara rebellion was therefore one positive feature of the organisation of the uprising.

This rebellion, like many other slave uprisings, was evidence of the discontentment of slaves with servitude. It occurred at a time when the institution of slavery was coming under increasing attack in Britain especially from Evangelical Christians, other philanthropists and some economists. The institution, however, was being strongly defended by apologists who contended that the lot of slaves was tolerable and that in general slaves were contented and much happier than they had been or would be in Africa. Rebellions like the 1823 Demerara uprising clearly demonstrated that this pro-slavery argument was a lie or myth.

In 1823 slaves on the East Coast of Demerara, especially those employed in the field and factory, were particularly discontented over the long hours of demanding work extracted from them. It was this excessive overwork which helped to make the receipt in July 1823 of the news of the initiative of the British government to improve the condition of slaves in the British West Indies a source of great excitement to slaves on the East Coast of Demerara and the immediate cause of the rebellion in August. The slaves, eager to escape from the increasingly severe system of servitude there, misinterpreted the policy of amelioration to mean emancipation.

The 1823 Demerara rebellion was also significant because many if its leaders were Creoles, that is, locally-born not African-born slaves. Most of the earlier slave revolts in the Caribbean had been led mainly by slaves who were born as free men in Africa in an effort to regain the cherished freedom which they had lost when they were purchased by Europeans and brought as captives against their will across the Atlantic to the Caribbean. Few rebellions had been due mainly to the initiative of Creoles who were slaves from birth and gained a reputation of being less hostile and more accommodating to slavery than African-born slaves. This belief which many Whites in the Caribbean shared about the relative passivity of Creole slaves was shattered by the occurrence in the early nineteenth century of three major rebellions which were led principally by Creole slaves- an uprising in Barbados in 1816, the 1823 revolt in Demerara and another rebellion in 1831 in Jamaica. These rebellions reinforced the argument made by anti-slavery advocates that all slaves - Creoles as well as African-born – resented slavery and longed to be free.

Another striking feature of the Demerara rebellion was the remarkable degree of restraint, self-control and humaneness demonstrated by the rebels who killed or injured very few Whites during the uprising. This virtual absence of deaths and injuries by Whites was attributed by the slaves to the effect on them of religious instruction which they had received at Bethel Chapel, the church established by the London Missionary Society at Plantation Le Resouvenir in 1808.

The 1823 Demerara slave rebellion was also significant because of two related factors. Firstly, one of the distinctive features of the revolt was the very prominent role played by Christianised slaves, especially deacons, class teachers and other devoted members of Bethel Chapel. In fact, this rebellion was probably the first revolt in the history of the Caribbean which was led mainly by Christianised slaves.

Secondly, the rebellion was a very rare occasion in Caribbean history when the supreme leadership of a slave revolt was attributed to a white man, namely, Rev. John Smith, the English clergyman in charge of Bethel Chapel. Perhaps the most distinctive feature of the rebellion was that many slave owners on the East Coast of Demerara believed that Smith was the main instigator of the uprising. As a result, he was arrested, charged, sentenced to death and died in prison. No previous slave revolt in the Caribbean had had such a calamitous end for a respectable white man at the hands of his fellow Whites. However, Smith's death eventually had considerable significance for it helped to influence the momentous decision made in 1833 to abolish slavery in the British Empire with effect from 1st August, 1834.

For Further Reading

Da Costa, Emilia	**Crowns of Glory, Tears of Blood. The Demerara Slave Rebelloion of 1823** (New York: Oxford University Press, 1994).
McGowan, Winston	**The Demerara Revolt,** 1823 (Georgetown: Free Press, 1998).

CHAPTER 16

THE 1763 AND 1823 SLAVE REBELLIONS: A COMPARATIVE PERSPECTIVE

The 1763 rebellion in Berbice and the 1823 uprising on the East Coast of Demerara are two of only three major slave revolts in Guyanese history, the third occurring in West Demerara in 1795. Major slave uprisings, in fact, were for several reasons a comparatively rare event in the history of most slave societies in the Americas. Slaves were often deterred from rebelling by three serious considerations. They were aware not only that it was difficult to plan and organise rebellions without detection, but also that uprisings were likely to fail and the participants, especially the leaders, would incur severe punishment.

The 1763 and 1823 uprisings were two of the most massive slave rebellions in the entire history of slavery in the Americas. Guyana is one of only a few countries in the hemisphere that experienced as many as two massive slave revolts. In fact, the vast majority of countries there did not experience a single major rebellion involving thousands of slaves.

It is estimated that about 3,000 slaves were involved in the rebellion in Berbice in 1763, while about 11,000-12,000 of them participated in the 1823 Demerara revolt. Though the number of slave rebels in 1823 was much greater than those who participated in 1763, the proportion of slaves who revolted in 1763 was much larger. The rebels in 1823 constituted about 1/6 or 1/7 of the entire slave population of about 75,000 of the colony of Demerara-Essequibo, while those in Berbice in 1763 were at least 75-80 per cent of that colony's estimated slave population of about 3,800. In short, in 1763 Berbice experienced what may be described as a colonial or almost total rebellion. In striking contrast, in 1823 the revolt was restricted to only one area of the colony of Demerara-Essequibo, namely, most of the East Coast of Demerara. Slaves in other parts of the colony did not participate, although, admittedly, the leaders of the rebellion hoped to obtain support from slaves at least in West Demerara.

There were some similarities in the origins of the two rebellions, but the differences were more striking. The most fundamental cause of both uprisings was probably the natural human desire of the rebels for freedom. This was no doubt particularly the case of the African-born slaves, who had been born free, but had lost that cherished liberty when they became victims of the transatlantic slave trade and understandably longed to regain it.

The slaves were also prompted to rebel in 1763 and 1823 by their wish to be free from the intolerably severe system of bondage to which they were subjected. In Berbice in 1763 the most disturbing feature of this severity seems to have been inadequate rations and physical brutality, especially by certain masters or managers of plantations in the Head Division of the Berbice River. On the other hand, in Demerara in 1823 the aspect of severity which was the subject of greatest complaint was excessive overwork, which was probably the most single specific grievance shared by the majority of slaves on the East Coast.

There were at least two major causes of the 1823 rebellion which were not factors in the earlier uprising in Berbice. One of them was the influence of Christianity and the grievances of Christianised slaves. The other factor was its immediate cause, namely, the erroneous belief of the slaves in the 1823 that the British government in London had granted them freedom, but that this liberty was being illegally withheld by the local authorities in Demerara and their masters.

In addition to the causes, the course, consequences and significance of the two uprisings can be compared meaningfully. The rebellions were similar in that they both ended in failure. They differed considerably, however, in their duration and in the extent of the threat which they posed to the slave-holding class and the institution of slavery.

The Berbice rebellion lasted about fourteen months and is one of the longest revolts in the history of slavery in the Americas. It also came nearer to overthrowing the system of slavery than any other abortive slave uprising in the hemisphere. The slave rebels in 1763 experienced considerable success in the early months of the uprising, virtually driving the Whites out of the colony. This success, which enabled them to assume control of the colony, was due largely to their unity and the initial military advantage which they enjoyed over the white troops, decimated by an epidemic. Their eventual defeat by April 1764 stemmed mainly from serious disunity which developed among them, a growing shortage of arms and ammunition, and the effectiveness of the reinforcements which were summoned by the Berbice government from other Dutch colonies and the Netherlands.

In striking contrast, the 1823 Demerara rebellion was suppressed within a week and did not pose a formidable threat to slavery there. Its early demise was due partly to the fact that it was confined to one area of the colony, namely, the East Coast of Demerara. This limitation enabled the colonial authorities to concentrate all their attention and military resources there rather than on several fronts as had been the case in Berbice in 1763, when fighting took place on both the Berbice and Canje Rivers.

The slaves in 1823 also suffered from a great disadvantage in armament, being armed mostly with cutlasses and pikes against troops with guns. The effect of this disparity was clearly seen in the crushing defeat which they experienced in the decisive military engagement at Bachelor's Adventure on the third day of the rebellion.

The marked difference in the number of casualties suffered by the two sides in this encounter was also due to one of the most striking features of the rebellion, namely, the remarkable degree of restraint and humaneness demonstrated by the slave rebels. The rebels hardly offered personal violence to any White, especially where they met no resistance. On a few plantations, however, where they were opposed with firearms, they returned fire. These rare clashes resulted in the death of two and the injury of four white estate personnel. This restraining attitude of the slaves, a result of the moderating influence of religious instruction on them, was one of the causes of the failure of the rebellion. It was in marked contrast to the extreme ruthlessness of the white troops.

As in 1763 in Berbice, the suppression of the 1823 Demerara uprising was followed by severe punishment of the leaders and other prominent participants. This severity was designed both as a punitive measure and as a means of engendering fear among slaves which, the Whites hoped, would serve as a deterrent against future rebellions.

The long duration of the Berbice revolt did great damage to the colony, ruining many plantations and causing a significant numerical decline in the slave population. The physical, material and economic damage there was far greater than that which Demerara suffered in 1823.

Both rebellions shattered the confidence of slaveholders and caused them to adopt new security measures. In Berbice, for example, the pass laws, which restricted the movement of slaves outside their plantations especially at night, were enforced strictly after the rebellion.

Finally, where consequences and significance are concerned, the 1823

Demerara revolt had an impact not matched by the earlier Berbice uprising. It attracted attention in England inside and outside Parliament to the terrible evil of slavery and the need to abolish it. Eventually, ten years later, it contributed to the momentous decision of the British government to abolish slavery in the British Empire with effect from 1st August 1834.

For Further Reading

McGowan, Winston	**The Demerara Revolt, 1823** (Georgetown: Free Press, 1998).

Chapter 17

The Impact of The Restriction and Abolition of The Transatlantic Slave Trade on Demerara-Essequibo, 1805-1831

In 1800 the area which today constitutes the Republic of Guyana consisted of two Dutch colonies, Berbice and the United Colony of Demerara-Essequibo which had been occupied by the British since April 1796. In 1814 the Netherlands ceded these colonies to Britain who unified them in 1831 into a new entity called British Guiana.

British occupation in 1796 resulted in many changes in Berbice and Demerara-Essequibo. Some of the most important early changes were in relation to the transatlantic slave trade from Africa which had peopled the region with a growing number of Africans since the beginning of Dutch colonization there in the late sixteenth or early seventeenth century. British occupation was followed by a massive increase in the volume of the trade in captive Africans to Demerara-Essequibo which had been undersupplied with them throughout the period of Dutch rule.[75] Within five years at least 28,000 captive Africans were landed in Demerara- Essequibo and by 1803 an average of about 8,000 of them was being supplied there each year.

Planters in Demerara- Essequibo looked forward to a long duration of this flourishing trade. Their hopes, however, did not materialize for the British government imposed severe restrictions on the Atlantic slave trade to Demerara- Essequibo and Berbice in 1805, before outlawing the traffic completely for all British subjects and possessions two years later. This chapter focuses on the reasons for the restrictions, the reaction of the planters in Demerara-Essequibo to them and to the subsequent abolition of the Atlantic slave traffic and the impact which these two developments had on the slave population of the colony.

The Restriction of 1805

The restrictions on the Atlantic slave traffic to Demerara-Essequibo were introduced in the wake of a dispatch dated 21st August 1805 sent by

Lord Castlereagh, the Secretary of State for the Colonies, to the governor of the colony. The instructions in the dispatch prohibited the importation of captive Africans into the colony to work on lands which were not already under cultivation. They, however, allowed planters to import each year under licence a maximum of three per cent of the colony's total enslaved population to make up for losses in their stock provided that this deficiency was not due to ill-health, neglect, overwork or sale. Importation could take place only under licence which would be denied to any slave owner who was proved to have knowingly sold enslaved people for new cultivation except provision grounds. After 1st January 1807 no captive Africans could be imported into the colony directly from Africa. The supply allowed could only be secured from the older British West Indian colonies, i.e. those which came under British rule before war broke out in Europe in 1793.

The Prohibitory Order of 1805 was issued by the British metropolitan authorities in response to complaints from planters, especially in the older British colonies of Barbados and Jamaica, who were becoming increasingly concerned about the competition being posed to their produce in the British market since 1796 by exports from Demerara-Essequibo and Berbice. Since British occupation that year these two colonies, mainly as a result of a substantial influx of labour and capital, had been experiencing considerable economic growth, especially a marked increase in the production of cotton and coffee. There was such a remarkable economic transformation that by 1800 these two colonies, whose development had been stifled under Dutch rule, had become the second largest producer of sugar in the British West Indies, the largest producer of coffee in the British Empire and the greatest producer of raw cotton in the world.

In short, by 1805 the booming export economy of Demerara-Essequibo and Berbice was viewed as an increasingly formidable rival by Barbadian and Jamaican planters, a concern shared by some British metropolitan officials especially because there was no certainty that Britain would retain these occupied Dutch colonies when peace was eventually made. Consequently, the Prohibitory Order was designed to restrict the investment of British capital and the supply of slaves to these newly acquired colonies before their future was definitely settled and to prevent the older British Caribbean possessions from being ruined by a competition with which they could not cope from Demerara-Essequibo and Berbice.

The implementation of the Prohibitory Order had an immediate effect on the volume of the slave trade to Demerara-Essequibo which declined from the 6631 captive Africans imported in 1805, the last year of unrestricted traffic. Slave imports from Africa dwindled further with the British abolition of the trade in all British possessions from 1st January, 1808.

Repercussions on the Enslaved Population

The restriction and then the abolition of the Atlantic traffic in captive Africans to Demerara-Essequibo had serious repercussions on a colony which had always depended on continuous importation from Africa, not on natural reproduction, for the maintenance and growth of its enslaved population. Aided by gender imbalance in favour of men, the low birth rate and the high incidence of mortality among the enslaved, caused mainly by overwork, underfeeding, disease, poor medical care and physical brutality, they resulted in a steady decline of its captive population, in spite of the efforts of the planters to secure new supplies of enslaved people by legal as well as illegal means. The colony's enslaved population fell from about 80,000 in 1808 to about 77,000 in 1817, about 75,000 in 1823, 71,000 in 1826 and 69,000 in 1829.

The decline in the number of enslaved people understandably was accompanied by a gradual decrease in the proportion of African-born compared with Creoles in the enslaved population. The percentage of the Africans, who were numerically dominant in 1808, fell mainly as a result of deaths from about 42,000 or 55% in 1817, to 39,000 or 51% in 1820, to 34,000 or 46% in 1823, to 30,500 or 43% in 1826, to 26,000 or 38% in 1829. In striking contrast, the Creoles, who in 1808 were much less than the Africans, rose from 45% in 1817 to 62% in 1829 and by 1832 almost doubled the latter.

The abolition of the slave trade also resulted in a loss in the effectiveness of the enslaved labour force, owing to the increasing proportion of old captives, females and children in the enslaved population. For example, whereas in 1817 an estimated 3,323 slaves (i.e. about four per cent) were over fifty years old, in 1832 9,204 (or 14 per cent) had attained that age. During these years female slaves, who constituted a smaller part of the captured cargoes than males before 1808, remained stationary numerically (about 33,000), but increased proportionally from 43 to 47 per cent.

In short, the restricted order of 1805 and the abolition of the transatlantic slave trade in 1808 in particular had a serious impact on the slave population of Demerara-Essequibo. The abolition of the Atlantic traffic greatly affected the size, composition and the effectiveness of the enslaved population.

The enslaved were also affected by the reactions of the planters to both the restriction and abolition of the slave trade to the colony.

Planter Reactions

The restrictive order of 1805 was a great disappointment to most planters in Demerara-Essequibo, especially new settlers. It occurred at a time when there was a great and growing demand for slaves there for at least two reasons. Firstly, the demand was due to an increase of the area under cultivation in the wake of the British occupation in 1796 which not only encouraged resident British planters to extend their plantations, but also resulted in a new influx of British settlers who purchased land and sought to establish viable cotton, coffee and sugar estates. Consequently, within four years the area under cultivation in Demerara-Essequibo increased by more than 10 per cent and the number of plantations grew from 392 to 490. Secondly, the high prices which were being offered in the British market for coffee, cotton and sugar were strong inducements to planters in the colony to seek to maximise production through the acquisition of additional slave labour. Furthermore, many of them were in a position to purchase this labour for they had long-term credit from merchants in Britain.

Many planters resented the restrictive order because it failed to take cognisance of the strategy usually employed in the colony to develop plantations. The common method was to secure a land grant, purchase a few slaves, cultivate the area as far as possible, and seek gradually to extend cultivation through the acquisition of additional slave labour year by year. The order therefore caught many planters, especially new settlers, in the midst of this process of development, much to their resentment. In fact, it is said that at the time of its introduction only 4 per cent of the total land granted in Demerara and 27 per cent in Essequibo was already under cultivation. The order, which posed the unwelcome prospect of a shortage of labour especially to work on uncultivated land, also ran counter to the plans and ambitions of many established planters. They viewed it as preventing them from taking advantage of the offer of a second grant, to which they were eligible, when they succeeded in cultivating all the land in their initial grant. In short, the order seemed likely to ensure that many plantations, especially recently established ones, would remain small and that few large estates would emerge.

These considerations made the Court of Policy and the planters in Demerara-Essequibo and many merchants in Britain protest against the order, especially against the three per cent limit which they contended was insufficient to replace the annual decrease in enslaved labourers, particularly in view of losses suffered from attacks by Spanish privateers and the high mortality rate which characterised the slave system. Their protests, however, proved futile.

The abolition of the Atlantic trade in captive Africans two years later was an even greater disappointment to planters in Demerara-Essequibo than the restrictive order of 1805. Although the supply of captive Africans to the colony had increased considerably after the British occupation of 1796, Demerara-Essequibo was still very short of enslaved workers. The planters therefore protested strongly to the British government about abolition, but again without success.

Planters resorted to a variety of expedients in order to address the labour problem. Some of them improved the treatment of their enslaved population with a view to prolonging their lives, while others extracted more labour form the captives, resulting in complaints about overwork. This complaint later proved to be one of the major causes of the massive slave rebellion which broke out on the East Coast of Demerara in 1823.

Many planters tried to acquire additional enslaved workers by legal as well as illicit means. They employed five legitimate methods. Firstly, they made serious efforts to recapture runaway slaves through the conduct of Bush Expeditions against Maroon settlements. They succeeded not only in recapturing many of the fugitives, but also in destroying their villages, which otherwise would have served as a perennial magnet to the plantations' servile labour force. Through the dispatch of letters and missions from the government of the colony, they also made several unsuccessful attempts to persuade the Spanish authorities in the Orinoco to extradite enslaved persons who had fled there especially from Essequibo.

Secondly, the planters and authorities in Demerara-Essequibo took steps to recover enslaved persons who had been captured in raids by Spanish subjects in the Orinoco, especially from coastal plantations in Essequibo. These overtures to the Spanish authorities there, however, were unsuccessful.

Thirdly, the planters purchased enslaved people from depressed estates. Fourthly, some of them depended on natural reproduction by the captives. Finally, the planters resorted above all to the legal importation of enslaved people from the older British West Indian colonies which the British government permitted. Between 1808 and 1825 this inter-territorial traffic resulted in the entry of about 7660 enslaved persons into Demerara-

Essequibo, mostly from Barbados and Antigua.

The planters in Demerara-Essequibo resorted also to two illegitimate means of acquiring slaves. The more fruitful one was the smuggling of enslaved people into the colony especially from neighbouring Suriname and from the more distant French colonies of Guadeloupe and Martinique. To curb this illegal practice, the government of Demerara-Essequibo enacted legislation in April 1818 and again in April 1820.

Some planters also secured labour by enslaving Amerindians, though Amerindian slavery had been outlawed by the Dutch government of the colony in 1793. This practice was dangerous for it was likely to antagonise the Amerindians whose assistance was often sought by the government and planters to pursue and recapture runaway slaves and to suppress slave rebellions.

The licit and illicit means employed by slave owners to secure enslaved persons were no substitute for the outlawed Atlantic traffic in captive Africans. They did not result in an increase of the enslaved population or in preventing its decline. What they did was to prevent it from declining at a faster rate.

The declining labour force also served to make the colony's planters extremely opposed to the idea of manumission of slaves. Demerara-Essequibo had the lowest frequency of manumission in the entire Caribbean, freeing only 27 slaves between 1808 and 1810 out of a slave population of about 80,000. Manumission was particularly rare there partly because until the late 1820s it required the consent of the slave owner. But even in the late 1820s, when pressure from the metropolitan government to apply the imperial policy of slave amelioration resulted in the highest incidence of manumission in the history of the colony, the number of slaves manumitted remained very small. For example, in the three years between 1826 and 1829 when the colony's slave population numbered about 70,000, only 254 were manumitted.

The labour problems created in Demerara-Essequibo by the abolition of the Atlantic traffic in captive Africans resulted in changes in land tenure. Some plantations were abandoned, while in some others the area under cultivation was reduced. In short, the normal practice of progressive extension of the cultivation of land grants was often discontinued. Sometimes insufficient labour led to the marked decline of cultivation in an entire district of the colony, notably the Pomeroon area.

The most important change in land use effected by the abolition of the slave trade, however, was a progressive switch from coffee and cotton cultivation to the planting of sugar cane which in 1808 ranked third among the colony's three main agricultural staples. From about 1811 the colony's cotton began to suffer effective competition from cotton grown in the southern United States, while its coffee exports began to be undermined by Jamaican and especially after 1825 by Ceylonese coffee. At the same time the prices of all three exports were falling on the British market. Sugar prices fell less steeply than coffee prices, while the latter fell less sharply than cotton prices.

In the circumstances, the cultivation of sugar cane appeared increasingly to be the most profitable option and most planters decided, if possible, to use their declining labour force to produce sugar instead of coffee and cotton. Consequently, sugar exports increased considerably, while coffee and cotton production decreased remarkably. For example, coffee and cotton production respectively dropped from 9,456,000 and 9,437,473 pounds in 1812 to 6,064,351 and 1,109,889 pounds in 1833, while sugar production increased from 26,532,688 to 92,960,560 pounds in these years. Thus by 1831, markedly unlike the situation in 1808, not more than one fifth of the colony's population was employed in the cultivation of coffee and cotton.

This change from coffee and cotton cultivation to sugar production had serious implications for the enslaved, who found the labour regime on sugar plantations far more demanding than that on coffee and cotton estates. In particular, enslaved persons who were required to make the transition from cotton to sugar production, which necessitated longer hours of harder work, were very discontented, complaining especially of overwork. This aspect of the transition was a major cause of the outbreak of the slave rebellion in August 1823 in the former cotton-growing area of the East Coast of Demerara.

The inability of most planters to maintain the size of their labour force after 1808 disturbed them immensely. In their view the effectiveness of the slave system depended largely on the ability to maintain numbers and authoritarian control of the slaves. The loss of the former made the planters determined to retain control of their enslaved property and to resist any challenge to the authority which they exercised over it. This helps to explain their hostility to the metropolitan government's policies of amelioration and then emancipation, both of which they recognized would have serious effects on their supply of labour.

Conclusion

The restrictive order of 1805 and the act of 1807 to abolish the Atlantic slave trade were important developments in the history of the colony of Demerara-Essequibo. Because the former was short-lived, being overtaken quickly by abolition, its effect on the colony was limited. The repercussions of the abolition of the trade, however, were drastic and prolonged, affecting both the captives and their masters in numerous important ways, some of which had lasting influence on the territory.

For Further Reading

Eltis, David	"The traffic in Slaves between the British West Indian Colonies, 1807-1833", **Economic History Review,** 2nd series, Vol. XXV, No. 1 (1972), pp. 55-64.
Higman, Barry	**Slave Populations of the British Caribbean, 1807-1834** (Baltimore: The John Hopkins University Press, 1984).
Mc Gowan, Winston	"The African Slave Trade to Guyana", in Mc Gowan, Winston, Rose, James and Granger, David, eds., **Themes in African - Guyanese History** (Georgetown: Free Press, 1998).
Mc Gowan, Winston	**The Demerara Revolt, 1823** (Georgetown: Free Press, 1998).
Mc Gowan, Winston	"The French Revolutionary Period in Demerara-Essequibo, 1793-1802", **History Gazette**, Number 55, April 1993.

CHAPTER 18

SLAVERY, ABOLITION AND EMANCIPATION

In spite of the evils of slavery, the institution for a long time had widespread support in Europe. It was encouraged by governments and sanctioned, surprisingly, by the Christian church. This situation of support, approval and toleration, however, eventually changed.

In the latter part of the eighteenth century Caribbean slavery began to come under increasingly serious attack especially from two sources. One of them was an essentially secular intellectual movement centred in France known by historians as the Enlightenment and led by renowned thinkers like Jean Jacques Rousseau who stressed ideas such as the liberty, equality and fraternity of the human race. The second source was a humanitarian movement in England which emerged largely from a major evangelical religious revival there.

The first major success by the new anti-slavery protesters was gained in the British Isles in the 1770s when slavery was outlawed in England in 1772 and in Scotland in 1778 by judicial decisions. These decisions in the English and Scottish courts, recognising the freedom of captive Africans in these two countries, were made in the famous Somerset case in England in 1772 and the less known Knight case in Scotland six years later. It was obviously somewhat easy to secure the abolition of slavery in these countries where there was an abundance of free labourers and only about 14000 – 15000 enslaved Africans. Time proved, however, that it was much more difficult to abolish slavery in the Caribbean, where the institution was pervasive and was considered indispensable, especially to the economy.

Opposition to slavery became more intense and better organised in the 1780s when British humanitarians in 1787 formed the Society for the Abolition of the Slave Trade, led by men such as Thomas Clarkson, Granville Sharp and William Wilberforce. Their initial focus was an attack on the Atlantic traffic in captive Africans not on slavery itself. They conducted a systematic campaign on two fronts, seeking to sensitise the British public to the evils of the traffic and endeavouring to persuade the British Parliament to outlaw it. Eventually their relentless efforts were successful for in 1807 the British Parliament declared the trade in enslaved Africans illegal for all British nationals and subjects.

This major success emboldened the Society to seek their ultimate objective, namely, the abolition of slavery itself. This goal was not achieved until 1833 when the British Parliament passed an Abolition bill which stated that slavery would be abolished in all British dominions with effect from 1st August 1834.

This momentous decision, taken somewhat reluctantly by the Parliament, was influenced by at least four major considerations apart from the continuing strong humanitarian pressure. Firstly, the British government was motivated partly by the failure of a policy which it had been pursuing especially since 1823 to persuade the authorities and slaveholders in the British Caribbean to improve the lot of the enslaved Africans. Among the reforms, which it had recommended, were the prohibition of the flogging of women, the cessation of the use of the whip in the field, the provision of religious instruction for slaves, the recognition of slave marriages, a reduction in the length of the working day, the provision of better food and clothing for captives and compulsory manumission. However, this policy of reforms, called the policy of amelioration by historians, encountered strong opposition from slaveholders and the governing authorities in Demerara – Essequibo, Berbice and other British territories in the Caribbean, especially Jamaica and Barbados, resulting in its virtual abandonment by 1831 as a failure.

The decision in 1833 to abolish slavery was also prompted by economic considerations. By 1830 the British West Indies and Africa had begun to feature differently in British thinking. The British Caribbean economy, based mainly on sugar production, was being seen increasingly as one on the decline. Soils, especially in the older British colonies such as Barbados and Jamaica, were becoming exhausted and sugar prices were falling on the international market. As a result, the British Caribbean increasingly was being regarded in Britain as a region with much less economic value to it than before.

On the other hand, Africa was no longer being seen in Britain as valuable for its supply of slave labour to the now somewhat depressed British Caribbean economies. Rather it was being valued especially in two new ways considered vital to the changing British economy which was in the process of being increasingly industrialised, namely, as a supplier of raw materials such as oils and cotton and as a market for British manufactured goods. This new thinking meant that it was now more in Britain's economic interest to have Africans remain in their homeland to produce these materials and to purchase these goods than to be taken as captives to the Caribbean.

The decision to abolish slavery was also influenced by the fear generated by the resistance of the captives, witnessed especially in two of the most massive slave rebellions ever seen in the Caribbean – in 1823 in Demerara and in 1831 in Jamaica. These uprisings convinced many residents in Britain that once slavery continued, violent resistance by the captives would occur, causing much loss of life and considerable damage to property in the Caribbean.

The final impetus to abolition was political. In 1832 a new parliament was elected in Britain under a new reform bill which altered electoral requirements. The new ruling party and parliament which came to power soon demonstrated that they were more committed to reform than their predecessors. It was they who took the decisive action which resulted in slavery being abolished partially on 1st August 1834 and completely on the same date in 1838, after the enslaved Africans had been required to endure four years of a modified form of slavery, euphemistically termed "apprenticeship".

For Further Reading

Williams, Eric	**Capitalism and Slavery** (London: Andre Deutsch, 1944).
Blackburn, Robin	**The Overthrow of Colonial Slavery, 1776-1848** (London and New York: Verso, 1988).
Green, William	**British Slave Emancipation: The Sugar Colonies and the Great Experiment, 1830-1865** (Oxford, 1976).
Thomas, Hugh	**The Slave Trade** (London: Papermac, 1998).
Walvin, James	**A Short History of Slavery** (London: Penguin Books, 2007).

Chapter 19

Slavery and Apprenticeship in Guyana

In 1833 the British metropolitan government, influenced by humanitarian, economic, political and other considerations, decided to make slavery illegal throughout the British Empire with effect from 1st August 1834. It also determined that enslaved persons in British Guiana and elsewhere in the British Caribbean would not become free immediately on that date. Instead, depending on the type of slave labour which they performed, the captives would serve an additional period of four or six years before they became completely free. In short, the British government in London decided that there would be a transitional period, called apprenticeship, between slavery and freedom. Eventually, in British Guiana this period was shortened with the result that all categories of apprentices were freed on 1st August 1838.

The introduction of the system of apprenticeship was prompted by three main considerations. Firstly, it was designed to give substantial benefit to slaveowners who in British Guiana were mainly white sugar planters. The planters would be assured of a continuous supply of labour and the maintenance of the slave system for at least four more years. They were being granted a breathing space to find an alternative source of labour, if necessary. This was deemed necessary for it was anticipated that when full freedom was granted after four or six years in 1838 or 1840, there would be a massive exodus of the apprentices from the sugar estates to establish an independent existence on waste land beyond the limits of the plantations.

Planters were therefore being granted time to prepare for this possibility of a labour crisis by taking appropriate action. For example, they could use the period of apprenticeship to introduce new labour – saving machinery or to experiment with new and better techniques of cultivation which required less manual labour. They could also utilise the period to modify their methods of labour management and treat the apprentices much better than before with the hope that a substantial number of them might be induced by improved treatment to remain on the plantations to work as wage labourers when full freedom was granted in 1838 or 1840.

It was also intended that planters could use the apprenticeship period to recruit an alternative labour force to their ex – slaves. Many planters took such action, bringing in immigrants as contracted labourers, notably West Indians, Portuguese mainly from Madeira from 1835 and East Indians from India in 1838. The first batch of East Indians indentured labourers arrived in British Guiana on 5th May 1838, almost three months before the full emancipation of the former slaves on 1st August 1838.

The planters also regarded apprenticeship as a part of the compensation which they felt was due to them for the ultimate loss of their slave property. They considered apprenticeship as a supplement to the monetary compensation which they received in 1834 from the British government for the withdrawal of what they perceived as their rights to their slave property.

The issue of compensation was a tendentious matter. The Anti – Slavery Society in Britain had tried unsuccessfully to convince the British government that it was the captives, not the slaveowners, who deserved compensation. The Society had stressed the moral injustice of slavery, pointing out that the captives had been brutally taken against their will from their home in Africa, transported across the Atlantic in completely sub-human conditions, and dehumanised and exploited cruelly by their owners in the Caribbean. Its appeal, however, was rejected by the metropolitan government, whose decision, as Eric Williams has eloquently pointed out, meant "it was compensation not for the deprivation of liberty but for the expropriation of Property".[76]

The second major objective of the British government in introducing the apprenticeship system was to prepare the slaves for full freedom. The government believed that because of their long experience of slavery – a way of life based on intimidation and coercion – the captives were not ready to enjoy immediate total freedom. Rather it thought that the captives needed to be specially prepared and trained for the enjoyment of citizenship. In particular, it felt that there was need to mould the thinking of the slaves, to encourage them in habits of industry, and to inculcate different ethical values before they were granted full freedom. It hoped that these ends could be achieved in a period of "apprenticeship" mainly through exposure to Christianity and western education. Thus, the apprenticeship period witnessed a great expansion of education and Christian missionary enterprise in British Guiana. It was then in a real sense that a formal school system was established in the country and the Christian faith spread to the masses.

The third major objective of the apprenticeship period was to provide the British metropolitan and local authorities with time to prepare the legal, administrative and other framework for the establishment and smooth function of a free society. For example, there was a need to prepare a new legal system to supersede and replace the now discarded slave codes which until then had governed the behaviour of the captives. The establishment of banking institutions to serve a free wage – based economy was another necessity. Furthermore, the period of apprenticeship would provide the ruling authorities with an opportunity to rectify serious monetary problems and to provide the colony with enough currency to pay the wages of free workers.

One interesting aspect of apprenticeship was its comparison with the system of slavery that it succeeded. In several respects the conditions encountered by apprentices were less onerous than those which they faced under slavery. For instance, the length of the working week was reduced by one sixth, from 54 hours to 45 hours. Apprentices were entitled to wages for any work which they were requested to do beyond 45 hours. Thus, it was during the apprenticeship period that captives for the first time were granted wages in return for some of their labour. It is true, however, that they did not have the freedom to bargain over wage rates for there was a fixed daily rate of 1s 4d. It was partly savings accumulated from wages for overtime work which the ex-apprentices used after emancipation in 1838 to purchase abandoned plantations and establish free villages.

The apprentices were also subject to a less oppressive system of discipline than during slavery. The disciplinary power of the planters, managers and overseers was legally reduced almost to nothing. Instead, a newly created stipendiary magistracy was created and entrusted with exclusive jurisdiction over disputes between apprentices and planters, including the sole responsibility for the punishment of apprentices. Understandingly, this change was not welcomed by the planters who viewed it as evidence of the philanthropic meddling of the British government in the affairs of the colony and accused the magistrates of being too sympathetic towards apprentices.

In a few respects, however, the lot of apprentices was worse than that which they had experienced before 1st August 1834. In particular, many planters withdrew customary privileges which enslaved persons had enjoyed but which they were not specifically compelled to grant by the provisions of the Apprenticeship Act. For example, they required pregnant apprentices to work harder and for longer hours than they had done previously. Thus whereas during slavery such women were not required to return to work until about six weeks after delivery, during the apprenticeship period they were obliged to resume to work after three or four weeks.

The stark truth was that the attitude of planters to their labour force did not change in any marked way with the introduction of apprenticeship. There was little evidence of a spirit of reconciliation and compromise. Labour relations continued to be marked by coercion and hostility. Yet it is probably true to assert that the apprenticeship system, in spite of major defects, as a whole gave the apprentices better working conditions and a moderation of discipline when compared with the period of unmitigated slavery before 1st August 1834. It also provided the planters with a valuable cushion between slavery and full freedom.

For Further Reading

Green, William	"The Apprenticeship in British Guiana, 1834-38", **Caribbean Studies**, No.9, July 1969.
Menezes, Mary	"The Apprenticeship System, 1834-1838: A Leap in the Dark", **History Gazette**, No.2, November 1988.
Moohr, Michael	"The Economic Impact of Slave Emancipation in British Guiana, 1832-1852", **The Economic History Review,** 2nd series, Vol. XXV, No.4, 1972.

Chapter 20

Slavery and Indentureship in Guyana: A Comparative Perspective

In 1834 the British metropolitan government legally abolished slavery in British Guiana. It decided, however, that the slaves should serve their white masters for a few additional years as what it termed "apprentices", before they became free. The grant of freedom on the 1st August 1838 was followed in the subsequent years by the exodus of a substantial number of former apprentices from the plantations to pursue an independent existence. This exodus, which was expected, created a labour crisis which threatened to ruin the country's plantation – based sugar economy.

In anticipation of this development some planters began during the apprenticeship period, (1834 – 1838), to seek to create an alternative labour force to Africans by bringing into the colony immigrants with whom they had concluded a contract to work for a fixed period, usually five years. This contract was called an "indenture". Consequently, in historical literature these labourers are often referred to as "indentured workers" and the system to which they were subjected is usually termed "Indentureship".

Some of the indentured labourers were Portuguese mostly from the Atlantic island of Madeira, about 30,000 of whom came to British Guiana between 1835 and 1880. There was also a small number of indentured immigrants from China, about 14,000 between 1853 and 1880. The vast majority of indentured workers, however, were Indians from India. It is estimated that about 238,000 of them were brought to British Guiana between 1838 and 1917. It was due largely to the labour provided by these contracted workers that the plantation system and the sugar industry in British Guiana survived and eventually recovered, after the marked decline which they suffered in the wake of the withdrawal of the labour of many of the ex-apprentices after 1st August 1838.

Indentureship was at least the third system of human labour exploitation in Guyanese history following unmitigated slavery which ended in 1834 and apprenticeship or modified slavery from 1834 to 1838. It is a matter of controversy in modern Guyana as to whether the experience of indentured labourers was identical or similar to that of African slaves. This issue became a matter of serious consideration among scholars especially after 1974 when a book written by a distinguished historian, Hugh Tinker, entitled **A New System of Slavery; the Export of Indian Labour Overseas, 1830 – 1920,** was published by the prestigious Oxford University Press. In general individuals who hold the view that these two systems of labour were identical or similar are much better informed about indentureship than about slavery. On the other hand, persons with reasonable knowledge of both systems tend to conclude that it is a falsification of history to equate them.

The consideration of indentureship as "a new form of slavery" is partly a reflection of the obvious fact that there are some basic similarities between all systems of labour exploitation in the same way that all forms of democracy or dictatorship, for example, have common elements. Both slavery and indentureship had the same fundamental objective. They were designed to provide a cheap, constantly available and easily controllable labour force. But more than anything else it was the regimented social and industrial control, buttressed by an unjust legal system, which placed indentured labourers at a marked disadvantage that has caused some scholars to regard indentureship as very much akin to slavery. For instance, the pass laws, that is to say, the requirement that slaves and later indentured labourers should have written permission from their masters if they wished to proceed beyond a certain distance from their plantation, existed in both systems. Both systems were designed to immobilize labour, binding it perpetually to the plantation. Planters were simply not happy with any system in which labour was free and mobile. This was the main reason why they sought to extend control over indentured labourers by inducing them to sign a second contract at the expiration of the first.

Apart from the immobilization of the labour force, slavery and indentureship had several other common features. Both slaves and indentured workers, especially the former, had little hope of gaining redress for abuses and other grievances. They were also both subject to ill – treatment by the "drivers" on the estates. Furthermore, the harshness of the system prompted slaves and indentured immigrants to resist in active and passive ways.

Ultimately, both slavery and indentureship were systems of human exploitation and manipulation. The indentured immigrants, like the captive Africans, found themselves in an intolerable situation for they were subject to laws in the formulation of which they had no say and over the application of which they had no control. In both systems the power of control was exercised by the planters through the local legislature and the executive and the administrative institutions.

These important similarities between slavery and indentureship, however, cannot or should not obscure the fact that there are many major differences between these two systems of labour. One very obvious difference was the fact that indentured immigrants, unlike the captive Africans, for the most part did not come to Guyana against their will. Although many Indian immigrants in particular were cajoled, enticed and even tricked into leaving India, they virtually all came to British Guiana as a result of a contractual arrangement. In striking contrast enslaved Africans were brought from Africa in chains against their will. This journey from the point of enslavement in Africa to Guyana was marked by resistance at every stage, demonstrating their total opposition to servitude and their forced migration, the largest in human history, from their beloved homeland, Africa.

A second major difference between slavery and indentureship was in the legal status of the victims. Slaves were legally the private property of their owners. Indentured immigrants, on the other hand, were not legally a piece of property. This difference helps to explain the disparity in their treatment. Thirdly, indentured immigrants, unlike captive Africans, were paid wages in return for their labour. Admittedly, however, the wage rates were very low and were not the result of any bargaining process between the workers and the planters.

There was also a very marked difference in discipline under the two systems. The discipline of slaves was legally left largely to the jurisdiction of their owners, who made the rules and imposed and executed the penalties on slaves whom they considered delinquent. Not surprisingly, such punishment was marked by excessive cruelty, including incredible torture. In marked contrast, the discipline of indentured labourers was entrusted to the magistrate courts, where decisions were guided by various ordinances passed by the local government to regulate relations between masters and indentured workers. Though the system weighed heavily against the indentured immigrants, the penalties to which they were subjected were far less onerous than those experienced by slaves, especially in terms of physical brutality.

Perhaps the most fundamental difference between the two systems of labour, however, was the most obvious one, namely, the fact that African slavery was almost invariably for life, whereas indentureship was for the duration of the contracted period, usually five years. Indentured immigrants could look forward to an end of their lot and the possibility or prospect of returning home, perhaps with savings, at the termination of their contract. About 75,000 or nearly one-third of the Indian indentured immigrants to British Guiana returned to India. In striking contrast, captive Africans had little chance of becoming free, except by running away or staging a successful rebellion for legal manumission was very rare and no prospect of ever returning to their home in Africa.

These and other major differences between slavery and indentureship are often overlooked or underemphasized in views which tend to approximate the two systems and to refer to indentureship as "a new form of slavery". Although there were similarities between these two forms of labour, the differences were much more striking. In short, in view of these and other considerations, it would be very wrong to present Indian and other indentureship as identical, equivalent or similar to the slavery experienced by captive Africans in Guyana. To do so would be to distort or falsify history.

Furthermore, although this is not the subject of this chapter, it would be even more ludicrous to equate the oceanic voyage of indentured immigrants from India and elsewhere to Guyana with the Atlantic crossing of captive Africans from Africa literally in chains to these shores. The very marked difference in mortality during these two types of voyages, just to cite one factor, is an indication of this indisputable fact.

For Further Reading

Chanderbali, David	"The Indian Indenture System: Evolution and Structure", **History Gazette,** No.5, February 1989.
Tinker, Hugh	**A New System of Slavery; the Export of Indian Labour Overseas, 1830-1920** (London: Oxford University Press, 1974).
Laurence, Keith	**A Question of Labour: Indentured Immigration into Trinidad and British Guiana, 1875 – 1917** (London: James Curry, 1984).
Mangru, Basdeo	"Trusteeship and East Indian Indentured Labour in British Guiana", **History Gazette,** No.33, June 1991.
Kale, Madhave	**Fragments of Empire. Capital, Slavery and Indian Indentured Labor Migration in the British Caribbean** (Philadelphia: University of Pennsylvania Press, 1998).
Roopnarine, Lomarsh	**Indo-Caribbean Indenture, Resistance and Accommodation, 1838-1920** (Kingston: University of the West Indies Press, 2007).

PART FOUR
ECONOMIC HISTORY

An early horse-powered sugar mill in Essequibo in the 17th century

Reverend John Wray

Chapter 21

The Beginning of the Sugar Industry in Guyana

For most of the last two hundred years of Guyana's history, the pillar of the export economy has been the sugar industry. That industry has been and continues to be the main single provider of employment and almost invariably the principal source of foreign exchange earnings. The production and consumption of rum has long been an important economic and social feature of the sugar industry, for prior to that development the only locally produced alcoholic beverages were various Amerindian liquors, notably piwarri, produced from cassava. This chapter will focus on the first phase of the sugar industry in the seventeenth and early eighteenth centuries.

The precise date of the introduction of sugar cane cultivation in the region that today constitutes the Republic of Guyana is not certain. What is known is that by the mid-1630s Dutch residents in what was then the Dutch colony of Essequibo had begun to plant sugar cane. Surviving documents indicate that in 1637 a small shipment of cane syrup was sent from Essequibo to Zealand in the Netherlands. This was the earliest phase of the industry, when sugar apparently was not refined locally and when cultivation may have been undertaken on an experimental basis.

Unlike several other European colonies in the Caribbean, notably Barbados, where sugar production made rapid strides after it was initiated, in Guyana the sugar industry developed very slowly. It was not until the 1650s that a significant impetus was given to sugar cultivation in Guyana, giving it a regular and unprecedented role in the economic life of Essequibo and, later it seems, in Berbice.

This impetus in the 1650s came principally from the arrival in Essequibo from Brazil of some Dutchmen, among whom were many Jews. Their arrival followed their expulsion or flight from Brazil, where since 1630 the Netherlands had been seeking, but ultimately unsuccessfully, to occupy a part of North-Eastern Brazil, which at that time was claimed by Portugal as its possession. Many of these Dutch immigrants settled in the Pomeroon, bringing with them some capital and considerable technical knowledge of sugar production. Immediately sugar cane cultivation in Essequibo expanded and its technology improved. It was from this period, especially from 1661, that sugar seems to have been exported regularly to the Netherlands. Dutch, English and Spanish documentary sources indicate that in the early 1660s the Pomeroon was a flourishing area with several sugar plantations. For example, a Spanish document in the 1660s stated that the Dutch Pomeroon settlement was "rich in produce, and the best trading establishment which they [the Dutch] have on the whole coast".[77]

In spite of the significant growth in the sugar industry in the Pomeroon and elsewhere in Essequibo in the 1650s and 1660s, these areas never experienced the so-called "sugar-revolution" which was occurring at that time in Barbados and took place later in most other British West Indian colonies. In Barbados, for example, the introduction of sugar in the early 1640s soon resulted in dramatic changes. Notable among them were the quick and virtual abandonment of earlier agro-based industries such as tobacco and cotton production, the importation of an ever-increasing number of African slaves to work on the sugar plantations, and great transformation of the system of land tenure as the small holdings used previously for tobacco and cotton cultivation gave way to the extensive plantations used to produce sugar.

In striking contrast, it was not until the early decades of the eighteenth century, especially after 1720, that a fairly thriving and influential sugar industry can be said to have developed in Guyana. There were at least three major reasons for the comparatively low initial progress of the industry.

Firstly, in the seventeenth century the Dutch settlers, especially those in Essequibo, were preoccupied with trading with the Amerindian population rather than with agriculture. They concentrated on exchanging European goods especially for anatto dye, utilised in the textile industry in the Netherlands. In the early eighteenth century, however, this trade dwindled as the Dutch found better sources of dyes elsewhere and the export economy of Essequibo and Berbice began to be based almost completely on plantation agriculture, especially sugar cultivation.

A second factor which hindered the progress of the sugar industry in Essequibo and Berbice was the destruction which these two Dutch colonies sometimes suffered from enemy attacks during periods of international warfare. For example, in 1665 an English expedition, led by one Major

John Scott, captured the Dutch colonies in Essequibo and the Pomeroon and two years later a French force also attacked the Pomeroon. During this period of hostilities many of the Dutch sugar planters in the Pomeroon fled and nearly all the sugar plantations there were destroyed or abandoned. The sugar industry in Pomeroon, unlike that in the Essequibo River, never recovered from these reverses.

The third cause of slow growth of the sugar industry was a serious shortage of labour, that is, African slave labour. This shortage was due largely to the fact that the Dutch West India Company, which until 1730 was entrusted with the responsibility to supply Essequibo and Berbice with captive Africans, was both unable and unwilling to do so for several reasons. One reason was that the company held Essequibo and Berbice, from which the Netherlands derived only minimal benefit, in low esteem and preferred to supply captives to the neighbouring Dutch colony of Suriname which had a flourishing and rapidly expanding sugar industry. This Dutch policy of preferential treatment to Suriname to the comparative neglect of Essequibo, Berbice and, later, Demerara, lasted until the 1770s when Suriname suddenly experienced a serious economic crisis.

In short, the initial Dutch preoccupation with trade with the Amerindians, the destruction suffered from enemy privateers and warships, and a severe shortage of labour combined to ensure that the sugar industry in Guyana made very slow progress at least until the 1720s.

FOR FURTHER READING

Goslinga, Cornelis	**The Dutch in the Caribbean and on the Wild Coast 1580 – 1680** (Assen: Van Gorcum & Comp., 1971).
Goslinga, Cornelis	**The Dutch in the Caribbean and the Guianas 1680-1791** (Assen: Van Gorcum & Comp., 1985).
Shahabuddeen, Mohamed	**From Plantocracy to Nationalisation. A Profile of Sugar in Guyana**. (Georgetown, 1983), especially Chapter 2.

Chapter 22

The British Guiana Sugar Industry In 1900

In 1900 the sugar industry in what was then British Guiana was, like today, the main pillar of the country's economy. It was not only by far the largest employer of labour, but also the main earner of foreign exchange. In 1900 the country exported 84000 tons of sugar, 385,000 gallons of molasses and 3,334,000 gallons of rum. Nevertheless, the sugar industry was experiencing a prolonged crisis, dating back to the year 1884.

The main cause of this crisis was the increasingly severe competition which Guianese cane sugar was encountering in its principal market in Britain from beet sugar supplied by producers in continental European countries, especially France, Germany and Austria, with the assistance of a substantial subsidy from their respective governments. As a result of this subsidy, beet farmers were able to offer sugar at a much lower price than that of Guianese and other Caribbean cane sugar, causing a massive decline of both the volume of sales and the price of cane sugar in the British market. Sugar prices there fell by more than 50 per cent between 1883 and 1900, from 22 pounds 4 shillings (sterling) a hundred weight in 1883 to 14 pounds 11 shillings in 1884 and finally 9 pounds 12 shillings in 1896.

The crisis proved to be the deathblow to many Guianese sugar estates, whose owners, including both large absentee planters and weaker residents, abandoned cultivation. The number of sugar plantations fell from 105 in 1885 to 84 in 1890 and then to 57 by 1900. Consequently, the area under sugar cultivation in the colony decreased considerably, from about 77,000 acres in 1884 to about 66,000 acres in 1900, a drop of 14 per cent. Not surprisingly, there was a concomitant decline in sugar production from an annual average of 125,000 tons in the period 1882-1884 to about 84,000 tons in 1900. The average value of the annual sugar exports of the colony also diminished from about 2.4 million pounds sterling in the period 1883-1885 to 1.9 million pounds sterling in the years 1898 to 1901, that is, a drop of about 20 per cent.

The difficulties faced by the sugar industry made it extremely difficult for the plantation proprietors to obtain urgently needed credit from increasingly cautious capitalists in Britain who were reluctant to take risks. The reluctance was understandable, for the abandonment of many plantations since 1884 had resulted in the collapse of several substantial merchant houses in England as a result of losses experienced through advancing money for the operation of estates in British Guiana and elsewhere in the British Caribbean.

In spite of the chronic depression in the sugar industry, many planters demonstrated remarkable tenacity, employing a variety of expedients in their effort to survive. For example, they directed their sugar exports increasingly away from the customary British market to the United States of America and, to a much lesser extent, Canada which offered better protection against competition from beet sugar. Thus whereas in 1884 only 15.3 per cent of British Guiana's sugar exports were sent to the United States, by 1900 this proportion had reached an unprecedented figure of 76 per cent. As a result, the share of Guianese sugar exports sent to Britain fell from 83.5 per cent in 1884 to 16.4 per cent in 1900.

Much more important, however, as a reason for survival than this shift in markets was the planters' ability to effect a substantial reduction in production costs from about 22 pounds 10 shillings sterling per ton of sugar in 1883 to about 11 pounds sterling a ton in 1900 to counteract the massive decline in sugar prices. This significant cost reduction was achieved, above all, by changes in the manufacturing process, especially the introduction of modern multiple-effect evaporators. It was also due to reduction in wages and in the number of indentured workers recruited from India, and the increased subsidisation of the sugar industry from public revenue. For example, in 1894 the responsibility for maintaining estate roads was transferred from the estate proprietors to the government.

Some estate proprietors also effected economies of scale by purchasing adjacent failing or abandoned plantations and amalgamating them with their estates. Thus 17 of the 63 plantations which disappeared between 1885 and 1904 were amalgamated with other estates.

Furthermore, by 1900 a growing number of estates had started to conduct successful experiments to introduce new varieties of cane which would give a more substantial yield than the Bourbon type, which had been the basic type in Guyana since the end of the eighteenth century. This change was prompted by the fact that in 1895 the Bourbon type began to be attacked in the colony by a fungus disease that had caused it to fail in other sugar-producing countries since the 1840s.

Estate owners in British Guiana in 1900 also sought to survive the sugar crisis by soliciting loans or grants from both the local and the metropolitan governments. In 1901 they received 69,000 pounds sterling of a grant of 250,000 pounds sterling which the British government gave to the entire British Caribbean sugar industry.

The main hope of Guianese planters for survival and the restoration of the prosperity enjoyed in the early 1880s, however, was to secure the abolition of the government subsidies granted to the European beet sugar producers. The suppression of these subsidies was finally achieved in 1903 as a result of strong diplomatic pressure which the British metropolitan government exerted on other European countries.

In spite of the severe crisis still facing the industry, in 1900 sugar continued to hold a commanding, though diminished, position in the economy of British Guiana. Thus whereas in 1884 sugar and its by-products, rum and molasses, contributed 91 per cent of the total value of the colony's exports, in 1900 this figure had fallen to 68.2 per cent, with sugar providing 56.5 per cent, rum 10.9 per cent and molasses 0.7 per cent. This diminished, but still important role, of sugar was due mainly to the fact that the profound crisis in the industry persuaded the local and metropolitan government, and even the very reluctant sugar planters, to countenance diversification of the hitherto narrow export economy, based in 1884 almost exclusively on sugar.

Since 1884 gold mining in particular had developed considerably so that gold exports increased from 250 ounces in 1884 to 112,000 ounces in 1900. In 1900 gold constituted 21.4 per cent of the value of the country's exports and 87.5 per cent of the value of exports other than sugar, rum and molasses.

Furthermore, by 1900 diamond mining had just begun, with the export for the first time in that year of a small quantity of 936 carats. Moreover, since 1885 the cultivation of rice was making new and steady progress, although it was not until 1903 that the initial rice exports were made. The colony, however, continued to import declining amounts of rice each year from India until about 1920.

The crisis in the sugar industry after 1884 was in some ways a disaster for British Guiana, for the value of the country's exports fell by about 28 per cent in 20 years mainly due to the decline of the price of sugar in international markets. On the other hand, the crisis ultimately benefited the country, for it led to the diversification of the economy which characterised the twentieth century, with sugar production being supplemented initially by gold mining and rice cultivation, and later by the mining of diamonds and bauxite. In 1900 the country's economy was in the process of this important transition.

Another permanent result of the crisis in the sugar industry was that it led to striking changes in the ownership of sugar estates with the emergence of a new and increasingly pronounced trend of individual proprietors being progressively replaced by liability companies, which had better access to capital and credit and protected individuals from the risk of excessive personal financial loss. Very significantly, in 1900 Booker Brothers merged with John McConnell, with whom they had long been closely associated to form a new partnership which would eventually dominate the country's sugar industry. By 1901, 70 per cent of British Guiana's 46 sugar plantations was owned by six companies with Booker Bros. McConnell and Company leading, possessing 17.2 per cent of them, followed by Curtis Campbell and Company with 14.9 per cent, the New Colonial Company with 14.9 per cent, Sandbach Parker with 11.6 per cent, the Ewing Estates with 5.8 per cent and S. Davson and Company with 5.3 per cent.

For Further Reading

Beachey, R.W.	**The British West Indian Sugar Industry in the Late Nineteenth Century** (Oxford, 1957).
Adamson, Alan	**Sugar Without Slaves. The Political Economy of British Guiana, 1838-1904** (New Haven: York University, 1972).
Rodney, Walter	**Guyanese Sugar Plantations in the Late Nineteenth Century. A Contemporary Description from the Argosy, Georgetown** (Georgetown: Release Publishers, 1979).
Rodney, Walter	**A History of the Guyanese Working People, 1881-1905** (Baltimore: The John Hopkins University Press, 1981)
Shahabuddeen, Mohamed	**From Plantocracy to Nationalisation. A Profile of Sugar in Guyana.** (Georgetown, 1983).

Chapter 23

The Beginnings of Rice Cultivation in Guyana

Guyana, then named British Guiana, began exporting rice in 1903 when five tons were sent abroad. Since then the rice industry has increased considerably in importance with about at least 300,000 tons being exported annually in recent times, and over 400,000 tons in 2011 and 2012, and over 500,000 tons in 2013, unprecedented figures. It is estimated that about thirty per cent of the current Guyanese population is employed in the rice industry.

The success of the rice industry is one of the major contributions of Indians to the Guyanese economy. Rice cultivation, however, was first practised in Guyana by Africans who were brought there as slaves by Europeans across the Atlantic from their homes in West Africa in the seventeenth, eighteenth and early nineteenth centuries. Many of these captive Africans came from areas of the Upper and Lower Guinea Coast where locally grown rice was a major staple of their diet.

Enslaved Africans initiated rice cultivation in Guyana in at least three kinds of circumstances. Firstly, some of them who worked on plantations, used a part of their free time to plant rice to supplement their meagre food allowance and to sell to other slaves. This practice continued until the end of slavery. Thus in 1826 the managers of the estates of Wolfert Katz, the leading plantation proprietor in Berbice, reported that

☙

> where a Bush, or uncultivated piece of land, is contiguous to the Estate they reside on, some of them [slaves] will clear away a space which they plant in Rice, and in the space of 3 Months one Negro has reaped 100 Bundles, which they sell at 2 Bitts each, making 50 Guilders in 3 Months by this Article

alone.[78]

❦

Secondly, enslaved Africans were required to cultivate rice by a small number of planters who used a part of their land for that purpose, no doubt to provide food for their slaves. This was a rare occurrence for almost invariably planters used their land exclusively to produce crops for export, especially sugar, coffee and cotton. It is known, for example, that rice was introduced on some Essequibo or Berbice plantations from South Carolina early in the eighteenth century and on at least one plantation in about 1782 from the French Colony of Louisiana at a time when the French had taken possession of Essequibo, Berbice and Demerara.

It was not unusual for planters to give slaves rice as part of their food allowances especially when there was a shortage of plantains, the main staple of the diet of enslaved Africans. As a Commission of Enquiry into slavery in Berbice reported in January 1826

❦

> by the Colonial Ordinance, Adult Slaves…are allowed two bunches of good plantains weekly… When plantains are not to be had, Slaves are fed on Rice, Corn Meal or Flour of which from 7 to 9 pounds are issued to adults & working Creoles weekly.[79]

❦

This rice was mostly imported from Europe and North America, and was not grown locally. In 1813, when supplies of rice from the United States of America were stopped because of an Anglo-American war, it was suggested that Demerara-Essequibo and Berbice should grow larger quantities of rice, but nothing seems to have resulted from this proposal.

The third and apparently the most common situation in which captive Africans initiated rice cultivation in Guyana was in the settlements of runaway slaves, who escaped from the plantations and established communities often in the forested hinterland. The colonial authorities who sent expeditions to recapture these fugitives and destroy their settlements were often amazed by the quantity of rice which was discovered there. For example, in 1810 Charles Edmonstone, a Demerara militia captain who led an expedition to the Mahaicony-Abary area, reported

> The quantity of Rice the Bush Negroes have just rising out of the ground is very considerable, independent of Yams, Tanias, Plantains, Tobacco etc.... Fourteen houses filled with Rice and several fields in cultivation (were) totally destroyed... On a moderate calculation the quantity of Rice that has been destroyed... would have been equal to the support of seven hundred Negroes for twelve months.[80]

Rice seems to have been the main staple in the diet of residents of many runaway slave settlements.

The role of enslaved Africans in pioneering rice cultivation in Guyana is largely forgotten today. The final end of slavery in 1838 resulted in a decline of African participation in rice cultivation for most of the ex-slaves opted to focus principally on the cultivation of ground provisions. An official report in 1848, however, does mention that rice was being planted in Berbice by Temnes, probably immigrants from Sierra Leone.

There was at that time a growing demand for rice in the colony to provide the staple diet of the increasing number of East Indian contracted labourers from India who since 1838 were being recruited to take the place of the ex-slaves, many of whom abandoned the plantations when and after full freedom was granted. Most of the rice required was imported from India. The quantity imported grew considerably in the 1850s and 1860s when Indian immigration experienced an unprecedented regularity and volume.

This situation prompted new efforts at rice cultivation in the colony. In 1853, for example, a company was formed in Georgetown for the cultivation of 150 acres of rice at Plantation Vive La Force on the west bank of the Demerara River, but this venture was not successful. In 1853 also another effort was made by A.V. Colvin, an Englishman who had migrated to Florida where he became a naturalized United States citizen and was involved in rice cultivation. Colvin came to Demerara to plant rice with seed from Georgia. His experiment is said to have been successful, but he was forced to abandon it owing to a lack of capital. A few years later, in April 1856, Colvin, in his new capacity of U.S. Consul in British Guiana, wrote the American Secretary of State recommending that American capital investment in rice cultivation in the colony would be "a valuable investment".[81]

Rice cultivation got a fillip in the early 1860s when, it seems, Indians began to plant the crop in the colony for the first time. This important development appears to have been initiated in the Leonora area of the West Coast of Demerara where about sixteen acres were cultivated for immediate subsistence with very successful results. The area under rice cultivation was extended yearly in various parts of the colony until about 1870 when for reasons which are not clear it was reduced. By 1872 only a small amount of cultivation of the crop was being conducted, notably in the Abary, Mahaicony and Canje districts.

The situation changed from 1873 when the practice of reindenture (i.e. contracting Indian labourers for a second five-year period of service) was discontinued. As a result, a growing number of Indians began to leave the sugar plantations and to establish themselves on small holdings which they leased or purchased especially to plant rice. By 1880 the Essequibo Coast had become arguably the most important rice-producing area in the colony. Anna Regina was a main centre as well as Better Success where 300-400 free Indians were reported to be working 1500 acres of land. In short, by 1880 indentured and free Indians had begun to give an unprecedented impetus to rice production.

In spite of these developments, until the early 1880s rice cultivation in Guyana can be described as haphazard and very limited. Most of the country's demand for rice was still being met by importation especially from India. The entire production of the colony was being used for local consumption, none for export. It was not possible yet to speak about a Guianese rice industry.

The very limited state of rice cultivation in British Guiana in the early 1880s was due to several factors, some historical, others more contemporary. Firstly, rice had not been a principal staple of the diet of most Africans resident on the plantations during slavery. Secondly, after full emancipation in 1838, it was ground provisions, not rice, which were by far the preferred crops and food of the overwhelming majority of Africans in the colony.

Thirdly, few Whites during or after slavery were willing to invest capital in rice production. Fourthly, there were ecological, climatic and technical obstacles to rice cultivation. For example, it was easier to transfer sugar land to plant ground provisions than rice. Furthermore, several efforts to plant rice especially in the 1850s and 1860s failed due to lack of knowledge and water. Production was also hindered by the fact that it was being done by hand, with cutlasses, hoes, grass knives and pestles being the only instruments employed.

Finally, rice production was hindered by the opposition of most sugar planters who used their political and other influence to ensure that land, labour and capital were not diverted in any significant measure from the dominant sugar industry to rice cultivation or any other economic enterprise. As a result, sugar and its by-products, rum and molasses, continued every year to provide about 90 per cent of the value of the colony's exports. This lack of diversification of the colonial economy ended in 1884 when the sugar industry experienced an unprecedented and prolonged crisis which gave a major impetus to rice cultivation. It was in this post-1884 period, especially the following forty years, that the real foundations of the modern rice industry may be said to have been established.

By the 1920s it could be said that an expanding rice industry had been established in British Guiana. This was clearly reflected in land usage in the colony. According to official statistics, in 1931 49,000 acres or 30 per cent of the cultivated land in the colony was planted with rice. This was a great change from the situation in 1880 when less than 2000 acres of land were in rice cultivation and the colony imported most of the rice needed from India.

Several factors were responsible for the considerable extension of rice cultivation in British Guiana between 1880 and 1920. The first and by far the most important one was a major crisis which the dominant sugar industry experienced from 1884 to 1904.[82] This prolonged crisis stemmed from the effective competition which Guianese and other Caribbean sugar encountered in the British market from subsidized beet sugar produced by several European countries. Perhaps its most important consequence was that it emphasized the need for the diversification of the colony's economy away from sugar monoculture.

The depression resulted in a significant reduction in wage rates and the amount of work available in the sugar industry. Wages became so low that many Indians at the completion of their indenture decided to end or reduce their employment on the sugar plantations and instead to rent or purchase land to cultivate rice and to sell it as their main source of income.

Rice cultivation was greatly stimulated by the availability of cheap land provided both by the sugar planters and the government who in order to avoid the heavy expense of a return passage to India offered the ex-indentured labourers land instead. Thus, there was a progressive relaxation of the terms of sale of Crown land, reducing the price immensely. Similarly, many planters rented parts of their estate to such labourers with the hope of recruiting them as workers especially at crop time. As a result, by 1904, 8561 acres of estate land were said to be under rice cultivation.

Rice cultivation was also encouraged by recurrent local shortages of ground provisions. Such shortage helped to make rice become a staple food of other ethnic groups apart from Indians, especially Africans and Chinese. Similarly, local rice cultivation was stimulated by shortfalls in rice production in India, still the colony's main external supplier. In particular, a major shortfall in 1901 limited exports to the colony, enabling local rice to fetch a much higher price than usual and encouraging more extensive cultivation. This development was aided by the belief that local rice was better than the imported article.

The Guianese rice industry also benefited from special assistance from the colony's Department of Agriculture, which from 1900 provided new varieties of seeds. It was also stimulated by the introduction of rice mills. By 1907 there were 44 mills in the colony, 24 in Demerara, 10 in Berbice and 10 in Essequibo.

Rice cultivation in the colony also profited from the impact of World War I (1914-1918) which adversely affected its food supply in several ways. For example, the war resulted in the high price of the limited quantity of imported wheat flour reaching the colony. Furthermore, there were transportation difficulties in respect to rice imports from India. The average annual importation of 2519 tons of rice between 1909 and 1913 dropped to 159 tons between 1914 and 1916 and 72 tons in 1917. These circumstances were exploited by the local rice producers who provided not only what was lacking from India but also rice flour as a substitute for wheat flour.

Rice cultivation in British Guiana got a major impetus from the introduction of more modern technology, modifying the earlier more rudimentary approach of ox-ploughing, hand cutting, etc. From 1917 tractors and other machines such as reapers and threshers were employed very successfully, especially by some of the bigger farmers. This development was evidence that the industry had begun to benefit from greater capital investment, some of which was provided by overseas companies.

Finally, the successful expansion of rice cultivation between 1880 and 1920 was due considerably to the tenacity and hard work of the farmers, mostly Indian peasants. They demonstrated these qualities in spite of the high mortality among them due to the frequent attacks of malaria. Mortality in the Indian community, a major social problem in the colony, was said to be highest among rice growers.

The expansion of rice cultivation between 1884 and 1920 took place in spite of many obstacles. The main obstacles were probably the related problems of recurrent unfavourable weather conditions and deficient drainage and irrigation. Inadequate rainfall, including the late arrival of the rains, often resulted in a lack of water to flood the rice beds. As a September 1905 report stated, "it is not unusual to hear of hundreds of acres of rice parched owing to a prolonged drought."[83] Droughts tended to be more frequent and severe in Berbice and a series of them affected the entire colony between 1911 and 1913.

Damage from prolonged drought was particularly great where irrigation was deficient. Rice cultivation also suffered from flooding which resulted from heavy rainfall and poor drainage. Flooding often hindered the planting of paddy and, when it occurred at harvest time, destroyed the crop.

In short, the lack of a good system of drainage and irrigation made certain rice-growing districts unable to provide against excessive rainfall and severe drought. As the British Guiana East Indian Association complained in 1922, "through the lack of a proper system of drainage and irrigation serious losses have been and are still being suffered by the rice farmers in times of drought and during rainy seasons."[84] The inability to deal effectively with these difficulties partly explains why at least until 1900 the acreage under rice cultivation was severely restricted and only one crop was harvested every year.

Rice cultivation was also adversely affected by several other problems, some of which were comparatively minor and others more serious. Among them were pests such as water-weevils and paddy bugs and the eating of growing rice plants by straying cattle. Cultivation was also hindered by inefficient methods and the frequent lack of proper seed selection which resulted in crops of poor quality and undesirable quantity. It was also checked by the slow introduction of mechanization owing to the limited financial resources of most rice farmers.

In spite of these various obstacles, rice cultivation in British Guiana expanded after 1884 with the estimated acreage growing from about 2,000 acres in that year to about 55,000 acres in 1920. The growing establishment of the rice industry had major effects on the Guianese economy.

Its most obvious and important effect was that it served to diversify or modify the economy which in 1884 was dominated by sugar production. There was some discussion locally in the 1890s as to whether rice production could become an alternative to the sugar industry in the colony's economy. This possibility, however, never materialized. Sugar continued to be the backbone of the economy, but enjoying reduced importance. By 1920, when almost all the former sugar plantations in Essequibo had been converted to rice lands, rice was second to sugar as the colony's main export. Nevertheless, its significance was still somewhat limited. In fact, rice production never assumed a position of major importance in the local economy until the early 1940s when it reached about 50,000 tons annually.

Rice cultivation resulted in a shortage of labour on the sugar estates which tried to address this disturbing problem in several ways. For example, many estate proprietors decided to grant Indians a portion of their estate for rice cultivation on a part-time basis so as to retain their labour except when these workers were planting or harvesting rice. Furthermore, the shortage of labour led to greater mechanization of the sugar industry with the introduction and growing use of tractors from 1917.

Rice cultivation also had major effects on food supplies in the colony. Rice gradually became a staple in the diet of other sections of the Guianese population other than Indians, especially among Africans and Chinese and the working class in general. This development helped to lead to a sharp decline in the level of imported food especially from the 1890s. For example, the value of all imported food into the colony fell by about 35 per cent between 1891 and 1913.

This development included a marked decline in imports of rice mostly from India which fell from an annual average of about 18,000 tons between 1888 and 1894 to about 8,000 tons between 1904 and 1908 to about 2500 tons between 1909 and 1913. By 1920 imports of rice had virtually ceased. By then local production was not only meeting domestic needs, but also the colony was exporting 8000 tons of rice a year mostly to the British West Indies and the other Guianas.

Rice cultivation had a severe effect on the production of several locally produced food items, especially vegetables and ground provisions. The high price obtained for locally produced rice, especially during World War I when there was a drastic fall in imports from India, helped to induce many small farmers to switch from the cultivation of vegetables and ground provisions to the planting of rice. The result was that by 1919 there was a great scarcity of local vegetables, fruits and ground provisions which were usually abundant in the pre-war years. The prices of these scarce commodities rose 100-150 per cent above those existing in 1914 and 1915. The shortage of ground provisions in 1919 also resulted in the importation of a considerable quantity of sweet potatoes.

Similarly, some farmers abandoned cattle raising and turned their efforts to rice cultivation. Thus by the end of the war in 1918 there was a severe shortage of milk in the colony and a sharp increase in its price from three pence a pint in 1915 to eight pence per pint in 1919.

Thus by 1920, due partly to the impact of World War I, rice cultivation in British Guiana had evolved from a somewhat minor peasant enterprise to become one of the more important sectors in the colonial economy. Rice had come to stay and one could speak of the existence of a rice industry, however fledgling. The colony had become the leading rice producer in the Caribbean. This significant development since the early 1880s was due primarily to the industry of Indian peasants.

For Further Reading

Adamson, Alan	**Sugar Without Slaves: The Political Economy of British Guiana, 1838 - 1904** (New Haven: Yale University Press, 1972).
Mandle, Jay	"Population and Economic Change: The Emergence of the Rice Industry in Guyana, 1895 – 1915", **Journal of Economic History**, xxx. No.4, 1970.
Moohr, Michael	"The Discovery of Gold and the Development of Peasant Industries in Guyana, 1884 – 1914: A Study in the Political Economy of Change", **Caribbean Studies**, Vol. 15, No.2, July 1975.
Potter, Lesley	"The Paddy Proletariat and the Dependent Peasantry: East Indian Rice Growers in British Guiana, 1895-1920", **History Gazette,** No 47, August 1992.
Rodney, Walter	**A History of the Guyanese Working People, 1881-1905** (Baltimore: The Johns Hopkins University Press, 1981).

Chapter 24

The Beginning of the Gold Mining Industry in Guyana

The production of gold occupies a special place in the history of Guyana for it was the first mining industry to be established in the country. A few centuries earlier it was the lure of gold, the fabled wealth of El Dorado, which first generated considerable interest by some Europeans in Guyana.

Although Amerindians were aware of some sources of gold and Europeans made gold discoveries there from the seventeenth century, gold was never found in sufficiently large quantities to result in the emergence of an organised and sustained industry. By 1750 the Dutch authorities in the colony of Essequibo, who in the 1720s and 1740s had sent a number of costly expeditions into the interior to locate gold and silver, had begun to give up the idea of mining. They were discouraged not only by the meagre results of these expeditions, but also by the resistance demonstrated by the African slave labour force, who resented greatly the physically demanding work required by mining and often rebelled or ran away.

As a result, the exports of the colonies of Essequibo, Berbice and Demerara in the latter half of the eighteenth century were almost completely agricultural, consisting largely of the three staples, cotton, coffee and sugar. This pattern continued after these Dutch colonies were occupied by the British in 1796. From 1811, however, Guyanese cotton, and coffee underwent a decline, owing largely to competition from American cotton and Ceylonese coffee, which enjoyed lower production costs. By the time the British government unified Demerara-Essequibo and Berbice into a single new entity, British Guiana, in 1831, many cotton and coffee plantations had been abandoned or converted to sugar.

By the 1840s the new colony had virtually ceased to export coffee and cotton and its exports had come to consist almost exclusively of sugar and its two by-products, rum and molasses. This essentially monocultural export economy persisted until the 1880s, when there was a sudden and remarkable change, ushered in by the emergence of a gold mining industry and a growing variety of peasant-dominated industries, of which the most important and largest was rice cultivation.

Until then, such initiatives were constantly blocked by the planter-dominated legislature which used its political power to ensure that labour and capital were not diverted away from the coast, where the sugar plantations were located, to the interior where there was potential for mining and forest industries, and from sugar to any other coastal enterprise, such as agriculture in the African villages. One of the strategies which the sugar planters employed to achieve this objective was to set an exorbitant price for Crown land to prevent its purchase. For example, the minimum price was eventually set at 10 dollars an acre and the minimum lot size which could be purchased at 100 acres.

Nevertheless, planter policy was challenged by local residents who were interested in other enterprises than sugar production. Thus the first serious effort at gold mining was made in 1863 and 1864 by a local syndicate in the Mazaruni River. However, it proved unsuccessful and was abandoned. Although other attempts to mine gold in the following fifteen years were also abortive, they made the local government recognize the need to have a policy in relation to mining. The result was the introduction in 1880 of an ordinance which made provision for the mining of gold and silver. This ordinance provided for the issuing by the government of licenses for the purpose of mining any portion of ungranted Crown lands not exceeding 500 acres. It also stipulated that there should be the payment of a royalty of two per cent on all gold and silver found.

The introduction of this ordinance, which gave a new legitimacy to mining, resulted in more vigorous prospecting for gold, especially in the area traversed by the Cuyuni, Mazaruni and Puruni rivers, tributaries of the Essequibo, and to a small extent in the Demerara River. While a part of this new activity was the work of individual gold prospectors, much of it was effected by companies established by local residents and capital. These companies sent prospecting parties into the interior, and while most them found traces of gold in the creeks and streams of these rivers, only a few of them found gold in paying commercial quantities.

As a result, there was no substantial increase of gold production immediately after the introduction of the mining ordinance of 1880. Nevertheless, 1882 was a significant year. For the first time gold appeared among the exports in the **Blue Book,** the colony's official administrative record. A small quantity of 40 ounces is recorded as being exported that year, but none in the following year, 1883. The colony could not yet be said to possess an established gold industry. None of the findings until then was large enough to anticipate the rise of a substantial and sustained gold industry.

The situation, however, began to change significantly in 1884 and 1885 when new discoveries of rich deposits of gold were made in the interior. Thereafter gold appeared every year in the country's exports. The quantity and value of the metal exported showed an annual increase for almost ten years. In 1884 250 ounces valued at 1,019 pounds sterling were exported, in 1885 939 ounces valued at 3249 pounds and in 1886 6518 ounces valued at £23,342 pounds.

This expansion was largely due to the fact that news of the new discoveries of gold encouraged many residents to abandon the coast in favour of the gold fields in the interior and stimulated the formation of new companies. By 1886 the scale of this migration had become so large that local government officials had begun to refer to it as a "gold rush". Furthermore, by 1887, when 11906 ounces of gold valued at 44,427 pounds sterling were exported, there were 16 gold companies with a total capitalization of more than £460,000 pounds.

In short, the beginning of a sustained gold industry in Guyana can be said to date back to the year, 1884. The remarkable early expansion continued, reaching 138,000 ounces in 1893-94, the peak year, and remaining over 100,000 ounces every year thereafter until 1903-4, when it fell to 90,000 ounces. This decline which set in was due initially mainly to the fact that the richer seams were gradually exhausted. Gold production never attained the level of the 1890s again until the post-independence era after 1966.

The establishment of a gold mining industry in the 1880s there was not only sudden, but also a great surprise, especially given the fact that for at least forty years prior to that time the colony's export economy was based almost exclusively on sugar and its by-products. The gold industry emerged mainly because of a major crisis which the dominant sugar industry was experiencing as a result of competition in its traditional market in Britain from subsidized beet sugar from European countries.[85] The crisis had a drastic detrimental impact on the production and profitability of the Guianese sugar industry.

The prolonged depression in the sugar industry from 1884 to at least 1903 made the British authorities in London and Georgetown decide to modify their long-standing policy of developing only sugar in the colony and placing obstacles in the way of the emergence of other industries on the coast and in the interior. In particular, the Colonial Office in London forced the planter-dominated administration in Georgetown to change Crown land policy by reducing the price of such land and the minimal acreage requirement. The initial legislation in this direction was Ordinance No.4 of 1887 which reduced the price of specific Crown lands, partly with a view to inducing the incipient gold industry to legalize its occupation of Crown Land. Subsequent ordinances of 1889 and 1890 extended this new land-disposal policy, further facilitating the granting of Crown Land concessions to the rapidly expanding gold industry.

In short, the gold mining industry was able to emerge in the mid-1880s because the crisis in the sugar industry made the long-standing argument of the planter-dominated local government that a modification of the Crown Land policy would be detrimental to both the sugar industry and the colony no longer persuasive. This was a major development, for as recently as 1872 the local government had rejected a suggestion from the Colonial Office, which wanted to make it possible for more labourers to become landed peasants, that the basic price of Crown Land be reduced by 50 per cent and the minimum lot size which could be purchased by 80 per cent. The planter-controlled legislature argued successfully then that such an innovation would attract labour away from the sugar estates and the coast, drive up wages and result ultimately in the destruction of the sugar industry in particular and therefore the colony as a whole.

The appearance and expansion of the gold mining industry in the 1880s and early 1890s occurred in spite of major problems which the industry faced. Some of these difficulties were a result of the topography of the country. The gold mining regions were remote and initially accessible only in row boats by rivers beset with rapids and cataracts. These conditions made transportation slow, difficult, expensive and dangerous. There was much talk about building roads or railways to circumvent these long dangerous river journeys and to open up the interior, but the cost proved prohibitive.

Among the other problems encountered by the miners was the difficulty of using dredges in the rivers and creeks which were encumbered with boulders and, particularly, numerous trunks of fallen trees. The industry also suffered from the unsystematic approach and rudimentary, often crude, methods used by the miners and a lack of capital. At first most of the capital came from local sources, but by 1895 such investment had virtually dried up and there was growing dependence on foreign companies, many of which soon or eventually collapsed.

Notwithstanding these problems the gold mining industry had major consequences for the colony economically, socially and politically. Because it provided an alternative source of work and income, it attracted labour from the coast, both from the depressed sugar estates and the African villages. Workers were attracted to the goldfields because the wages offered there were high (approximately three times higher than those on the coast), but employers recuperated much of this expenditure through payment in kind at prices which were often 200 per cent higher than on the coast. By 1891 there were an estimated 8,000 persons involved in gold mining, more than one-tenth of the size of the large labour force of the sugar industry.

The seasonal withdrawal of labour from the coastal villages to the goldfields resulted in the decline or stagnation of cultivation there, especially in the older villages of the East Coast of Demerara and a serious shortage of ground provisions and vegetables in the coastal towns and villages. This development was also a consequence of the decrease in the quantity of land leased from the sugar estates for the cultivation of provisions from about 4355 acres between 1885 and 1889 to about 2,250 acres between 1901 and 1904.

The establishment of the gold mining industry also served to diversify the colony's essentially monocultural export economy, modifying its exports significantly. Whereas since 1838 each year sugar, rum and molasses had accounted for at least 88 per cent of the total value of its exports, their share fell after 1884 progressively to 81.7 per cent between 1889 and 1891, 71.5 per cent in 1892 to 1894, to 66.1 per cent between 1895 and 1897. This changing proportion was due to the increasing importance of gold which by 1897 was contributing about 25 per cent of the value of the colony's annual exports. Gold exports served to limit the decline of the colony's total exports in this period of depression in the sugar industry.

The modifications made initially in the regulations governing the sale and use of Crown Land to accommodate the emerging gold industry greatly increased the accessibility of land to the entire population of the colony. This soon permitted the flow of labour into a number of other industries which developed both on the coast and in the interior. Notable among these new industries were rice cultivation, the cattle industry, the production of three major forest commodities (timber, balata and charcoal), and diamond mining. In short, gold mining was the principal catalyst to the growing diversification of the country's economy, a major development.

Finally, the gold mining industry helped to bring about constitutional reform in British Guiana. In 1891 the colony's archaic constitution, which gave the sugar planters a monopoly of political power, was modified to permit merchants, representatives of the mining industry, and professionals to share constitutional power. This was a goal which non-sugar interests had struggled for without success since at least 1838.

For Further Reading

Adamson, Alan	**Sugar Without Slaves: The Political Economy of British Guiana, 1838-1904** (New Haven: Yale University Press, 1972).
Moohr, Michael	"The Discovery of Gold and the Development of Peasant Industries in Guyana, 1884-1914: A Study in the Political Economy of Change", **Caribbean Studies**, Vol.15, No 2, July 1975.

Chapter 25

The Origins of the Fishing Industry in Guyana

One important development in the economic life of Guyana during the past sixty years has been the increased utilisation of its riverain and marine resources. Fish and prawns have become a significant addition to the country's exports and a valuable source of foreign exchange. Fishing also provides a means of livelihood for a growing number of Guyanese, while from a nutritional standpoint fish is an important source of protein.

The development of a thriving fishing industry in the "land of many waters", as Guyana is often called, may be considered by many as "inevitable", but this had not been the case historically. Difficulties have been encountered in the various phases of the development of the industry.

The beginning of a fishing industry in the area that constitutes the Republic of Guyana has to be attributed to the first Guyanese, the ancestors of the current Amerindian population. From time immemorial the Amerindians depended on fish as a vital part of their diet to supplement the food supplies which they obtained from hunting, gathering and, later, agriculture.

The early Amerindians devised a variety of methods to enable them to exploit the abundance of fish which could be found in the numerous rivers and creeks of the territory. Their expertise in fishing impressed European settlers in Essequibo and Berbice in the seventeenth century, when they were employing three main methods to catch fish.

Firstly, they depended considerably on the use of the hook and line, especially in the dry season in deeper waters. Secondly, in some circumstances they employed a method which modern fishermen would consider strange- namely, the use of poison. At certain times of the year they blocked up the creeks and streams and put poison in the water, causing the fish to rise and float insensibly on the surface where they were taken easily.

The third main Amerindian method of catching fish particularly impressed European eyewitnesses, who were amazed by their dexterity. The Amerindians shot fish with bows and arrows, especially as the fish sought food near the banks of rivers and creeks. This occurred particularly in the rainy season, when seeds and fruits fell into the water from trees on the banks and the fish crowded to the banks to feed on them.

Some Amerindians caught only enough fish for their own subsistence. Others, however, deliberately sought to secure a surplus, which they smoked or salted to exchange with other Amerindians or Europeans for foodstuff and other necessities. They also sold fresh fish to Europeans who pickled it, receiving in return articles of European manufacture such as axes and knives.

Among the Amerindian groups, the Warraus, in particular, had a reputation for being expert fishermen, who possessed a remarkable aim with the bow and arrow. In the eighteenth century they could be found mainly on the coastlands, particularly in the area between the Barima and Pomeroon Rivers and their tributaries. They had a diet in which fish and crabs featured prominently.

Some of Guyana's earliest fisheries developed in areas, such as the Moruka region, dominated by the Warraus. Early descriptions of these Amerindians reflect the importance of fishing in their lives. For example, in the 1670s Adriaan van Berkel, a Dutch official, observed that the Warraus in the Berbice River "do not bother with planting or reaping and gain their livelihood just by fishing and hunting for the Europeans".[86]

The coming of the Dutch settlers from the Netherlands to Essequibo and Berbice in the early decades of the seventeenth century and to Demerara after 1745 ushered in the second major phase in the development of a fishing industry in Guyana. Until their arrival fishing seems to have been conducted by the Amerindians in the region's rivers and creeks and their estuaries on a relatively small scale. It does not seem that fishing was conducted then by Guyanese Amerindians away from the coast, although they are known to have travelled at least as far as Trinidad on other business.

The Netherlands, especially the northern Maritime Provinces, had for centuries been the centre of a substantial fishing industry. Not surprisingly, the Dutch immediately brought their knowledge of fishing to Essequibo, Berbice and Demerara, giving a significant impetus to fishing there. They valued fish not only for their nutrition, but also as the cheapest and most available form of protein food for the slaves whom they exploited to cultivate sugar cane, coffee and cotton.

The Dutch settlers played an important role in developing fishing in some inland fisheries, notably the one in the Canje River. They also embarked on marine fishing, especially in fisheries off the Waini, Barima and Orinoco rivers and possibly near Trinidad.

Their fishing operations, however, were often interrupted by Spaniards-coastguards, pirates and other individuals and vessels-from modern Venezuela and Trinidad, who seized their boats. Such disruption was particularly frequent in the second half of the eighteenth century. In the early 1760s the situation became so difficult that Laurens Storm van's Gravesande, the Director-General of Essequibo and Demerara, decided not to risk sending the Dutch West India Company's boats to the Orinoco, though, as he recognized and lamented, "the loss of the fishery is most injurious to the Colony".[87]

The limited supply of fish obtained from the marine and inland fisheries forced the Dutch in Essequibo, Berbice and Demerara to depend considerably on importing salted fish from North America. This situation was a source of grave concern to the Dutch planters for two reasons.

Firstly, when supplies of local fish failed, the Amerindians took advantage of the situation to raise the price of their commodity. Secondly, in times of shortage, when the planters were unable to provide slaves with their normal ration of three pounds of salt fish per fortnight, the slaves often responded by running away or resorting to other forms of resistance. The fish which the slaves caught in their free time in the evenings or on Sundays in the canals or trenches in or adjacent to the plantations was no substitute for the loss of their regular allowance.

This somewhat problematic second phase in the development of Guyana's fishing industry ended with the occupation of Demerara-Essequibo and Berbice by the British in 1796 and the subsequent official cession of these Dutch colonies to Britain in 1814. These two events prompted the departure of most of the Dutch residents there and ushered in a new and third phase in fishing activities in these territories. Fishing seems to have declined, for it was not a major preoccupation of the British, who were largely content to depend on imported dried, smoked and pickled fish. The recognized inland fisheries of the Dutch period of colonization in the Canje and Upper Essequibo River, for example, lost their importance.

This situation of reduced importance of fishing did not change after the amalgamation of Demerara-Essequibo and Berbice into a single entity, British Guiana, in 1831. This is evident in the **Blue Books**, the official annual statistical records of the new entity, which attest that for a long time after the unification in 1831 there was nothing which could truly be called fisheries or a fishing industry. For example, in the section headed "Manufacturers, Mines and Fisheries" in the Blue Book of 1838, it stated: "No fisheries whatever. There are two or three small boats kept by Individuals who supply the inhabitants with fish."[88] These boats supplied small quantity of fresh fish to the residents of the colony's two towns, New Amsterdam and, especially, Georgetown.

While this off-shore fishing continued on a small scale, there was increased fishing in the coastal creeks, canals and trenches after 1838 by the emancipated Blacks and East Indian indentured immigrants largely for their own subsistence. Furthermore, the gradual growth of the population of Georgetown and New Amsterdam eventually created a growing but still limited demand for fish which was supplied by the owners of a small number of vessels which operated off-shore and in the estuaries of the main rivers that flowed into the Atlantic Ocean. Thus the Blue Book for 1868 states: "A few Boats are engaged in supplying the Town Markets with a small quantity of fish of several descriptions."[89] No record was kept of the quantity or species of fish supplied or of its monetary value.

The colony, however, still did not have any recognised or established inland or marine fisheries. Thus the Blue Books for 1854 and 1860 respectively stated: "There are no Mines in Work and no Fisheries" and "There are not any Fisheries established in this colony".[90]

In these circumstances the dependence on salted, smoked and pickled fish, imported mainly from North America, continued. In 1868, for example, British Guiana imported about 82,000 hundredweight of dried fish, 19,200 hundredweight of pickled fish and 375 hundredweight of smoked fish-in short, over 100,000 hundredweight of fish costing nearly 70,000 pounds sterling. These fish imports constituted just over four per cent of the colony's total imports. They were surpassed in value by only four other imports, namely, flour, machinery, rice and manure.

This reliance on imported fish was strengthened by the decreased involvement of Amerindians in fishing, especially after 1884 when the beginning of the gold mining industry resulted in the opening of the interior of the country. Amerindians there began increasingly to depend on salted fish which they purchased from pedlars from the coast. Furthermore, the small quantity of smoked fish which Amerindians previously had been sending or bringing to Georgetown for sale declined substantially by the 1890s.

By 1890 fishing in the colony was distinguished by at least five features. Firstly, it was restricted to its rivers, creeks, canals, estuaries and areas in the sea relatively near the coast. There was no deep-sea fishing. Secondly, few efforts were being made to preserve fish. Fish curing in the colony was very limited partly because the limited supply could always be sold while fresh.

Thirdly, fish did not feature among the colony's exports, except a small quantity of the imported fish which was re-exported especially to Suriname, French Guiana and the British Caribbean islands. Fourthly, apart from these re-exports, the only fish product exported was fish glue or isinglass, which was made from the sounds or air bladders of certain species of fish, especially gilbacker, caught off-shore. Since about 1860 a comparatively small quantity of this commodity was being exported each year to the United Kingdom. In 1890, for example, 4203 pounds of fish glue, valued at about 225 pounds sterling, were exported.

Fifthly, the off-shore fishing was dominated by Portuguese residents. The Portuguese had been brought to the colony as early as 1835 as agricultural labourers, but they eventually abandoned the plantations and became involved in a variety of business enterprises, including fishing.

By 1890 the colony's limited involvement in fisheries was being increasingly lamented by local officials and other residents who complained that when compared with the emphasis on agriculture and gold mining, fishing was being neglected. For example, the Blue Book for the late 1880s and early 1890s in the "General Remarks" on "Fisheries" repeated the following observation: "There is abundance of Fish in the waters of the Colony, but as an industrial pursuit fishing is comparatively neglected, nor has any attempt been made to meet the existing demand by fishing in the Rivers and Creeks of the Colony which teem with valuable fresh water species."[91]

Similar remarks were made in 1893 by James Rodway, a local historian and one of the colony's prominent residents, in the publication, **Hand-Book of British Guiana**. In the book's last chapter, entitled "Resources and Capabilities", Rodway stated

☙

> The fisheries of the colony are also capable of development to a considerable extent. At present the supply is unequal to the demand, from the fact that very few persons are

engaged in the industry, the result being that salt cod is imported in immense quantities. Really good fish of a great many kinds are, however, plentiful both on the coast and in the rivers.[92]

☙

Shortly afterwards, however, a significant development took place. In 1894 deep-sea fishing, abandoned since the departure of Dutch settlers early in that century, was resumed on a small scale. Thus the Blue Book for 1894-1895 reported: "Deep sea fishing has been established during the year, and the market is well-supplied with Grouper, Dolphin, Red Snapper, etc."[93]

The beginning of sustained deep-sea fishing in 1894 was the first of several important developments which played a major role in expanding the fishing industry, enhancing its value, and causing fishing eventually to become a significant feature in the economic life of the country.

Chapter 26

British Guiana's Fishing Industry: Progress and Problems, 1894-1960

1894 was an important year in the history of fishing in Guyana for it marked the beginning of sustained deep-sea fishing. This development ushered in a new phase in this history. This phase lasted until the 1940s and was marked by a number of significant developments.

Among these developments was a modest expansion in deep-sea fishing after 1910 when every year at least three or four vessels were involved, instead of the single schooner operating in previous years since 1894. This limited expansion seems to have been stimulated largely by the provision of ice storage in Georgetown at an ice-manufacturing establishment.

Partly for the same reason the years after 1910 also witnessed a great increase in off-shore fishing. Not only was there an increase in the number of boats owned by Portuguese fishing especially for gilbacker, but also fishing spread to almost every village on the East and West Coasts of Demerara, whose fishermen supplied mainly the Georgetown market. By the early 1940s more than half of the colony's coastal fishermen and seamen were resident on the East Coast of Demerara, where the main landing points for fish were the kokers of Plaisance, Beterverwagting, Buxton, Clonbrook and Greenfield.

This increased supply of fish was partly a response to a significant growth in local demand for fish in the 1920s, owing to two factors, namely, growth in the population and a rise in the price of imported salt and pickled fish. But although fish imports declined, they still remained substantial, requiring the expenditure of a considerable amount of foreign exchange. For example, as late as 1940 nearly five million pounds of salted, smoked, pickled and canned fish worth $362,000.00 were imported.

The first years of the twentieth century saw initiatives in research, education and fish curing. The first serious study of the colony's fish resources was undertaken by a Fisheries Committee or Commission established in 1901 by the Royal Agricultural and Commercial Society to collect information about the colony's fishes, including the species found, their habits, breeding seasons, etc. In 1903 a brochure on the colony's fishes was published by the local Argosy Press, promoting interest in fishing. Furthermore, in that same year or in 1904 the first curing enterprises were established.

The growing interest and involvement in fishing were evident in other areas. For example, it was reported that fishing was becoming a hobby or recreational activity for some residents. More importantly, working-class Blacks and Indians began to exploit the coastal shrimp and prawn resources more intensely than before. This practice must have begun much earlier in the nineteenth century, but it was not until the early years of the twentieth century that it was first mentioned in the colony's official records. The somewhat terse or vague comment in the **Blue Book** of 1902-1903 that "Prawns, Shrimps and Crabs are caught in large quantities"[94] is amplified in the **Blue Book** of the following year, 1903-04, where it is reported that "The amount of Shrimp consumed in the colony is enormous and must run to tons weekly. The coolies use them in their curries and the black people in their foo-foo."[95]

Perhaps the most significant development in fishing in British Guiana between 1900 and 1940 was the growing interest showed by the colonial government in fishing. The 1920s witnessed the provision for the first time of somewhat precise statistics in relation to deep-sea fishing. The **Blue Books** began from that time to record the quantity and value of the catch, the species caught and the number of deep-sea as well as off-shore fishing craft. For example, it was reported in 1928 that the colony had three two-masted schooners engaged in deep-sea activities and 161 small fishing boats involved in off-shore operations.

The government commented often on the possibility of improving various aspects of the fishing industry, especially marine fishing. For example, each year from 1910 to 1919 the **Blue Book** stated that "There is room for development on the lines of curing and canning as well as catching."[96] This comment was understandable in view of a further decline in the amount of smoked fish being supplied by the Amerindians. Similarly, the colony's administration report of 1927 stated that "There is room for considerable development in many directions, especially in deep-sea fishing."[97]

Government officials, however, were not yet confident that there would be expansion in deep-sea fishing. Their statements of optimism were often contradicted by somewhat pessimistic observations such as those which appeared in the **Blue Book** of 1928, where it is stated

> The local demand is being amply met and should it increase, additional schooners would be forthcoming. There seems little prospect, however, of development, the tendency being the other way.[98]

This observation was repeated virtually in every year's **Blue Book** until 1940. Nevertheless, the important point to note is that the colonial government was showing a far greater interest in fishing than it had done in the nineteenth century.

Although by 1940 the colony's fishing industry was making progress, it was being hindered by a number of factors. Among them were the poor quality and condition of fishing gear, the relatively small number of boats, the limited state of development of the trench fisheries and the failure to exploit the pelagic fisheries in the off-shore waters. Pelagic fish are those which have no relation to the sea floor and live for the most part a floating existence in the upper waters of the sea. Up to at least the early 1940s the pelagic fisheries off the coast of the colony were entirely untouched and their possibilities unknown.

Perhaps the major hindrance to the fishing industry of British Guiana was the lack of adequate facilities for the distribution of fish in the rural areas. There was a great need to establish insulated depots in the countryside and to develop sea, rail and road transport, including the improvement of important roadways such as the East Coast of Demerara road.

The early 1940s were a watershed in the history of fishing in Guyana, ushering in its final phase, namely the early modern and contemporary period from 1946 to the present day. Two events between 1940 and 1945 had a major impact on the country's fishing industry. One was the Second World War. The other was the visit to the colony in December 1942 of Herbert Brown, the British Colonial Office's Director of Fisheries Investigation, and the recommendations which he made about the British Guiana fishing industry.

World War II had at least four principal effects on this industry. It resulted in a general rise in operating costs, the risk of loss of the deep-sea schooners by German submarine action, a decrease in the quantity of imported fish and an increased demand for locally produced fish. This increased demand was due not only to the reduced ability to import fish, but also to the consumer needs of the United States base at Atkinson Field. By August 1942 the quantity of fish available to the local population began to decline owing to three factors, namely, the deterioration of road transport on the East Coast of Demerara, consumption by the U.S. base and the shortage and increased cost of fishing gear replacements and imports of tar, the main preservative of fishing nets.

The colony's fishing industry profited after the war from a continuation of the decreased importation of fish which the insecurity of the sea lanes had caused during the war. This was due partly to the increased supply of local fresh fish after the war as a result of a growth in the number of fishing boats. In 1946 more than two million pounds of skin and scale fish were landed in Georgetown and 491 fishing boats are said to have been operating in the colony.

The colony's fishing industry was also greatly affected by the recommendations of Herbert Brown, the British Director of Fisheries Investigation, who visited British Guiana in December 1942. Some of his recommendations were to deal with the wartime exigencies, while others were more long-term. Brown's wide-ranging recommendations for stimulating local fish production included the following:

1. The prompt provision of fishing gear replacements.
2. The institution of a better distributive system for marketing fish.
3. The development of trench fisheries.
4. The conduct of commercial fishing research.
5. The provision of information about new fishing techniques and demonstration of those techniques.
6. The provision of cheap ice through the establishment of ice plants.
7. The introduction of salting projects.
8. The improvement of wharfage facilities.
9. The provision of credit facilities to fishermen.
10. The formation of fishermen's associations

to obtain cooperative credit and to purchase supplies in bulk.

Brown stressed that British Guiana possessed at least three advantages over the other British Caribbean colonies where the fishing industry was concerned. Firstly, there was a strong local demand for fish. Secondly, Georgetown had a well-organised system of iced fish distribution through the firm, Weiting and Richter, whose fishing operations had developed as an ancillary to their manufacture of ice. Thirdly, British Guiana enjoyed shorter passages to and from the fishing grounds which resulted in less loss of fishing time and other benefits. An awareness of these advantages had prompted Weiting and Richter to increase its deep-sea fleet from three to six between 1938 and 1942 by the purchase or charter of three Barbadian vessels.

Some of Brown's recommendations were implemented during the war, most of them after the war, giving a great impetus to the colony's fishing industry which entered a new phase, unprecedented for the degree of change and growth. This new phase can be said to have begun with a critical administrative development. In February 1946, a Fisheries Division was established within the Department of Agriculture staffed by a Junior Fisheries Officer and nine Technical Assistants and supervised by the Marketing Officer. The initial mandate of the Division, the earliest precursor of the modern Ministry of Fisheries, Crops and Livestock, was to develop inland fisheries and fish farming and to conduct a survey of potential fisheries in the colony's off-shore waters. Much of the credit for the subsequent growth of the Guyanese fishing industry can be attributed to the work of the Division and its successors.

Mainly as a result of the work and influence of the Fisheries Division, the year 1946 witnessed several achievements, some of which represented new developments in the fishing industry. Fourteen fishing organisations were formed; bulk purchasing of gear and equipment was effected by the Division on behalf of fishing associations; refunds were given of customs duty paid on fishing gear and equipment; and the facilities were improved at the major landing points for fishing vessels in Georgetown. Fishermen's Associations were also encouraged and educated to start cooperative movements such as credit unions.

The industry also got a fillip from a successful experiment conducted by the Fisheries Division in August and September 1947 in the use of the otter trawl to promote inshore fishing in accordance with a recommendation made by Herbert Brown. The purpose of this experiment, which was to introduce trawling in the colony, was achieved, as several prominent fishermen who witnessed the trawling operations were convinced that this method of fishing would be successful and profitable. A similar important and successful experiment was conducted ten years later in 1957 when the colonial government secured an extended loan on a British Fisheries research vessel, the "Cape St. Mary", to conduct a trawl survey of off-shore waters of depths from 10 to 100 fathoms.

All these developments enabled the fishing industry to make unprecedented strides in the late 1940s and the 1950s. Other factors contributing to the development of the industry in this period included the establishment of a wholesale fish market and processing centre and the provision of better facilities for docking, cold storage and shore accommodation for fishermen.

All these improvements led to the expansion of the industry which was clearly reflected in all the relevant statistics. For example, the quantity of fish landed in Georgetown increased from 2.1 million pounds in 1948 to 5 million pounds in 1953 to over 8 million pounds in 1957. Similarly, the number of fishing gear units increased from 737 in 1952 to 981 in 1957, while the number of powered fishing boats grew from 58 in 1952 to 185 in 1957. Most significantly, the colony began to export fish in this period, an important development which enhanced the value of the industry as a foreign revenue earner.

In short, in the period from 1946 to 1960 the British Guiana fishing industry experienced a major transformation in nature, scope and status, greatly enabling it to become the industry which it is today. Since the 1950s numerous significant developments have occurred in the industry. These include the development of aquaculture, the trade in ornamental fish, the establishment of fish complexes, the eclipse of fish by prawns in Guyana's exports, the involvement of foreign capital, boundary problems, regional and bilateral projects, the impact of international agreements and regulations and recently the injurious effects of piracy.

The growth of the fishing industry has been achieved in spite of the fact that it has been adversely affected by numerous problems of varying nature and gravity during its long history. Some of these problems were unique to a period, others were recurrent periodically, while some have been persistent and virtually continuous.

Some of the problems have been beyond the ability of the industry to avert or address effectively. These include problems of water pollution which has sometimes resulted in massive fish deaths, and climatic problems. For example, in 1951 the fishing industry suffered considerably from climatic and other geographical factors. According to the Director of Agriculture in his annual report

> The prolonged floods of the earlier part of the year, the excessive and prolonged freshening of coastal and estuarine waters affected fishermen operating smaller craft, and those operating larger craft reported a longer period of adverse winds and an unusual amount of changes in the mud banks suitable for fishing.[99]

Occasionally the source of problems has been political, especially boundary disputes with the country's neighbours. For example, from time to time the operations of Guianese fishermen in the Corentyne river and its estuary have been disrupted by Surinamese authorities.

The most persistent political problem, however, has been internal – namely, the insufficient attention frequently paid to the fishing industry by the local administration, both in the colonial and post-independence periods. In the period of British rule this inadequate attention, which at times bordered on indifference, stemmed from any one or a combination of the following factors – inertia, a lack of confidence in the future of the industry, satisfaction with dependence on imported fish, and the need to spend financial resources on other areas, notably agriculture, which seemed more critical to the colonial economy or more profitable to British capitalism.

The fishing industry in modern Guyana is accorded an importance which it did not have in earlier periods of the country's history. This contemporary importance attached to fishing is largely a result of five main considerations. Firstly, fish is regarded as valuable as a source of protein. Historically, it has been a main element in the diet at first especially of lower-income groups and later of the more privileged classes as well. By at least the 1930s it had become a very important part of the country's food supply as a comparatively low-priced source of animal protein.

Secondly, fish and prawns are valuable as a source of foreign exchange, though, admittedly, it took a long time before the country began to export fish or any fish products. Thirdly, the fishing industry is valued because it has freed Guyana from the need of spending a substantial amount of foreign exchange in purchasing imported fish, as was the practice at least until the 1940s. Fourthly, fishing is important as a means of livelihood, not only for fishermen, but also for other workers, including vendors, boatbuilders and providers of fishing gear. Finally, the industry is also important because it has led to the formation and development of fishing-based coastal communities.

These five contrasting factors, some social and some economic or political, largely explain the value attached to fishing in contemporary Guyana. The country's fishing industry today involves three types of operations

1. Inland fishing, that is, fishing in the country's numerous rivers, creeks and trenches as well as aquaculture, the rearing of fish in ponds, etc.
2. Off-shore or coastal operations, i.e. fishing in the Atlantic in areas relatively near the coast.
3. Marine or deep-sea operations, i.e. fishing in the blue waters of the Atlantic far away from the muddy coastal waters in the depths of 360 to 600 feet near and beyond the edge of the continental shelf.

These three operations to a large extent require the use of different fishing gear and methods and result in the catching of different species of fish. Each of them is expanding, making progress in spite of the problems that its operators face.

For Further Reading

| Brown, H. | **The fisheries of British Guiana. Appendix to Roth, Vincent, Notes and observations on fish life in British Guiana** (Georgetown: The Daily Chronicle, 1943). |
| Roth, Vincent, | **Notes and observations on fish life in British Guiana** (Georgetown: The Daily Chronicle, 1943). |

CHAPTER 27

GUYANA'S PURSUIT OF A DIVERSIFIED EXPORT ECONOMY

One of the distinguishing features of most European colonies in the Caribbean in the seventeenth, eighteenth and nineteenth centuries was the possession of a restricted export economy. That economy often centred on the export of one commodity, usually sugar, produced by the colony. Only a few colonies escaped this restriction for any considerable time. Among them were the colonies of Essequibo, Berbice and Demerara which were unified in 1831 into a new entity, British Guiana. During much of its colonial experience, Guyana managed to have a diversified export economy.

Initially in the seventeenth century the export economy of the Dutch colonies of Essequibo and Berbice centred on forest products acquired from trade with the Amerindians. In particular, it was based on the export of one commodity, annatto, used as a dye in the buoyant textile industry of the Netherlands. Trade with the Amerindians continued to be the principal economic activity of many Dutch settlers in Essequibo and Berbice until about the 1720s when it came to a virtual end partly because the Dutch developed new and better resources of dyestuffs elsewhere in the world.

By then, however, the export economy of the Guiana colonies was somewhat diversified with two main commodities, annatto and sugar. The cultivation of sugar-cane was introduced in Essequibo at least by the late 1630s, with the first export of sugar to the Netherlands being a small shipment in 1637.[100] Sugar production, however, did not begin to become a significant element in the local economy until after the arrival in the late 1650s of Dutch immigrants from Brazil who brought capital and great technical expertise in sugar cultivation, giving an impetus to the sugar industry especially in Essequibo.

Nevertheless, the growth of sugar production in Essequibo and Berbice was comparatively slow. This was due partly to a shortage of labour provided mostly by slaves from West Africa. The Dutch West India Company and later the Dutch free traders preferred to supply slaves to the neighbouring Dutch colony of Suriname, which at least until 1770 was far more prosperous than Essequibo, Berbice and Demerara. Thus whereas in 1762 the slave population of Suriname was estimated to be about 74,500, that of Berbice and Essequibo was said to be 3824 and 2571 respectively. For similar reasons Dutch creditors preferred to invest their capital in Suriname, from where they expected to derive more handsome returns than from Essequibo, Berbice and Demerara.

Not surprisingly, in these circumstances of limited labour and capital, the diversified economy of Essequibo and Berbice grew very slowly. When the trade in annatto virtually ended in the 1720s, the export economy of these two colonies threatened to revert to its original dependence on one commodity, on this occasion sugar. About that same time, however, the cultivation of two new agricultural staples, coffee and cotton, was introduced into Essequibo and Berbice. After discouraging initial efforts, the production of coffee and cotton developed, thereby diversifying the export economy. Dutch governors of these colonies were instructed to encourage the cultivation of these two crops and sugar-cane.

Because of the perennial problem of a shortage of slave labour, however, the plantation economy continued to expand slowly. Sugar was the main plantation crop and initially coffee was more favoured than cotton, which only began to be cultivated on a significant scale in the 1760s. By the 1780s coffee and cotton began to pose an increasing threat to sugar as the main commodity exported by Essequibo, Berbice and Demerara, which became a Dutch colony in 1746. Their cultivation appealed to many planters because it required less labour and capital than sugar-cane cultivation. For example, it was estimated that whereas it required on the average one slave per acre to cultivate sugar-cane, one man could cultivate 1 1/2 acres of coffee and two acres of cotton. This was obviously an important consideration in a context where labour was short. Not surprisingly, after the death or escape of many slaves during the massive slave rebellion in Berbice in 1763 and 1764, several sugar plantations there switched to coffee cultivation. Essequibo, however, continued to be mainly a sugar colony, with only a small quantity of cotton being produced along the coast.

The labour situation in these colonies improved significantly in the 1770s when there was a serious economic crisis in Suriname which resulted in the withdrawal of credit, the bankruptcy of planters, the abandonment and sale of plantations and a marked fall there in the demand for, and price of, slaves.

The crisis prompted most Dutch slave traders who arrived in Suriname after 1772 to refuse to sell their slaves there and to proceed instead to neighbouring Berbice, Demerara and Essequibo to dispose of them at higher prices. It is estimated that these three colonies were supplied with 7000-8000 slaves in this way instead of Suriname in the 1770s. Some of these slaves were used to promote cotton cultivation which expanded especially in the 1780s in the wake of a growing realisation that saline coastal soils, particularly in Demerara, were the lands most suited for its growth.

Although the supply of slaves had improved, it was still not sufficient to meet the demand for labour. This situation, however, changed to some extent after 1796 when Britain took possession of Demerara, Essequibo and Berbice. Consequently, British traders, who were dominating the transatlantic slave trade, were able for the first time to supply these colonies with slaves without restrictions over an extended period. They supplied Demerara- Essequibo and Berbice with an unprecedented number of slaves. Within five years at least 28,000 enslaved Africans were landed in Demerara-Essequibo, while the imports into Berbice were so massive that its slave population doubled by 1802.

Many of these new slaves were used to develop cotton and coffee plantations, established by new British immigrants who settled in these colonies and purchased land there after the advent of British rule in 1796. The number of plantations in Demerara, for example, grew from 392 in 1795 to 490 in 1800 an increase of 25 per cent. These developments were financed mainly by British creditors, attracted by the good returns gained from their investment. In 1802 it was estimated that British merchants in London, Bristol and Glasgow had extended ten million pounds sterling in credit to planters in Demerara-Essequibo since 1796.

By 1800 there was such a remarkable growth and transformation in the economies of Demerara -Essequibo and Berbice that sugar was no longer their main export. Rather sugar had been superseded in importance by cotton and coffee and relegated to the third spot in what was now a more fully developed diversified export economy being experienced by both colonies. Thus while in 1800 the export of sugar from Demerara – Essequibo remained at the same level as in 1795, the average annual export of coffee increased by 65 per cent between 1796 and 1800 compared with the years 1792 to 1795 and that of cotton grew by 350 per cent during the same period. This marked expansion of coffee and, especially, cotton production after 1796 was due largely to the rapidly growing demand for these articles in Britain, the increasingly high prices which they were fetching there and the fact that they required less capital and labour to produce than sugar.

By 1800 the economy of Demerara-Essequibo and Berbice had developed so much that these colonies combined had become the second largest producer of sugar in the British West Indies, eclipsed only by Jamaica, the greatest producer of coffee in the British Empire and the biggest producer of raw cotton in the world. It is doubtful whether Guyana's economy has ever been as buoyant at any time in its long history as it was in 1800. The diversified export economy of Demerara-Essequibo and Berbice could not be matched then by that of any other British possession in the Caribbean, not even by Jamaica. Its growth, in fact, had begun to become a source of concern and envy to planters in the older British Caribbean possessions, especially Barbados and Jamaica, who saw these former Dutch colonies as formidable competitors in supplying the British market with tropical produce.

In short, by 1800 Guyana's quest for a diversified export economy had made remarkable progress since the 1720s. In the nineteenth century, however, the country suffered a number of severe setbacks with the result that the gains were lost and its export economy reverted to a dependence on sugar and its by-products, rum and molasses, for several decades.

The first setback which the colonies encountered was the restriction in 1805 of the slave trade from Africa and, more importantly, the outlawing in 1807 by the British government of this traffic for British subjects.[101] These measures deprived the planters in Demerara-Essequibo and Berbice of their main source of labour and rendered it impossible for most of them to maintain, much less extend, their area of cultivation.

From about 1810, when cotton and coffee production reached their peak, the export economy began to suffer increasingly from another setback, namely, the challenge to Guyanese coffee and cotton in the British market from competition from cheaper products from other countries – cotton from the southern United States and coffee from Turkey and, later, Ceylon. As a result of this competition the export of cotton from Demerara-Essequibo declined from 9.4 million pounds in 1810 to 1.1 million pounds in 1833, while that of coffee, which declined more slowly, decreased from 9.4 million pounds in 1812 to about 6.1 million pounds in 1833.

As the prices which Guyanese coffee and cotton fetched on the British market continued to fall, the planters faced declining profits and even bankruptcy. Those who were able switched to sugar production which was more profitable, but required more labour and capital. Many cotton and coffee planters who were unable to make the transition to sugar cultivation abandoned agriculture completely. Thus between 1809 and 1824 111 cotton and 21 coffee estates in Berbice were abandoned and only 19 of these were converted to sugar plantations.

In short, after 1810 the Guyanese diversified export economy progressively declined, with a growing dependence on sugar and increasingly less emphasis on coffee and, especially, cotton. It suffered an even more formidable blow in the 1830s, firstly with the legal abolition of slavery in 1833 and the introduction of apprenticeship in 1834 and secondly, and more importantly, with the full emancipation of the slaves in 1838.

Emancipation in 1838 plunged most planters in British Guiana into a labour and financial crisis, It was followed by a massive exodus of the former apprentices from the plantations to seek their own independent existence mostly in villages which they established, thus creating a shortage of labour in the plantations. Labour problems, including the impact of national strikes in 1842 and 1847-48, and the need for the first time to finance a huge wage bill for labour brought the ruin of many planters.

In these circumstances, many plantations were abandoned - 135 between 1838 and 1853, including virtually all the surviving coffee and cotton plantations and many of the smaller sugar estates. By 1850 the Guianese diversified economy had disappeared and there was a reversion to a dependence almost exclusively on one export, namely, sugar and its by-products, rum and molasses. In fact, from about 1850 to 1880 sugar, rum and molasses almost every year contributed at least 90 per cent of the value of the exports of British Guiana.

The colony's export economy also suffered a further major blow from a change in British imperial commercial policy which gradually deprived Guyanese and other British West Indian sugar from a privileged position which it had long enjoyed in the British market from protective tariffs which gave it advantages in customs duties payable over sugar from other countries. The progressive elimination of these protective tariffs commenced in 1825 and ended in 1854, when sugar from all countries began to enter Britain on identical terms. This meant that Guianese sugar then had to face formidable competition from the slave-grown sugar of Cuba and Brazil and later from European beet-sugar.

Because of the challenges which Guianese sugar planters faced in the 1830s and 1840s, sugar exports declined considerably from an annual average of about 51,000 tons between 1834 and 1838 to an annual average of about 31, 000 tons between 1838 and 1846, a decrease of about 38 per cent. By the mid1850s, however, the sugar industry had begun to recover. This recovery was due primarily to the exploitation of a growing number of indentured immigrants, especially East Indians, who provided a new, cheap, reliable and controllable labour force. It was also facilitated by the failure of the black village economies as a viable way of life and the application of new technology and scientific knowledge, making the industry more efficient, productive and competitive. As a result of these developments, the amount of sugar exported from British Guiana doubled between 1855 and 1880.

The sugar industry benefited from the fact that the planters who controlled the local legislature, deliberately and consistently used their political power to ensure that sugar would remain ascendant in the economy and that labour, capital and national revenue would not be diverted to any other industry. They stubbornly resisted all attempts to encourage developments away from the sugar estates, both in the black villages and in the interior. In these circumstances, the possibility of developing again a diversified export economy could not and did not materialise.

This situation of an export economy centred essentially on one commodity, sugar, continued until 1884 when the sugar industry faced its most formidable crisis in the nineteenth century. This crisis stemmed from competition from government-subsidised beet sugar produced by France and other continental European countries.[102] The great increase in the volume of beet sugar entering the British market and other factors resulted in a drastic fall of sugar prices from £22.4s a ton in 1883 to £14.11s a ton in 1884. The fall in the price of sugar and the competitiveness of the British market resulted in reduced sugar production in British Guiana, where production fell by about 20 per cent between 1884 and 1900.

The sugar crisis lasted until 1903 when Britain finally succeeded in persuading the relevant European governments to withdraw subsidies to beet farmers. It led to significant changes in the Guianese economy. The deepening crisis made the British Government lose faith in sugar and become willing to countenance and encourage diversification in the Guianese economy by promoting the emergence and development of new industries and thus remove the danger of having an export economy based on only one commodity, sugar. The collapse of many plantations and the retrenchment of sugar workers during the crisis resulted in the availability of a large pool of unemployed labourers who could be employed in new industries.

It was in these circumstances that gold mining began seriously in 1885 in the interior in Essequibo, attracting mostly unemployed Blacks from the coast.[103] Gold production increased rapidly from 939 ounces in 1885 to 6518 ounces in 1886 to over 138,000 ounces in 1894, the peak year in the early phase of the industry. Simultaneously, East Indians, with reduced opportunities for work on the struggling sugar estates, began to be actively involved in the cultivation of rice.[104] In short, these new industries profited from their ability to attract labour from sugar at a time of depression in the sugar industry.

With the growth of the production of gold and rice, and the beginning of diamond mining in the late 1890s, the Guianese export economy regained the diversified character it had lost earlier in the century. Even after sugar recovered from the crisis posed by beet sugar, this diversified economy survived and continued, for the sugar industry never regained the same degree of ascendancy it had enjoyed between 1838 and 1884, though it remained the country's largest employer of labour and greatest source of foreign exchange. In fact, its dominance was further eroded somewhat after the commencement of bauxite production in 1917. In short, in the twentieth century Guyana, unlike its experience in the nineteenth century, never lost its diversified export economy.

For Further Reading

Adamson, Alan	**Sugar Without Slaves: The Political Economy of British Guiana, 1838-1904** (New Haven: Yale University Press, 1972).
Moohr, Michael	"The Discovery of Gold and the Development of Peasant Industries in Guyana, 1884 – 1914: A Study in the Political Economy of Change", **Caribbean Studies,** Vol. 15, No.2, July 1975.
Granger, David	"The Diversification of the Economy of British Guiana, 1880-1930", **Guyana Historical Journal**, Vol. IV &V, 1992-1993.

Part Five

Church History

St. Andrew's Kirk

Front cover of "Building Bridges", the autobiography of Philip Mohabir, the visionary and main founder of Full Gospel Fellowship

Chapter 28

The Beginnings of The Congregational Church in Guyana

The establishment in Guyana of what came to be known as the Congregational Church, one of the country's main historic churches, was the work of the London Missionary Society (LMS), a British Protestant missionary body which was founded in 1795 in London, England. The LMS was one of the products of a great spiritual awakening which England experienced in the eighteenth century and is described by many historians as "The Evangelical Revival". The central figures of this awakening were two brothers, John and Charles Wesley, the founders of Methodism. As a result of it, many residents of England were converted to Christianity and English Christian churches were revived, becoming much more devoted to Christ and spiritual matters than before.

One expression of their new devotion was the demonstration of an unprecedented concern for the spread of the gospel of Christ to non-Christian people in other lands. The closing years of the century witnessed a rapid increase of missionary activity through the formation of several new missionary bodies. In the 1790s at least five such bodies were formed in Britain: the Baptist Missionary Society, the Church Missionary Society, the London Missionary Society, the Glasgow Missionary Society and the Scottish Missionary Society. The first three of these organisations were to enjoy a long and notable history. However, only one of them, namely, the London Missionary Society, had any special relevance to Guyana.

In the first ten years of its existence from 1795 to 1805, the LMS concentrated its efforts on countries in Asia and Africa, where it sent several missionaries. In that period it displayed little or no interest in the West Indies. It was therefore a surprise when in 1808 it established its first mission in the Caribbean by sending a young English theological school graduate, Rev. John Wray, as a missionary to Demerara. It is Wray who is considered the pioneer of the Congregational Church in Guyana.

The inauguration of missionary work in Demerara in 1808 was largely the result of overtures made to the LMS by Hermanus Hilbertus Post, a Dutchman who was the owner and resident of the Plantation Le Resouvenir located on the East Coast of Demerara about eight miles from the colony's capital, Stabroek, which was renamed Georgetown in 1812. In 1808 Le Resouvenir was a large cotton estate cultivated by about 400 predominantly black slaves.

At that time Christianity in Guyana was almost exclusively a religion for Whites. From the beginning of Dutch settlement and colonisation in Essequibo, Berbice and Demerara the local authorities and the white plantation owners had strongly and consistently opposed the Christianisation of the slaves. This opposition stemmed from the fear that exposure to Christian teaching would make the slaves more discontented with servitude and consequently more rebellious.

This policy and attitude continued when Demerara, Essequibo and Berbice passed from Dutch to British rule in 1803. Thus in 1805, for example, John Hawkshaw, a Methodist clergyman from Nevis, was expelled from Demerara by the governor after a stay of only eight days because he announced his intention to give religious instruction to slaves. Slaves and free Blacks, who out of curiosity sometimes approached the public place of worship to view the proceedings, were invariably driven away from the doors and windows by members of the exclusively white congregation.

This hostile attitude to the Christianisation of Blacks, however, was not shared by at least one white man in the colony, namely, Hermanus Post. Post was a rare example in Demerara of a devout and humane planter. Born in Holland in a deeply religious family, he had settled in 1765 in Demerara, where he continued to lead a God-fearing life. He felt very guilty about his failure to attend to the spiritual welfare of the slaves whose labour he exploited. His guilt and concern were reflected in a letter which he wrote in April 1807 regretting the failure of efforts which he had begun in the previous year to secure a Moravian missionary from Europe to come to Demerara to give his slaves religious instruction. In that letter Post wrote

☙

> It was always laid heavy on my mind and not ceased to do so that we only endeavour to profit by the labour of this people, without considering that some among them may through the grace

of God be made happy for ever by being made acquainted with the message from heaven which offers peace to fallen mankind.[105]

❦

Since the 1730s Moravian missionaries had been working among slaves in Suriname and in several islands in the Danish and British West Indies. On the whole their work had given satisfaction to governments and slaveholders for they managed to improve the spiritual and moral condition of the slaves without apparently making them more discontented with their servile lot.

Post was very impressed with what he described as "the wonderful successes" which the Moravians had in the art of effectively communicating the gospel of Christ to Africans from different linguistic and ethnic backgrounds. His effort, however, to recruit a Moravian missionary failed partly because the letter which he sent to a friend in England in 1806 seeking his assistance in this endeavour did not reach its destination.

Disappointed but still anxious and determined to so something to promote the spiritual welfare of his slaves, Post decided to employ an individual whom he described as a "Black schoolmaster". This personage was apparently a pious free Black who had some education and a rudimentary knowledge of Christianity. He was given the responsibility of teaching ten of Post's adult slaves (probably domestics) and their children. He also gave his students talks on religion and on Sundays read prayers and scripture lessons of the Anglican church to them and taught them to sing psalms along Methodist lines.

Although the "schoolmaster" was quite industrious and possessed an unblemished character, his limitations were very obvious. Not only was he lacking in physical energy, but he also did not possess sufficient knowledge of the Christian faith nor the personality and ability to establish a proper rapport to enable him to communicate effectively with the slaves. He was therefore not considered by Post as a suitable or permanent substitute for a white missionary from overseas.

Post, however, was very particular about the kind of missionary whose services he wished to acquire. He made it very clear that he did not desire an Anglican clergyman, but rather a missionary from a nonconformist group. Such groups, he believed, practised a form of Christianity which was nearer than Anglicanism to the pristine faith explained and described in the New Testament.

Post had several misgivings about the Anglican Church. In his opinion Anglicans

> have rather too much outward show and formalities… and the manner of the distribution of the Lord's Supper, the dresses of the Clergie, theiyr saently power and high living, the bowing by the name of Christ… all seem… things quite unfounded on the holy word.[106]

Furthermore, he was not satisfied with the preaching of Anglican clergymen whom he had encountered. He believed that their message did not focus sufficiently on what he regarded as "the main point"[107] of the Christian gospel, namely, the doctrine of Christ, especially His death on the cross as an atonement for human sin and the new life and eternal life which He offered to those who placed their faith in His.

Post's agent in London, knowing his preference in terms of the type of missionary whose services he desired, decided in 1807 to approach the London Missionary Society, one of the new nonconformist organisations in England. The Society, prompted by several considerations, responded by acceding to Post's request and sending John Wray to Demerara.

The LMS was influenced partly by the prospect of extending its work to an entirely different hemisphere of the world. Since its founding in 1795, the Society had concentrated its attention on Africa and Asia and as yet did not have any missionary in the Caribbean or South America. It was Wray therefore who inaugurated missionary work by the Society in the Americas and partly for this reason the Demerara mission was regarded with great importance in London.

The LMS was also attracted to Demerara by the opportunity to share the Christian faith with African slaves whom it rightly recognised as "the much injured Negro race".[108] Since its formation it had done nothing to help these exploited Blacks, though its members, like many other English Christians, were beginning to experience growing pangs of conscience over the injustice of the transatlantic slave trade and Caribbean slavery. Understandably therefore, the Society attached much sentimental value to Wray's work in Demerara as its first mission to slaves.

Furthermore, the LMS was attracted to Demerara by the size and anticipated scope of this mission field. The united colony of Demerara - Essequibo had an estimated slave population of 75,000, of whom 50,000 lived in Demerara. This was a larger slave population than that of any other British West Indian territory except Jamaica (about 350,000 slaves) and Barbados (also about 75,000 slaves). Moreover, the LMS noted with concern that the slaves of Demerara, many of whom were said to possess "a disposition towards Religion",[109] were completely neglected by the two established churches there, the Anglican and Dutch Reformed denominations, which catered exclusively for Whites who constituted only about 10 per cent of the population of the colony. Some Whites believed that Blacks were outside the pale of spiritual salvation, while others feared that exposure of black slaves to Christianity would make them more discontented and rebellious. Partly for these reasons no attempt was made by the established churches to share the Christian faith with Blacks, making Christianity a minority religion, practised seriously almost exclusively by only a segment of the small white population.

In these circumstances only two groups of Blacks in the colony had been Christianised by 1808 when Wray arrived. One was the small group of slaves on Plantation Le Resouvenir who had been instructed by the "Black schoolmaster" whom Hermanus Post had employed in 1807. The second group, which was larger and had greater exposure to Christianity, consisted of a small number of freemen and slaves residing in Stabroek, who had migrated or been brought by their masters to Demerara from islands in the British West Indies, where they had been converted to the faith mainly as a result of the work of Methodist missionaries. This influx was particularly pronounced after Britain occupied Demerara – Essequibo in 1796. Among them were two devout and zealous freemen from Nevis, William Claxton and William Powell, who were deeply committed Methodists. Soon after their arrival in Demerara in 1801, Claxton and Powell began to organise and conduct religious meetings along Methodist lines in Stabroek for Blacks. These meetings continued, although they evoked suspicion from slaveholders as well as from the colonial government. The efforts of Claxton and Powell, the pioneers of Methodism in Guyana, to secure a white Methodist clergyman from overseas were initially defeated by the governor's expulsion of John Hawkshaw in 1805, but were finally successful in 1815.

Apart from these Blacks in Le Resouvenir and Stabroek, in 1808 Blacks in Demerara were mostly adherents of animism and ancestral worship, the two dominant types of West African faith. A few of them, mostly from the Senegambia and Hausaland areas in West Africa, were Muslims.

In these circumstances the LMS anticipated that it would provide an invaluable service by giving many Blacks in Demerara, especially slaves, the opportunity to hear the gospel of Christ for the first time. Though this was to be the main and immediate purpose of Wray's mission, the society hoped that he would also be able to attend to the spiritual welfare of the minority white residents. The latter were reported to be irreligious and were notorious for the dissolute lives which they led with the result that in Demerara "there was little esteem made of Divine Worship in general".[110]

This lack of religious devotion among Whites, the Society was informed, was due to several reasons. It was partly a result of the unsatisfactory character and conduct of the two clergymen in Demerara, Rev. Ryk, a minister of the Dutch Reformed Church, and Rev. Straghan, an Anglican who was chaplain of the resident garrison in the capital, Stabroek, whose behaviour was said to be a hindrance to Christianity gaining credibility. It was also facilitated by the inadequate provision of opportunities for worship in Demerara where, in addition to the marked paucity of ministers there, there was as yet no building specially constructed and reserved for public worship and only two services weekly. These services, one conducted by each of the two ministers, were held on Sunday exclusively for Whites in a small room in the Court House in Stabroek, the first in the morning and the second after noon. The congregation at these meetings was very small and consisted mostly of residents of Stabroek.

In short, in 1808 white residents in the rural districts of Demerara had little or no opportunity of attending religious meetings and of being instructed in the Christian faith because of the complete absence of churches and clergymen there and their distance from Stabroek. One planter on the East Coast of Demerara whom Wray met in February 1808 shortly after his arrival told him "that he had no opportunity of obtaining divine knowledge, for he had not heard a Gospel Sermon for 33 years".[111] This planter's wife, who had a deep interest in spiritual matters, felt particularly deprived. Wray commented about this situation in his journal thus:

> He [the planter] spoke of his wife as having received a pious education, and loving spiritual things, and frequently lamenting that she had

not had an opportunity of hearing the Gospel preached. What I can learn concerning her, she appears to be a woman who wishes to be devoted to God.[112]

☙

In short, in 1808 the church in Demerara was not sufficiently established to cater for the spiritual needs of even the minority white population. This situation prompted a small group of Whites on the East Coast to begin to meet in a home on Sundays to sing psalms and to read the Bible. The LMS hoped that though Wray's mission was intended mainly to attend to the black slaves, that services which he conducted would provide opportunities for spiritual assistance to both pious and irreligious Whites and that his life would commend the Christian faith better that that of the Anglican and Dutch Reformed clergymen.

Apart from the prospect of catering for the spiritual needs of Blacks, especially slaves, and Whites in Demerara, a minor inducement to the LMS to send a missionary there was the possibility of extending missionary work to the neglected Amerindians in the interior who, like the slaves, were still unevangelised. Even more attractive to the LMS, in terms of an extended mission field, however, was the hope that it could use its mission in Demerara eventually to evangelise residents of the colonies of Berbice and Suriname.

The decision of the LMS to send Wray as a missionary to Demerara was influenced partly by the growing British presence there, a territory once dominated by the Dutch. Since the British occupation of Demerara in 1796, many Englishmen had purchased land and settled there with the result that by 1807 it was estimated that about 90 per cent of the estates there had English proprietors. Furthermore, the LMS was informed that many of the estates had British managers and overseers and that a considerable proportion of the slaves, especially those brought from British possessions in the West Indies, could speak and understand English. It was anticipated therefore that Wray would not encounter any language barrier in his efforts to communicate the gospel to the slaves. This proved to be a miscalculation for, as Wray soon discovered, Dutch Creole was far more comprehensible to many slaves than English.

The invitation to inaugurate a mission in Demerara was also attractive to the Directors of the LMS because it was extended by someone possessing the status of Hermanus Post, a long-standing resident and a respectable planter. Post had resided in Demerara for 33 years and possessed one of the largest and most prosperous estates on the East Coast of Demerara. Furthermore, the LMS anticipated that the expenditure it would have to incur to establish a mission in Demerara would be minimal because Post had intimated his willingness not only to protect and promote the mission but also to give it financial support. The Society also anticipated that other planters might contribute financially to the mission once they were satisfied that the Christianisation of their slaves did not and would not make them more discontented and rebellious.

It was a combination of these considerations that made the LMS decide late in 1807 to send its first missionary to Guyana. Ultimately the invitation by Post to send a missionary was interpreted by the Society to be a sign of divine providence and sanction. As a result John Wray left London in December 1807 and arrived in February 1808 in Demerara, where he pioneered what later became known as the Congregational Church.

Wray was sent to Demerara to work principally among Africans-born and Creole slaves on Plantation Le Resouvenir and other estates on the East Coast of Demerara. Though it was sympathetic towards the exploited slaves, the LMS had no desire or intention to cause discontent among them. It realised that any unrest created among slaves by their Christianisation would make the Society and its Demerara mission incur the animosity of the planters whose goodwill and support were regarded as indispensable for the success of missionary work in the colony.

The LMS was not sure what response it should expect from planters in Demerara apart from its host, the devout, Hermanus Post. It hoped that other planters there would also encourage the introduction of religious instruction among their slaves, but anticipated that their response would be based on the impact of Wray's work on slaves. Thus a report on Demerara which helped to convince the Society's Directors to send Wray there stated in relation to the planters that

> It appears probable also that a disposition to enourage the introduction of Religious knowledge among their negroes… will increase rapidly as soon as they perceive it does not tend to produce any political change among them but leads to due subordination and peaceableness of conduct. It is

even highly probable that a prudent and diligent Missionary would find a comfortable and ready support without requiring any aid from the Society.[113]

☙

These considerations were reflected in the instructions which the LMS gave to Wray in December 1807 at the time of his departure from London to Demerara. These instructions obviously were influenced largely by a desire to avoid giving offence to slaveholders in Demerara and, if possible, to win their confidence and support. Wray was told not to try change the slave system, but rather to seek to improve the morals and behaviour of the slaves and to lead them into spiritual, not physical, freedom. Furthermore, he was instructed both to encourage the slaves to be faithful and obedient to their masters and to seek to promote peace and good order in the colony.

Wray was told

☙

You are going to preach the Gospel to poor Africans in a state of slavery to man. They have been torn from their native country and reduced to a low and degraded situation. As such, they will be the objects of your commiseration. But it is not to relieve them from their servile condition that you visit them – that is out of your power. Nor would it be proper, but extremely wrong to insinuate anything which might render them discontented with a state of servitude or lead them to any measures injurious to their Masters. This would be to defeat the object of your mission and excite such opposition as might eventually prevent many other missions. These poor creatures are slaves in a much worse sense – they are the slaves of ignorance, of sin, and of satan; it is to rescue them from this miserable condition by the gospel of Christ that you are now going.[114]

☙

Identical instructions were given to the other missionaries such as John Davies who were sent later to assist Wray in Demerara and to extend and establish the fledgling Congregational Church there.

For Further Reading

Rain, Thomas	**The Life and Labours of John Wray, Pioneer Missionary in British Guiana. Compiled from his own MSS and Diaries** (London: John Snow & Co. 1892).
Lovett, Richard	**The History of the London Missionary Society**, 1795 – 1895. 2 Vols. (London, 1899).

CHAPTER 29

CHRISTIANITY AND SLAVERY: REACTIONS TO THE WORK OF THE LONDON MISSIONARY SOCIETY IN DEMERARA, 1808 – 1813

1808 was a very significant year in the history of Christianity in Demerara. It witnessed the beginning of the first serious effort to propagate the faith among the slave population there. This work was undertaken by Rev. John Wray, who was sent there by the London Missionary Society in response to a request from Hermanus Post, the owner of Plantation Le Resouvenir, a large cotton estate on the East Coast of Demerara for a missionary to work among his slaves.

From the beginning of Wray's ministry at Le Resouvenir in February 1808, his work assumed a basic pattern. He maintained a day school where religious and secular education was provided for black as well as white children. His main services were on Sundays, but he also held meetings most evenings especially to instruct and catechize adult slaves and to teach them to read and pray. Although his work was primarily among slaves, a small number of Whites and free Blacks attended the services. The meetings were held in one of the buildings on the plantation until September 1808 when a chapel, named Bethel Chapel, with a seating capacity of 600 and built there mainly at Post's expense, was opened. In 1808 also Wray began to preach regularly on another plantation further up the East Coast.

The work of the LMS was also extended by the arrival in January 1809 of a second missionary, John Davies who, like Wray, came out from England at Post's request and expense. Davies began by assuming responsibility for a secular school in Stabroek, the capital, for white and free coloured children. However, he soon used the school as a centre for preaching the Gospel, at first to Whites and free Coloureds, but eventually also to an ever-increasing number of slaves, mostly from suburban plantations and from across the Demerara river. The work in Stabroek assumed such great proportions that Providence Chapel, which Davies built there in 1812, was soon unable to accommodate the whole congregation, although it had a seating capacity of

1000.

Both Davies and Wray received invaluable support from their wives, who worked effectively among the women and children. The Demerara mission also benefited from the services of Adam and Purkis, two other missionaries who spent a few months there in 1809 before proceeding respectively to Trinidad and Tobago. It also received assistance from Richard Elliot, another LMS missionary, who paid a short visit from Tobago in 1812 and returned later to take charge of the station at Le Resouvenir which Wray left permanently in 1813 to work on slaves on the Crown estates in Berbice.

OBSTACLES

The growth of the mission took place in spite of several difficulties and obstacles such as the slaves' lack of knowledge of Christianity and the inability of most of them to read. There were also serious problems of communication resulting from the inability of many slaves, especially Dutch Creole speakers and recent arrivals from Africa, to understand preaching in English and the missionaries' lack of knowledge of Dutch Creole. To overcome these problems, Wray and Davies decided to concentrate on catechising the slaves and on training those who understood both English and Dutch Creole to teach others. Their work was also hindered by the limited amount of time available to instruct the slaves even on Sundays, legally a free day for slaves. Many slaves, if not required to work on the plantation or to remain there to collect their weekly allowance of food, preferred to spend Sunday fishing, cultivating their plots of land or taking their produce and stock to the market in Stabroek or Mahaica.

RESPONSE OF THE PLANTERS

The greatest obstacle faced by the missionaries, however, was the opposition which they encountered from the vast majority of planters, whose understanding of the history of slavery in the British West Indies made them view Methodists and other nonconformists with great mistrust and suspicion. The planters' main fear was that instruction in the Christian faith would result in slave rebellions. Many of them wrongly believed that the missionaries would deliberately teach doctrines which would undermine the slave's duty to his master. In fact, Wray and Davies stressed faithfulness, obedience and submission to the extent of declaring that it was wrong for a slave to run away from or to rebel against a cruel master. Nevertheless, some planters felt that a struggle for freedom was inevitable because the doctrines of Christian brotherhood and the equality of man in the sight of God seemed incompatible with slavery. Their sentiments were echoed publicly in 1808 by a correspondent in the local **Gazette** who stated

> It is dangerous to make slaves Christians, without giving them their liberty. He that chooses to make slaves Christians let them give them their liberty. What will be the consequence when to that class of men is given the title of "beloved brethren" as is actually done? Will not the Negro conceive that by baptism, being made a Christian, he is as credible as his Christian white brethren? [115]

Most planters, however, believed that the two most likely sources of slave revolts would be the evening meetings conducted by the missionaries and their efforts to teach slaves to read. They feared that slaves who learnt to read would be more reflective, subject to the influence of anti-slavery literature, and likely to interpret the Bible in a way detrimental to the perpetuation of slavery. The aversion of the planters to having slaves taught to read was so strong and widespread that for at least one year Wray restricted membership of his reading classes to the slaves of his patron, Post, whose initial repugnance he had managed to overcome.

The planters, who had long been encountering difficulty in restricting the movement of slaves, were also deeply fearful of evening meetings which provided slaves with a good reason or excuse for leaving the plantations in large numbers without proper supervision. Past experience had shown that this gave slaves a splendid opportunity to plan and stage revolts.

The fear of slave revolts was acute and understandable. The planters' long –standing belief in the basic rebelliousness of slaves, reinforced by a series of revolts and conspiracies since 1795, was strengthened further by the discovery in December 1807 and May 1808 of plans for rebellion among slaves on several plantations near Le Resouvenir. Most planters found the prospect of a general slave uprising alarming, especially in view of the fact that the colony's military forces were deficient and slaves outnumbered Whites by about twenty-five to one.

Apart from the fear of slave uprisings, other considerations prompted the opposition of planters to the missionaries' work among the slaves. Some planters believed that the missionaries were agents or supporters of the anti-slavery party in Britain and that emancipation of the slaves was their secret and ultimate objective. Others at least believed that the missionaries sent reports to London denouncing slavery and giving the colony a bad name. The moral content and effects of the teaching given to the slaves were also a source of friction. Many Whites were annoyed by the missionaries' severe denunciation of drunkenness, concubinage and dancing, and their assertion that all participants in these practices would be condemned to hell, a subject which they believed was given too much emphasis. They seem to have been particularly disappointed with the change which the preaching of the missionaries effected in the morals and sexual behaviour of free and slave women with whom they had hitherto enjoyed liberal sexual favours.

Some planters also objected to missionary work among the slaves because they feared that it would adversely affect the efficiency and supply of labour on the plantations. A small number of them contended that Christianity would make slaves indolent. Although this did not generally happen, there is evidence to suggest that house slaves sometimes neglected their responsibilities in order to attend evening services. The late return of slaves from these services was a grievance of some planters who complained that it made them somewhat unfit for work on the following day. A more common complaint, however, was the loss of labour on Sundays. Many planters became enraged and jealous when some of their slaves, in response to the missionaries' call for the Sabbath to be kept holy, began to attend services regularly on Sunday instead of continuing to work on the plantations.

Some of the planters who opposed the work of the LMS were sceptical of the Christian religion. Others, however, were professing Christians, some of whom felt that slaves were beyond the pale of spiritual salvation. Among the most bitter critics of Wray and Davies were planters who were members of the Anglican Church. They regarded the missionaries as "inveterate enemies of the established church"[116] who were bent on opposing and vilifying it.

Planters who were ill-disposed towards the missionaries showed their displeasure in a variety of ways. They prohibited their slaves from attending services or hindered and discouraged them by the use of sanctions and other expedients. Whippings, additional work, the withdrawal of food allowances, and confinement in the stocks were used both as penalties and deterrents. Although these measures did not succeed in deterring some slaves from attending services or from becoming serious Christians, others demonstrated remarkable patience, determination and courage as they sought religious instruction and so became the special object of their master's resentment. Some planters, however, used less drastic methods in opposing the work of the missionaries. They placed practical obstacles in the way of the slaves by deliberately requiring them to work or collect their food allowances when services were being conducted. They also ridiculed the slaves who attended services, discouraged them from catechising and instructing others, and refuted the teachings of the missionaries.

The planters also aimed their animosity directly against the missionaries and their white supporters. After an unsuccessful attempt to persuade the governor to expel Wray from the colony, they used criticism as their major weapon. They accused the missionaries of introducing discontent and disorder among the slaves and dubbed planters who gave them access to their slaves fools or lunatics. They charged Post in particular with misguided zeal which might result in Demerara becoming a second Saint-Domingue.

As in the West Indies, the planters also sought to discredit the missionaries by questioning their background, education, training and vocation for the ministry. They denounced them as ignorant hot-headed fanatics, idle members of the British lower class who had come out to Demerara mainly to secure an easy means of livelihood. At times their opposition became more positive and practical. In 1809 angry Whites withdrew their children from Davies' school in Stabroek when he introduced religious instruction into the curriculum. Later they stoned the building as a protest against his efforts to transform it into a place of worship. Generally, however, the opposition by planters in Demerara to the work of the LMS stopped short of violence. The security of the person and property of the missionaries was seldom threatened.

The opposition which the LMS missionaries encountered was tempered from the outset by the firm support which they received from a small number of planters and, above all, managers and attorneys of absentee proprietors. At first this group consisted mainly of friends of Post and individuals who had had personal experience in the British West Indies or Suriname of the "good effects" of the missionary work on slaves. In particular, they were convinced that religious instruction would diminish the necessity of severe punishment and compulsion to work by making the slaves more industrious and obedient.

The band of supporters grew slowly as some planters abandoned their original opposition to the religious instruction of slaves. This volte-face at first was due to two factors. Firstly, some planters, often out of curiosity, decided to attend some of the LMS services and became acquainted with the teaching, character and objectives of the missionaries whose work they discovered did not undermine the slaves' duty to their masters, but rather tended to make them better servants. Secondly, several planters were influenced by the satisfactory changes which they witnessed in the lives of slaves who were receiving religious instruction. Furthermore, from 1812 a third factor became operative. The willingness and ability of the missionaries to intervene to restore order and submission among rebellious slaves on the plantations dispelled the prejudices of many planters.

The planters who supported the LMS work had reservations. Some of them were not prepared to allow their slaves to attend meetings on weeknights. Most of them were also unwilling to allow the missionaries to teach their slaves to read or to preach on their plantation. Very few of them gave any regular substantial support to the mission. All of them desired only missionaries who would not seek to interfere with the political state of the slaves.

Response of the Slaves

The missionaries, grateful for the support of these planters, were encouraged especially by the response of the slaves in terms of numbers, attentiveness and seriousness. The congregation at Le Resouvenir grew from about 50 in February 1808, to about 600 in 1813. Apart from a small number of Whites and Coloureds, the rest were slaves who came mostly from plantations within a three- mile radius of Le Resouvenir. A few slaves, however, came from considerable distances, notably from Mahaica, thirteen miles away. In Stabroek the average attendance increased from about 60 in June 1809 to more than 1000 in 1813. At least half of these came from plantations, several miles away on the West Coast and West Bank of Demerara.

The LMS continued to be the church of the Blacks, even though the Anglican Church began in 1810 to hold special services for slaves and free Coloureds. Slaves played an important role in promoting the work of the LMS They encouraged others to attend services, instructed and catechised absentees and those who had difficulty understanding the missionaries, and supported the work financially. Out of their meagre earnings from the sale of agricultural produce and poultry, they contributed more than £60 towards the construction of Providence Chapel in Stabroek.

The eagerness of some slaves to receive religious instruction provided masters with an additional means of social control. Permission to attend services was held out to such slaves as an inducement to industry and good behaviour, and withdrawal of the privilege was used as an effective sanction. For example, in May 1812 when a dispute arose between the manager and slaves of Plantation Success over the question of food allowances, instead of inflicting corporal punishment, he prohibited them from going to the chapel. The slaves soon submitted and the prohibition was withdrawn. "Thus", the manager said, "by making Religion a reward of good conduct, beneficial effects may be expected, and more severe punishment avoided."[117]

On the other hand, some slaves used their relationship with missionaries, whom they regarded as their friends, counsellors and protectors, to promote their interests. Sometimes they complained to them about the ill-treatment and injustices which they suffered and solicited and secured their advice and other assistance. In 1812, for instance, Wray not only advised some of the slaves of Le Resouvenir to complain to the Fiscal about the cruelty of the new manager of the estate, but also gave evidence against him.

Christian instruction seems to have had a profound effect on the morals, values and behaviour of many of the slaves who attended. According to missionary reports, confirmed by some planters and Free Coloureds, there was a marked decline in the incidence of drunkenness, theft, fighting, quarrelling, and swearing among slaves who attended services regularly. Many of these slaves are also said to have become more industrious and less prone to feign illness, to run away or to rebel. They also began to abstain from dancing, drumming, and other forms of traditional slave entertainment and culture, and to seek to conform to the Biblical requirements in relation to marriage. Thus is March 1809, Wray reported that

> The manager [of Plantation Success]...says he is astonished at the wonderful change which has taken place among them [the estate's slaves]. They formerly were of a very rebellious disposition, and not at all backward to insurrections, and generally spent three or four nights in a week in drumming, dancing, intoxication, and other wicked employments so that they disturbed the whole neighbourhood, indeed they say themselves they

were notoriously wicked and used to spend their nights in such vain pursuits that they destroyed their constitution and made themselves unable to do their Master's work. But now their leisure time is spent in prayer and praise and in receiving, and communicating religious instruction and instead of making them discontent and indolent in their work as some ignorant persons suppose it has quite the contrary effect.[118]

☙

This moral and spiritual reformation, however, was not welcomed by all planters. To some of them it represented an unnecessary and undesirable distortion of the slave's personality and to others an unwholesome preoccupation with religion. It prompted at least two masters to withdraw the permission they had given their slaves to attend services at Le Resouvenir. One of them complained that Wray, "had spoiled his slave by making him leave off swearing",[119] while the other was annoyed and disturbed because "they [his slaves] think more about it [the Gospel] than anything else".[120]

The converse, however, was also sometimes true. A few planters lost some of their enthusiasm for the work of the LMS because they failed to see any substantial change in the character and conduct of their slaves. This provided welcome ammunition for critics of the LMS work among the slaves. Thus, the fact that a slave was found drunk the day after he attended one of Davies' meetings was regarded "as an instance of the immoral effect of the Preaching Christianity to Negroes, or at least of its inutility".[121]

The eager response of some slaves to the LMS missionaries could not conceal the fact that the vast majority of slaves, even on Plantation Le Resouvenir, did not attend their services. Wray estimated that by March 1809, just over a year after the commencement of his ministry in Demerara, about 1000 slaves had attended Bethel Chapel on at least one occasion, but this figure represented only a small part of the slaves who lived on the 25 plantations within a three-mile radius of the Le Resouvenir. Slaves who refused to attend the LMS services were influenced partly by their attachment to their own African religion, the lack of interest shown by many local Whites in the Christian faith, and their unwillingness to renounce obeah and other African customs and beliefs which the missionaries denounced strongly. Some of them were also affected by an erroneous belief that the missionaries were influenced by mercenary motives and had come to Demerara to get rich from subscriptions, offerings, and gifts solicited from slaves. They showed their opposition to the missionaries not only by ignoring or boycotting their meetings, but also by ridiculing slaves who attended them and informing hostile masters of slaves who went there without their knowledge.

Response of the Officials

Although the missionaries were disturbed by the attitude and activities of these slaves, their main concern was the strong opposition which they encountered from most members of the plantocracy and the Court of Policy. The Court, which consisted of the Governor, the Commander of Essequibo, and the Fiscal, the Colony's three principal officers, and three elected representatives of the planters, was normally a strong upholder of planter interests. It was subject to the commanding influence of the Governor, the sovereign's representative. Some of its members, notably Joseph Beete, were opposed to the LMS work among the slaves not only because they were planters, but also because they were committed Anglicans who hated dissenters. According to Wray, the greatest opponents in the colony of his work were a member of the Court, who was a planter, and F.P. Van Berckel who, until 1811, was the Fiscal or supreme law officer.

There was a strong disposition in the Court to obstruct and, if possible, suppress the LMS work in its infancy. Fortunately for the missionaries, however, they were protected during this critical early period by two acting governors, Lieutenant-Colonels Robert Nicholson and Andrew Ross, military officers who had no vested interests in the colony nor instructions from the metropolitan government about the policy to be adopted towards the LMS It was Nicholson, who administered the colony from September 1807 to June 1808, who gave Wray permission to settle and preach there. This was a surprise and great disappointment to many planters who had requested and expected him to expel Wray from the colony as Governor Beaujon had done to the Methodist clergyman, John Hawkshaw, a few years before.[122] Nicholson, however, believed that the instruction of slaves would have good effects and the planters' opposition to it would eventually subside. Although he intended to be very careful before he permitted anyone to preach to slaves, he was quickly satisfied when he discovered that Wray was not only a trained and ordained minister, but also a student of David Bogue of Cosport in England with whom he was personally acquainted.

Although Nicholson maintained a very friendly disposition towards

Wray and a keen interest in the work at Le Resouvenir, it seems that he did not wish to antagonise the plantocracy unduly or to lose all the esteem they had for him. So in April 1808, when Post applied for permission for Wray to begin to preach occasionally to the black population in Stabroek with the ultimate view of building a church and establishing a second mission station there, Nicholson felt it was prudent to bring the request to the Court of Policy. The Court, fearful of evening meetings and slave revolts, rejected the application.

A few weeks later Nicholson handed over government to Andrew Ross, a less cautious administrator. Ross's high esteem for the work of the Moravian missionaries among slaves in St. Croix where he had served made him decide to give strong support to the LMS. He promised Wray protection and encouraged him to seek to overcome the opposition of the planters by securing written testimonials from Whites who were in favour of his work. He also encouraged planters to allow their slaves to receive Christian instruction. Moreover, in December 1808 he supported Wray when he had his first serious public controversy with the planters as a result of a misrepresentation of a sermon which he delivered at the funeral of a white doctor. Finally, he enabled Davies to continue missionary work in Stabroek by giving him permission to conduct services in his home for his relatives and friends, thus rescinding a prohibition which the Fiscal had imposed on the missionary. This permit gave the LMS work in Stabroek valuable protection from the white opponents who had begun to resort to violence in an attempt to destroy this incipient missionary station.

The LMS work continued to enjoy the protection and support of the governors of Demerara- Essequibo until May 1809, when Henry Bentinck assumed office. Unlike his three immediate predecessors, Robert Nicholson, Andrew Ross and Samuel Dalrymple, military officers, Bentinck was a civilian who had vested interest in the colony. He was the owner of a plantation near Le Ressouvenir and had refused to allow his slaves to receive religious instruction. Before he came to Demerara, the LMS Directors in London had tried in vain to influence him in favour of their mission in the colony. He was sympathetic towards the Church of England, but strongly opposed in principle to dissenters. His principal objection to the LMS work in Demerara was its evening meetings which he feared would result in slave rebellions. He also felt that the teaching of Wray and Davies was irrelevant, abstruse and detrimental to the slaves. Thus he told Davies that "the Negroes ought not to be instructed respecting Eternity for it is too difficult for them to understand and thinking of it makes them mad". [123]

Response of the British Government

Not surprisingly, Bentinck's administration witnessed the first serious conflicts between the LMS and the local government. Although the Colonial Office in London had indicated to him that he should adopt a policy of religious toleration, Bentinck consistently opposed the LMS work. In 1810 he successfully opposed Wray's efforts to get permission to preach on Plantation Kitty, a large suburban estate near Stabroek, on the ground that it was too near to the newly – built Anglican Church, St. George's. He also refused to grant the LMS land to build a chapel at Mahaica, giving no answer to a petition of about fifty inhabitants, although it was before him for nearly eighteen months. Finally, he raised serious objections to the missionaries' evening services. To placate him Wray tried to hold the meetings earlier, but the late return of the slaves from the plantations frustrated his efforts.

Eventually, on 25th May 1811, Bentinck and the Court of Policy issued a Proclamation prohibiting slaves to assemble for religious meetings before sunrise and after sunset. Their action, allegedly taken in response to representations by some planters on the East Coast of Demerara, may have been inspired by the introduction of similar legislation in Jamaica.

The proclamation was a great blow especially to Wray, for the evenings were the most convenient time for instructing the slaves, especially field labourers. Its introduction meant that it was no longer possible to have meetings during the week, for slaves worked then at least from sunrise to sunset. Wray tried in vain to persuade the governor to recall the proclamation. Undaunted, he sailed to London to urge the LMS Directors to seek the help of the metropolitan government. There he became part of a LMS delegation which in October 1811 made successful representations to Lord Liverpool, the Colonial Secretary. Liverpool decided to order Bentinck to recall the proclamation and to issue a new one permitting slaves to assemble for worship and religious instruction on Sundays between 5:00am and 9:00pm and or week–days between 7:00pm and 9:00pm.

Instead of carrying out this order, Bentinck decided to submit it to the Court of Policy for discussion. Pending these deliberations, he wrote a lengthy letter to Lord Liverpool in January 1812 explaining the reasons for his proclamation and justifying his action. This act of disobedience annoyed Liverpool so much that he decided immediately to summon Bentinck to London to answer queries about his administration. Major–General Hugh

Lyle Carmichael was sent out to replace him, with specific instructions to execute the order with which Bentinck had failed to comply.

On 7th April 1812, the day after he assumed office, Carmichael rescinded Bentinck's proclamation and issued the new one, in the preamble of which he stated that he had received instructions from the Prince Regent "to give every aid to missionaries in the instruction of religion".[124] This was a great triumph for the missionary cause. It made it possible for Wray and Davies to resume evening meetings. It also served to undermine the opposition of some planters to the work of the LMS for they now became aware that the metropolitan authorities were supporting the missionaries and that the missionaries were not insignificant, as they had assumed, but possessed influence in London.

During Carmichael's tenure of office, which lasted from April 1812 to May 1813, the LMS work in Demerara received an unprecedented degree of sympathy and support from the local government. He assisted the missionaries not only because he knew this was the desire of the Secretary of State whom he was eager to please, but also because the findings of an inquiry which he made about the character, principles and teaching of Wray and Davies convinced him that they were worthy of his confidence and support. Carmichael was also convinced that religious instruction would be of great benefit to the slaves in this life as well as in the hereafter, and was encouraged when he discovered that a growing number of planters were beginning to share this view.

Expansion

Carmichael's support encouraged Davies to press ahead with plans to build a chapel in Stabroek and extend his labours to the West Bank and West Coast of Demerara. The governor accepted Davies' invitation to be the patron of the building fund and gave a generous donation to the cost of a chapel, which was opened early in 1813. He facilitated Davies' work by lending him the government boat to visit plantations up and across the Demerara River and by giving him letters of introduction to the planters. He also granted the LMS its long-standing request for a piece of Crown land at Mahaica, invited Davies to instruct the Crown slaves, and accepted his offer to instruct the children of the soldiers of the garrison. His gratitude for Davies' offer made Carmichael even more firmly committed to the missionary cause. Wray and Davies had ready access to him and they had a regular exchange of friendly correspondence. The governor even consulted them on policy to be pursued in relation to the instruction of slaves.

Carmichael introduced a policy of using the missionaries' known and growing influence with the slaves to restore peace and order on plantations where slaves were discontented and insubordinate. In 1812 Davies accepted the governor's invitation to visit Plantations Vive La Force and De Hague, respectively located on the West Bank and West Coast of Demerara, where he encouraged refractory slaves to be patient and law-abiding and succeeded in restoring them to order and submission. He was glad for the opportunity to demonstrate that the missionaries were promoting order and not rebellion as feared. His success at Vive La Force in August 1812 proved to be a major turning point in the progress of the LMS Demerara mission. Within three months he was allowed to preach on five other plantations on the West Bank either by invitation or at his request.

Carmichael's favourable policy towards the LMS was continued, at least initially, by his successor, Brigadier –General John Murray, who took over the government when Carmichael died suddenly in May 1813. Murray believed that Christian religious instruction would make the slaves become more obedient servants. At his recommendation, Davies successfully petitioned the Court of Policy for financial assistance. Thus in April 1813 he received 100 pounds to help meet the expenses incurred in building Providence Chapel and three months later he was granted 2200 guilders for his personal support during the following years.

The ready grant of these allowances was clear evidence of the considerable change which had taken place in the attitude towards the LMS of the Court of Policy and many planters since 1808. In fact, the fear of opposition had discouraged Davies in the past from seeking financial support from the court. Since 1811, however, opposition in the Court had declined. This was due partly to a change in its composition, especially the departure of Van Berckel, who had been relieved of his post of Fiscal after a dispute with Governor Bentinck. Above all, it was due to the Court's realisation that the Colonial Office was supporting the missionary cause and its gratitude to Davies for bringing order among refractory slaves on the West Coast and West Bank of Demerara.

Prospects

Thus in 1813 the prospects facing the LMS mission in Demerara were far brighter than at any time since its inauguration in 1808. The mission was now firmly established and was expanding. A small but growing number of planters were beginning to invite the missionaries to instruct their slaves on their own plantations. Much of the original prejudice which planters had against the mission had subsided. The Directors in London regarded Demerara as the Society's most fruitful field in the Caribbean, certainly much more encouraging than Tobago, where they were considering curtailing their operations.

The survival and growth of the work in Demerara were due largely to the determination, industry and sagacity of the missionaries and the invaluable support and protection which they received from all the governors, except Bentinck, and from the British metropolitan government after 1811. Much of the opposition which the missionaries encountered stemmed from the fact that they were a nonconformist body which, to make matters worse, many planters in Demerara associated with the feared and detested Methodists. It was this realisation which prompted Governor Carmichael to mention in a letter to the Burgher Captains in September 1812, that "these Missionaries are not of that Sect usually called Methodists; they are persons properly qualified and employed by the Missionary Society for the Propagation of Religion"[125] The Established Church met with little or no opposition when it began in 1810 to work among slaves.

Though the situation was encouraging in 1813, the LMS was still encountering some mistrust and opposition. Very few slaveholders were prepared to allow their slaves to learn to read. Furthermore, there were still a few Whites who were advocating the expulsion of the missionaries from the colony, although this then seemed a very remote possibility, no longer feared by the missionaries. Such opponents, when questioned by the missionaries, sometimes admitted that they could not point out any definitely adverse effect that instruction in Christianity had on the slaves or on the interests of the planters. They, however, expressed the view that some disastrous consequence would occur sometime in the future, especially because of the evening meetings. These fears assumed reality ten years later, in 1823, when a massive slave uprising, centred on Bethel Chapel, broke out on East Coast of Demerara.

For Further Reading

Rain, Thomas	**The Life and Labours of John Wray, Pioneer Missionary in British Guiana. Compiled from his own MSS and Diaries** (London: John Snow & Co. 1892).
Lovett, Richard	**The History of the London Missionary Society, 1795 – 1895**. 2 Vols. (London, 1899).

Chapter 30

The Origins of The Presbyterian Church in Guyana

The Presbyterian Church in Guyana dates its formal organised beginnings back to September 1818 when its first church building, St. Andrew's, located on the Avenue of the Republic in Georgetown opposite the Parliament Buildings, was opened for public worship. St. Andrew's proved to be the first of many Presbyterian churches which were established in all three counties of Guyana.

The beginning of the Presbyterian Church in 1818 occurred at a significant period in the religious history of Guyana. That period was distinguished by a significant expansion of the Christian faith in the Demerara region of the United Colony of Demerara- Essequibo. There were at least three striking aspects of this extension of Christianity.

The first aspect was the establishment of an increasing number of church buildings. Although Demerara had existed as a Dutch colony since 1746, as late as 1808, 62 years later, there was no building in the colony constructed specifically for public worship. The only building in Demerara used regularly then for that purpose was the Court House in the capital, Stabroek, where a room was utilised on Sundays by the Anglican and Dutch reformed Churches who held separate services for their adherents. Some private religious meetings were also held in homes in Stabroek by two free Black Methodist laymen.

The first church building to be erected in Demerara was Bethel Chapel at Le Resouvenir on the East Coast by the London Missionary Society in 1808. In 1810 the Anglican Church built St. George's Chapel, the earliest precursor of what today is St. George's Cathedral, in Stabroek. Three years later, in 1813, the LMS erected its second church building in the Charlestown district of Georgetown. The establishment of St. Andrew's in 1818 therefore meant that there were then four church buildings in Demerara, mostly in Georgetown.

The second facet of the extension of Christianity in Demerara in the early nineteenth century was in terms of the number of resident ministers of religion. In 1800 there were only two resident clergymen in Demerara: Rev. Straghan, the Anglican chaplain of the resident British garrison who in 1810 became the first minister of St. George's, and Rev. Ryk, a Dutchman who was minister of the Dutch Reformed Church which during the period of Dutch rule was the official established Christian church in Guyana. In 1808 and 1809 they were joined by John Wray and John Davies, the first two clergymen sent by the LMS In 1815 the incipient Methodist church in Demerara secured its first minister, Rev. Thomas Talboys, who preached in Georgetown and Mahaica, although the Methodist congregation there as yet did not have a building specially constructed for worship. Two years later, in 1817, Rev. John Smith arrived from London to assume responsibility for Bethel Chapel as an intended permanent replacement for John Wray who had moved to Berbice in 1813. In September 1818 this growing number of resident Christian ministers in Demerara was further increased with the arrival of Rev. Archibald Browne, the first minister of St. Andrew's.

The growing influence of Christianity was also evident in a third significant development, namely, the spread of the Christian faith to the non-white population of Demerara-Essequibo which consisted mainly of black slaves. From the introduction of Christianity in Guyana in the early seventeenth century, the faith had been deliberately restricted to the small minority of white residents in Essequibo, Berbice and, later, Demerara. The white local government and planters consistently opposed the spread of Christianity to the black slaves for fear that it would make them more discontented and rebellious. In 1794, for example, an application by the Methodist Missionary Society in London for permission to send missionaries to Demerara to work among the slaves was rejected by the States General in Holland because of the strong objections raised by the Dutch colonial authorities in Demerara - Essequibo.

This policy of opposing the Christianisation of slaves continued when Demerara – Essequibo and Berbice passed from Dutch to British rule in April 1796. It was only in 1808 that the Christian church in Guyana began to allow the Christianisation of slaves. This new development was initiated by the LMS through the mission which it established on Plantation Le Resouvenir at the invitation of the owner, Hermanus Post.[126]

This example eventually stimulated the older churches to change their policy of debarring Blacks from their services. The Anglican Church, for example, abandoned this policy after the erection of its first church building, St. George's Chapel, in 1810. Furthermore, from its official organised beginning in Guyana in 1815, the Methodist Church also catered for Blacks.

This was also the policy of the Presbyterian Church from its official establishment in 1818. Shortly after the membership of St. Andrew's began to include Blacks, especially slaves. Scores of slaves were baptised within the first two years of the church's existence, as the baptismal records, which are still available locally, indicate. In short, St. Andrew's contributed significantly to the spread of Christianity to the non-white section of the population of Georgetown, though initially its principal focus was the white residents.

The opening of St. Andrews's Kirk in 1818 was largely a result of a little-known fact, namely, that a significant proportion of the British residents of Demerara and, to a lesser extent, Essequibo in the 18h century and the early 19th century consisted of Scots. The influx of substantial numbers of Scots had begun in the 1740s when the Dutch authorities in Essequibo and Demerara opened these two Dutch colonies to settlement by Europeans of all nationalities. Their numbers increased in particular after April 1796 when Britain took possession of Demerara - Essequibo and Berbice. As the number of Scottish residents grew, they began to express a desire for the establishment in Demerara – Essequibo of the Presbyterian faith which they had followed in their homeland, Scotland. The fulfilment of this desire, however, required the satisfaction of two crucial needs, namely, the acquisition of a church building and the provision of an appropriate clergyman, both of which financially were costly undertakings.

The acquisition of a church building occurred in somewhat fortuitous circumstances, where Dutch residents in Demerara proved unable to continue their efforts to erect a building for public worship by members of the Dutch Reformed Church. This project was begun in 1810 by the Dutch residents, who were jealous of the fact that Englishmen in Demerara, mostly newcomers, had succeeded in erecting a church building, St. George's Chapel, in the capital Stabroek, soon to be renamed Georgetown. As a correspondent remarked in the 26th June, 1810 issue of the **Essequibo and Demerara Gazette**

☙

> I am informed that their [the Anglicans'] good example had induced the members of the Dutch Church to remove the Opprobrium that so long

> hung over it, by subscribing to the erection of a decent and respectable place of worship for themselves.[127]

In August 1811 the foundation of this proposed Dutch Reformed Church building was laid on a spot of land donated by the government, which also contributed a grant of 15,000 guilders to help defray the expenses of the project. Efforts to secure by public subscription the remainder of the finances necessary to complete the project were not very productive. By the end of 1812 work on the building, which was only partly completed, ceased.

This unexpected development was due to three main factors. One of them was a lack of funds. The second was the sudden death in September 1812 of the Rev. Gabriel Ryk, the sole Dutch Reformed minister in the colony, who was the driving force behind the project. The final factor was the growing exodus from Demerara to the Netherlands of Dutchmen, who were becoming convinced that the colony, now occupied by the British, would never be restored to Dutch rule.

There was a suggestion that the government should purchase the unfinished building, complete the construction and convert it for use for public offices. In particular, it was suggested that the completed building should be used to house the Court of Policy, for the existing Court House was in a state of disrepair, No action, however, was taken in this direction. As a result, the building remained unfinished, unused and exposed to the weather, in spite of the warning of the Inspector General who reported: "as the building stands now, it will soon be rotten. The rain beats in at all parts."[128]

Eventually, in 1815, the Dutch proprietors of the unfinished building, made an offer to the Scottish inhabitants of Demerara of joint ownership of the property, provided that they shared in the expense of its completion. In response to this proposal, in September 1815, 33 Scottish residents held a meeting in a hotel in Georgetown at which several important resolutions were passed, including the following two:

> That it is highly desirable and would be conducive to good morals, to establish a Presbyterian Church in the Colony.

> That proper measures shall be immediately adopted for purchasing or erecting a suitable building for this purpose.[129]

Eventually the Scotsmen decided to seek to become the sole owners of the building by refunding the Dutch proprietors the expenditure which they had incurred in its construction and by completing the building by themselves. Within about four months they raised the substantial sum of 4,200 pounds sterling necessary for these two undertakings. Thus in February 1816 tenders were issued for finishing the "Building intended for a Dutch Church". On its completion the building became the exclusive possession of the Presbyterian Church and was named St. Andrew's. These developments angered Thomas Talboys, the first Methodist minister in Demerara, who claimed that at one stage he had been promised the unfinished building to erect a Methodist chapel.

In February 1816, before work to complete the building began, the Scottish residents of Demerara successfully petitioned the local government for a grant to enable them "to invite a clergyman of respectability to settle in these Colonies, provided with such a stipend as will be sufficient to maintain him in that station in Society which his public character would make it necessary from him to support."[130] The Court of Policy, the local legislature, agreed to grant 3,800 guilders each year towards the support of a minister for this Scot church.

Efforts were then made to secure from Scotland a minister who, residents in Demerara requested, should be a man of "complete education, intelligence, ability, strict moral habits, eloquence suited to the nature of his office, and at the same time a man of liberal and enlightened sentiments and gentlemanly address".[131] About eighteen months afterwards, Rev. Archibald Browne, a 31-year old Scotsman, was appointed to be the first minister of St. Andrew's Kirk, which was opened to public worship on September 27, 1818.

For Further Reading

Cruickshank, J.	**Pages from the History of the Scottish Kirk in Britrish Guiana** (Georgetown, 1930).
Lord, Wellesley	**A History of St. Andrew's Kirk 1818-1968** (Georgetown, 1968).

Chapter 31

100 Years of The Salvation Army in Guyana, 1895 – 1995

The last week of June 1995 was a special occasion for the Salvation Army, one of the better known and more highly respected, though numerically comparatively small, Christian groups in Guyana. During that week the Salvation Army held a four – day "Centenary Congress" celebrating the 100th anniversary of its official establishment in Guyana. Each evening there was a special feature at the National Cultural Centre in Georgetown to which the public was invited. Over one hundred delegates from overseas joined local members of the Army for the celebration. The most distinguished of them was the second highest officer in the international movement, Chief of Staff Earl Maxwell, an Australian resident in London, England, where the headquarters of the worldwide organisation is located.

The Salvation Army was founded in London in 1865 by an English couple, William and Catherine Booth. William Booth, born in 1829, was converted to Christ in a Methodist meeting in 1844 at the age of fifteen and later became a Methodist preacher. Eventually he left Methodism out of a conviction that it was too middle-class to reach the truly needy in society. For years thereafter he functioned as an independent itinerant evangelist with no denominational connection. Finally, he began to devote most of his attention to the poor of the east end of London where in 1865 he pioneered a movement known initially as " The Christian Mission". Thirteen years later in 1878, Booth , using colourful imagery, changed its name to Salvation Army. This term, he believed, graphically described the serious battle in which he was engaged with the forces of evil for the souls of men whose greatest need he stressed was spiritual salvation. His workers were called "soldiers", members of a "corps" based at a "citadel".

The Christian Mission/Salvation Army at first encountered bitter, often violent, opposition, especially from mobs who assaulted their workers and damaged their buildings. They, however, persevered and won many converts to Christ. The Salvation Army spread to all parts of the United Kingdom and then abroad, first to English – speaking countries, reaching the United States of America in 1880 and Australia in 1881, and later to nations speaking other languages.

Today the Salvation Army is a worldwide movement organised in five zones: Africa, the Americas and the Caribbean, Europe, South Asia (especially India, Pakistan and Sri Lanka) and the South Pacific and East Asia (including Australia, New Zealand, Papua New Guinea, Hong Kong, Japan and Korea). Everywhere it is known for its forthright evangelistic preaching and its practical concern for the material and social welfare of people, especially the underprivileged and the destitute.

As part of its spread abroad, the Salvation Army eventually reached the Caribbean, commencing with Jamaica in 1887 and then British Guiana in 1895. The beginnings of the organisation in Guyana are somewhat reminiscent of the origins of Methodism there in the first two decades of the century. Then, as was the case of the Salvation Army later, the official commencement of the church's work was preceded by unofficial activities by devout individuals who did not possess the requisite authority to initiate and develop an internationally recognised Methodist ministry.

The official work of the Salvation Army in Guyana started in April 1895 with the arrival in Georgetown from England of three officers, Adjutant and Mrs. Edward Wedgery and Lieutenant George Walker. This official beginning was a direct response to the efforts and appeals of three individuals. Two of them, namely, Samuel Marshall and Alexander Alexander, were resident in the colony, while the third Mr. Coburn, was a regular visitor.

Samuel Marshall, a shoemaker by vocation, was born in Barbados and was converted to Christ in a Methodist chapel in Grenada. Later he began to read Salvation Army literature and became a salvationist in spirit. In 1883 he moved from Grenada to British Guiana, where he continued to pursue his trade as a cobbler during the day. He used the evening, however, to preach and testify at street corners, where he won many converts to Christ and trained them along Salvation Army lines. Eventually Marshall wrote to the Army's headquarters in London requesting to be recognised as a "soldier" and petitioned its founder, William Booth, to send officers "to the only British possession on the South American continent".[132]

A similar petition was also received at the London headquarter from one Brother Coburn. Coburn was a English seaman who a member of the Salvation Army in England and worked on a vessel plying between Liverpool and Georgetown. He often brought out Salvation Army supplies, such as song books and badges, for use by "Marshall's Army ", as Marshall and his converts were called. Sometimes he joined Marshall in his meetings.

The third major antecedent to the official establishment of the Salvation Army in Guyana was the work of Alexander Alexander, a Scotsman who was employed as an overseer on a sugar estate in Demerara. Alexander was converted to Christ in a Salvation Army meeting in 1886 while on a visit to Scotland to recuperate from an injury. On his return to British Guiana later that year, he began to conduct open – air evangelistic meetings. As a result, several persons, mostly Blacks and East Indians, were converted to Christ. Eventually Alexander, like Marshall and Coburn, wrote the Army authorities in London requesting that an officer be sent to work in British Guiana.

It was in recognition of the work of Alexander, Marshall and Coburn and in response to their repeated appeals that a decision was finally taken in London in 1895 to send three officers to British Guiana to establish officially the work of the Salvation Army there. After an uneventful journey by sea, these officers arrived in Georgetown on 24 April 1895.

Initially the Army, with its military language and its unorthodox aggressive evangelistic preaching in the open air as well as indoors in venues such as the Hand of Justice Society Hall, the Rose of Sharon Hall and the Town Hall in Georgetown, encountered considerable opposition. This opposition was due partly to gross misunderstanding of the motive and mission of the movement by the government, other Christian denominations, numerous individuals, and even the police. As a consequence, the three officers from England were imprisoned for preaching the Gospel at street corners in Georgetown. The Salvation Army also had to contend with bricks, bottles, rotten eggs and flour which were all used by its opponents to impede its work.

Eventually, however, this opposition subsided and the Salvation Army became acceptable to other Christian bodies and the government, which sought its assistance in meeting social welfare needs and in solving other special problems. By then the Salvation Army had succeeded in winning many converts to Christ, most of who became "soldiers", as members of the movement were called. Within the first year of its establishment, the work in Georgetown had 40 local officers and over 500 members, serving in eight areas.

In addition to the initial opposition which it encountered after April 1895, a second major feature of the Salvation Army in the early phase of its work in British Guiana was that it was able to penetrate two ethnic groups, namely, East Indians and Chinese, who until then had been influenced by Christianity in only a limited way.

Credit for the Salvation Army's influence among East Indians belonged especially to the Scottish estate overseer, Alexander Alexander. Alexander returned to British Guiana from the United Kingdom in 1896 after a period of leave with a determination and special commitment to spread the Gospel among East Indians. He dressed like an Indian, adopted an Indian name, Ghurib Das (meaning "servant of the poor"), and went about preaching barefooted. He created quite a stir among East Indian estate workers. Moreover, when he got married in Georgetown at the Town Hall in 1901, to identify further with the East Indians, he insisted that his white bride wear a sari, while he appeared barefooted dressed in a dhoti.

Ghurib Das eventually was promoted to the rank of Major in the Salvation Army. Owing partly to his efforts, by 1920 there were eight centres among the East Indians. One of the best known Indians who became a member of the Salvation Army as a result of Major Alexander's ministry was Clement Moonsammy. Much later, in 1971, Moonsammy became divisional commander or leader of the Salvation Army in Guyana, the first of four Guyanese to have occupied that important office.

Alexander's influence among East Indians stemmed partly from the fact that he often championed their causes. On one notable occasion, for example, his relentless struggle eventually secured the release of three Indian men who had been sentenced wrongly to life imprisonment.

Appreciation for Alexander's work among East Indians was a accorded him at the time of his final departure from the colony in 1926 when he was admitted to the order of the Founder with a citation which read: "for 30 years he laboured with outstanding devotion and enterprise in seeking the safety and salvation of East Indians settled in British Guiana." His achievements occurred at a time when only the Canadian Presbyterian Church and the Lutherans had been particularly effective in the evangelisation of East Indians in the colony. Significantly, after his departure in 1926 the Salvation Army gradually lost its influence among this element of the multiracial Guianese population.

Similarly, at one stage the Salvation Army also had an impact on the colony's Chinese population. Its work among Chinese began with the conversion from time to time of a few individuals in the first decade in the twentieth century. Among was one Mrs. Chung, who was converted in

New Amsterdam and became a deeply committed member and worker of the Army in Georgetown. She became the first local Chinese officer in the Caribbean, serving as a manageress of a lunch room and bakery which the Salvation Army operated in Georgetown. Furthermore, in 1912 a Chinese merchant in New Amsterdam donated land to the Salvation Army for the erection of a new building there which was built with financial assistance from the foreign mission board.

It was not until 1917, however, that really fruitful evangelism was conducted by the Salvation Army among Chinese. It began with the conversion in Georgetown of a well-educated young Chinese who was born in Peking, but had come to British Guiana at an early age with his parents and could speak several languages. He and an older Chinese Salvationist, Sergeant Wong, were so successful in winning their countrymen to Christ that by August 1917 the first Chinese Salvation Army Corps was established. This was a separate corps, an indication of the distinctiveness and lack of integration of the Chinese in Guyanese society.

The work by the Salvation Army among Chinese was enhanced by the training as an officer of one of their number, Sergeant – Major (later Captain) Chin Kee Fat. It continued with a fair measure of success until the 1940s when it was weakened by outward migration, deaths and other factors. As a result, the Chinese corps ceased to function as a separate unit. Instead, Chinese joined the Georgetown Corps of the Army.

In addition to its early influence on Chinese and East Indians, a significant feature of the Salvation Army was that it was an evangelical body. The Salvation Army, in fact, was the fourth evangelical denomination to be established in British Guiana, following the Christian Brethren, a short-lived Baptist group in the1860s, and the Christian Mission founded in 1892. It immediately gave a significant impetus to the spread of Evangelical Christianity especially through its frequent indoor and outdoor meetings on Sundays as well as on other days to proclaim the Gospel of Jesus Christ.

Like other evangelical bodies, the principal doctrine of the Salvation Army was man's indispensable need for salvation from sin and its temporal and eternal consequences through repentance and personal faith in Christ. As the core of the Army's doctrinal statement says

༄

> We believe that the Lord Jesus Christ has by his suffering and death made atonement for the whole

world so that whoever will may be saved.

We believe that repentance towards God, faith in our Lord Jesus Christ and regeneration by the Holy Spirit is necessary to salvation.

We believe that continuance in a state of salvation depends upon continued obedient faith in Christ.[133]

☙

The Salvation Army is best known to many Guyanese for its service in the sphere of social welfare, especially its kind assistance to the poor, the unfortunate and the destitute. Although such philanthropy is a pronounced and important feature of its work, the Salvation Army emphasises that this service is secondary to its major objective, the evangelisation of the lost. This combination of spiritual ministry and practical care is reflected in its fundamental guiding principle of "Heart to God and Hand to Man", as Major Cleo Damon, a former head of the Salvation Army in Guyana, expressed it in 1987.

Thus from its inception in 1895 the work of the Salvation Army in Guyana was diverse, being designed to cater for a wide range of human needs, especially spiritual, moral, physical, material and social needs. The church developed a complex network of evangelistic, medical, social welfare, educational and other activities. As a recent Salvation Army publication put it, the church is committed to "preaching a round-sided Message of Soup, Soap and Salvation".[134]

Initially, the philanthropic services of the Salvation Army in British Guiana consisted primarily of the provision of food for the poor and accommodation for the homeless. For example, by the time the two pioneer Army officers, Adjutant and Mrs. Wedgery, left the colony in December 1897, the Army had a 'night shelter' for East Indians, accommodating 200 men. As the Army's social services expanded, the number of 'shelters' increased and a lunch room and a 'salvation bakery' were opened.

From its early days the Salvation Army was also actively involved in prison and probation work, rendering invaluable and deeply appreciated assistance to the authorities in these spheres. The pioneer in these developments seems to have been Mrs. Bax, the wife of Charles Bax, the leader of the Salvation

Army in British Guiana from 1898 to 1904. Mrs. Bax became famous for her effective intervention which resulted in the reduction of the sentences of several women for whom she pleaded in court.

The Army's ministry in this area was extended significantly from 1904 when the Inspector-General of Police, Colonel Lushington, granted the Army's three principal officers permission to visit local prisons at any time. A further development took place twelve years later in 1916 when the local divisional commander, Adjutant Charles Smith and Mrs. Smith were appointed prison chaplains. This enabled them to hold weekly services in the jails, as a result of which some prisoners were converted to Christ.

By then Salvation Army officers had begun to serve in another capacity, namely, that of probation officers, and were entrusted with the responsibility for distributing discharged prisoners' aid. The Army's responsibility was increased further in 1911 when one of its officers, Captain Bennett, was appointed inspector for the penal settlement for young offenders located in the Essequibo River. In short, within the first fifteen years of its operations in British Guiana, the Salvation Army was active in prison, probation and rehabilitation or after-care work.

In the 1940s the Army extended its ministry to young delinquents with the opening of the Belfield School for girls in March 1944 on the East Coast of Demerara. This development was undertaken in response to a request from the government for the Army to care for delinquents and other girls between the ages 13 and 16 who needed care and protection. By 1950 the school was accommodating 30-40 girls, providing them with moral and spiritual training as well as instruction in academic, domestic and vocational subjects, especially agriculture.

In 1952 the school, in response to another request from the government, became a co-educational institution through the addition of a boys' section. This section catered for boys between the ages of nine and twelve years whom it was not wise to accommodate in the Essequibo school for older delinquent boys.

This valuable service provided by the Salvation Army continued until July 1980, when the school was handed over to the government of Guyana. By then many young people had become converted to Christ and had been trained to be respectable law – abiding citizens.

Another principal feature of the Salvation Army during most of its history in Guyana has been ministry of song and music. This dates back at least to 1910 when a songster brigade and a brass band were formed. Singing and music played an important part in attracting people to the Army's street meetings. For many years the band also performed in monthly programmes in the bandstand of the Botanic Gardens in Georgetown and later in regular radio broadcasts.

The Salvation Army in Guyana, with a present committed membership of about 1000 soldiers, is numerically a comparatively small organisation. Its influence, however, belies the size of its membership which, like that of all other local churches, has suffered since the 1970s from substantial outward migration especially to North America. Admittedly, however, its membership has increased recently owing to the influx especially of young people, influenced by the introduction of new programmes geared to attract youths.

The Salvation Army at its centenary in 1995 had eight churches located in the three counties of Guyana in the following places: four assemblies in Georgetown and one in Linden, Vergenoegen, Bartica and New Amsterdam. As throughout its history in Guyana, notwithstanding the popular image of the Salvation Army as an organisation that is concerned primarily with social welfare, the main objective of the army remains the spiritual salvation of all Guyanese through repentance from sin and personal faith in Jesus Christ and the subsequent pursuit of a holy life. Much of the Army's evangelistic activity is in open – air meetings in which its musical band plays a prominent role.

Social work, however, continues to be a pronounced feature of the Army's service to the nation. It consists mainly of four types of activity: the provision of food, accommodation, education and comfort. There is a feeding programme for elderly citizens in four locations in Georgetown, Linden and Bartica, providing lunch in particular for 300 persons on five days of each week. The Salvation Army also maintains three hostels – one for elderly women in the Wortmanville area of Georgetown, one for men in Linden and another for males in Kingston in Georgetown. In New Amsterdam there is a programme of continuing education for school dropouts which currently caters for about 35 young people. Furthermore, the Army recently established a new facility in Bartica, providing residents there with a day-care centre, a play school and a programme for youths.

Another important element in the social work of the Salvation Army is the service provided by its 'League of Mercy'. This predominantly female arm of the Army in general investigates social needs and in particular visits homes, hospitals and other institutions to offer words of comfort and practical help.

The Army also has an organised "Medical Fellowship", comprising members who are doctors and nurses, which renders assistance in the field of health.

The Salvation Army is extremely grateful to the government of Guyana, the business community, banks, individuals and the general public for financial support which helps to meet a significant part of the substantial expenditure incurred in maintaining this diverse programme of social welfare. Its services are offered to all Guyanese irrespective of race, colour, religion or political affiliation. As Major Sydney McKenzie, the current head of the organisation in Guyana, put it recently in an interview, "where there is a need, there is the Salvation Army".[135]

Today, as in the past, the Salvation Army maintains a non-political approach in its activities. It is committed to work harmoniously with whatever government is in power at a given juncture, without seeking to become involved in a partisan way in national politics.

The present strength of the Salvation Army lies particularly in three areas, namely, its work among women, youths and children. The women's ministry falls under the oversight of the wife of the local head of the work in Guyana who bears the title of 'Director of Women's Organisations'. There are fifteen women's groups in the country, reaching about 1500 ladies. The local women's arm has been upholding the Army's reputation worldwide of having one of the strongest women's organisations.

The Army's Youth arm, known as the Torchbearers Youth Club, is particularly strong in the rural areas. Its aim is to attract and win young people to Christ. It is divided into a junior section called "Junior Soldiers", which caters for children and youths between the ages of seven and fourteen, and a senior section known as "Senior Soldiers", comprising young people aged fifteen and above. The Army's ministry among children, unlike that of many other churches, is not restricted to "Sunday School". There are also activities for children on other days of the week, including sessions to train them in singing, the playing of musical instruments, and learning the Bible.

The diverse programme of activities of the Salvation Army, which occupies all seven days of the week, keeps its members very busy. Nevertheless, the present objective of the Army is to expand its ministry. Very crucial to its current and future operations are its buildings which serve not only as places of worship but also as centres for its social welfare activities.

The Army is currently concentrating on reconstructing and refurbishing several of its buildings with a view to the improvement and extension of the already invaluable service being rendered by it to the nation. In one case the plan is to add to a building a hall specially geared for youth activities. One urgent need is to rebuild the men's hostel in Kingston in Georgetown. The Army plans to transform this building into a multi-faceted centre which can be employed to rehabilitate drug addicts, to offer training in vocational skills to young people, and to care juveniles on remand. The men's hostel in Linden is presently being refurbished, while a new building with a variety of facilities was recently constructed at Bartica.

This recent and current emphasis on the construction and rehabilitation of buildings is one of the major contributions to the work of the Salvation Army by its local head, Major Sydney McKenzie, who has been Divisional Commander of Guyana since October 1991. McKenzie, a Jamaican by birth, has been involved in the work of the Salvation Army for 26 years, including a previous stint of four years in Guyana from 1977 to 1981 in another capacity. He has served in four other Caribbean territories, Jamaica, Trinidad and Tobago, Barbados and St. Vincent.

McKenzie's title of "Divisional Commander" is the name given to the local head of the Salvation Army in most countries. The holder of this office is appointed by the Army's highest regional authority in the Caribbean, namely, the Territorial Commander based in Jamaica, and his advisory board. The work in Guyana also falls administratively within the Americas and the Caribbean, one of the five divisions or zones into which the worldwide Salvation Army movement is organised. Each of these five divisions or zones is under the oversight of an officer, called a Commissioner or International Secretary who is based at the International headquarters in London, England. The Commissioner is the third highest-ranking officer in the Salvation Army as an international organisation, being subject only to The General and the Chief of Staff, the top two positions.

Initially the leading officer of the Salvation Army in Guyana and elsewhere in the Caribbean was a white expatriate. This practice continued for a considerable time, but eventually the responsibility of leading the work was entrusted to Guyanese or other Caribbean nationals. This was particularly the case after Guyana and other Caribbean territories achieved political independence in the 1960s and 1970s.

In the hundred years which have elapsed since the official establishment of the Salvation Army in Guyana in 1895, there have been 31 local heads, usually occupying the office for relatively short terms of two to four years before being transferred to another territory. Four of these 31 leading officers have been Guyanese: Major Clement Moonsammy (April 1971 to

June 1974), Captain (later Major) David Edwards (September 1974 to June 1976), Captain (later Major) Mortimer Jones (August 1976 to 1982) and Major Cleo Damon (October 1986 to July 1990).

The Guyanese who has made the most substantial contribution to the work of the Salvation Army as an international movement is David Edwards. Edwards joined the Army as a youth in what was then British Guiana in the 1950s through the influence of a grandaunt with whom he went to live after his mother migrated to England. In 1960, while working as a school teacher, he felt a divine call to full-time service as a Salvation Army Officer. He proceeded to Jamaica, where he spent two years receiving the requisite training. He was then commissioned to the field, serving in Trinidad and Jamaica before returning home. In 1974 he became Divisional Commander of Guyana, the second Guyanese to hold that office.

Edwards' committment to God and the Salvation Army, his industry and his effectiveness brought him an ever-growing reputation and more responsibility, with the result that eventually he became the first Guyanese, and in some instances the first West Indian, to hold certain offices in the regional and international movement. In 1982 he became the youngest chief-secretary for the Caribbean region and when he was promoted to Lieutenant – Colonel and later Colonel, he was the first Guyanese and the youngest Caribbean national to be appointed to such high ranks.

In 1990 Edwards became the first West Indian to be appointed Territorial Commander of Central America and the Caribbean. Early in 1995, a few months ago, he was promoted to the position of Commissioner in London, with responsibility for overseeing the work of the Salvation Army in the entire Americas and the Caribbean, again the first Caribbean person to hold such a high office in the international movement.

Not surprisingly, Guyanese Salvationists have a special sense of pride in David Edwards' achievements as they celebrate this year the hundredth anniversary of the official establishment of the work in Guyana in 1895.

FOR FURTHER READING

Hobbs, Doreen	**Jewels of the Caribbean. The History of the Salvation Army in The Caribbean Territory** (St. Albans, U.K:The Campfield Press, 1986).
Anon.	**The Salvation Army 1895-1995 A Century of Service. The Guyana Division Centenary Congress June 21-26, 1995** (Georgetown, 1995).

CHAPTER 32

FROM OBSCURITY TO PROMINENCE: THE STORY OF THE FULL GOSPEL FELLOWSHIP, 1964 - 2014

This year, 2014, is the fiftieth anniversary of the foundation of the Full Gospel Fellowship of Churches in Guyana. From very obscure inauspicious beginnings in April 1964 in an old rented house at the corner of Waterloo and Murray (since renamed Quamina) streets in Georgetown, the Fellowship has developed into one of the leading Christian denominations in Guyana today. Now a national organisation, the Fellowship presently consists of about 125 churches located in all ten administrative regions of our country and served by over 200 ministers.

After fifty years the Fellowship continues to pursue vigorously the objectives outlined in its Mission Statement which asserts that

> The Full Gospel Fellowship is an Apostolic Ministry Consisting of Apostolic Teams and Churches, pioneering and establishing autonomous local churches in the towns and villages of Guyana in particular, the other Guianas, the Caribbean and other nations. Such churches should be in strategic areas and function as Models and Bases to express Kingdom of God Concerns. The Apostolic Teams and Churches will train, develop and release ministries, resources and services in the communities and nations.[136]

The birth of the Fellowship was due largely to the vision, initiative and faith of Philip Mohabir. Mohabir, the visionary and principal founder of the Fellowship, is one of the unsung heroes of Guyanese church history. Born and brought up a Hindu in the little-known village of Enterprise on the East Coast of Demerara, Mohabir was converted to Christ in 1952 at the age of fifteen as a result of reading the Gospel of Mark during a Religious Education lesson in secondary school.

This important unexpected experience resulted in a remarkable change in the nature and direction of his life while still a teenager. As the inside cover of his last major book, **Hands of Jesus,** states: "In a personal encounter with Jesus he heard a distinct call to be a missionary. In obedience to that call he arrived in the United Kingdom in 1956 totally trusting the Lord to meet all his needs."[137]

According to Mohabir, on two occasions while he was abroad, in December 1956 in London and in 1963 in France, he received a vision from God directing him to return to what was then British Guiana to do pioneer evangelism and church planting in eleven specific areas. These areas were Skeldon in the Upper Corentyne, Rosehall in the Lower Corentyne, New Amsterdam, Buxton, Georgetown, Leonora/Anna Catherina, Vergenoegen/Parika, Bartica, Mabaruma, Moruka, and some unidentified villages on the East Bank of Demerara. He understood that these would be the strategic places where the work which he was being directed to undertake would be established, serving also as bases for its expansion.

Philip Mohabir returned to his homeland, British Guiana, in 1964 to fulfil this vision. With him were his wife, Muriel, a Jamaican trainee nurse of African descent whom he met and married in London in 1958, their three young children, all girls, and two friends, a white British couple, Bryn and Edna Jones.

With such limited human resources and virtually no finances, the task of fulfilling the vision seemed impossible. Surprisingly, however, this small, apparently ill-equipped team was able to pioneer what today is the Full Gospel Fellowship. Initially the work of Mohabir and his small team of co-labourers significantly bore the name Centre of Evangelism. It was joined in 1967 by the work of another converted Hindu, Harry Das, an outstanding evangelist who had pioneered a few churches in the Corentyne in Berbice. This united work was incorporated under laws of Guyana in November 1968 under the name Full Gospel Fellowship, with Mohabir as leader and Das as Chairman and pursuing Mohabir's God-given vision with considerable success.

The leaders of the Fellowship attribute its remarkable success, above all, to two factors which sceptics will find difficult to understand and appreciate, namely, divine purpose and divine providence. They also acknowledge the importance of several other factors, two of which will now be mentioned.

One of them is the genuinely multi-ethnic character of the Fellowship throughout its history. This factor was particularly critical in its early years when the country was torn by ethnic friction and violence. The unity and love demonstrated especially by East Indian and African ministers and church members, and visibly exemplified in the life of Philip and Muriel Mohabir, enabled the early pioneers to gain considerable respect and influence in a country where people needed reconciliation both to God and each other.

This factor is emphasised by Philip Mohabir in his instructive autobiography, entitled **Building Bridges**. He observes

> The remarkable thing about this band of people who worked together in Guyana, a country torn at the time by inter-racial feuds, is how mixed we were, both in race, culture and social class. People of African and Indian descent working together in love and harmony in Guyana in the early nineteen sixties and onwards – truly it was a miracle which only God could have achieved.[138]

The second factor which has contributed immensely to the Fellowship's progress is its full-time residential missionary training programme, conducted initially for a few months in Georgetown, then for a year on the Essequibo Coast and about nine years at Stanleytown on the West Bank of Demerara, but since 1975 at Hauraruni on the Soesdyke – Linden Highway. This programme, a rare feature among Christian denominations in Guyana, has provided a steady flow of trained personnel to maintain and expand the work of the Fellowship, in spite of the high incidence of outward migration of ministers, leaders and ordinary church members witnessed in recent decades.

The Fellowship's most important single activity each year is what it calls a "Ministers' and Leaders' Conference". Held for many years in the somewhat remote location of Hauraruni, at least from 2004 the event had been staged in Georgetown at the National Cultural Centre from Tuesday to Thursday usually in the second week of March. The shift in venue is designed to expose a larger and wider audience to the proceedings. The morning sessions of the conference are restricted to ministers and local church leaders, while the evening sessions are open to the general public.

Each conference has a pertinent theme, addressed by a team of able local and foreign speakers. One of its main sessions is its official opening, normally the first evening, to which many of the nation's political and civic leaders and other important personalities are invited. At that session in the 2004 conference, for example, the keynote address was delivered by the Fellowship's current leader and superintendent, Elsworth Williams, on the subject, "The Guyanese Nation – The Way Forward: a Christian Perspective".

Like the main founder of the Fellowship, Philip Mohabir, Williams, the Fellowship's chief apostle, has had a remarkable life. Brought up in the deprived area of Albouystown in Southern Georgetown, he was converted to Christ in 1968 in his youth. After serving in the police force for a few years, he felt a divine call to the Christian ministry. He has been instrumental in the establishment or development of two of the Fellowship's largest and most vibrant churches, one in Plaisance on the East Coast of Demerara and the other in Cooper Street in Albouystown, where he presently serves as Senior Pastor in addition to his other important functions.

Like the other leaders and members of the Full Gospel Fellowship, Rev. Williams is humbled by the progress the work has experienced over the past fifty years. He acknowledges that it is ultimately due to God's sovereignty and grace that the Fellowship, an indigenous body, has been able to move from obscurity to a position of prominence and greater influence.

For Further Reading

Mohabir, Philip	**Building Bridges**. 2013 Reprint, originally published in 1988 (London: Hodder and Stoughton, 1988).

Chapter 33

The Evangelical Witness in Guyana – A Historical Outline

One of the most striking features of the modern history of Christianity in Guyana is the growing strength of the Evangelicals. Until 1803, when Britain took possession of the country (then consisting of the two Dutch colonies of Demerara-Essequibo and Berbice) from the Netherlands, Protestant Christianity, although introduced at least 185 years before, had made very little progress. This was due mainly to a serious shortage of money and ministers and the neglect of the Amerindians and Blacks by the dominant Dutch Reformed and Lutheran churches, which catered only for the small white population. Thus in 1803, there were only two church buildings and a few clergymen in the two colonies. Moreover, except for an unsuccessful Moravian mission among Amerindians in the Berbice River, no significant efforts had yet been made to evangelize the Amerindians or the large black slave population. In fact the evangelization of the blacks had been prohibited by the Dutch authorities and planters, who feared that this would make the slaves more discontented and rebellious.

Drastic Change

This situation changed drastically between 1808 and 1840 owing to the arrival of several white missionaries sponsored by four British missionary bodies: the London, Methodist and Church Missionary Societies and the Society for the Propagation of the Gospel. Extensive evangelization was undertaken and many Blacks and some Amerindians were converted. As the nineteenth century advanced, however, less emphasis was placed on the preaching of the Gospel and the membership of the established churches came increasingly to consist considerably of nominal Christians rather than devout born-again believers.

Growing Need

The growing need for serious evangelism and Christian living was partly met initially mainly by the Christian Brethren Church, the first distinctly evangelical group to emerge. Its founder was Leonard Strong, a former Anglican missionary, who between 1827and 1848 established two Brethren assemblies in Demerara, one in Georgetown and the other in Peter's Hall on the East Bank of the Demerara River. The work grew steadily and by the 1920s there were about 25 Brethren assemblies in the country. By then a few other evangelical bodies had been established, including the Christian Mission in 1892, the Salvation Army in 1895, the Pilgrim Holiness (later renamed the Wesleyan Church) in 1908 and the Church of God in 1915. These bodies were followed later, especially after 1945, by at least twelve other evangelical denominations including the Assemblies of God, the Elim Mission, the Church of God of Prophecy, the Christian Catholic Church, the Church of the Nazarene, the Baptists, the Bible Missionary Church, the New Testament Church of God, the Full Gospel Fellowship and the Church of Christ. Furthermore, a growing number of independent evangelical churches have been established, especially in recent decades. Today, the evangelical churches are estimated to have a total membership and following of at least 100,000 persons or at least 15 per cent of the country's population.

Evangelical Faith

Evangelicals emphasize certain fundamental truths of Christianity such as:

1. The unity of the Father, Son, and the Holy Spirit in a sovereign Godhead.
2. The divine inspiration and the complete trustworthiness of the Bible and its supreme authority in all matters of faith and conduct.
3. The universal sinfulness and guilt of all men, rendering them subject to God's condemnation and wrath.
4. Freedom from the guilt, penalty, power, and pollution of sin only through the sacrificial death of the Lord Jesus Christ, the Son of

God.
5. The bodily resurrection of Christ from the dead and His ascension to the right hand of God the Father in heaven.
6. The salvation of the sinner by the grace and mercy of God through personal faith in Christ.
7. The existence of one universal church, the Body of Christ, to which all true believers belong.
8. The expectation of the personal return of Christ to rule and judge the world and to complete God's purposes for the whole universe.

A Serious Matter

Evangelicals stress the absolute need for people to turn from their sinful way of living and commit their lives to Christ as their Lord and Saviour. Converts are baptized in water by immersion as a public testimony of their decision to abandon their old sinful life and to follow Christ in a new life. They are expected daily to live a holy life totally committed to Christ. Evangelical Christianity is thus not a Sunday affair, but a serious and costly matter, daily affecting every area of one's life.

Pentecostals

Certain Evangelicals, known as Pentecostals, also emphasize the supernatural. They pray for the sick and diseased, cast out demons, and urge believers to seek the power and supernatural gifts of the Holy Spirit mentioned in I Corinthians, Chapter 12. The leading Pentecostal denominations are the Full Gospel Fellowship, the Assemblies of God and the New Testament Church of God. Prominent among the independent Pentecostal churches are the Love and Faith World Outreach group in Sophia, Georgetown and the Covenant Church in Lodge, also in Georgetown.

Other Distinctive Features

Evangelical churches are known for their wide range of activaties throughout the week. In addition to Sunday services, there are usually weekly prayer meetings, Bible studies and special meetings exclusively for women and young people, who constitute a substantial part of most evangelical congregations. The zeal and numerical strength of evangelical youths are remarkable especially in view of the difficulty encountered by many other churches in winning and maintaining the interest of young people.

Evangelical Youth Camps

One of the important undertakings of Evangelical churches and groups in Guyana is the organisation of Christian Youth Camps. The feature was introduced about 1950 when a non-denominational organisation named "Youth for Christ" began to run camps on an inter-denominational basis. The marked spiritual impact of these camps eventually encouraged local churches to begin to hold camps for the benefit of their own young people. As this trend became more pronounced, "Youth for Christ" left the responsibility for the Evangelical camp ministry mainly in the hands of the churches.

The pioneers in this new trend of essentially denominational camps were the Church of the Nazarene in 1956 and the Kitty Bible Church (now the Kitty Baptist Church) in 1957. Their example has been followed by almost all the other evangelical churches. The idea of the inter-denominational camps, however, persisted mainly due to the work of the Inter-School Christian Fellowship which has been holding camps every year since 1958, especially for students of secondary schools.

The main purpose of most Evangelical camps is to strengthen and deepen the spiritual life of Christian young people. Only a few camps, sponsored mostly by the Inter-School Christian Fellowship, are designed primarily to win non-Christians to Christ. There are also a few camps, such as those organized by the Inter-School Christian Fellowship for the students and teachers who direct Christian groups in schools, which are intended to provide training in spiritual leadership.

The spiritual objectives of camps are achieved through a multi-faceted programme. This programme includes talks, Bible studies, quizzes, group and panel discussions, debates, counselling, prayer, Question and Answer sessions, skits, films and videos. Among other activities are games, swimming, physical training and handicraft.

Until the early 1970s the most popular venue for camps was the government-owned campsite at Madewini near the modern motor-racing circuit at Timehri. Its virtual unavailability since 1973, however, resulted in the increasing use of other sites, especially the Roman Catholic camp at Kayuka off the Soesdyke-Linden Highway, and the Baptist and Adventist camps at Goshen near Bartica.

A growing number of Evangelical churches have decided to establish their own camp sites, though this is a difficult and costly undertaking. The Pilgrim Holiness Mission, now known as the Wesleyan Church, and the Full Gospel Fellowship, for example, have been holding their annual youth camps for many years at their respective sites at Wesleyana and Hauraruni off the Soesdyke-Linden Highway. The Assemblies of God began using their site, Camp Alpha near Wesleyana as the venue for their youth camp in 1977, while the Church of the Nazarene started to utilise its own facilities at Goshen in 1978.

The organisation of evangelical youth camps is undertaken by committees consisting largely of able young people. It is a challenging task rendered difficult by many factors, particularly by inadequate sleeping accommodation and the high cost of accommodation and food. Though camp fees have increased considerably since the 1970s, several camps have to be subsidized in order to cover the cost.

Because of their desire for good fellowship and spiritual renewal and growth, Evangelical youths have displayed a keen interest in camps. Attendance at the Nazarene camps increased from almost twenty-five youths in 1956 to seventy in 1962, and later to over one hundred, the largest number of campers before the late 1970s being about one hundred and forty. The Assemblies of God had by then as many as three hundred campers on one occasion, while the attendance at Full Gospel Fellowship camps rose phenomenally from forty at its first camp at Stanleytown on the West Bank of Demerara in 1966 to over five hundred in Hauraruni in 1977. Most Evangelical camps, however, are organized on a much smaller scale, usually catering for about sixty to one hundred persons.

Camps are occasions of great spiritual challenge and blessing, resulting in the conversion to Christ of sinners, the restoration, renewal, sanctification and consecration of Christian lives, and the acceptance by some youths of God's call to full-time Christian service. They have also served to create better unity among Christian young people, an increased awareness of their spiritual and other potential, and a clearer understanding of the problems and challenges facing youths.

Evidence of the tremendous spiritual impact of Evangelical youth camps is seen in the following extract from an official report on the first Nazarene

Camp held in August 1956 at Madewini.

&

"Our young people are taking a greater interest than ever before, due primarily to our first youth camp. …What a time of blessing and victory it was! …Before the nearly five-day camp closed everyone who came to the camp without victory obtained the blessing needed. From this camp the revival fires spread to the young people's respective churches, especially the Queenstown Church. The young folks made confessions, sought holiness as well as forgiveness and carried this spirit into their homes and churches. Glorious it was! Praise the Lord."[139]

&

Evangelical church leaders continue to praise God for His rich blessing on the camps which have challenged and revolutionized the lives of thousands of young people since their introduction. These camps are certainly one of the sources of strength of the Evangelical witness in Guyana.

For Further Reading

Chapman, E.	**History of The Christian Brethren in Guyana** 2nd Edition, no date. 1st Edition, 1955.
Cockfield, Alfred	**The History of the Assemblies of God in Guyana** (New York: Christian Times, 2008).

Part Six

Education

Rev. William Piercy Austin, the Anglican Bishop of British Guiana and the founder of Queen's College

The official opening of the University of Guyana in 1963

Two renowned Guyanese historians, Professors Elsa Goveia and Walter Rodney

Three locations of Queen's College - in 1870 on Carmichael Street, in 1920 on Brickdam and in 1960 on Camp Road

CHAPTER 34

THE BEGINNINGS OF ELEMENTARY EDUCATION, 1800-1840

The beginnings of primary education in Guyana can meaningfully be dated back to the first half of the nineteenth century. In 1800 opportunities for formal education in Guyana were extremely limited. They were restricted to the small minority of politically, economically and socially dominant white residents, many of whose children attended private schools especially in Stabroek, the capital of the United Colony of Demerara-Essequibo. Other white children were either educated by their parents at home or were sent to Europe for their education.

There were no facilities in 1800 for the education of the numerically dominant Africans and Amerindians. In particular, there was strong opposition by Whites to the idea of educating enslaved Africans. Whites feared that education, especially literacy, would cause captive Africans to become more reflective and to be able to read anti-slavery literature, thereby making them more insubordinate and rebellious. Between 1800 and 1840, however, three important developments occurred which gave a significant impetus to the growth of primary education.

The first development was in 1808 when the London Missionary Society in England sent a clergyman, Rev. John Wray, to teach Christianity to enslaved persons on Plantation Le Resouvenir on the East Coast of Demerara in response to a request from its Dutch proprietor, Hermanus Post. Wray persuaded Post to allow him and his wife to conduct a school there attended by the children of slaves, free Blacks and Coloureds and Whites.

The education of these captive Africans enraged and unnerved other slaveholders and met with the disfavour of the colonial authorities. Thus, when Wray's successor, Rev. John Smith, indicated to Governor Murray on his arrival in 1817 that his intention was to educate slaves, he received a sharp response: "If you ever teach a Negro to read and I hear of it, I will banish you from the colony."[140] Nevertheless, Smith continued Wray's work of teaching free and enslaved children and adults to read and imparting other rudiments of primary education. Admittedly, however, only a very small number of children benefited from this opportunity and from a few other schools established by Christian missionaries.

The second major impetus to the extension of primary education was given by the British metropolitan government who in 1823 introduced a policy of amelioration of slavery in Demerara- Essequibo, Berbice and the other British Caribbean colonies. One aspect of this new policy encouraged the education of both enslaved Africans and freedmen. As a result, in 1824 the St. George's "free" school, conducted separately for boys and girls, was established. A similar school was set up in Georgetown, as Stabroek was renamed in 1812, under the patronage of the colonial government for enslaved boys and girls owned by the Crown. Later, in 1829, the Anglican Church opened a school- All Saints- in New Amsterdam, where education was provided separately for boys and girls.

The establishment of these schools under the influence of the imperial government's amelioration policy may have inspired the setting up of other educational facilities. Certainly, this period of the 1820s witnessed the birth of several private schools especially in Georgetown and New Amsterdam which catered particularly for free Blacks, free Coloureds and poor Whites. The best-known of these new private institutions was the De Saffon Institute which was opened in Georgetown in 1825, financed from the legacy of Pierre Louis De Saffon, who had requested in his will that admission to the school should be limited to poor white children.

Owing to these developments, by 1830 the number of children who were receiving at least a measure of primary education, though still small, had increased significantly since 1800 especially in Georgetown and New Amsterdam. Education in British Guiana, the name given to the new entity resulting from the unification of Demerara- Essequibo and Berbice in 1831, received a third and more formidable fillip in the late 1830s in the wake of the imperial government's decision to abolish slavery in the British Empire from 1st August, 1834. This stimulus was received during the four-year apprenticeship period which enslaved persons were required to serve before they became completely free in 1838.

One purpose of the apprenticeship period was to prepare the apprentices for full freedom. The imperial government decided that the Christianisation and education of the apprentices should be regarded as vital components of this preparatory process. It therefore allocated £20,000 sterling from the imperial treasury to promote education in the entire British Caribbean. The money was distributed to various Christian missionary societies according to the number of schools they proposed to build and based on an undertaking that they would bear one third of the cost of each building.

As a result of this appropriation, missionary organisations in British Guiana- namely, the Anglican Church, the London Missionary Society, the Methodist Missionary Society and the Church Missionary Society- received a total of about £2,000 sterling. They used this "Negro Education Grant", as it was called officially, to build many new schools with the result that by 1840 72 schools were established in the colony by these bodies partly with aid of the imperial financial subsidy. Forty of these schools belonged to the Anglicans, 22 to the M. M. S., and five each to the LMS and C.M.S.

Other church organisations, who were not recipients of the imperial grant, were also active in opening schools. For example, the Church of Scotland established 27 schools and the Independent Dissenters seven schools.

Thus by 1840, due mainly to the perceived need of preparing the enslaved for full freedom which occurred on 1st August 1838, there were 115 primary schools in British Guiana, with about 9500 children registered. The overwhelming majority of these students were Blacks and represented about 45 per cent of the estimated 21, 170 African children of school age. Some of the schools in Essequibo, however, catered mainly for Amerindian children. The C.M.S. in particular concentrated on extending education mainly among Amerindians in the rivers and creeks in Essequibo. Surprisingly, although by 1840 schools were established in most parts of the country, Demerara was less endowed with educational institutions than Berbice and Essequibo.

In short, by 1840 the foundations for primary education in Guyana were established with the Christian churches, not the colonial government, playing the dominant role. Admittedly, the system of education had many deficiencies. For example, there was a great paucity of competent teachers in a system where much use was made of the monitorial approach, in which older children were trained to help in instructing the younger ones. Furthermore, the curriculum, consisting of a modicum of the three R's, reading, writing and arithmetic, was very limited. Moreover, the educational system lacked an administrative structure. Not surprisingly, in the late 1840s the colonial authorities began to address some of these salient weaknesses in the system.

For Further Reading

Gordon, Shirley	**A Century of West Indian Education** (London: Longman 1963).
Cameron, Norman	**150 Years of Education in Guyana (1808-1957)** (Georgetown: The Author, 1968).
Chase, Marguerite	"The Development of Primary Education in Post-Emancipation British Guiana," **History Gazette**, No. 62, November 1993.
Bacchus, M.	"Education in the Pre-Emancipation Period (with Special Reference to the Colonies which later became British Guiana)", **Guyana Historical Journal**, Volume 11, 1990.

Chapter 35

Primary Education in Guyana 100 Years Ago

This chapter will focus on some of the main problems experienced in the system of elementary education in British Guiana at the beginning of the twentieth century. At that time, and at least until 1930, the interest of the public and the policy of the government in regard to education were almost entirely confined to the provision of primary schools throughout the country. In 1900 there were very few secondary schools and no tertiary institution. Queen's College, the leading secondary school, had then only 69 students on the register.

In 1900 primary education was largely in the hands of Christian denominations who owned and ran schools with the aid of a grant from the public revenue. With the exception of 14 schools called "estate schools", all the 214 existing primary schools were under the control of Christian churches, but were open to children of all religions. Of these schools 72 were run by the Church of England, 37 by the Church of Scotland, 30 by the Congregational Church, 29 by the Methodists, 28 by the Roman Catholics, two by the Moravians and one each by the Lutherans and the Canadian Presbyterian Mission.

One of the glaring weaknesses of the system of primary education then was that the government of the colony did not take sufficient responsibility. Furthermore, there was not a clear demarcation of responsibilities between the two parties, namely, the churches and the state, in charge of education. As the Commissioner of Education, Major Bain Gray, observed in his famous report of 1925

> My objections to the present methods of administration do not prevent me from appreciating to the full the great services which

the churches have rendered to education in the past. I appreciate, also, the fact that it will be a long time before the Commissioner of Education can hope to find elsewhere than in the Churches any organised body of public opinion which will take more than a languid interest in educational progress. But the present insanitary condition of many schools, and the general lack of furniture and equipment, are due to the fact that each party- the churches and the state- has been able to prove to its own entire satisfaction that the responsibility rested on the other. In the meantime the physical welfare of the children has been lost sight of. It is essential, therefore, that in the future the relations of the two parties should be clearly defined, and that each should accept full responsibility within its own sphere.[141]

One of the principal concerns in 1900 in relation to primary education in British Guiana was the high level of absenteeism of students, especially in rural areas. This was particularly disturbing in a country which since 1876 had passed an ordinance making elementary education compulsory. Of the 27, 512 students on the registers of primary schools in 1900- 1901, the average attendance was 16, 397 or only 59 per cent. H. A. Matthews, a leading Education District Officer, lamented in his July 1902 report that "the difficulties of thoroughly enforcing the compulsory clauses of the Ordinance are very great."[142]

Absenteeism was due to several circumstances. Among them were factors such as drought or heavy rains in some months, the truancy of some children to whom school life appeared uninteresting, and the poverty of many parents which made them unable or unwilling to equip their children for school. Another important cause of absenteeism in the case of East Indian children was the reluctance of their parents to send them to Christian schools for fear that they might be converted to Christianity, although there was a conscience clause which allowed them not to attend religious instruction classes. Furthermore, many parents, especially East Indians, for economic reasons preferred to send their children to work rather than to school.

The question of East Indians, who were predominantly Hindus and Muslims, attending Christian schools, had been a matter of discussion and debate since the introduction of the Compulsory Education Ordinance in 1876. For instance, in August 1881 the **Argosy** newspaper, had asked its readers

> Do you consider it right and just that the Government should compel Mohammedans, for example, to send their children to the Church of England, and other denominations of Christians?[143]

Poor attendance of schools by East Indian children was, in fact, encouraged later by a January 1902 circular issued by Governor Swettenham addressed to all Stipendiary Magistrates. According to the circular, penalties imposed by the 1876 Ordinance were not to apply to "children of Asiatic immigrants" during the first ten years of residence in British Guiana, and after that period the governor was inclined to think that "no penalty should be inflicted where the parents (or parent or guardian) have a conscientious objection to the school on account of the religion taught there, or to the instruction in the school of girls, on account of prejudices in favour of seclusion."[144]

These circumstances help to explain why in the early twentieth century the composition of the school population showed a significant ethnic imbalance. For example, the 36, 113 pupils on the roll of primary schools in 1914 included 25, 404 Blacks, and 7,148 East Indians, 1,764 Portuguese, 814 Chinese and 609 Amerindians, notably at a time when East Indians constituted the largest single ethnic group in the country's population. In fact, it was not until after the withdrawal in 1933 of the Swettenham Circular that the attendance of East Indian children at primary school increased appreciably. For instance, the attendance of East Indian girls grew from 3,144 in 1933 to 8,573 in 1938, an increase of about 172 per cent.

The fact that defaulting parents could be prosecuted for failing to send children to school did not prove to be a significant deterrent for several reasons. Firstly, the penalties were not severe, with a maximum fine of two dollars. Secondly, the process was somewhat slow, discouraging the prosecution of offenders. A defaulting parent had first to be cautioned by an Education District Officer before he could be summoned. The magistrates would usually warn the offender before taking more severe action. Furthermore, teachers were usually unwilling to play an active role in the prosecution, "fearing that they might thus be brought into too sharp collision with the people."[145]

Education District Officer H.A. Matthews lamented in his 1902 report that the judicial process was "probably the greatest stumbling block of all". According to him

> One has to put up with the law's delays and the cold cynical sneer of an unsympathetic Magistracy. I have here and there met with the support of a Magistrate, but, in most cases, even where the order is made against the parent, the remarks uttered from the bench are neither pleasant nor kind. Saying the least, I cannot help feeling that the Magistrates, exceptions apart, regard the present compulsory system of Education as something not palatable.[146]

This alleged apathetic or uncooperative attitude of many magistrates was no doubt due partly to the fact, as Matthews himself realized, that the parents summoned were "for the most part poor women with illegitimate children, or East Indians, and the destitute appearance of some of these at once arrests the attention and excites the pity of the Court."[147]

In 1904, however, the courts began to deal less leniently with the offending parents. In the early months of that year 250 summonses were applied against parents in Georgetown, resulting in the prosecution of 138 of them. In fact, cases of school attendance began to occupy so much of the time of the court in Georgetown that in February 1904, apparently for the first time in the country's history, a magistrate was required to sit regularly (each Monday) to hear education cases. About that time the Education Ordinance was amended to specify that compulsory attendance by children meant at least 25 sessions of school each month for those in Georgetown and New Amsterdam and at least 15 sessions for those in rural districts.

The earnest efforts of the education authorities eventually resulted in a reduction in the rate of absenteeism. By 1928 the average attendance in Demerara had increased to 70 per cent and to 75 per cent in 1938. Increased attendance and enrolment, however, resulted in an acute problem of insufficient staffing. Thus in 1939 the Moyne Commission reported that there is "the very unsatisfactory state of staffing in the schools".[148] This view was endorsed by the Director of Education who observed that "staffing in schools to meet the increasing school population remains a difficult problem."[149]

In 1900, apart from the question of absenteeism, the most serious problem in primary education was in relation to the teaching staff, which was deficient not only in quantity but also in quality. As late as 1925 the Commissioner of Education Major Bain Gray expressed grave concern about "the employment of unqualified and underpaid teachers who are a danger to the schools and the community."[150] He was right in his conclusion that it was "the lack of a training institute which has led to the multiplication of inferior practitioners."[151]

The staffing situation, especially the paucity of certified teachers, which was so obvious in 1900, improved gradually after 1928 when the Government Teachers' Training Centre in Georgetown was opened to train primary school teachers, and especially after 1938, when the institution was reorganized to train 20 teachers every year instead of 30 every two years.

In 1900 the primary education system had other difficulties. There were problems of a material nature such as the inadequate accommodation and maintenance of school buildings and the shortage of furniture and equipment. The curriculum also had obvious deficiencies, especially the lack of vocational training, Science and Physical Education. These defects, however, were dwarfed by the more serious problems of absenteeism and staffing.

For Further Reading

Cameron, Norman	**150 Years of Education in Guyana (1808-1957)** (Georgetown: The Author, 1968).
Gordon, Shirley	**A Century of West Indian Education** (London: Longman 1963).
Gordon, Shirley	**Reports and Repercussions in West Indian Education 1835-1933** (London: Ginn and Co. Ltd. 1968).
Thorne, Alfred	"Education in British Guiana", **Timheri**, Vol. 1 (third series), 1911.
Thorne, Alfred	"Education in British Guiana – Part II", **Timheri**, Vol. 4 (third series), 1912.

CHAPTER 36

THE STORY OF QUEEN'S COLLEGE: ITS FIRST 150 YEARS, 1844-1994

1994 was a very special year for Queen's College, the most prestigious educational institution in the history of Guyana. It marked the 150th anniversary of the foundation of this renowned secondary school. Understandably, it was distinguished by a week of memorable celebrations attended especially by past and current students and staff of the school. One salient feature of the celebrations was the launching of an impressive souvenir magazine, named the **Queen's College Sesquicentennial Souvenir Magazine 1994**.

The school, originally known as the Queen's College Grammar School, was opened on 5 August 1844. Its establishment was due mainly to the vision, initiative and zeal of Rev. William Piercy Austin, the Anglican Bishop of British Guiana and its first principal.

The Ordinance of 14 August 1848 to incorporate the school stated that it was designed

> To provide an efficient system of education at a moderate expense- open to all members of the community without distinction. The Plan of Education to be Classical and Commercial- to combine Theological Training with the Study of Classics, Mathematics and Modern Languages.[152]

and a few other subjects on the principles of King's College in London, England. While the school was open to all boys, irrespective of race, colour or class, the three forces which dominated Guianese society then, it was founded particularly to provide good local instruction for white sons of middle-class origin whose parents could not afford to send them to England to be educated in a comparable institution.

From its INCEPTION, Queen's College provided a quality and level of education hitherto unavailable in the country. It was the only local school of distinction until the Roman Catholic Grammar School (later renamed St. Stanislaus College) was opened in 1866. Queen's proved to be the best secondary school not only in British Guiana, but also eventually in the entire Caribbean. One of the first clear signs of the stature of Queen's in the region appeared in 1872, when one of its students, Charles Sinclair Mc Kenzie, won the prestigious Gilchrist Scholarship, open to intercolonial competition in the English-speaking Caribbean. By 1960, it was not uncommon for Queen's College to win at least three of the six or seven highly competitive open scholarships awarded annually by the University College of the West Indies in Jamaica to candidates from the entire Caribbean seeking admission into this premier regional tertiary institution. In fact, in one exceptional year, 1960, students from Queen's won five of these scholarships, awarded on the basis of results attained in a special entrance examination conducted by the university. It is not surprising therefore that the UNESCO Educational Survey Mission to British Guiana from November 1962 to March 1963 reported that

> Queen's College has won for itself the unenviable position of the premier school of British Guiana … there is a great deal of evidence to support the claim for it as the premier school of the Caribbean. The whole tone of the school is permeated by the tradition and reputation built up over the years.[153]

Since its modest beginning in 1844, Queen's College has undergone many notable changes. One of the most significant early developments was a change of OWNERSHIP. Originally the school was a church body, owned and governed by the Anglican Church, but supported from 1849 by an annual Government financial grant and open to students irrespective of creed. In 1876, however, it became a government institution, reflecting a growing demand by some residents, for at least two decades, for a secular system of education.

By then the school had acquired its own PREMISES. Originally located temporarily in the buildings of the Colony House, it moved soon to a rented property at the corner of what today are Main and Quamina Streets in Georgetown. It remained there until its own buildings were erected in 1854, on the current site of The Bishop's High School in Carmichael Street, at a cost of £5,000. This first Queen's College building was vacated in 1918, when the school was moved to Brickdam to the premises occupied today by the Ministry of Health. The school remained there until 1951, when its current facilities at Camp and Thomas Roads were constructed. The provision of these more spacious facilities, with 24 classrooms, six modern science laboratories, a library, a workshop for woodwork, a large auditorium with an excellent stage and an extensive playing field, ensured better academic offerings, an increase in student intake and an expansion in the school's recreational, cultural and other extra-curricular activities. Queen's soon became the main centre of cultural activities in the country.

Time also witnessed substantial improvement in the school's CURRICULUM which increasingly became more balanced, modern and relevant to the country's needs. Initially, and for much of the rest of the nineteenth century, there was a concentration on classical and, to lesser extent, commercial studies, with almost no attention being directed to instruction in science. The major concern then, as the Principal reported in 1880, was to "keep up efficiently the full course taught on the classical side of an English Public School or First Grade Grammar School".[154] Thus in the mid-1880s, for example, the curriculum consisted of the following subjects: Divinity, English Language, English Grammar and Composition, Dictation, Writing, History, Geography, Greek, Latin, French, Arithmetic, General and Commercial Geometry, Algebra, Accounts, Higher and Applied Mathematics (for Forms 5 and 6), Theory of Chemistry (Forms 3 to 6), Drawing (Forms 1 and 2) and Drill (Forms 1 to 3).

Most time for instruction was allotted to Latin and Greek, usually four hours each week throughout the school, and to French (normally three hours a week). Although the teaching of Chemistry had been introduced in about 1870 for at least the senior school, and a modicum of Physics was taught to the upper forms in intermittent years, for a long while very little progress was achieved in this area of science education. Thus the Principal, in 1886, lamented in his Annual Report that "in science it is impossible at school to get more than a preliminary training".[155] As late as 1890, science education at Queen's was limited to one lesson a week in elementary Chemistry and the country continued to pursue a policy of recruiting from abroad at high salaries the engineers, chemists, electricians and mineralogists it needed.

This deficiency began to be addressed gradually but increasingly seriously after 1896, when a new science laboratory and classroom were added to the school's facilities. This trend was encouraged further by the recommendation of a Special Committee set up in 1898 "to inquire into the education afforded by Queen's and to report as to the advisability of changing the standard of the same."[156] In its Report, the Committee urged that greater provision should be made for the teaching of Science. In 1899, the Principal was able to observe with some satisfaction that "Senior Division classes in Chemistry and Physics are now supplemented by Lectures in Zoology".[157]

Thereafter science began to occupy an increasingly significant place in the school's curriculum, eventually resulting in 1953 in the practice of dividing students from the fourth form into predominantly Science ("Modern") and Arts ("Classical") streams. In 1953 Queen's also began to offer students especially from other schools the opportunity to pursue studies and careers in science by entering a special fifth form, named "Remove Modern", where they were prepared for the GCE Ordinary and Advanced Level examinations in Science and Mathematics. By then, a growing number of students from Queen's, specialising in science subjects, had begun to win the coveted Guiana Scholarship, introduced in 1882 and dominated initially by students pursuing studies in Classics and other Arts subjects.

As science grew in importance, the dominance of Classics declined. Latin remained a compulsory subject on the curriculum at least in the lower school until the 1950s, but eventually disappeared completely in 1972, being progressively undermined by Spanish, which was introduced in 1956. At the same time, in the 1950s, some local flavor was introduced in certain subjects, notably History, where West Indian history began to rival British history owing to the recruitment to the staff of several History graduates from the University College of the West Indies in Jamaica. Other innovations in the curriculum included the beginning of instruction in Economics in 1960.

The balance eventually achieved in the school's curriculum between science and the humanities was only one aspect of the sound, balanced, all-round education which became the hallmark of Queen's College. Another facet was the fact that the curriculum, which also included music, physical education, woodwork and other non-examination subjects, was complemented by a full range of extracurricular activities, with a high score set on participation in games in particular.

By the 1950's students at Queen's could participate in at least seven games: cricket, football, hockey, athletics, volleyball, table tennis, chess, and, for a few years, rugby, and the school was represented in local competitions in these sports. Students also benefited from involvement in the school's numerous societies and clubs, which included a Literary and Debating Society, a Junior Debating Society, a Historical Society, a Science Society, a Dramatic Society, a Photographic Society, a Bee-Keeping Society, a Philatelic Society, a Co-operative Society, a Bible Club, a Radio Club, a Poultry Club, an Educational Tour Club and a Pen Pals' Club. The school also had a Cadet Corps and a Scout Troop. Exposure to these activities made an invaluable physical, educational, intellectual, aesthetic, cultural, technical, moral and spiritual contribution to the lives of students at Queen's.

The twentieth century witnessed important changes in the composition of the STUDENTS' BODY in terms of its size and character. At its foundation in 1844, Queen's had 15 students, the sons of the more affluent members of the top and middle classes, who could afford to pay the substantial fees charged for admission into the school. In short, it was a school for the privileged, especially Whites, with members of the working class and the other lower socio-economic groups unable to gain entry because of financial incapacity. This situation continued with relatively minor modifications until the 1930s with the size of the student body growing slowly, but reflecting essentially the same class character. Numbers were restricted by the level of fees, the shortage of teaching staff and limited accommodation. Though fluctuating, they increased to 40 in 1851, 70 in 1866, 109 in 1889, 140 in 1905 and 164 in 1931. Thereafter, owing to a reduction in fees and other factors, they increased rapidly, while continuing to fluctuate, to 218 in 1933, 242 in 1934, 260 in 1939, and 335 in 1944, 459 in 1951, 600 in 1955 and 650 in 1956, when the two other leading secondary schools for boys, St. Stanislaus College and Berbice High School, had 365 and 350 students respectively.

By the 1950s Queen's College had a growing proportion of students of lower middle-class and working-class origin. This development was made possible because from 1945, the government of the country began to offer a rapidly increasing number of scholarships or free places to students to enter Queen's and the other leading government secondary schools such as The Bishop's High School based on their performance at the annual secondary schools entrance examination. As a result, the portion of fee-paying students at Queen's fell from about 70 per cent in 1947 to 58 per cent in 1959. By 1964, all entrants to Queen's were holders of "free places", many of them being children from the lower socio-economic groups.

By 1960, all the ethnic groups in the country, except Amerindians, were represented amply in the school's population. Particularly noticeable was the rapidly growing number of students of East Indian origin who, after 1945, began to demonstrate an unprecedented degree of interest in secondary education. Thus the proportion of East Indian students at Queen's increased from about 18 per cent between 1946 and 1950, to 28 per cent in 1951-1955, to 31 per cent in 1956-1960, to 36 per cent in 1961-1965, to 44 per cent in 1967, figures increasingly more reflective of this ethnic group's numerical strength in the country's population.

The last significant change in the composition of the student population of Queen's occurred in 1975 when the school ceased to be an institution exclusively for boys. In that year female students were admitted to Queen's for the first time, in keeping with a new policy of the government of making all learning institutions co-educational.

The history of the school also witnessed significant changes in the size and composition of the teaching STAFF. At its inception in 1844, the staff consisted of a principal and two teachers, all three of whom were white clergymen. In fact, until the school became a government institution in 1876, all the principals, Rev. William Piercy Austin (1844-1851), Rev. George Fox (1851-1871), Rev. G.H. Butt (1871-1874), Rev. W.G. Austin (1874-1875) acting and Rev. Arthur Gwyther (1875-1876), and some of the teachers were clergymen. Thereafter, the principals were laymen, the first being Exley Percival (1877-1893), in whose memory "A" House was later named.

The staff continued to be relatively small into the twentieth century. As late as 1905, when Queen's had 140 students, there were only seven members of staff. As the staff increased later, a practice developed of recruiting them, except expatriates and females, almost exclusively from among former students of the school, thus facilitating a continuation of the school's traditions. Since the 1970s, however, only a small proportion of the staff have been former students of Queen's. Throughout most of the history of the school, the staff have been almost exclusively male. As late as 1960, for example, there were only four females among the thirty six members of staff. This situation, however, changed drastically after the school became a co-educational institution in 1975. Not only did the number of female teachers increase until they became a majority, but also, for the first time, females have occupied the top positions of principal and deputy head.

Since its foundation Queen's College DOMINATED and continues to dominate the local academic scene, winning, for example, 80 per cent of the Guyana Scholarships between 1882 and 1945 and six of the seven awarded in 1993. The school has made an invaluable contribution to the country, producing many of the outstanding Guyanese in every field of endeavour. The academic, professional, political, and cultural life of the country has depended largely on Queen's College and its former students have served with distinction in many other countries and in regional and international organisations. History continues to endorse and confirm the view of a late nineteenth-century principal who reported that "the old boys of Queen's College are to be found everywhere and in every capacity in the ranks of workers, acquitting themselves as loyal and useful citizens of the land."[158]

Since the late 1970s, however, Queen's, though maintaining its unchallenged position as the best secondary school in Guyana, has been experiencing serious PROBLEMS as a result of a number of unwelcome developments. Foremost among them are a decline in the quantity and quality of the teaching staff owing mainly to migration overseas and a marked reduction in financial support from the government of Guyana, especially since its introduction and pursuit of an ill-conceived policy of building an elitist institution, the President's College, at the expense of Queen's and the other leading secondary schools. As a result, Queen's has been unable to maintain its laboratories, playing fields and rich extracurricular life and its students have been forced to take the unprecedented step of seeking private "lessons" externally to supplement the tuition received at school.

In these trying circumstances, the survival of Queen's as a credible institution has been due largely to the commitment of some of the teachers, the commendable and unprecedented amount of support from the alumni and its Parent-Teachers' Association. As a result, Queen's continues to demonstrate to the nation and the wider world that it is the only educational institution in Guyana which can, with justification, be considered a "school of excellence". It has had a great past and seems likely to have a great future.

For Further Reading

Cameron, Norman	**A History of the Queen's College of British Guiana** (Georgetown: F.H. Persick, 1951).
Clarke, Laurence	**Queen's College of Guyana. Records of a Tradition of Excellence (1844-1994)**. (Gaborne, 1994).
Mc Gowan, Winston	**A Concise History of Queen's College, 1844-2009** (Georgetown: The Queen's College of Guyana, 2009).
Trotz, Clarence	"My Recollections of Queen's College (1945-1980)" in the **Queen's College Magazine**, 2000.

Chapter 37

Landmarks in The History of Queen's College, 1844-1894

1844 - Formal opening of Queen's College Grammar School (5 August) in the Colony House in the Victoria Law Courts compound with 15 students and two teachers.
1845 - The local government awards 10 exhibitions to students, granting them free places at Queen's.
1848 - Ordinance is enacted incorporating Queen's.
1851 - The appointment as principal of Rev. George Fox (1851-1871).
1854 - New College buildings are opened on 5 September at Carmichael and Murray Streets.
1866 - The year with the largest student body (70 students) during the period when the school was a private institution.
1872 - A QC student, Charles Sinclair Mc Kenzie, becomes the first Guyanese to win the prestigious Gilchrist Scholarship.
1876 - QC becomes a government institution.
1877 - Exley Percival, the youngest principal in the history of QC, after whom an Exhibition and "A" House were later named, assumes office at the age of twenty nine.
1880 - Formation of the school library.
1881 - Publication of the school's first newspaper, called **Our College Gazette.**
1882 - J.H. Conyers, a QC student, becomes the first winner of the Colonial Scholarship of British Guiana, later known as the Guiana (Guyana) Scholarship.
1889 - Formation of the first QC Cadet Corps, 48 boys enlisting.
1893 - Death of Exley Percival, who is succeeded as principal by J.A. Potbury (1893-1903).
1894 - The first award of the newly introduced Percival Exhibition to B.W. Braithwaite, the top QC fifth-form student at the

1896 - Cambridge Local Examination.
1896 - The opening of a new Science Laboratory and Classroom, giving a major impetus to education in Science subjects.
1898 - An official enquiry into the standard of education afforded at QC results in a recommendation that more attention should be directed to Science.
1903 - Death of the principal, J. A. Potbury, who is succeeded in January 1904 by Trevelyan Pope, after the short acting appointment of Geoffrey Franks.
1905 - A Barbadian, Edward Oliver Pilgrim, who was to become the longest-serving master at QC (53 years), begins his teaching career there as an Assistant Master.
1909 - Formation of the first QC scout troop.
1913 - One of QC's most brilliant students, E.M. Duke, wins the Guiana Scholarship at the age of 15 ½ years, specialising in Mathematics.
1915 - QC scout troop wins the Challenge Flag in an open competition among scout troops in the West Indies. Introduction of the system of prefects, initially called monitors.
1916 - Introduction of the House system, with the school's 99 students being divided into two Houses, "A" House and "B" House.
1918 - The school is removed from Carmichael and Murray Streets to the Orphan Asylum buildings at Brickdam and Vlissengen Road.
1919 - The school song, Carmen Collegii Reginae, of which the music was composed by Governor Sir Wilfred Collett and the words by the Colonial Secretary, Cecil Clementi, is sung publicly for the first time at a concert at the Assembly Rooms.
1920 - E.R.D. Moulder, a Guiana scholar and a member of staff from 1901 to 1914, becomes the first "old boy" to be appointed principal, succeeding T.A. Pope and serving until 1928.
1921 - A third House, "C" House, is formed and the names of the three Houses are changed to Percival, after a former principal, Raleigh after the famous British explorer, and Austin after the famous Anglican bishop, Rev. Piercy Austin, who founded QC. Provision of shields by former students for Inter-House competition in cricket, football and athletics.
1924 - Introduction of the system of Form Monitors.
1925 - The school football team wins the Russell Cup and its most distinguished athlete, Phil Edwards, breaks three records at the

1931 - school's annual sports and lowers several national records later in the year at an open meeting.
1931 - Assumption of office of Capt. Howard Nobbs, the longest-serving principal of QC (1931-1952).
1932 - Formation of a fourth House, D'Urban, named after Sir Benjamin D'Urban, Governor of British Guiana a century before.
1933 - Introduction of a Preparatory Form, initially with nine students, conceived as a potentially valuable feeder to the main school. Beginning of inter-collegiate sports competition between the three leading boys' schools of QC, St. Stanislaus and Berbice High School, in athletics and cricket, the latter for the Jacob Cup, named after the donor, C.R. Jacob, a prominent local businessman and citizen.
1935 - Beginning of competition between these three secondary schools in football for the Dias Cup, donated by the Hon. Francis Dias, the Acting Chairman of the QC Board of Governors.
1938 - Decision taken to award annually a Junior QC Scholarship and a number of Junior QC Exhibitions.
1940 - Introduction of hockey at QC.
1942 - A QC student, Linden Forbes Sampson Burnham, a future Prime Minister and President of the country, wins the coveted Guiana Scholarship, gaining distinctions in Latin and English.
1945 - Addition of two Houses, Pilgrim ("E"), named after a long-serving member of staff, and Weston ("F"), named after another staff member who was recently killed while serving in World War II.
1947 - QC's best cricketer, Bruce Pairaudeau, is selected to represent British Guiana against Jamaica in an intercolonial game and scores a century.
1950 - Publication in March of the first issue of the school's new newspaper, **The QC Lictor.**
1951 - The school moves from Brickdam to its current premises in Thomas Lands.
1954 - Introduction of four new Houses: Moulder ("G"), named after a former principal, Woolley ("H") after the then governor of the colony, Sir Charles Woolley, Cunningham ("K") after an old boy who became an admiral in the British Navy and Nobbs ("L") after a recent principal.
1956 - Formation of a new club, the QC Educational Tour Club, to

1962 - provide recreation and education for senior boys of the school in the vacation periods.

1962 - Retirement of Norman Cameron who in 1959 had become the first Guianese to be appointed Deputy Principal of QC, having joined the staff in 1934 and having been awarded a MBE in June 1962 for his devoted service to the school.

1963 - Appointment of the first Guyanese, Doodnauth Hetram, a Latin teacher, as substantive principal.

1968 - A change in school regulations permits fourth-form students to wear long trousers to school.

QC students achieve a record of 29 distinctions at the General Certificate of Education (GCE) "A" Level examination, surpassing the previous highest of 18 distinctions obtained in 1965 and 1967.

1969 - Change in school uniform- the wearing of ties is discontinued and the use of a crest is introduced.

QC students attain 35 distinctions at the GCE "A" Level examination and win four Guyana Scholarships, both achievements being unprecedented.

1975 - QC becomes a co-educational institution, admitting female students for the first time.

1978 - QC wins five of six available Guyana scholarships, three of the students creating history by offering five subjects at the GCE "A" Level examination, and one of them by gaining four distinctions.

1989 - Appointment of the first female principal of QC, Mrs. Dianah Rutherford.

The school celebrates its 145th anniversary.

1993 - An outstanding academic year in which QC wins six of the seven available Guyana Scholarships and produces the top four students in the country in the Caribbean Examinations Council (CXC) examinations.

1994 - Celebration of the school's 150th anniversary.

For Further Reading

Cameron, Norman	**A History of the Queen's College of British Guiana** (Georgetown: F.H. Persick, 1951).
Clarke, Laurence	**Queen's College of Guyana. Records of a Tradition of Excellence (1844-1994)**. (Gaborne, 1994).
Mc Gowan, Winston	**A Concise History of Queen's College, 1844-2009**

	(Georgetown: The Queens' College of Guyana, 2009).
Trotz, Clarence	"My Recollections of Queen's College (1945-1980)" in the **Queen's College Magazine**, 2000.

CHAPTER 38

U.G. FORTY YEARS LATER, 2003

Throughout this year, 2003, the University of Guyana has been celebrating its fortieth anniversary with a variety of commemorative events. U.G. was established by the Parliament of British Guiana in April 1963 and began its operations in October of the same year with an official opening in the auditorium of Queen's College, the country's most prestigious secondary school. Its noble goal was "to provide a place of education, learning, and research of a standard required and expected of a University of the highest standard, and to secure the advancement of knowledge and the diffusion and extension of arts, sciences and learning throughout Guyana."[159]

The reasons advanced by the P.P.P.-led government for this momentous step were primarily educational, financial and philosophical or ideological. For example, it was argued that there was great need for trained qualified teachers in a country where 366 out of 500 secondary school teachers were unqualified. The country also needed trained scientists, technologists and technicians, and able personnel for the civil service. It was said not to be deriving sufficient benefit from the substantial investment of an estimated ¾ million dollars it was making each year to train Guianese students at the University College of the West Indies, the British Caribbean's regional university with campuses at Mona in Jamaica and St. Augustine in Trinidad. In the fourteen-year association between 1948 and 1961 only 41 of 97 Guianese students trained at UCWI had returned home at the completion of their studies. Moreover, the government believed that the education being provided at UCWI was elitist and essentially capitalist and inappropriate or irrelevant to the social, cultural and philosophical needs and ideals of a country on the road to political independence from Britain and favouring socialism. A national university, it was felt, would be a major step towards academic and professional independence and would provide a facility to train and educate large numbers of Guianese at a low cost, many of whom would remain at home to serve after graduation.

Over the last forty years the university has developed and expanded considerably from its inauspicious beginnings in 1963. It was then an evening institution without a permanent building, using the facilities of Queen's College as a temporary measure, holding classes there from Monday to Friday from 6:30pm to 10:30pm until its own buildings could be erected. Today it has its own main campus at Turkeyen on the lower East Coast of Demerara opened in October 1969. Initially, the university was also virtually without a library faced with the disturbing question as to whether its degrees would gain international recognition, and disparagingly referred to as "Jagan's Night School".

In striking contrast to the small group of 164 students who entered the institution in 1963, the annual enrolment in recent years has been almost 5000 students. The original number of three Faculties (Arts, Natural Sciences and Social Sciences) subsequently increased to seven with establishment of the Faculties of Education in 1967, Technology in 1969, Agriculture in 1979, and Health Sciences in 1981. This figure, however, has now been reduced to six with the recent merger of the Faculties of Arts and Education to form a new entity called the School of Education and Humanities. Degree programmes have expanded to include disciplines such as Law, Medicine and Computer Science which were not initially envisaged as part of the institution's offerings. The establishment in 1985 of a training programme for medical practitioners was a major development.

At its inception the university offered only general Degree programmes, but today it also provides several Certificate and Diploma programmes, a development which began in 1966. Initially it had only part-time evening classes, but today most of its classes are full-time. Full-time classes were first introduced within the Faculty of Technology in 1969, but only became available to most students on campus in 1973. Initially, and for a long time afterwards the university's academic programme was organised in three terms, but today the semester system is in place. This system was introduced in the Faculties of Education and Social Sciences in the 1993-94 academic year and in the other Faculties in the following year.

One area of university life which has witnessed change over the years is that of tuition fees. Initially students were required to pay what was more or less a token tuition fee of $100.00 per annum, but this was abolished in 1974. Education at U.G. then became free, but this concession was counterbalanced somewhat by the introduction in 1975 of a requirement that students should participate in National Service. This requirement, which evoked controversy both on and off the university campus, was discontinued in 1994, when the government abolished mandatory National Service for students at tertiary level education institutions. About the same time, the 1994-95 academic year, tuition fees were reintroduced in a requirement described euphemistically as a "cost recovery" arrangement. Most students are required to pay $127,000.00 per annum with the exception of those registered for the Law, Medical and Tourism programmes who pay $300,000.00, $500,000.00 and $154,000.00 per annum respectively.

Striking changes have taken place over the years in other aspects of the university, notably in the number and gender composition of its graduates. The small number of 32 graduands (28 men and four women) at its first convocation in 1968 has grown immensely, with over 1277 students, of whom about 60 per cent were females, receiving degrees, diplomas and certificates last year.

Similarly, the range and reach of the university have also expanded with growth of its extramural arm, which was created in 1976 and now has centres in four areas, namely, Georgetown, Linden, New Amsterdam and Anna Regina. Furthermore, in 2000 the university's second campus was established at Tain in the Corentyne in Berbice. The programmes offered there include Degrees in Agriculture, Education, English, and Public Management, Diplomas in Accountancy, Marketing, Public Management, Social Work, English and History and a Certificate in Education.

Apart from these developments, during the past forty years the university has had many other notable achievements. It has provided tertiary education to thousands of Guyanese who otherwise would not have had the opportunity. U.G., in fact, has trained most of the leading personnel in the local public and private sectors. Moreover, through its extramural arm, now called the Institute of Distance and Continuing Education (IDCE), it has been able to provide education at both pre-tertiary and tertiary levels to students in various parts of the country, including some remote areas away from the coast where previous access to such training was extremely difficult.

In addition to traditional Departments, U.G. has established a number of important institutes and units which provide critical research, valuable support services, and, in several cases, tuition functions. Among them are the Amerindian Research Unit, the Centre for the Study of Biological Diversity, the Environmental Studies Unit, the Institute of Development Studies, the Jenman Herbarium and the Learning Resource Centre.

The University of Guyana has also provided a solid foundation for the successful careers of its graduates and teaching staff who have since migrated to all parts of the world. The performance of these migrants, both in employment and in further studies, has helped to gain U.G. international recognition, which is reflected partly in the growing number of collaborative arrangements which U.G. has with prestigious overseas universities.

U.G.'s achievements are remarkable in view of the limited financial resources which it almost invariably has had over these forty years. Severe underfunding has impeded its development and has been largely responsible for many of its current critical problems and needs. For example, poor remuneration has made it virtually impossible to attract and retain experienced and highly qualified staff. Funds are also urgently needed to strengthen and modernize the library, to retool the laboratories and to expand the physical plant, especially to provide more lecture room space.

There is also a great need at U.G. for the extension of graduate programmes which are presently offered in only a few departments and faculties. The first such programme, a Master's Degree in Guyanese and West Indian History, was started in 1973, followed by Master's Programmes in Biology and Education in 1976, Chemistry and Economics in 1977, and Political Science in 1978. Since then only a few additional graduate programmes have been introduced such as the Graduate Diploma in Development Studies in 1984. All the graduate programmes are undersubscribed by students and there are immense difficulties in sustaining most of them.

In spite of the existence of serious problems and needs, U.G. is Guyana's premier educational agency. It is a national institution of incalculable value to the country. Its graduates continue to play leading roles in every facet of national life, making a major contribution especially to political, economic, social and cultural development.

For Further Reading

Menezes, Mary	"A Brief History of the University of Guyana" in Menezes, Sr. Mary, **Guyana and the Wider World** (Georgetown: Guyenterprise, 2017), 39-40.
The University of Guyana Guild of Graduates	**The University of Guyana. Perspectives on the Early History** (Toronto, Ontario, Canada: The University of Guyana Guild of Graduates, 2002).

Chapter 39

Walter Rodney and the University Of Guyana

One of the most shameful and most damaging events in the University of Guyana's 50 years of history was the unjust denial of a teaching position to Walter Rodney, one of the Caribbean's most distinguished historians and one of the most renowned Guyanese scholars of all time. Rodney was born in Georgetown in March 1942 of humble parentage and his influential life came to an end in June 1980 at the relatively young age of thirty-eight when he was, in the opinion of this writer, assassinated in a car in a street there by means of a remotely detonated bomb disguised as a walkie-talkie. At that time Rodney was in the prime of his life both as a scholar and a political and social activist. His regrettable death is one of the most tragic and shameful events in the modern history of Guyana and is remembered each year in June by many Guyanese with profound sorrow.

Ironically in August 2005 the University of Guyana hosted a special event honouring Rodney. This event was a two-day conference designed to celebrate and evaluate his life and work. It was a collaborative effort between the University and the Faculty of Humanities and Education of the St. Augustine Campus of the University of the West Indies in Trinidad. It was one of many commemorative events staged in the Caribbean, Europe, North America and Africa that year to mark the 25th anniversary of his tragic demise. Its striking theme was "Walter Rodney Twenty Five Years Later: Facing the Challenges of History, Poverty, Underdevelopment and Globalisation."

Rodney's considerable academic ability first came to prominence between 1953 and 1960 when he was a student of Queen's College, the country's top secondary school. There he not only enjoyed academic success but also demonstrated athletic prowess in the field of high jumping, and brilliance as a debater. He culminated this phase of his life in 1960 by winning one of the seven prestigious University College of the West Indies (UCWI) Open

Scholarships, for which students throughout the Caribbean competed to enable them to pursue studies at that institution, which at that time was an external college of the University of London in England.

In 1963 Rodney graduated from UCWI in Jamaica with a first-class Bachelor of Arts Honours Degree in History. That impressive performance enabled him to win a UCWI external postgraduate scholarship which he used to pursue studies in African History in London, England at the famous School of Oriental and African Studies (SOAS), the college of the University of London which specialized in African studies. Three years later in 1966 the university conferred on him a Doctorate Degree in African History. The local press in newly politically independent Guyana acclaimed this achievement, honouring him as the youngest Guyanese ever to attain a PhD. Degree. Rodney was then only 24 years old.

At the completion of his postgraduate studies Rodney's primary ambition was to return to the Caribbean to introduce the teaching of African History initially at his alma mater in Jamaica. Before doing that, however, he felt that it was imperative to visit Africa to obtain first-hand knowledge and experience of the continent which would be the subject of his teaching. Consequently, as soon as he completed his PhD. Degree in London, he proceeded to Tanzania in East Africa in July 1966 to take up a teaching position in the Department of History of the University College of Dar es Salaam.

Rodney remained there for nineteen months until February 1968 when he accepted a similar post in Jamaica in the Department of History of the Mona campus of what had by then become the independent University of the West Indies (U.W.I.). While there, in addition to his university teaching, he became actively involved with the poor of urban Kingston. He instructed them about Africa, learnt about their grave socio-economic problems, and sought to help them find a solution to their terrible plight. He received an overwhelming response from them.

This enthusiastic response from the urban poor disturbed the Jamaican government, then under the leadership of Hugh Shearer. Consequently, in October 1968, only eight months after joining the U.W.I staff, while Rodney was abroad attending the Congress of Black Writers in Montreal, Canada, the ruling Jamaica Labour Party banned him from Jamaica, thus preventing his return to the island. The government's action provoked massive protest demonstrations in Kingston and a parliamentary crisis for the government and the ruling party.

It was these circumstances which created the first clear link between Rodney and the University of Guyana, founded five years before in 1963 during his undergraduate career at U.C.W.I. U.G. staff and students made headlines in the local press when for the first time they demonstrated a united front and joined with members of the public in staging a protest march to the residence of Prime Minister Forbes Burnham to voice their strong objection to Rodney's debarment from Jamaica. The response of the Guyana government, led by Burnham, to the banning of Rodney and three other Guyanese, Colin Moore and Harold and Kathleen Drayton, previously from Jamaica as undesirables was defensive and somewhat evasive. The government contended that it would be improper to criticise, or interfere with, a decision taken by another sovereign country.

Rodney was a patriot who had always looked forward to making a contribution to the development of his fledgling national university. His ban from Jamaica provided the first opportunity, little known and hardly remembered, for him to join the staff at U.G. A few days after the ban the University of Guyana's Staff Association proposed to the University's Board of Governors that "as soon a vacancy occurs that the Board of Governors makes an immediate offer of appointment to Dr. Walter Rodney, to be taken up by him as soon as he may be available."[160] The motion, however, was defeated, with Anson Sancho and Winston Verbeke apparently playing leading roles in its rejection.

Rodney, banned from Jamaica, returned to teach at the University of Dar es Salaam, where he remained until 1974. It was in these years that he made his first concrete links with the University of Guyana through two developments in 1970. Firstly, he acceded to a request from U.G.'s Department of History to serve as the external examiner for a newly introduced course on the history of West Africa initiated by Alvin Thompson, a former classmate of Rodney at Queen's College and a contemporary during his tertiary career at U.W.I. and S.O.A.S.

Secondly, Rodney also accepted an invitation from the History Department to deliver a series of special lectures at Turkeyen. These "guest lectures" were given in May 1970 on the theme, "An Examination of the Confrontation of West Africans and Europeans from the Beginning to the Present." They were simulating and informative and were well-received. He examined the evolving relationship between Europeans and the people of West Africa from the 1440s when the first Europeans, the Portuguese, began to visit that section of the African continent. He discussed the nature and impact of the European presence in West Africa through successive historical phases. These phases included the era of the transatlantic trade in captive Africans which lasted until the 1860s, the age of the European conquest and partition of Africa in the late nineteenth century, the period of classic colonial rule in the first half of the twentieth century, the age of decolonisation in the 1950s and 1960s and the subsequent era of neo-colonisation after formal political independence was achieved from Britain and France.

Some of the issues which Rodney addressed in these lectures were examined at greater length and in more depth in a book which he was preparing at the time. This book was published two years later in 1972 with the title **How Europe Underdeveloped Africa**. With its appearance Rodney was keen to return to his homeland to live and work. He applied to the University of Guyana for a teaching position that very year, and was disappointed to receive a response informing him that there was no vacancy then in the Department of History.

Rodney remained two more years in Tanzania. Early in 1974 he decided that he would return to Guyana to reside whether or not there was a vacancy at U.G. Therefore he did not renew his contract with the University of Dar es Salaam which was due to expire in July 1974. Shortly afterwards, in March 1974, Rodney saw an advertisement by the University of Guyana for a new post of Professor of History and immediately dispatched an application. His application was acknowledged by the University's administration. He did not receive any further official communication from the university until a terse letter, dated August 23, 1974, informed him that he had not been selected for the post. By then he had learnt that his application had been unanimously approved by the institution's properly constituted Appointments Committee, but the Committee's decision had been revoked by the government-dominated Board of Governors. This matter immediately became a subject of great controversy and catapulted Walter Rodney from relative obscurity in Guyana into national prominence.

For several reasons the rescinding of the decision to appoint Rodney to the U.G. teaching staff came as a surprise to many members of the academic community and other informed Guyanese who regarded it as strange and unjust. Firstly, Rodney was eminently qualified academically for the position. By 1974 he was already one of the Caribbean's most renowned historians and arguably Guyana's most internationally acclaimed scholar, especially in the wake of the publication in 1972 of **How Europe Underdeveloped**

Africa, his most famous and most influential work.

Secondly, Rodney was the only applicant for the advertised position of professor and already was serving the university creditably for three years as the external examiner for its course on West African history. He was expected to assume responsibility for this course as well as to teach another course which the Department of History was planning to introduce on the history of revolutionary change in the world since the eighteenth century.

Thirdly, the denial of employment to Rodney at U.G. seemed contradictory to several of the claims and avowed policies of the ruling P.N.C. regime. For example, it occurred at a time when the regime was encouraging, in fact urging, skilled Guyanese resident overseas to return home and assist in national development. It also seemed ideologically incongruous that a self-styled socialist government which claimed to be committed to African liberation would deny a job at its national university to one of the most influential socialist and African scholars who was a strong advocate of African liberation.

Finally, the process involved in denying Rodney a job at U.G. was very unusual. Particularly strange and unacceptable was the vulgar attempt by the government-controlled Board of Governors to make the Appointments Committee change its principled decision to offer the position to Rodney. That unsuccessful attempt failed for the simple reason that there were no valid reasons which could have been or were advanced to warrant such action. Faced with the resolute stand of the Committee, the Board of Governors rescinded, revoked or reversed the Committee's decision to appoint Rodney.

Initially the Board of Governors did not offer any public or official explanation for its unusual action. It was abundantly clear, however, that the reasons for the denial of employment to Rodney were political, not academic. This was a flagrant violation of the university's statutes and the nation's constitution. The U.G. Statutes, for example, state unambiguously that

> no religious, political or social test should be imposed on or required of any person in order to entitle him to be a student or member of the University, or to occupy any position in or on the staff of the University.[161]

In short, as Dr. Clive Thomas, the university's most renowned academic who was abroad at the time, rightly pointed out in an "Open Letter to the Vice Chancellor, the Staff and Students" of U.G., the Board of Governors had assumed "powers greater than those given to it by the Ordinances and Statutes of the University" and had "acted outside of the powers of its own enabling legislation."[162]

In retrospect, the decision of the government-dominated Board of Governors to deny Rodney a job at the university should perhaps not have been so surprising. It took place at a time in the history of Guyana when the ruling P.N.C. regime was seeking actively to exercise dominant control over the nation and in the process was deliberately and arbitrarily transforming the political character of the Guyanese state into an autocracy, which Rodney later would dub "the Burnham dictatorship."

Where the University of Guyana was concerned, the P.N.C. regime sought initially to establish paramountcy and control by at least two main means. These methods were firstly by determining the composition of the teaching staff by influencing appointments and the renewal of contracts and, secondly, by harassing dissenting academics. Later the regime devised a third major strategy, namely, that of determining the executive of the U.G. Students Society by manipulating the Society's annual elections.

In short, by the mid 1970s there was growing evidence of the government's interference in the university to stifle dissent and independent thought and expression and to restrict the institution's autonomy. Among the signs of this overt political interference was the Board of Governors' refusal to approve the renewal of the contracts of two lecturers, Kathleen Drayton and Mohamed Insanally. Though requested specifically for the reasons for its action, the Board proffered none in the case of Drayton and in that of Insanally gave the vague reason that his presence on the staff was "bad for the image of the University."[163]

The explanation that the government spokesman on the Board of Governors eventually gave for its refusal to grant a job to Rodney was that he was "a security risk", implying that he was a threat to national security. Often in the developing world, however, the term, "security risk"[164] was employed consciously by ruling regimes to refer to individuals, especially critics or potential opponents, whom they conceived to be a threat to their continued possession of political power.

This was particularly the case in Guyana in the early 1970s. The ruling P.N.C. regime felt insecure especially in the wake of Black Power disturbances in Trinidad which unsettled Eric Williams' People's National Movement government. The sense of insecurity was rendered greater by the P.N.C.'s awareness that it was enjoying political power as a result of blatantly rigged elections in 1968 and 1973.

Rodney could not by any objective criteria been deemed a risk or threat to the security of Guyana. Some leading P.N.C. politicians, however, had the foresight and astuteness to perceive and anticipate that he might be or become a threat to their continued safe, but illegitimate, enjoyment of political power. It was therefore in their interest to have him excluded from the university and hopefully the country. The hope or expectation was that Rodney, unemployed and unemployable, might migrate as Drayton had done and Insanally would eventually do. The move, however, backfired. Rodney, though unemployed, refused to migrate as intended and expected, declaring that he would not be exiled from his own country. Instead, he lectured abroad periodically at prestigious universities and other institutions in Europe and North America to be able to provide a livelihood for himself and his family, but spent most of the remainder of the time residing in Guyana until his death in June 1980.

In this period from 1974 to 1980 Rodney continued to do valuable historical research. His distance from, and limited accessibility to, documentary sources on African History prompted him to shift the focus of his research to a large extent from Africa to Guyana. He was able in these years to produce three major pieces of research.

The first was a lengthy paper on "Barbadian Immigration into British Guiana, 1863-1924," which was presented at the ninth annual Conference of Caribbean Historians in Barbados in April 1977. Secondly, he produced a text entitled **Guyanese Sugar Plantations in the Late Nineteenth Century,** published locally in 1979. This work consisted of a reproduction of a description of sugar estates in British Guiana which had appeared in issues of the **Argosy** newspaper between February and September 1883. It was edited and introduced by Rodney. The most important of the three works was an authoritative monograph entitled **The History of the Guyanese Working People 1881-1905**, published by The Johns Hopkins University Press in Baltimore in Maryland in the United States of America in 1981, a year after his death.

The denial to Rodney of a teaching position at the University of Guyana by the ruling P.N.C. regime left him with a considerable amount of time not only to undertake historical research and writing but also to participate in local politics. He became increasingly involved in the activities of the various forces that eventually coalesced to form the Working People's Alliance (W.P.A), originally an organised pressure group, in 1975. This orgainsation, of which he was a founder and co-leader, finally declared itself a full-fledged political party in 1979.

By 1980, the year of his death, Rodney had grown considerably in political stature and was becoming an increasingly popular political figure. By then he had become the W.P.A.'s leading spokesman and its popularly acclaimed leader, although the party and he continued to stress that its leadership was collective with a rotating chairman. By 1980 also, Rodney was being regarded as their spokesman by a growing number of Guyanese, exasperated by the deteriorating conditions of life which the country experienced in the latter half of the of 1970s. This decline had resulted in Guyana, which in the early 1970s was one of the most progressive and prosperous countries in the Caribbean, being relegated to the position of being the poorest nation in the entire region, with the exception of Haiti, by the end of the decade. By then Rodney had become the non-elected spokesman or representative for countless Guyanese who were adversely affected by this disastrous change but who were fearful of expressing publicly their discontent with a ruling regime that employed intimidation, coercion and victimisation to keep its suffering subjects in submission.

Rodney believed that the cause of, and cure for, Guyana's increasingly terrible plight were complex. In his opinion one of the fundamental reasons for it was the marked lack of democracy in Guyana, witnessed not only in recurrent fraudulent national elections since 1968, but also in the growing authoritarianism of the ruling P.N.C. regime which he dubbed "the Burnham dictatorship." His analysis of the situation led him to conclude that one of the most vital preconditions for the cure of the country's growing ills was the removal of the illegitimate dictatorship from power.

He advocated strongly a change of government that would bring to power a democratic regime that would be more seriously and sincerely committed to the welfare of the country, especially to the interests of ordinary people, than the P.N.C. and would pursue non-racist politics. He became famous for his clarion call, "People's Power, No Dictator".

In short, by 1980 Walter Rodney had become not only the most bold, strident and persuasive spokesman of the local political opposition and many other dissatisfied Guyanese, but also the one most feared by those enjoying, and apparently bent on retaining, by any means, political power.

And so on June 13 of that very year they killed him. At the time he was still unemployed by the University of Guyana and for a growing number of Guyanese the brightest or the only hope on the political horizon.

The matter of Rodney's appointment at U.G. dragged on for several years. Notwithstanding protests, representations, overtures, appeals and negotiations from a wide range of groups within and outside Guyana, the university's Board of Governors maintained its unjust decision to deny him a job at the university. Leading P.N.C. politicians on the Board, notably Minister Hamilton Green, played a pivotal role in the saga. This was not surprising. The U.G. academic community, however, was somewhat surprised and very disappointed by the prominent role played by one of Rodney's former schoolmates and undergraduate colleagues, leading to the conclusion that he had become or was becoming more of a politician than a scholar. In general, it was disappointing that none of the government appointees on the Board had the independence or courage to support Rodney's appointment, although it seemed evident that at least some of them believed that the denial of a job to him was unjust. This sacrifice of justice on the altar of personal expediency lost these members of the Board the respect of the academic community.

The refusal to appoint the internationally renowned scholar to the staff of the struggling fledgling national university because of the fears and narrow-mindedness of the insecure regime which then ruled the country had momentous consequences for him, the institution, the government and the nation. Those responsible for this travesty of justice owe the university and the nation a profound apology. They also must accept some of the responsibility for the degeneration of the university, which was one of the consequences of their action. Part of the incalculable damage which their unwarranted short-sighted act did to the university was that it injured the institution's image locally and internationally and dissuaded many academics and institutions from rendering much-needed service to the university.

For Further Reading

Lewis, Rupert	**Walter Rodney's Intellectual and Political Thought** (Kingston: The University of the West Indies Press, 1998).
Mc Gowan, Winston	"Remembering Walter Rodney", **The Journal of Caribbean History,** Vol. 39:2, 2005.

CHAPTER 40

WALTER RODNEY THE HISTORIAN

June 2005 may go down in Guyanese History as the time when the nation celebrated in a special way the life of Walter Rodney, one of its most outstanding sons. Twenty- five years after his assassination on June 13, 1980, Rodney was remembered in Guyana and abroad with a degree of honour and appreciation seldom or never extended to any other Guyanese, including past presidents. It is ironic that those, dead or alive, who were responsible for denying him a job at the national university in the 1970s and for his death in 1980 are today either completely or virtually forgotten, or are held in much less esteem than this scholar and political and social activist.

Because of his active involvement in local politics in the final years of his life, many Guyanese remember Rodney primarily or exclusively as a politician. However, throughout most of his adult life his principal accomplishments were realised in his capacity as an historian, researching, writing and teaching the history especially of two areas, namely, Africa and the Caribbean.

The June 5, 2005 edition of the **Stabroek News** newspaper contained an instructive account by Dr. Robert Moore, one of Rodney's early mentors, of the beginning of the formative period in his development as an historian. This was in the middle years of his secondary school career at Queen's College, his country's leading secondary institution, where Dr. Moore transformed History from being a somewhat boring subject into one of the most absorbing and enjoyable offerings on the school curriculum. Dr. Moore's impact was instrumental in making at least two other of Rodney's classmates at Queen's (Professor Alvin Thompson and myself) opt to pursue the study of history as a career. Rodney was also influenced immensely several years later by Elsa Goveia, another distinguished Guyanese historian and the first female Professor at the University College of the West Indies in Jamaica, who taught him during his brilliant undergraduate career there between 1960 and 1963. Rodney eventually became not only one of the Caribbean's most outstanding historians, but also one of the most renowned and internationally acclaimed Guyanese scholars of all time.

This enviable reputation stemmed largely from the nature, quality and quantity of his historical writing. By Caribbean standards Rodney was a very prolific writer. Thus in his comparatively short academic career, which ended prematurely at the relatively young age of thirty-eight, he produced three major books, one edited work on Guyanese sugar plantations in the late nineteenth century, several pamphlets and booklets and over seventy articles in academic and other journals. His acclaim as a historian was due mainly to two somewhat related factors, namely, his approach to History and the distinctive traits of his scholarship.

Rodney was essentially a revisionist historian, that is, an historian who sought to correct false or deficient statements, ideas and interpretations about historical events. One of his major specific objectives was, in his own words, "to uproot the numerous historical myths which have been implanted in the minds of black people".[165] He considered such myths, born of prejudice, ignorance, loss of memory and other factors, as *formidable* obstacles to the realization of urgently needed socio-economic change in Africa and the Caribbean. In his view mental liberation as a result of the acquisition of true historical knowledge was an indispensable, though not the only, precondition for the Black man's total liberation.

Rodney regarded History as a *multi-disciplinary* subject. His historical writing profited from approaches and insights which he derived from the social sciences, especially his knowledge of Economics and Political Science. He also viewed History as didactic, providing guidelines for the proper understanding and solution of current problems. Thus he sought to show that many of the serious problems, such as poverty, underdevelopment and dependency, facing Africa today are the result of immense damage which the continent suffered during the long era of the notorious transatlantic trade in captive Africans and the much shorter period of European colonial rule. This was the focus of his second major publication and best-known and most influential book, **How Europe Underdeveloped Africa,** written during his second period of residence in Tanzania after his return there following his ban from Jamaica in 1968. The work stemmed from what he described as "a concern with the contemporary African situation".[166] In it he not only sought to give a historical explanation for current African underdevelopment, but also to present what he called "a correct historical solution".[167]

His conclusion was that "African development is possible only on the basis of a radical break with the capitalist system, which has been the principal agency of underdevelopment of Africa over the past five centuries".[168] This proposed solution was partly a reflection of the fact that Rodney's philosophy of History was essentially Marxist. His Marxist orientation caused him to be preoccupied with questions of class and economy and to devote inadequate attention to cultural history. It also prompted the strong anti-capitalist and anti-imperialist character of his writings, expressed in his graphic description of colonialism as "a one-armed bandit".[169]

Rodney's scholarship was marked by an approach that academics sometimes describe as "history from below", that is, history written from the perspective, and often for the benefit, of the disadvantaged or dispossessed. In some contexts this expression means history written from the viewpoint of the largely poor and non-white developing world, including Africa and the Caribbean, rather than from the standpoint of the wealthy white developed world, especially of Europe and North America. The approach is clearly evident in **How Europe Underdeveloped Africa**.

In other circumstances, "history from below" means history from the perspective of the working class, the masses, the ordinary people in the society, the poor and the powerless, rather than from that of the more privileged middle and ruling classes. This approach is particularly evident in Rodney's final book, **The History of the Guyanese Working People, 1881 – 1905**, published posthumously in 1981 and, from the standpoint of the historian's craft, probably his finest work, though not as famous or influential as **How Europe Underdeveloped Africa**.

Rodney's historical writing is well-known for its many distinctive traits. It was very diverse in content as well as character. Most of his publications were academic, while some, such as **The Groundings with My Brothers**, which focused on his experiences in Jamaica in 1968, were polemical. Furthermore, many of them were localised, dealing with specific issues in African and Caribbean history, whereas others were global in perspective, addressing more universal themes, such as the history of capitalism, socialism, colonialism, neo-colonialism, pan-Africanism and Third World dependency and underdevelopment.

Rodney's works were generally marked by a great degree of dependence on original independent research. He seldom produced works of synthesis, based largely on the findings of other scholars. Rather his work was often pioneering and creative. He was always seeking to break new ground. He was a prominent member of the vanguard of a new genre of scholars who in the 1960s and 1970s began to write African history from a new perspective, reconstructing it, exposing and dispelling existing myths and misconceptions and correcting its hitherto Eurocentric character. His work was usually distinguished also by clarity of thought, convincing logic, rigorous analysis of the ideas or events he was examining, and a concise, effective literary style. These traits were partly a result of the perceptive, critical, analytic mind he possessed and were pivotal to his achievements.

Among Rodney's achievements as a historian five stand out. The first was through his doctoral thesis and his first major book, **A History of the Upper Guinea Coast, 1545 – 1800**, which was published by Oxford University Press in 1970. In it he presented a skilful reconstruction of the history of the first area in West Africa to be settled by Europeans and a penetrating analysis of the organisation of the transatlantic trade in captive Africans from Africa to the Americas and its detrimental effects on West Africa. Through this work he established himself as one of the leading authorities in the world on this important subject and his book became the starting point or standard of reference for most subsequent studies on the trade.

Secondly, as noted above, he produced **How Europe Underdeveloped Africa**, the first major study of the current underdevelopment of Africa, examining in depth its historical roots, attributing it largely to the negative political, economic and social consequences of the transatlantic slave trade and European colonial rule. Thirdly, his final major publication was the first authoritative, detailed, systematical historical study of the working class anywhere in the Caribbean, especially written from the perspective of that class. It made a major contribution to the knowledge of the history of the working class and racial division in Guyana.

Fourthly, in the last years of his life Rodney began to make a unique contribution to the historiography of Guyana which was unusual for a professional historian, especially one of his stature, accustomed to function at university level and to write almost invariably for an adult readership. That contribution was in the form of illustrated histories written specifically for children. He planned to produce a series of such books telling the story of each of the various racial groups which constitute the population of Guyana. The books were designed to enable Guyanese, especially children, to understand the origins, history, role and culture of all the country's ethnic groups and to have respect for all of them. His ultimate purpose and hope was that the books would contribute to multi-racial understanding, harmony and unity, an urgent national need.

The first of the series, Kofi Baadu, **Out of Africa**, was at the printer when Rodney was assassinated in 1980 and appeared a year later. The second book, **Lakshmi: Out of India** was printed in 2000 on the twentieth anniversary of his death. At the time of his death he had completed some of the work on three other books in the series which he planned to complete by writing the story of the indigenous Amerindians. Understandably none of these four proposed works, however, ever appeared.

Fifthly, Rodney's work won him many prestigious prizes and other honours. For example, his final major publication, **A History of the Guyanese Working People, 1881 – 1905** won him at least two such awards posthumously. Firstly, in 1982 the American Historical Association awarded him the Albert J. Beveridge Prize. Secondly, in the following year, 1983, the book became the first winner of the much- coveted Elsa Goveia Memorial Prize, awarded by the Association of Caribbean Historians for the most outstanding work on Caribbean history published every triennium. Furthermore, Rodney was invited to be a contributor to two prestigious projects designed to produce a multivolume history of Africa, one organised by UNESCO and the other by Cambridge University in the United Kingdom. He wrote chapters for both of these projects.

Any evaluation of Walter Rodney's work as an historian must emphasise that he was not an "Ivory tower" historian. His philosophy of history compelled him to be both a scholar and a social reformer. He believed strongly that teaching, research and writing should be accompanied by serious social involvement – that historical knowledge should be put to beneficial practical social use. His work on the history of Guyana went hand in hand with his political and social activism. He used his knowledge of Guyanese history to better understand the grave contemporary problems of his beloved native land and to help in finding solutions for them.

It is this aspect of Rodney's work as a historian which is emphasised in the tribute given in his honour at the time of his death by the International Scientific Committee responsible for organising the UNESCO General History of Africa. In its memorial the committee stated:

In evaluating Walter Rodney one characteristic

stands out. He was a scholar who recognised no distinction between academic concerns and service to society, between science and social commitment. He was concerned about people as well as the classroom. He found time to be both a historian and a sensitive social reformer.[170]

For Further Reading

Hill, Robert (ed.)	**Walter Rodney Speaks** (Trenton: Africa World Press, 1990).
Lewis, Rupert	**Walter Rodney's Intellectual and Political Thought** (Kingston: The University of the West Indies Press, 1998).
Mc Gowan Winston	"Walter Rodney The Historian", **The Journal of Caribbean History**, Vol. 39:2, 2005.
Anon.	"Bibliography of Works by Walter Rodney", **Ibid**.
Mc Gowan Winston	**Walter Rodney The Historian**, (Turkeyen: Department of Social Studies, 2006).

CHAPTER 41

GRADUATE STUDIES IN HISTORY AT THE UNIVERSITY OF GUYANA

Since 1973 the Department of History of the University of Guyana has been offering a Master of Arts Degree Programme in Guyanese and West Indian History, the first graduate programme to be introduced in the institution. The introduction of the programme was due largely to the vision, initiative and organising ability of Dr. Mary Noel Menezes, a senior member of staff. Dr. Menezes was mainly responsible for the programme until her retirement from the university in 1990. The M.A. Degree in History is awarded to candidates on the basis of the satisfactory completion of two courses and a thesis.

The two required courses are entitled "Comparative Guyanese and West Indian History" and "Techniques of Assessing, Evaluating and Analysing Historical Documents". The former investigates in a comparative manner the major historical events in Guyanese and British West Indian history in the nineteenth and twentieth centuries. The latter course not only focuses on the techniques of analysing historical sources, but also embodies a more thorough study of research techniques in general.

On completion of these two courses, normally taken in the first year, students proceed to the second and much more challenging part of the programme, namely, original research largely on primary sources in local archives and libraries with a view to producing a thesis of about 30,000 words on some facet of Guyanese history. Students, who for the most part are part-time evening students, are given a maximum of five years to complete and submit their thesis. During this period before submission they are required to present four papers to be read and discussed at periodic postgraduate seminars. These seminar papers are invariably preliminary drafts of a part of their proposed thesis or a more thorough investigation of an aspect of their research which will appear in a much more concise or limited form in the thesis submitted.

The following is a list of the theses already completed, submitted and approved and the year of acceptance or approval;

ADAMS, Estherine	Sydney King [Eusi Kwayana] and National politics in British Guiana, 1950 – 1961 (2012).
AZEEZ, James	The Apprenticeship System in British Guiana, 1834 – 1838 (1979).
CHANDERBALI, David	Sir Henry Light: A Study in Protection and Paternalism (1977).
CHASE, Marguerite	The Development of a System of Primary Education in British Guiana, 1833 – 1857 (1977).
DRAKES, Francis (now NEHUSI, Kimani)	The 1905 Protest in British Guiana: Causes, Course and Consequences (1981).
GEORGE, Gwyneth	The Development of the Road Network in Guyana up to 1978 (2001).
GRAVESANDE, Nigel	The Question of Spanish and Dutch Occupation in the Venezuela – Guyana Boundary Dispute (1981).
JOSEPH, Shammane	History of the British Guiana Railway: Georgetown to Mahaica, 1837 – 1972 (2012).
KARTICK, Reuben	The Administration of Francis Hincks as Governor of British Guiana, 1862 – 1869 (1979).
LANCASTER, Alan	An Unconquered Wilderness: A Historical Analysis of the Failure to Open up the Interior of British Guiana, 1838 – 1919 (1977).

MANGAR, Tota	The Administration of Sir Henry Turner Irving as Governor of British Guiana, 1882 – 1887. A Study in Astuteness and Resoluteness (1987).
MANGRU, Basdeo	Imperial Trusteeship in British Guiana with Special Reference to the East Indian Indentured Immigrants 1838 – 1882. Myth or Reality? (1976).
MANGRU, Simon	The Role of the Anglican Church in Christianising the East Indians in British Guiana, 1838 – 1898 (1977).
Mc CALMONT, Cecelia	The Honourable Peter Rose: A Study in Opposition (1979).
MOHAMED, Khaleel	Planter Patronage and Creole Response to Portuguese Immigrants in British Guiana, 1835 – 1856 (1977).
MUNRO, Arlene	The Administration of Sir Gordon Lethem: selected issues 1941 – 1946 (1995).
PIERRE, Laureen	Stephen Campbell, First Amerindian national politician of British Guiana, 1957 – 1966 (1993).
ROSE, James	The Plight of the British Guiana Creoles, 1838 – 1873: A Study of Antagonistic Class Relations (1981).
SIMMONS, Terrence	An appraisal of the economic conditions of a colony during World War 1 : British Guiana, 1914 – 1918 (1996).
WILLIAMS, Denis	The Aishalton Petroglyph Complex in the Prehistory of the Rupununi Savannahs (1980).

WOOLFORD, Hazel   The Press and the Compulsory Denominational Education Bill of 1876 (1985).

These 21 theses have served to enhance greatly our knowledge of Guyanese history, especially our understanding of the post – Emancipation period of the nineteenth century. Their number would have been greater had it not been for the outward migration of several students who in some cases were in the advanced stage of thesis preparation.

For Further Reading

Anon.   "Graduate Studies in History at the University of Guyana", **Guyana Historical Journal**, Volume 1, 1989.

CHAPTER 42

THE UNIVERSITY OF GUYANA HISTORY SOCIETY

One of the most influential student bodies in the history of the University of Guyana is its History Society which was founded in October 1988 twenty five years after the establishment of the university in 1963. Its foundation was due largely to the vision, initiative, industry and organising ability of David Granger, the current leader of the political opposition in Guyana, who was at that time a second-year student pursuing studies leading to the acquisition of a Bachelor of Arts Degree in History.

Granger persuaded his fellow undergraduates majoring in History to form themselves into an organisation called "The History Society", run by an executive committee consisting of students with advice from a board of three Trustees chosen from senior members of staff of the Department of History. The Society was established as "a non-profit educational organisation for diffusing historical knowledge".[171]

At that time, as now, there were hardly any student societies on the U.G. Campus organised for academic or other intellectual purposes. From its inception the History Society proved to be a very dynamic organisation. It arranged an active programme of monthly lectures and symposia on the U.G. Campus on subjects of historical significance which brought a new and welcome stimulus to extra-curricular life at Turkeyen. Such activities, of course, are normal for students on university campuses around the world. The U.G. History Society, however, soon began to be involved in another kind of enterprise which is rare among university student clubs and was unique at Turkeyen.

At its inaugural meeting in October 1988 the society took a decision to embark on a policy of regular publications "to disseminate data of historical interest to members, staff, other students and, if necessary, to libraries". Shortly afterwards, the society decided to seek realise this objective by producing a monthly publication called the **History Gazette**. To those who were aware of the immense difficulties then of maintaining a regular publication in Guyana, this decision seemed not only courageous, but also overambitious to the extent of being almost foolhardy.

The Society, however, managed to maintain the publication for seven years, though sometimes not on schedule owing to administrative, technical or financial problems. So far 76 issues of the **Gazette** have appeared. This is a remarkable achievement for a society in a Third-World university, especially one located in a country adversely affected by serious economic and other difficulties.

The **History Gazette** normally consists of a previously unpublished essay on a subject of historical importance, especially to Guyanese. From the inception its main purpose was declared to be "to provide a forum for the presentation of ideas and information of interest principally to teachers and students of history".[172]

The first issue of the **Gazett**e appeared in October 1988. It consisted of the text of a brilliant address delivered by Dr. Ali Mazrui, an African scholar who was at the time Professor of Political Science, Afro-American and African Studies at the University of Michigan in the United States of America. This address, entitled "Collective Martyrdom In Modern History", was given in July 1988 at the opening session of the Second International Conference on the Genesis of the Guyanese Nation at the National Cultural Centre in Georgetown.

Twenty of the seventy six issues of the **Gazette** which have appeared present the work of scholars, mostly Guyanese, who are resident overseas and are conducting research on Guyanese history or a closely related field. These scholars include Percy Hintzen, Basdeo Mangru, Perry Mars, Kimani Nehusi (formerly Francis Drakes), Lesley Potter and Roberta Walker-Kilkenny. Another twenty odd issues consist of essays by historians resident in Guyana, mostly members of staff of the Department of History of the University of Guyana. The remaining thirty three issues comprise seminar papers or thesis chapters produced by students enrolled since 1973 in the Department's M.A. Degree programme in Guyanese and West Indian History, the first graduate programme introduced at the University of Guyana. In short, this final category, i.e. essays by postgraduate students, constitutes the largest group of **Gazettes**.

All but two of the seventy six issues of the **Gazette** focus on some facet of Guyanese history.[173] The two exceptions were the first issue mentioned above and the third issue. The latter examined the resistance showed by individual Africans and African states to the transatlantic slave trade, the forced migration of millions of Africans from West, Central and East Africa to the Americas from the fifteenth to the nineteenth century.

The other seventy four **Gazettes** address a wide range of important themes in the political, economic, social, cultural, and ethnographic history of Guyana. They constitute a significant addition to the comparatively limited historical literature on Guyana, greatly increasing the body of knowledge on the history of Guyana especially in the nineteenth and twentieth centuries.

Admittedly, only a few of the **Gazettes** deal with Guyanese history in the less known seventeenth and eighteenth centuries and only one issue relates to the even less explored prehistoric or preliterate period when the Guiana region was occupied exclusively by Amerindians. This solitary publication on this ancient period is the seventh issue, entitled "The Archaic of North – Western Guyana" and produced by the late well-known local archaeologist, Denis Williams.

The five issues of the **Gazette** which deal with developments in the seventeenth and eighteenth centuries focus on three themes: firstly, Amerindian jurisdiction in the Guiana region in this period (No. 44), the British occupation of Demerara-Essequibo in 1796 and the early years of British rule of these territories (No.55); and, thirdly, African resistance to slavery in Demerara – Essequibo and Berbice, especially the activities of runaway slaves and Maroons and the famous 1763 Berbice slave uprising (Nos. 4, 29 and 30).

Sixty-eight of the seventy-six issues of the **Gazette** deal with the history of Guyana in the nineteenth and twentieth centuries. This concentration on these two centuries to the virtual neglect of the earlier period has been due mainly to two factors, namely, the limited amount of archaeological work conducted in Guyana and the lack of competence of most historians in Dutch, the language of most of the documentation relating to the seventeenth and eighteenth centuries when Essequibo, Berbice and later Demerara were Dutch colonial possessions.

The **Gazettes** enhance our knowledge and understanding of many of the major developments in Guyana in the nineteenth and twentieth centuries. A few of them deal with certain aspects of the important question of slavery, such as slave society in Berbice in the early decades of the nineteenth century (No. 45), the initial Christianisation of the slaves (No. 24), resistance by runaway slaves and Maroons (No. 5), and the compensation granted to slaveholders for the loss of their slave property at the legal abolition of slavery in 1834 (No. 12). One issue focuses on the period of apprenticeship after August 1, 1834 which preceded the full emancipation of the slaves in August 1838 (No. 2).

Greater attention, however, is given by the **Gazettes** to the Post-Emancipation decades of the nineteenth century than to the period between 1800 and 1838, beginning with the difficulties faced by the ex-slaves as workers and villagers. Thus issues of the **Gazette** deal with the little-known general strikes of 1842 and 1848 (Nos. 13 and 23), the new taxation policy introduced after 1838 (No. 38), the power exercised by the planter class in the decades immediately after 1838 (No. 10), and the village policy of Francis Hincks, governor of British Guiana between 1862 and 1869 (No. 32).

Understandably, many Gazettes are devoted to the examination of immigration by Portuguese (No. 60), Chinese (No. 6), Africans (No.31), and especially East Indians after the abolition of slavery, as the planters sought to find a substitute labour force to replace ex-slaves who had abandoned the plantations at the grant of full freedom in 1838. For example, twelve **Gazettes** address various aspects of East Indian immigrantion and indentureship between 1838 and 1917, including the structure and evolution of the indenture system (No. 5), resistance and insurgency by sugar workers (Nos. 8 and 15), rice cultivation (No. 47), the voyage from India to British Guiana (No. 28), the Madrasis (No. 16), imperial trusteeship (No. 33), village settlement and relations with Africans (No. 48), and Christianisation (Nos. 57 and 61).

Three other major themes are given considerable examination in the **Gazettes**. One of them is education in the nineteenth century, especially the development of primary education between the beginning of the apprenticeship period in 1834 and the introduction of compulsory primary education in 1876 (Nos. 9, 39, 62 and 63). Secondly, much attention has been devoted to the struggles of the working class in the twentieth century. In particular, the **Gazettes** provide very informative accounts of major working-class protests in 1905 (Nos. 22 and 37) and 1924 (Nos. 67 and 68) in Georgetown, in 1939 at Leonora (No. 46) and in 1948 at Enmore (No. 69).

The third area of knowledge to which the **Gazettes** have made a major contribution is constitutional and other political developments in the late nineteenth century and the twentieth century. These developments include the constitutional changes of 1891 (No. 40), the work of the People's

Association (No.36), the involvement of women in social and political struggle from the 1946 to 1953 (No. 49), constitutional changes during the Second World War (No. 50), perceptions of the People's Progressive Party in 1953 (No. 72), the suspension of the constitution in 1953 (Nos. 25 and 51), race relations and ethnic politics after 1950 (No. 65), the role of Stephen Campbell (Nos. 73 and 74) and the political disturbances of the early 1960s (No. 70).

Individual Gazettes also address other specialised subjects. Among them are the labour force and demographic changes in Georgetown between 1781 and 1881 (Nos. 18 and 56), the failure to open up the hinterland between 1838 and 1919 (Nos. 58 and 59), St. George's Cathedral (No. 75), the Guyana – Venezuela border dispute (No. 21), and profiles of influential individuals such as Peter Rose (Nos. 19 and 20), Chief Justice Joseph Beaumont, 1863 – 1868 (No. 35), Immigration-Agent-General James Crosby (No. 34), Hubert Nathaniel Critchlow (No.43) and Elsa Goveia and Walter Rodney (No.66).

The following is a list of the authors and titles of the **Gazettes** which the Society has published.

No. 1   Ali Mazrui "Collective Martyrdom in Modern History".
No. 2   Mary Menezes "The Apprenticeship System, 1834 – 1838: A Leap in the Dark".
No. 3   Winston McGowan "Some Aspects of African Resistance to the Atlantic Slave Trade in West Africa: A Preliminary Analysis".
No. 4   James Rose "Runaways and Maroons in Guyanese History".
No. 5   David Chanderbali "The Indian Indenture System: Evolution and Structure".
No. 6   Marlene Crawford "Scenes from the History of the Chinese in Guyana, 1853 – 1988".
No. 7   Denis Williams "The Archaic of North – Western Guyana."
No. 8   Pulandar Kandhi"East Indian Insurgency on the Sugar Estates of British Guiana, 1869 – 1913".
No. 9   Hazel Woolford "The Introduction of the Compulsory Denominational Education Bill in British Guiana, 1876".
No. 10   Tota Mangar"Planter Class Power and the Struggle for Constitutional Reforms in Nineteenth Century British Guiana".
No. 11   Francis Drakes   "The Middle Class in the Political Economy of British Guiana: 1870 – 1928"

No. 12 James Azeez "The Compensation Controversy".
No. 13 James Rose "The Strike of 1842".
No. 14 Hazel Woolford "The Press in British Guiana, 1856 – 1876"
No. 15 Pulandar Kandhi "The Leonora Riot of 1869".
No. 16 Elappa Visswanathan "A Preliminary Study of the Madrasis in Guyana".
No. 17 Hugh Payne "From Burgher Militia to the People's Militia".
No. 18 Desiree Khayum "The Labour Force in Georgetown, 1781 – 1881".
No. 19 Cecelia McAlmont "Peter Rose: The Years before 1835".
No. 20 Cecelia McAlmont "Peter Rose: The Report of 1850".
No. 21 Mary Menezes "The Background to the Venezuela – Guyana Boundary dispute".
No. 22 Francis Drakes "The Causes of the Protest of 1905".
No. 23 James Rose "The Strike of 1848".
No. 24 Winston McGowan "Christianity and Slavery: Slave, Planter and Official Reaction to the London Missionary Society in Demerara, 1808 – 1813".
No. 25 James Rose "The Suspension of the British Guiana Constitution, 1953".
No. 26 Hazel Woolford "Social Issues Behind the Introduction of the Compulsory Denominational Education Bill of 1876".
No. 27 Francis Drakes "The Development of Guyanese Political Organisation up to 1953"
No. 28 Basdeo Mangru "Crossing Kala Pani : Mortality on Indian Emigrant Ships to the Caribbean in the Nineteenth Century".
No. 29 Ineke Velzing "The Berbice Slave Revolt of 27th February 1763.
No. 30 Anna Benjamin "The Origins of the Berbice Slave Revolt of 1763".
No. 31 Anand James "The Immigration of Liberated Africans to British Guiana, 1841 – 1852".
No. 32 Reuben Kartick "The Village Policy of Francis Hincks, 1862 – 1866".
No. 33 Basdeo Mangru "Trusteeship and East Indian Indentured Labour in British Guiana".
No. 34 Reuben Kartick "James Crosby: Immigration Agent General".
No. 35 Reuben Kartick "Joseph Beaumont: Chief Justice of British Guiana, 1863 – 1868".
No. 36 Francis Drakes "The People's Association, 1903 – 1921".
No. 37 Francis Drakes "The Reaction of Sir Frederick Hodgson to the

Protest of 1905".
No. 38　James Rose "The Taxation Policy of Sir Henry Light, 1838 – 1848".
No. 39　Hazel Woolford"The Reaction of the Press to the Compulsory Denominational Education Bill of 1876".
No. 40　Harold Lutchman"The British Guiana Constitutional Change of 1891".
No. 41　Harold Lutchman "Patronage in Colonial Society : A Study of British Guiana, 1891 – 1928".
No. 42　Tota Mangar "The Rural and Interior Development Policy of Henry Irving, 1882 – 1887".
No. 43　Hazel Woolford "Hubert Nathaniel Critchlow: The Crusader".
No. 44　Caesar Gravesande"Amerindian Jurisdiction in the Guiana Region in the Seventeenth and Eighteenth Centuries".
No. 45　Eirene O'Jon "Slave Society in Early Nineteenth Century Berbice".
No. 46　Roberta Walker-Kilkenny "The Leonora Strike of 1939"
No. 47　Lesley Potter "The Paddy Proletariat and the Dependent Peasantry: East Indian Rice Growers in British Guiana, 1895 – 1920".
No. 48　Lesley Potter "Indian and African – Guyanese Village Settlement Patterns and Inter – Group Relationships, 1871 – 1921".
No. 49　Roberta Walker- Kilkenny "Women in Social and Political Struggle in British Guiana, 1946 – 1953".
No. 50　Harold Lutchman "Constitutional Developments in British Guiana during the Second World War".
No. 51　Hugh Payne "The Expulsion of the People's Progressive Party from the Government of British Guiana in 1953".
No. 52　Lesley Potter "The Amerindians of Guyana and their Environment".
No. 53　Harold Lutchman "Historical Perspective on the Problems of Political Change and Administrative Adaptation in Guyana".
No. 54　Harold Lutchman "Historical Perspective of Race and the Public Service in Guyana".
No. 55　Winston McGowan "The French Revolutionary Period in Demerara – Essequibo, 1793 – 1802".
No. 56　Desiree Ramdayal "Demographic Change in Georgetown, 1820 – 1881".
No. 57　Simon Mangru "The Role of the Anglicans in the Evangelisation of the East Indians in British Guiana, 1838 – 1919".

No. 58 Alan Lancaster "The Unconquered Wilderness: A Historical Analysis of the Failure to Open the Hinterland of British Guiana, 1901 – 1919".

No. 59 Alan Lancaster "Proposals for Hinterland Settlement and Development of British Guiana, 1884 – 1890".

No. 60 Khalleel Mohamed "The Establishment of the Portuguese Business Community in British Guiana".

No. 61 Simon Mangru "Anglican Efforts to Evangelise the East Indians in British Guiana, 1873 – 1898".

No. 62 Marguerite Chase "The Development of Primary Education in Post – Emancipation British Guiana ".

No. 63 Marguerite Chase "The Education Bill of 1855".

No. 64 Tota Mangar"The Immigration Policy of Henry Irving, 1882 – 1887".

No. 65 Percy Hintzen "The Colonial Foundations of Race Relations and Ethno – Politics in Guyana".

No. 66 "Proceedings of a Commemoration Symposium in Honour of Professor Elsa Goveia andProfessorWalter Rodney".

No. 67 Silvius Wilson "The Background to the Ruimveldt Incident of 1924".

No. 68 Silvius Wilson "The Causes of the Ruimveldt Incident of 1924".

No. 69 James Rose "The Enmore Incident of 1948".

No. 70 Perry Mars "The Significance of the Disturbances, 1962 – 1964".

No. 71 Kimani Nehusi "Writing the History of Villages in Guyana and the Caribbean".

No. 72 James Rose and John Williams "International Perceptions of the People's Progressive Party by 1953".

No. 73 Laureen Pierre "Stephen Campbell: The Evolution of an Amerindian Political Advocate in a Colonial State".

No. 74 Laureen Pierre" Stephen Campbell: Legislator and Statesman"

No. 75 William McDowell "St. George's Cathedral: An Historical Study of a National Monument".

No. 80 Arlene Munro "Sir Gordon Lethem and the Grow More Food Campaign, 1941 – 1947"

(Owing to special circumstances Numbers 76 to 79 were never published) Apart from the **History Gazettes**, the University of Guyana's History

Society has two other publications, namely, a newspaper column, entitled initially **History Today** and later **History This Week** and a magazine, originally intended to be annual, called the **Guyana Historical Journal**. The newspaper column originally appeared in the **Guyana Chronicle** but from May 1993 it was published in the **Stabroek News** daily from Monday to Saturday and later weekly on Thursdays under a new title, **History This Week**.

The newspaper column consists, for the most part, of revised forms of the texts of talks presented during the Society's popular broadcast, named **Living History**, which is aired on local radio stations five times a week from Monday to Friday. This column and the **Living History** broadcast are the main components of the Society's public education programme which aims at disseminating historical knowledge to the general public. They cover a wider range of subjects than the **History Gazettes** and are not necessarily the work of trained professional historians.

Broadly speaking, the content of the **History Today** and **History This Week** column has two aspects. It tends to be either commemorative or current. Some articles, such as those which usually appear each May on East Indian immigrants, and every August on the abolition of slavery, are designed to remind readers of important past events at a time when the anniversary of these events is being celebrated or recognized in some other way. Other articles, such as those published recently on West Indies Test Cricket, aim to focus attention on some current event or development. In short, the Society's newspaper column seeks to make readers reflect on both the past and present.

The least frequent of the Society's three publications is the **Guyana Historical Journal** which it intended to produce annually. It is the first exclusively historical journal to appear locally and may be compared with the now defunct **Jamaica Historical Review**. A survey of the Caribbean indicates that such journals, focusing on a single territory, are rare and they seldom survive. Scholarly journals, such as the **Journal of Caribbean History**, which focus on the entire Caribbean, and can depend on the input of a larger body of contributors drawn from the whole region, have shown a greater capacity to survive than publications such as the **Guyana Historical Journal**, which rely largely on the resources of a single country or university.

So far, the History Society has produced four issues of this journal which is conceived as an important complement to its **History Gazettes**. Compared with the **Gazette**, the content of the journal tends to be more comprehensive, analytical, specialised and authoritative, though aimed at essentially the same readership, namely, school teachers, university staff and students and professionals.

The **Journal** is the History Society's most scholarly publication. The first issue was published in 1989 and is the only one that has a specific theme, namely, "Slavery and Immigration". It was greatly influenced by the fact that in the previous year the University of Guyana and the Guyanese nation celebrated two important events, namely, the 150th anniversary of the end of African slavery in Guyana and the arrival of the first East Indians, the major immigrant group which settled in the country in the Post-Emancipation era. This influence is reflected in the titles of the four articles which comprised most of this issue: "The African Slave Trade to Guyana", "The Winged Impulse: The Madeiran Portuguese in Guyana. An Economic Socio–cultural Perspective", "O Tye Kim and the Establishment of the Chinese Settlement of Hopetown"; and "The Repatriation Controversy and the Beginning of an East Indian Village System".

Each issue of the **Journal** is divided into three clear – cut sections. The first and most important and extensive section consists of three or four articles embodying the most recent research on an issue in Guyanese History. In addition to the four subjects just mentioned, the following themes have been addressed in the leading articles in the **Journal** : education in the pre-Emancipation period, East Indian political representation in British Guiana from 1890 to 1917, the imposition of Crown Colony government on the colony in 1928, United States of America relations with British Guiana during the Second World War (Volume II); mating patterns and gender relations among East Indians in the nineteenth century, gender and women in Guianese politics from 1812 to 1964, and the education policy during the governorship of Henry Irving in the 1880s (Volume III); Amerindians and the Dutch Plantation system in the 17th and 18th centuries, hook – swinging among East Indians in the 19th century, the diversification of the Guyanese economy between 1880 and 1930 and the Guyana – Venezuela border problem (Volume IV). These well-researched lengthy articles have served to increase significantly knowledge and understanding of Guyanese history.

The second section of the **Journal**, entitled "Notes and Documents", is designed to "publish original source materials, reports on current research and bibliographic information" about Guyana. Three important, and hitherto little – known documents have been published so far: the correspondence between the attorney of Goldstone Hall estate in Berbice and its absentee proprietor in 1845 (Volume II); the account of a voyage to Berbice from the Netherlands in 1735 by an unknown Dutchman and his initial experience there as a resident planter (Volume III) and observations made by Thomas Pierronet, an American resident, of what today is Georgetown in 1798 (Volume IV). The "notes", on the other hand, cover three themes: the content and history of postgraduate studies in History at the University of Guyana (Volume I), bibliographies of the works produced by and about the late Walter Rodney, Guyana's most renowned historian, (Volume II and III), and a bibliography of the works of Mary Noel Menezes, the university's most distinguished historian (Volume IV).

The third section of the **Journal** consists of reviews of recent publications on Guyana, especially its history and politics. Its purpose is to inform readers of new works which appear on Guyana and to provide a critical appraisal of these publications, many of which are usually unknown locally. Among the books which have been reviewed are the following: Brian Moore, **Race, Power, and Social Segmentation in Colonial Society. Guyana after slavery 1838 – 1891** (New York: Gordon and Breach, 1987) in Volume I; Basdeo Mangru, **Benevolent Neutrality: Indian Government Policy and Labour Migration to British Guiana 1854 – 1884** (London: Hansib Publishing limited, 1987), in Volume II; Chaitram Singh, **Guyana: Politics in a Plantation Society** (New York: Praeger, 1988) in Volume III; Colin Baber and Henry Jeffrey, **Guyana: Politics, Economics and Society** (London: Frances Pinter Publishers, 1986) and **Madan Gopal : Politics, Race and Youth in Guyana** (San Francisco: Mellen Research University Press, 1992) in Volume IV.

Each issue of the **Journal** endorses the fact that the publication is a valuable contribution to our knowledge of the history of Guyana and the historical literature of the nation. Through the **Journal**, the **History Gazette** and its newspaper column, **History Today** and **History This Week**, the University of Guyana's History Society has made a significant contribution to the university and the nation.

Part Seven

CRICKET

Edward Wright, the first outstanding Guyanese/Caribbean circketer

The Parade Ground, Georgetown, the initial venue of first-class cricket, 1865

Rohan Kanhai   Clive Lloyd

Trinidadian Jeffrey Stollmeyer and Robert Christiani, the first Guyanese Test Centurion

The famous G.C.C. Bourda Cricket Ground

Lance Gibbs

Carl Hooper   Shivnarine Chanderpaul

Chapter 43

Some Major Developments and Landmarks in The History of Guyanese Cricket

For at least the last hundred years cricket has been the most popular spectator sport in Guyana. No other sport or pastime has had such a grip on Guyanese of every class, colour, ethnicity, age, religion, vocation and even gender as cricket. Cricket has been and continues to be Guyana's national game. Notwithstanding its importance in the socio-cultural life of the country, the history of Guyanese cricket is a comparatively neglected subject in the historiography of Guyana.

The origins of cricket in Guyana are quite obscure. The exact or even the approximate date of the beginning of the game in the country is not known. It is believed that the sport was introduced into Guyana in the middle decades of the eighteenth century by newly arrived British residents, merchants and the owners of sugar and other plantations and their white employees. Since its introduction cricket in Guyana has undergone major developments.

Perhaps the most significant development was the gradual spread to other races of the game which initially was played exclusively by the Anglo-Saxon Whites. In particular, it evoked considerable interest among Blacks and Coloureds and later among the Portuguese, East Indians and Chinese. By 1900 it had become extremely popular among Blacks. As Henry Kirke, who served as a magistrate in British Guiana for twenty-five years, observed in 1897

✵

> The black and coloured people are madly fond of cricket, every available open space of ground is full of them playing the game in one form or another. Little boys play on the sides of the street with an empty kerosine oil tin for wickets, and the rib of a

palm leaf for a bat. Some of them attain a certain proficiency in the game.[174]

☙

By then all the other ethnic groups in the colony, except the Amerindians, had become actively involved in cricket, the Portuguese embracing the game earlier than the East Indians and Chinese. By the 1890s the game had spread to most coastal villages and sugar estates, to the latter mainly through the instrumentality of British overseers who had played cricket in England and Scotland. Owing to this development, by 1900 cricket was challenging horse-racing for the distinction of being the most popular outdoor sport for adult males of all classes and all races except the Amerindians. As the twentieth century progressed, it attained an unrivalled supremacy over all other outdoor sports, especially where male adults were concerned.

The remarkable progress which the game has made in Guyana especially during the past 150 years has been due to a number of factors. Notable among them are the establishment of teams and, later, organized clubs, involvement in matches against Caribbean and other foreign teams, and the influence of outstanding Guyanese cricketers.

The formation of cricket teams and clubs is probably the most important single impetus to the progress of cricket in Guyanese history. This development gave a major impetus to the game by attracting new players, encouraging regular practice, enhancing skills and stimulating competition. Initially, and for a long time afterwards, this competition consisted of friendly matches. It seems that it was not until early in the twentieth century that regular organized local inter-club competitions were introduced, firstly in Georgetown with two divisions – a First Division competition for the Parker Cup and a Second Division competition for the Garnett Cup. Games were confined to Saturday afternoons, with play lasting from 1:30 or 2:00 until 5:30 or 6:00.

From the beginning clubs in Guyana were greatly influenced by the society's three dominant forces, namely, race, colour and class. The first clubs were exclusively white organisations, whose existence seems to have stimulated the establishment of completely black clubs, initially especially on the East Coast of Demerara and the West Coast of Berbice. For much of the nineteenth century competition was restricted by this ethnic approach to cricket which made teams and clubs, especially white ones, initially play games only against those of the same race.

SOME MAJOR DEVELOPMENTS AND LANDMARKS IN THE HISTORY OF GUYANESE CRICKET

One of the earliest clubs to be formed, certainly the most famous and influential, was the Georgetown Cricket Club (G.C.C.) in 1858, with its membership restricted initially to the colonial elite, especially senior government officials, proprietors, attorneys and managers of sugar plantations and wealthy merchants, all of whom were British by nationality. The G.C.C. is the oldest surviving cricket club in the entire Caribbean. It was the most formidable club in British Guiana until the early decades of the twentieth century and immediately became the headquarters of cricket in the colony. To a considerable extent it managed or controlled cricket there until the establishment of a national board, the British Guiana Cricket Board, in 1943.

At first the G.C.C.'s. main rival was another exclusively white club, the Garrison, comprising British soldiers. Other white teams of British nationals were formed by senior sugar estate personnel on the East Coast of Demerara, in Essequibo and Berbice. Furthermore, in 1865 the Berbice Cricket Club was established in New Amsterdam, the country's second town, with about twenty members. By the 1890s, however, it had collapsed, owing to the paucity of Whites in Berbice and an apparent unwillingness of its members to modify its exclusively racial character.

The 1870s saw the emergence of exclusively Portuguese clubs. The Portuguese, who were regarded as inferior or second-class Whites by residents of British nationality, were excluded initially from membership of the G.C.C. The best-known of the originally exclusively or predominantly Portuguese clubs was the Demerara Cricket Club (D.C.C.) which later became dominated by Blacks.

By 1900 most of the teams and clubs in both the towns and the rural areas were black. The earliest black teams and clubs emerged on the East Coast of Demerara and the West Coast of Berbice. The strongest and best-known of them, however, were formed later in Georgetown, reflecting considerations not only of race and colour but also of class. Among them were the now defunct British Guiana Cricket Club (B.G.C.C.), later renamed Guyana Sports Club, which was founded in 1896 to cater for black and colored professionals and men of means. In striking contrast, the Maltenoes Sports Club, which was founded in 1902 by a Barbadian immigrant who was a master tailor, catered especially for unprivileged working – class Blacks.

This trend of racially based cricket teams and clubs was also followed by the Chinese and East Indians. The earliest Chinese clubs were in existence at least by the 1890s, long before the best-known such club, the Chinese

Sports Club, was established in 1929. East Indians, the last of the post-slavery immigrant groups to take cricket seriously, formed their first club, the Asiatic Cricket Club, in Georgetown in 1895. Their best-known club, the British Guiana East Indian Cricket Club (B.G.E.I.C.C.) was founded in 1914 and gave a great impetus to Indian interest and participation in cricket.

In spite of these developments, however, by 1900 a measure of change had begun to occur in the racial character of the country's cricket. A few clubs had begun to have teams which were ethnically mixed. Furthermore, some teams had started to play matches against teams from other ethnic groups. Eventually all teams began to play against other sides, regardless of considerations of race, colour or class.

Nevertheless, ethnicity, especially the pattern of racially-based clubs continued to be prominent in Guyanese cricket throughout the colonial period, resulting in many ills, including favouritism and prejudice in the selection of national teams and captains. Some salutary change, however, has occurred since the country won political independence from Britain in 1966. Owing mainly to pressure from the government, clubs were forced to alter their membership criteria to exclude, or place less emphasis on, considerations of race and colour.

This major adjustment was reflected in some cases partly in changes of nomenclature. East Indian Cricket Club was renamed Everest Cricket Club and the Chinese Sports Club became the Cosmos Sports Club. The most striking change, however, was witnessed in the membership of the G.C.C. which finally abandoned its long-standing policy of predominantly white membership (British national and later Portuguese) and opened its doors to other ethnic groups. This explains why players such as Shivnarine Chanderpaul and Ramnaresh Sarwan and Reon King can presently belong to, and even lead, a club from which their forbears would have been debarred. The change is also reflected in the administration of the club which in recent times has been having non-white presidents.

An important development in Guyanese cricket was the introduction of matches against foreign teams, initially and mostly against other Caribbean teams. The first match which British Guiana played against another territory seems to have been in March 1859 against a visiting team from Bermuda. Six years later, in February 1865, a Guyanese cricket team had its first venture overseas with a visit to Barbados, where it was defeated decisively by 138 runs by the Barbadian national team in a low-scoring game. That visit was returned by the Barbadians later in the year in September, when British Guiana came from behind to win a keenly-contested game by two wickets. In 1868 the G.C.C. were hosts for the first time of a Trinidadian team, the Sovereign Cricket Club, and in the following year visited Trinidad to play two games against its national team, losing the first by five wickets and winning the second by 27 runs.

These matches set a pattern for the next twenty-five years which witnessed periodic encounters between British Guiana and Barbados and Trinidad at home as well as abroad. British Guiana lost games against Barbados in 1871 in Georgetown and in 1883 and 1891 in Barbados, but defeated the Barbadians twice in 1887 in Georgetown. It enjoyed greater success against Trinidad, with decisive victories in 1882 in Georgetown and 1891 in Barbados and one loss in 1876 in Georgetown. It was not until 1896 that British Guiana had its first encounter with distant Jamaica. British Guiana won both matches in Georgetown against the Jamaicans, the first by an innings and 35 runs and the second by the narrow margin of one wicket.

These early intercolonial matches had several distinguishing features. They were due largely to the initiative of British Guiana, especially the G.C.C. British Guiana was one of the two teams engaged in the first ten of these games which occurred over the long period of twenty-five years between 1865 and 1890. Secondly, beginning with the two historic encounters between British Guiana and Barbados in 1865, they were the first games in the history of Caribbean cricket which were accorded first-class status by the Marleybone Cricket Club (M.C.C.), the international governing body. Thirdly, partly because of the difficulty of financing them, they were very intermittent, often separated by as many as five or six years. They did not include Jamaica which was too distant especially in an era when travelling was by sea and did not begin to participate regularly in regional intercolonial cricket until 1946.

Furthermore, although the Guyanese teams consisted exclusively of Whites, almost invariably members of the G.C.C., the spectators who witnessed the games included persons of every class and colour, males and females from Georgetown as well as the countryside. Moreover, initially, most members of the Guyanese teams were expatriates, of whom the most outstanding was Edward Fortescue Wright, an Englishman who had played county cricket for Gloucestershire before coming to British Guiana in 1878 to work as a senior police officer. In 1882 Wright created history by becoming the first person to score a century in an intercolonial match or any other first-class game in the Caribbean. In what is arguably the most remarkable innings ever played for Guyana, Wright, batting at Number Five and coming to the wicket with the score at seven for the loss of three wickets, made 123 out of his team score of 169 against Trinidad in Georgetown. This still remains the highest proportion of runs (72 per cent) in an innings made by a batsman representing a Caribbean national or regional team in first-class cricket.

Finally, some of these early intercolonial cricket matches were the chief event of what was publicised as "a sports season". The visiting team, as in the case of Trinidad in 1882, brought not only cricketers but also other sportsmen to compete in athletics, rifle-shooting, lawn tennis, rowing and billiards.

The pattern of haphazard matches between British Guiana, Barbados and Trinidad continued until 1891 when the three territories agreed to have a regular tournament for which a cup was subscribed in 1893. The arrangement was that the winning team would receive a bye into the final of the following tournament and the tournament would be contested in each territory in turn at two-year intervals. The tournament was contested roughly every two years up to 1909 and then virtually annually up to 1912. Owing to the disruption caused by the outbreak of the First World War in 1914, however, it was not resumed until 1921. It then continued more or less annually until 1939, when it was interrupted by the outbreak of the Second World War.

In 1895 British Guiana won the regional tournament for the first time at home, owing mainly to the brilliant batting of Clement King and the excellent all-round performance of Edward Wright.[175] In the game against Trinidad which British Guiana won decisively by an innings and 217 runs, Wright made 96 and King 135, only the second century ever in Caribbean intercolonial cricket. In the following final game, in which British Guiana defeated Barbados easily by 175 runs, Wright had innings of 26 and 85, the top score in the match, and captured 10 wickets for 111 runs, three for 58 in the first innings and seven for 53 in the second.

After this victory in 1895, British Guiana did not win the intercolonial tournament until 1929, although it was held on 17 occasions in the period. It emerged victorious, however, in three of the following seven tournaments, namely, in 1934, 1936 and 1937, before the disruption caused by the Second World War. It won the first three tournaments held after the war, namely, in 1956, 1961 and 1964, before the regional competition became an annual affair in 1966 with the introduction of the Shell Shield. This contest for the Shell Shield was dominated by Barbados who emerged the winner on twelve of the 21 occasions it took place between 1966 and 1987 with Guyana being victorious only four times, in 1973, 1975, 1983 and 1987. Similarly, since the introduction of the Red Stripe Cup in 1988 and subsequent tournaments Guyana has had only limited success.

One interesting feature of the evolution of this regional competition has been the improvement in the playing conditions and the increase in the member of venues utilized in Guyana. Initially grounds where cricket matches were played left much to be desired. In the absence of regular ground staff and adequate equipment, pitches were poorly prepared. Often they were uneven and irregular in pace and bounce and were never covered to protect them from rain. Furthermore, the outfields were uneven and grassy, affecting fielding and making the scoring of boundaries from strokes along the ground difficult, unless the batsman hit the ball very hard.

Such conditions favoured bowlers immensely. As a result, individual and team scores were low. Before 1900 it was extremely rare for any team to score more than 150 runs in any match in the colony. Rather it was common for both teams to be dismissed for a total of less than 100 runs, especially in friendly games. Such low team scores, however, also occurred on several occasions even in first-class intercolonial games. For example, in the first two such games, which British Guiana played against Barbados in 1865, its innings totals were 22 and 58 and 82 and 146 for a loss of eight wickets. In its next international games against Trinidad in 1896, British Guiana scored 103 and 103 and 68 and 83.

These low team scores explain why the century (123) by Edward Wright, British Guiana's captain and star batsman, against Trinidad in Georgetown in 1882, was regarded as a phenomenal achievement. Until then the highest score by a Guyanese in an intercolonial match was 65 by Charles Rawlins against Trinidad in Port of Spain in 1869 and the best score in a regional first-class game was 75 by the Trinidadian middle-order batsman, Edgar Agostini, in 1876 against British Guiana in Georgetown. In short, in those days to score fifty in a first-class match in the Caribbean was a prodigious feat and to score a century seemed a virtual impossibility.

The prevalence of low scores then is very evident in an analysis of the thirteen intercolonial games which were played in the Caribbean in the first phase of regional competition between 1865 and 1891. In the 24 innings in these matches the highest team total was 168 by British Guiana against Trinidad in Georgetown in 1882 and in fifteen of them the side was dismissed for less than a hundred runs.

These extremely low scores were a clear reflection of the playing conditions which were very unfavourable to productive batting. This indisputable fact was emphasised in reports about matches in the local press. Typical of such reports was one which appeared in the **Daily Chronicle** in September 1887 on a practice game at Bourda in preparation for visit by the Wanderers Club of Barbados. The reporter observed that "the state of the ground was unfavourable for the making of large scores and in fact, no large score was made". [176] He was correct for one team was dismissed for 50 runs and the other for 91 runs. With time, especially after 1920, batting conditions improved considerably and as a result individuals and teams began to make bigger scores.

Initially the only venue for first-class cricket in British Guiana was the Parade Ground, located in Georgetown opposite the Promenade Gardens and so named because of the parades and other military activities conducted there. The ground, renamed Independence Park after the colony gained its freedom from Britain in 1966, was owned by the Town Council. From its formation in 1858 the G.C.C. was given special permission to use the ground for its activities.

All intercolonial matches in British Guiana until 1882 were held at this ground. On such occasions special benabs were erected to provide accommodation for spectators, while the pavilion was reserved for the two teams and members of the G.C.C. The general public viewed the proceedings from the roads north and east of the ground.

Because of the dual purpose and use of the ground, it was often not clear who was responsible for its general maintenance and for its preparation for intercolonial matches. Consequently, its condition was not always satisfactory. As a newspaper reported in 1882 shortly before a match between British Guiana and Trinidad

> We hear loads of complaints on all hands about the condition of the Cricket Ground, and there seems to be a general agreement that it is decidedly unfitted to be the scene of an intercolonial contest for supremacy. At present, it is as rough as any piece of macadamized road in the colony.[177]

Some Major Developments and Landmarks in The History of Guyanese Cricket

෴

In particular, the venue suffered from a grassy, uneven outfield, late preparation of the pitch and inadequate accommodation.

This unsatisfactory situation eventually prompted the G.C.C. to seek its own facility, now the famous Bourda Ground, which it secured in 1885 and where the first intercolonial games were played in 1887 – a historic occasion when British Guiana defeated Barbados, its most redoubtable opponent, in two games. This ground, which eventually developed a reputation of being "a batsman's paradise", remained the only local venue for first-class cricket until the early 1960s when a few matches began to be played in other venues, initially at Skeldon, Rose Hall and Albion in the Corentyne in Berbice and in 1985 at Hampton Court in Essequibo. More recently, first-class cricket has been played at several new venues in Demerara, notably at Uitvlugt on the West Coast of Demerara, the Everest Cricket Club ground in Georgetown, and the National Stadium built at Providence on the East Bank of Demerara for the 2007 International Cricket Council's World Cup.

In short, today Guyana has several venues for first-class cricket, unlike the single ground used for much of the past. Until 2007, however, the Bourda ground remained the first choice for any type of cricket and the only venue for international Test cricket. It has now been replaced by the Providence Stadium as the venue for Test and international limited-over cricket.

Test cricket is another factor which has been a major impetus to the progress of cricket in Guyana. It was at Bourda in 1930 that the West Indies, led by Marius Fernandes, its first Guyanese shipper, won a Test match for the first time. Although there were Guyanese in almost all West Indian Test teams from the initial series in England in 1928, their contribution to the regional team's efforts was usually negligible until the late 1950s. Admittedly, however, in this early period there were some significant achievements by Guyanese in Tests.

Firstly, in 1948, Guiana's star batsman, Robert Christiani, became the first Guianese to score a century in Test cricket, 107 against India at Delhi, batting at Number Eight. Secondly, John Trim, a fast bowler and the first Berbician to play Test cricket, became the first Guianese to capture five wickets in a Test innings and to head the West Indies' bowling averages in a Test series. He headed the averages both in India in 1948 – 49 with 10 wickets at an average of 18.80 runs each and in Australia in 1951 – 52, when he took five wickets for 59 runs in the single Test in which he played. Those five wickets were taken in 12 overs at a cost of 34 runs in the first innings of the exciting fourth Test at Melbourne which Australia won by one wicket.

The third major achievement by Guianese in Tests up to the early 1950s was the first-appearance century scored by Bruce Pairandeau, 115 against India at the Queen's Park Oval in Trinidad in 1952. He was the first of only three Guyanese to have this distinction, preceding the Berbicians Alvin Kallicharran in 1972 and Leonard Baichan in 1975.

Notwithstanding these three achievements, until the 1950s Guianese players on the whole were not critical to the West Indies team. This situation, however, changed remarkably in the late 1950s with the emergence of Rohan Kanhai, Basil Butcher, Joe Solomon and Lance Gibbs. In the following twenty-five years, the West Indies owed much of its success to Guyanese players, including also Clive Lloyd, Roy Fredericks, Alvin Kallicharran and Colin Croft. Since Lloyd's retirement from Test cricket early in 1985, however, the value of the Guyanese contribution to the regional team has declined considerably. For much of the next fifteen years, Guyana often had only one or two representatives on the West Indies Test team. Presently, in 1913, Guyana has only one regular member of the team, Shivnarine Chanderpaul, the pillar of the team's batting.

Cricket today is the preeminent sport in Guyana. Over the past one hundred and fifty years it has grown immensely in importance and has exerted considerable influence on historical developments in the country. It has been both a source of racial division and racial integration in a multiethnic society, plagued throughout by racism, tension and friction. Its potential to unite Guyanese makes cricket a very important factor in the current political climate in the country.

For Further Reading

Nicole, Christopher	**West Indian Cricket** (London: Phoenix House Ltd, 1957).
Ross, Gordon	**A History of West Indies Cricket** (London: Arthur Barker, 1976).
Manley, Michael	**A History of West Indies Cricket** (London: Andre Deutsch, 1988).
Goble, Ray and Sandiford, Keith	**75 Years of West Indies Cricket 1928-2003** (London: Hansib Publications, 2004).
Mc Gowan, Winston	**The Origins and Development of Guyanese Cricket** (Turkeyen: Department of Social Studies, 2006).
Richards, J. & Wong, M.	**Statistics of West Indies Cricket 1865-1989** (Kingston: Heinemann Publishers, 1990).
George, Mortimer	**A Time in Our History: Berbice Cricket from 1939 to**

	2012 (2012).
Seecharran, Clem	**Hand-in-Hand History of Cricket in Guyana 1865 – 1897** (Hertford: Hansib Publications Ltd., 2016).

Chapter 44

Robert Christiani: Guyana's First Test Centurion

In November 1948, an unprecedented event occurred in the history of Guyanese cricket. British Guiana's star batsman and most highly acclaimed cricketer, Robert Julian Christiani, became the first Guyanese to score a century in a Test match. He achieved this distinction on November 12, 1948 at the age of 28, in his fifth Test appearance in his career and his first Test outside the Caribbean. He performed this feat in the 27th Test in which the West Indies were involved since they began to play Test cricket in 1928, twenty years before.

Christiani or R.J. as he was fondly called by his many admirers, was an exciting bespectacled right-handed middle-order batsman. He possessed a wide range of attractive strokes, especially in front of the wicket. He was particularly quick-footed. It is doubtful whether any other batsman in the history of Guyanese cricket has advanced down the wicket as far and as often to slow bowling as Christiani did. Yet he was seldom dismissed stumped. He was also a brilliant fieldsman, especially close to the wicket, a reserve wicket-keeper, and an occasional leg spin – googly bowler.

R. J., arguably the most outstanding member of a distinguished cricket family, was born on July 19, 1920 and began his first-class career just before the Second World War as a wicket - keeper – batsman. His scores in his initial three first-class games _ three not out and 14, 0 and 23 and 1 and 30 – were disappointing. Nevertheless, he impressed some observers with his talent and potential and only narrowly missed selection at the young age of eighteen in the West Indies team which toured England in 1939 under the captaincy of the Trinidadian, Rolph Grant.

It was during the War, which completely interrupted Test cricket and greatly disrupted Caribbean regional competition that Christiani really came to prominence in the occasional matches which were contested between British Guiana, Barbados and Trinidad and Tobago. In his first such match against Trinidad and Tobago at the Queen's Park Oval in Port of Spain in March 1944, Christiani scored his maiden first-class hundred (126 runs) and followed it up with a half century (54 runs)in the second innings out of modest team totals of 208 and 292 in a game which Trinidad and Tobago won comfortably by 101 runs. Later in the year he made his first such hundred at home, 128 runs at Bourda against Barbados, who nevertheless won the game by 72 runs.

Christiani was even more successful with the bat in intercolonial matches immediately after the war. He scored 129 and 45 against Barbados at Bourda in September/ October 1946, 10 and 133 and 31 and 89 in two matches against Trinidad and Tobago at the Queen's Park Oval in March 1947, and 67 and 45 and 39 and 181, his highest score in first-class cricket, against Jamaica at Bourda in October 1947. Thus he became the first West Indian to score at least one century against all the other principal regional teams.

These impressive performances enabled Christiani to gain selection in the West Indies team against England in 1948 in the Caribbean, the region's first Test series in nine years. He made his Test debut in the first match at Kensington Oval in Barbados along with several other debutants, including his compatriot, Berkeley Gaskin, an opening bowler, and the Barbadian middle-order batsmen, Clyde Walcott and Everton Weekes. Christiani was dismissed leg-before-wicket in both innings, scoring a single in his first knock and 99 in the second. Understandably, he shed tears over the disappointment of just failing to achieve the much-coveted distinction of a first-appearance Test hundred _ a feat performed later by three Guyanese, namely, Bruce Pairaudeau in 1953, Alvin Kallicharran in 1972 and Leonard Baichan in 1975. However, he surpassed the highest Test score until then by a Guyanese _ 80 by Francis De Caires on the same ground in 1930, eighteen years before.

Christiani also made a delightful half-century (51 runs) in the third Test at home at the Bourda ground. In the series he had an aggregate of 176 runs in six innings, with an average of 29.16 runs an innings. He played all four matches and was the only Guyanese in the regional team in the final Test at Sabina Park in Jamaica, a frequent experience in his Test career.

Later in the year Christiani proceeded to India as a member of the West Indies team on a historic tour which witnessed the first encounter ever between the two sides. There were two other Guyanese in the touring party, namely, the newcomer, Clifford McWatt, a wicket-keeper batsman, and John Trim, a fast bowler who, like Christiani, had made his Test debut earlier in the year against England.

It was in the high-scoring drawn first Test in Delhi, where he scored 107 runs in his team's only innings, that Christiani created history. Until then British Guiana was the only one of the four principal Caribbean cricketing countries that had not yet produced a Test centurion. Of the 19 centuries scored by West Indian batsmen in Test cricket since 1928, 13 had been made by Jamaicans (including 10 by George Headley) and three each by Barbadians and Trinidadians.

In the historic game in Delhi in November 1948 when Christiani removed this major blot from the Guianese cricket record, the West Indies won the toss and elected to bat. The team, however, had a disastrous start, losing its first three wickets for only 27 runs – the openers, Jeffrey Stollmeyer and Allan Rae being dismissed for 13 and eight respectively and George Headley, the Number 3 batsman, for two. It was rescued from this critical situation by a dominating fourth-wicket partnership of 267 runs by Clyde Walcott and the able Trinidadian all-rounder, Gerry Gomez, who both made their maiden Test centuries, 152 and 101 respectively. The captain, John Goddard, batting at Number 6, above Weekes and Christiani, made 44.

The score was 403 for the loss of six wickets when Christiani, the only Guianese in the team, came to the wicket just before lunch on the second day to join Weekes, who was then 62 not out. From the outset he batted with great confidence. According to one reporter,

> Christiani soon got off the mark with a splendid cover drive for four off Mankad… It was Christiani's cover drives which featured the after – lunch cricket for his timing was superb. Christiani often jumped out to drive Mankad and one shot for four raised the 500 in 485 minutes.[178]

With the score at 521 Christiani lost the company of Weekes who was caught off Vinoo Mankad, a successful all-rounder who was an effective orthodox slow left-arm bowler, for 128, after sharing a partnership of 118 runs with him for the seventh wicket. Shortly after, the Jamaican, Francis Cameron, was dismissed for two. Christiani, however, proceeded to reach

50 in 104 minutes and 62 not out by the tea interval.

After tea Christiani batted steadily, refusing to take risks and obviously determined to reach the coveted landmark of a Test century. Eventually he succeeded when he crashed a short delivery from Mankad to the boundary for four in the last over of the day. His hundred, which contained nine fours, had taken three hours. He was involved in a second century partnership of 106 runs with the Barbadian, Denis Atkinson (45), for the ninth wicket.

Early on the following day Christiani was dismissed for 107, caught off an out swinger from Commandur Rangachari, a right-arm fast bowler, who took five wickets in the innings. His entire innings lasted 197 minutes.

This proved to be the first and only century by Christiani in his career of 22 Tests, then the largest number of Test appearances by a Guianese cricketer. It was a rare occasion in West Indian cricket when a Number 8 batsman scored a century in a Test. It was also the first of only two occasions in the history of Caribbean Test cricket that four batsmen scored centuries in the same innings. This was repeated in 1983 thirty four years later against India at the Recreation ground in Antigua, where Gordon Greenidge (154), Desmond Haynes (136), Jeffrey Dujon (110) and Clive Lloyd (106) made centuries in a team total of 550 runs.

Christaini's hundred at Delhi enabled the West Indies to amass a total of 631 runs which was then the highest score made by the regional team in a Test innings. This total, achieved in only 655 minutes, surpassed the previous Caribbean record Test score of 535 for seven wickets declared achieved against England at Sabina Park in Jamaica thirteen years before in 1935 when George Headley made his career-best Test score of 270 not out.

Christiani remained the sole Guianese Test centurion for over four years, that is, until January 1953 when Bruce Pairaudeau scored 115 against India at the Queen's Park Oval. Like Christiani's hundred at Delhi, this was the only Test century which Pairaudeau made.

Christaini, in fact, set a pattern of success by Guyanese batsmen against India. Most Guyanese who have scored Test hundreds made their first such century and in several cases (Christiani, Pairaudeau, Joe Solomon and Faoud Bacchus) their only Test century against India. In short, Christiani's maiden Test hundred and his other achievements in the historic initial encounter with India at Delhi in 1948 are part of a substantial amount of evidence which demonstrates convincingly that Guyanese batsmen (and bowlers too) have enjoyed greater success against India than against any other country in Test cricket.

For Further Reading

Goble, Ray & Sandiford, Keith	**75 Years of West Indies Cricket 1928 – 2003** (London: Hansib Publications, 2004).
Lawrence, Bridgette with Scarlett, Reg	**100 Great West Indian Test Cricketers** (London: Hansib Publishing Ltd, 1998).
Lawrence, Bridgette & Goble, Ray	**The Complete Record of West Indian Test Cricketers** (Leicester: ACL and POLAR Publishing Ltd., 1991).
Mc Gowan, Winston	**Guyanese in India – West Indies Test Cricket** (Georgetown: The Author, 1997).
Ramchand, Kenneth with Teelucksingh Yvonne (eds.)	**The West Indies in India 1948. Jeffrey Stollmeyer's Diary 1949** (Macoya: Royards Publishing Co. Ltd., 2004).
Weekes, Everton with Beckles, Hilary	**Mastering the Craft** (Kingston: University of the Caribbean Press, Inc. 2007).

CHAPTER 45

THE BOURDA CRICKET GROUND AND ITS HEROES

Until 2007, when the National Stadium was built in Providence on the East Bank of Demerara to accommodate the International Cricket Council's World Cup, by far the best known sports arena in Guyana was the famous cricket ground in the Bourda ward of the capital, Georgetown. It is the home of the Georgetown Cricket Club (G.C.C.), which was founded in 1858 and is the longest surviving cricket club in the entire Caribbean.

Initially the G.C.C. did not possess a ground. By a special arrangement with the Georgetown Town Council, the club used the Council's ground, the Parade Ground, for practice and matches. Difficulties which developed between the club and the Council eventually prompted the G.C.C. to acquire its own ground by purchasing and developing a piece of land. The new facility in Bourda immediately replaced the Parade Ground as the venue for all first- class cricket matches in the country, beginning with two games between British Guiana and Barbados in September 1887 which the home team won by 108 runs and six wickets.

From the 1960s other venues, initially in Berbice and later in Essequibo and elsewhere in Demerara, began also to be used for first- class matches. Bourda, however, remained the only venue for Test cricket, which was first played there in 1930, until 2007, when it was replaced by the Providence National Stadium.

The long history of first-class and Test cricket at the Bourda ground has been distinguished by numerous outstanding performances by players who may be regarded as its heroes. These performances occurred in each of the five main chronological periods into which this history may be divided.

THE EARLY YEARS, 1887-1909

The earliest heroes of Bourda are hardly remembered. The first two were the brilliant Guyanese all-rounders, Edward Wright and Clement

King, who were both superb batsmen as well as penetrative pace bowlers. Their brilliance was instrumental in British Guiana winning the regional intercolonial tournament for the first time in 1895, imposing heavy defeats on Trinidad and Barbados.

In the following year, 1896, excellent bowling by King enabled British Guiana to win its first matches against Jamaica. In these games at Bourda King had match analyses of 10 for 102 (three for 43 and seven for 59) and 11 for 92 (six for 43 and five for 49). He represented British Guiana until 1901, scoring 104 in his final game against Trinidad, only the second first-class hundred at Bourda and only the third such innings by a Caribbean batsman, following his innings of 135 against Trinidad in 1895 and Wright's 123 against Trinidad at the Parade Ground in 1882.

The third hero of this early period was the Trinidadian skipper and fine attacking middle-order batsman, Bertie Harragin. His knocks of 73 and 53 in 1901 and a century (123) in 1907 enabled Trinidad to defeat British Guiana by 75 runs and nine wickets in two games at Bourda. These early years of cricket at Bourda were followed by a period dominated for the most part by one man, Cyril Rutherford Browne.

THE BROWNE ERA, 1910-1939

Browne, a Barbadian by birth, was a bowling all-rounder. He bowled quick leg-breaks and googlies and was a hard-hitting attacking lower-order batsman. In his early first-class career between 1909 and 1911 he represented Barbados in nine games, including one against British Guiana at Bourda in 1910 in which the eight wickets which he took (three for 11 and five for 26) were a major contribution to his team's decisive victory by eight wickets.

After World War I he migrated to British Guiana and represented his new home in 21 first- class matches between 1921 and 1939. In these games he captured 104 wickets at a low cost of 19.19 runs each and scored 891 runs, including one hundred and six fifties, with an average of 26.50 runs an innings. Almost invariably he was the main architect of the victories which British Guiana achieved at Bourda in this period. His most outstanding performance was in a game against Barbados in October 1925. He scored a century (102) and captured 13 wickets for 135 runs (five for 77 and eight for 58) in 74 overs, enabling his team to win the match by eight wickets. This was British Guiana's first victory over its most redoubtable opponent, Barbados, since 1895 and Browne's eight and thirteen victims remain the highest number of wickets taken by a player representing British Guiana/

Guyana in an innings and match in first-class cricket.

Browne is also remembered for a scintillating innings of 70 not out which he played against England for the West Indies in February 1930 in the historic first Test played at Bourda. He reached fifty in only 34 minutes, one of the fastest half-centuries by a West Indian in Test cricket. It was also a historic occasion because the West Indies were led for the first time by a Guyanese, Marius Fernandes, and gained their first victory in a Test match.

This victory by a massive margin of 289 runs was due largely to excellent fast bowling by George Francis and Learie Constantine and brilliant batting by Clifford Roach and the gifted young Jamaican, George Headley. Roach, the Trinidadian opener, scored 209, the first double century by a West Indian in a Test, while Headley, then only twenty years old, made 114 and 112, the first West Indian to score a century in each innings of a Test.

The Browne era had at least two other Bourda heroes, namely, the middle-order Guianese batsmen, Peter Bayley and Chatterpaul Persaud. In a game against Barbados in 1937, Bayley (268) and Persaud (174) shared a record fourth-wicket partnership of 381 runs. Bayley's innings is the highest score at Bourda and remained the best score by a Guyanese in first-class cricket until 1996 when it was surpassed by Shivnarine Chanderpaul's triple century (303 not out) against Jamaica at Sabina Park. It was played in the penultimate match at Bourda before the outbreak of the Second World War in 1939 severely disrupted both regional and international cricket.

THE WAR YEARS AND THEIR AFTERMATH, 1939-1955

Matches at Bourda during and immediately after the war were distinguished above all by the attractive productive batting of the stylish Guianese right-handed middle-order batsman, Robert Christiani, the country's most respected cricketer until his retirement in 1954. Christiani scored three centuries at Bourda: 128 and 149 against Barbados in 1944 and 1946 and 181, his highest first-class score, against Jamaica in 1947. These impressive innings helped him to gain selection on the West Indies team for its first Test series after the war against the visiting Englishmen in 1948.

In the early 1950s two other Guianese batsmen, the openers, Leslie Wight and Glendon Gibbs, also scored three centuries at Bourda in intercolonial matches. They gained renown especially for their massive record opening partnership of 390 runs there against Barbados in 1951, Wight scoring 262 not out and Gibbs 216. This remains the highest partnership for any wicket at Bourda. It enabled British Guiana to amass an innings total of 692 for nine wickets declared, its highest score in first- class cricket and the largest innings total at Bourda in any level of cricket.

The 1950s also witnessed the best innings bowling analysis in a Test at Bourda- seven for 44 in April 1955 by the Australian skipper, Ian Johnson, with his flighted off- breaks. This performance enabled the visitors to win the fourth Test of their first series in the Caribbean easily by eight wickets and the series by three games to nil with two matches drawn.

The late 1940s and early 1950s were a difficult period for Guianese cricket. The national team, in spite of the exploits of Robert Christiani, Leslie Wight and Glendon Gibbs, suffered several defeats in intercolonial matches at Bourda and overseas. This period of depression ended in 1956 which marked the beginning of a new era in Guianese cricket at the same time as the country struggled for and eventually achieved political independence from Britain in 1966.

The Immediate Pre- and Post- Independence Era, 1956 - 1975

These years were a very important era in Guyanese cricket because of three major related developments. Firstly, the country regained ascendancy in regional cricket for the first time since 1937. Secondly, for the first time Berbice became a force in national cricket. Thirdly, British Guiana began to make an unprecedented major contribution to West Indies Test and other first- class cricket.

These developments were closely linked to the emergence and development in the mid and late 1950s of four players who were all Bourda heroes: the off- spinner, Lance Gibbs, and the three Berbician middle- order batsmen, Rohan Kanhai, Basil Butcher and Joe Solomon. Their contribution was continued or extended by the advent in the 1960s and early 1970s of three other Bourda heroes, namely, the left-handed batsmen, Clive Lloyd, Roy Fredericks and Alvin Kallicharran.

The turning point in 1956 was British Guiana's victory in the first regional quadrangular tournament held at Bourda. This success was due mainly to penetrative spin bowling by Lance Gibbs and the Berbician wrist spinner, Ivan Madray, and brilliant batting, especially by Kanhai and Solomon who both made two hundreds and Butcher and the opener, Bruce Pairaudeau, who both scored one century. History was created in the game against Jamaica when as many as four Guianese batsmen scored centuries in the same innings- Pairaudeau (111), Kanhai (129), Butcher (154 not out) and Solomon (144 not out). Butcher and Solomon shared an unbroken sixth-wicket partnership of 281, enabling the team to reach a mammoth total of 601 for five declared.

Guyanese batsmen continued to be Bourda heroes in the years up to 1975. For example, in 1964 Solomon (107 and 100 not out) in a match against Trinidad became the first Guianese to score two hundreds in a first-class game at Bourda, a feat emulated there three years later by the opener, Roy Fredericks (127 and 115), against Barbados. In the following year, 1968, Kanhai had the distinction of becoming the first Guyanese Test centurion at Bourda when he scored 150 against England, sharing a 250 – run fourth – wicket partnership with Garfield Sobers who made 152. Furthermore, in 1972 Alvin Kallicharran, who made 100 not out against New Zealand, became the first batsman of any nationality to score a hundred at Bourda on his Test debut. In 1973 Clive Lloyd played a memorable innings of 178 in a Test there against Australia, his highest innings in a Test in the Caribbean.

The most successful Guyanese batsman at Bourda in this era from 1956 to 1975 was Basil Butcher, who scored seven hundreds there, two more than Fredericks, Kanhai and Solomon. His success there, however, was surpassed by Garfield Sobers who was the most outstanding batting hero at Bourda in this era. In this period Sobers scored seven hundreds there, two in intercolonial games and five in Tests, including a century in both innings (125 and 109 not out) in a Test against Pakistan in 1958. He holds the record for the highest number of both runs and centuries in Tests at Bourda (853 runs, average 94.77).

Two of the batting heroes at Bourda in this period were from New Zealand during its first tour of the Caribbean in 1972. Glenn Turner (259) and Terrence Jarvis (182) shared a mammoth opening partnership in the fourth Test of the series. These innings were their career-highest in Tests and their partnership of 387 the highest for any wicket in a Test at Bourda. Turner's Test double century, which followed an identical score of 259 in his previous innings in a game against Guyana, lasted 704 minutes and remains the highest and longest Test innings at Bourda. It became and remained the highest score in all Tests by a New Zealander until 1991 when it was surpassed by Martin Crowe's 299 against Sri Lanka at Wellington. Turner's partnership of 387 runs with Jarvis enabled his team to reach what was then its highest Test innings total of 543 for three declared, which was also the highest total in a Test at Bourda until 1991 when the West Indies scored 569 against Australia.

In the 1960s three bowlers had impressive performances in Tests at Bourda. The first were Lance Gibbs and the Australian opening bowler, Neil Hawke. Gibbs's achievement of nine wickets for 80 runs (three for 51 and six for 29) in the third Test against Australia in 1956 enabled the West Indies to win the game and eventually the series, their first series victory against the Aussies.

In that same game Hawke became the first bowler to capture ten wickets in a Test at Bourda. His match analysis was 10 for 115 (six for 72 and four for 43). This feat was repeated at Bourda three years later in the final Test of a series by the English fast bowler, John Snow, who took 10 for 142 (four for 82 and six for 60).

By 1975 many of the Bourda heroes of the era since 1956 had retired or were past their peak. New players emerged to take the limelight in the following years.

The Last Thirty-Two Years, 1975 – 2007

There were several heroic bowling performances at Bourda in this period. Among them were the feats of the two contrasting Guyanese off-spinners, Clyde Butts and Roger Harper in interterritorial matches. Harper had the most impressive match analysis in such games – 11 for 102 (six for 72 and five for 30) against Barbados in 1984, enabling his team to win the match easily by nine wickets. On five occasions in these matches at Bourda in the 1980s Butts captured at least five wickets in an innings.

The 1980s also witnessed the best bowling analysis in a Test at Bourda. In a game against the West Indies there in April 1988, the Pakistani skipper and opening bowler, Imran Khan, took 11 wickets for 121, seven for 80 in the first innings and four for 41 in the second. His excellent bowling enabled his team to win this opening match of the series against the world champions convincingly by nine wickets.

Where batting is concerned, the most memorable performance in regional first-class matches at Bourda was a partnership for the seventh wicket by Guyana's best two batsmen, Alvin Kallicharran (184) and Clive Lloyd (144) against Trinidad in January 1981. Lloyd, batting at Number 8, joined skipper Kallicharran with the team in crisis with a score of 112 for six. Their productive stand enabled Guyana to reach a respectable total of 439 in a drawn game.

Another drawn game 14 years later witnessed a rare brilliant all-round performance in which a player scored a double century and took 5 wickets in an innings in the same match. This rare feat was performed by Roger Harper in 1995 at Bourda against the Windward Islands. Harper took five for 98 in 53.2 overs when the visitors batting compiled a solid total of 414 runs and made 202 in Guyana's reply of 479. This was only the third occasion that such a feat was performed in regional cricket in 130 years and the first time in 28 years. Harper was following the example set by two Barbadians, namely, Garfield Sobers (204 and six for 66) against British Guiana in 1966 at Kensington Oval and Geoffrey Greenidge (seven for 124 and 205) against Jamaica in the following year at the same venue.

One of the most outstanding batsmen in Tests at Bourda since 1975 is the Antiguan, Richie Richardson, who scored 766 runs in eight innings at an average of 95.75 runs an innings. His achievements included three substantial centuries _ 185 against New Zealand in 1985, 194 against India in 1989 and 182 against Australia in 1991, his three highest Test scores. This last innings enabled the West Indies to reach a total of 569 runs, their highest Test score at Bourda and to gain their first victory there since their win against Australia in 1965.

In recent times Bourda's main heroes have been the two local stars, Carl Hooper and Shivnarine Chanderpaul. Hooper's renown is largely the result of several good all – round performances which have contributed immensely to Guyana's success. Particularly impressive were his feats in the regional tournament in 2001 when he scored 954 runs, including four hundreds and four fifties, in 12 innings at an average of 95.40 runs an innings, took 11 catches and captured 25 wickets at 25.42 runs each.

Chanderpaul's acclaim has been due mainly to his productive batting, especially in Tests where he has scored several centuries. In 1998, for example, he scored 118 against England, the first Test hundred by a Guyanese at Bourda in twenty-five years, that is, since Clive Lloyd's 178 against Australia in 1973. In his seven Test appearances at Bourda Chanderpaul has scored 758 runs, including one double century, three single hundreds and two fifties, at a remarkable average of 108.28 runs an innings.

There was great jubilation at Bourda when Chanderpaul (140) and Hooper (233) set a new fifth-wicket partnership record for Tests there of 293 against India in 2002. This was Hooper's first Test hundred at Bourda and his maiden and only Test double century.

Chanderpaul further established his reputation as a Bourda hero when he in his first game as captain of the West Indies made a Test double century (203 not out) against South Africa in 2005, surpassing his previous highest

Test score of 140 against India in 2002. He shared a massive fourth-wicket stand of 284 with the Jamaican, Wavell Hinds, who also scored a double hundred (213). It was only the second occasion in the history of West Indies cricket that two batsmen made double centuries in the same innings and only the second time since international cricket began in 1877 that a captain scored a double century on his debut as skipper.

Chanderpaul's most remarkable innings at Bourda, however, is probably his uncharacteristically aggressive hundred against Australia on the first day of the initial Test of a series in 2003. Made off only 69 deliveries, it is the third fastest Test hundred in terms of balls faced. This "innings of glorious cavalier defiance",[179] as one writer in the famous **Wisden Cricketers' Almanack** described it, enabled the West Indies to recover from a paltry score of 47 for four when he came to the wicket to reach a more decent, though inadequate, total of 237.

In short, the famous Bourda cricket ground has had heroes throughout its history. Because of its reputation as a "batsman's paradise", it should not be surprising that most of its heroes are batsmen. The relatively small number of excellent performances by bowlers is therefore all the more laudable.

For Further Reading

Woods, John	**Test Cricket Grounds** (Cheltenham: Sportsbooks Ltd., 2004).
Hand in Hand Group of Companies	**Cricket at Bourda** (Georgetown: Sheik Hassan Printing Inc, 2007).
Seecharran Clem	**Hand-in-Hand History of Cricket in Guyana 1865-1897** (Hertford: Hansib Publications Ltd, 2016).

Chapter 46

Profiles of Two Successful Test Cricketers: John Trim and Clive Lloyd

John Trim, a right-arm fast bowler, was born in Port Mourant, Corentyne, Berbice in January 1915 and died in November 1960. He began his first-class cricket career in March 1944 at the age of 29 years with two matches against Trinidad at the Queen's Park Oval in Port of Spain, British Guiana's first such matches since 1939 when the outbreak of the Second World War severely disrupted regional cricket. In the following three years he represented British Guiana in seven matches against Barbados and Trinidad.

Trim's performance in these nine games was, on the whole, rather unimpressive. He captured only 18 wickets at an average of over 51 runs each with a best performance of four wickets for 158 runs in 31 overs in a drawn game against Trinidad in September – October 1944. He was usually greatly overshadowed in these games by his senior opening partner, Berkeley Gaskin, who took 43 wickets at an average of 29 runs a wicket.

Trim's fortunes, however, changed dramatically in 1948, when England visited the West Indies, the first international tour after the War. He bowled magnificently for British Guiana against the tourists in the colony game immediately before the third Test at Bourda. He had a match analysis of nine wickets for 104 runs, capturing four for 68 in 27 overs in the first innings and five for 36 in 20 overs in the second, by far his best performance in a first-class game in his entire career. Six of his nine victims were bowled in a fine demonstration of hostile fast bowling.

This brilliant performance enabled Trim to gain selection for the West Indies in the third Test at the expense of Gaskin, who had bowled accurately with little success in the first two Tests, taking two wickets for 158 runs in 79 overs, including 24 maidens. Thus Trim made his Test debut at home at the comparatively old age of 33 years. He took two wickets for six runs in 10 overs in the first innings and one wicket for 38 runs in 13 overs in the second innings.

This modest performance did not enable him to retain his place in the team for the fourth and final Test at Sabina Park in Jamaica, where he and his opening partner at Bourda, the Trinidadian, Lance Pierre, were replaced by the Jamaican pace men, Hines Johnson and Esmond Kentish. Nevertheless, he was selected to be a member of the West Indies touring party which left at the end of the year for its first encounter with India. There he represented the West Indies in the final two Tests and had commendable success. His bowling was a major contribution to the team's victory in the fourth Test at Madras which enabled the West Indies to win the series by one game to nil with the other four matches drawn. He was the team's most successful bowler in this Test, taking seven wickets for 76 runs, four for 48 in 27 overs in the first innings and three for 28 in 16 overs in the second innings.

Surprisingly, in spite of this success, Trim was not slected in the West Indies' touring team for its next encounter in 1950 against England. He, however, was a member of the party that went to Australia for the following series in 1951 – 2 and performed well in the only Test for which he was selected. In short, Trim represented the West Indies in four Tests in three series against England, India and Australia between 1948 and 1952. Notwithstanding the late start and the brevity of his international career, he occupies a special place as a Guyanese in the history of Test cricket for several reasons.

Firstly, he was the first Berbician to represent the West Indies in Test cricket, the precursor of Rohan Kanhai, Basil Butcher, Joe Solomon, Roy Fredericks, Alvin Kallicharran and several others, including Devendra Bissoo and Narsingh Deonarine. Secondly, he was the first genuinely fast Guyanese bowler to be selected to play Test cricket for the West Indies, an example followed later by Sven Stayers, Colin Croft, Reon King and Colin Stuart.

Thirdly, Trim was the first Guyanese bowler to be effective in Test cricket. Until his appearance no Guyanese had taken more than two wickets in a Test innings. He did that on four occasions, including once in Australia at Melbourne in January 1952 when he took five wickets for 34 runs in 12 overs, the first five-wicket haul by a Guyanese in Test cricket. He was also the first Guyanese to head the regional team's bowling averages in Test cricket, achieving this honour on two occasions, in India in 1948-9 and Australia in 1951-2. In his entire career Trim took 18 wickets in Tests at an average of 16.16, the best career statistics by any West Indian bowler with more than a few victims in the entire history of Test cricket dating back in 1928. It is still puzzling why his success did not gain him more Test appearances.

Trim's short international career was a striking contrast to the duration of the career of Clive Hubert Lloyd, the first of only three Guyanese to have over one hundred Test appearances. Lloyd a left-handed middle-order batsman was born in Georgetown on 31st August 1944. His interest in cricket was stimulated partly by the fact that he lived near the Demerara Cricket Club ground in Queenstown and was a cousin of the famous Guyanese and West Indies off-spinner, Lance Gibbs. At least from his early teens, when he was a student of the now defunct Chatham High School and the school's cricket captain, he demonstrated undoubted talent and promise.

After growing success in local cricket competitions, his first-class career finally began when he was included in the national team in 1964 at the age of nineteen. He failed dismally in his first two matches for British Guiana against Jamaica and the Australian tourists, scoring only thirty runs in three innings, but his fortunes changed dramatically in 1966 in the newly introduced Shell Shield competition, when he made two splendid centuries in consecutive innings, 107 against Barbados at Kensington Oval and 194 against Jamaica ta Sabina Park.

These performances and a vacancy created by the end of his compatriot Joe Solomon's international career enabled Lloyd to gain selection for the West Indies tour of India at the end of 1966 as a middle-order batsman. In the first Test of that tour at Bombay in December 1966. Lloyd made an impressive debut, scoring 82 and a match – winning 78 not out. This proved to be the beginning of a long Test career which ended in 1985 at the conclusion of a tour of Australia.

This career can be divided into two phases. The first one was from his initial Test appearance to his appointment as captain of the West Indies team in 1974. He played several outstanding innings in this period, including a knock of 118 against England at Port-of Spain in 1968, his maiden Test hundred. The most salient feature of his batting in this period, however, was its inconsistency, which finally resulted in his omission from the team for several Test matches in 1972 and 1973, after commanding a regular place for 23 matches since 1966.

A remarkable change took place after his appointment as captain in 1974, an event which ushered in the second phase of his career. He began to bat more responsibly, scoring more heavily and with greater consistency. By the end of his international career in January 1985, Lloyd had scored a total of 7515 runs, including 19 hundreds and 39 half centuries, in 110 Tests at an average of 46.67 runs an innings. The most distinctive traits of his batting were his aggression and the fearsome power with which he hit the ball, especially off the back foot.

Lloyd made an invaluable contribution to Guyanese and West Indian cricket as a batsman, fieldsman and captain. His number of Test appearances, hundreds and half centuries surpasses those of other Guyanese cricketers except Shivnarine Chanderpaul, while his Test career average is inferior to that of only two Guyanese, Rohan Kanhai and Chanderpaul. Lloyd also has the distinction of scoring the largest aggregate by a Guyanese in a Test series – 636 runs against India in the subcontinent in 1974-75. His highest Test score, 242 not out at Bombay in the final Test of that series, is the fifth highest innings by a Guyanese in Test cricket, surpassed by innings of 291 and 261 by Ramnaresh Sarwan, 256 by Kanhai and 250 by Faoud Bacchus. He once had the honour of making the highest score by a Guyanese in a Test at Bourda, 178 against Australia in 1973, until this score was eclipsed by Carl Hooper's 233 against India in 2002. His innings of 178 was at the time the highest Test score by a Guyanese in the Caribbean. It was equalled by Hooper in 1993 against Pakistan and then eclipsed by him 2002.

Lloyd was also a superb fieldsman, initially in the outfield, especially at cover point, but later in the slips. He has taken more catches (90) in Test cricket than any other Guyanese except Hooper (115). He was also a very successful captain and the longest-serving skipper in the history of West Indies international cricket. He led the West Indies in 74 Tests in 18 series over a period of eight years. The West Indies won fourteen of these rubbers, drew two and lost two and became the cricket champions of the world for only the second time since the region began to play official Test cricket in 1928. In 1983 he led the Guyanese team to a unique double success in the Shell Shield and the Geddes Grant – Harrison Line regional competitions.

Lloyd has exerted more influence on West Indian cricket than any other Guyanese. In recognition of his services to cricket, he received many awards, including the Order of Roraima from the Government of Guyana, the Order of Australia from the Government of Australia, and honorary doctorate degrees from at least two universities.

For Further Reading

Lloyd, Clive	**Living for Cricket** (London: WH Allen & Co, 1983).
Lawerence, Bridgette & Goble, Ray	**The Complete Record of West Indian Test Cricketers** (Leicester ACL & Polar Publishing, 1991).
Goble, Ray &	**75 Years of West Indies Cricket 1928 – 2003** (London:

Sandiford, Keith Lister, Simon	Hansib Publications Ltd., 2004). **Supercat the authorised biography of Clive Lloyd** (Fairfield Park: Fairfield Books, 2007).
Ramchand, Kenneth (ed.) with Teelucksingh Yvonne Sambhudat (Known as Shako), Ramnarine	**The West Indies in India 1948. Jeffrey Stollmeyer's Diary 1949** (Macoya: Royards Publishing Co. Ltd.,2004). **WI in Test Matches. Facts and Feats, 1938 -2013** (2014).

Chapter 47

Lance Gibbs, Bowler Par Excellence

Ever since Lancelot Richard Gibbs made his debut in first-class cricket at the age of nineteen at Bourda in 1954 for British Guiana against the visiting M.C.C. tourists, I have followed his career with keen interest. It was not obvious then that he would have become one of the greatest exponents of off-spin bowling the world has seen. In that game which the visitors won by an innings after compiling a mammoth score of 607, Gibbs took two wickets for 126 runs in 41 overs. His performance was not better in two games against Barbados at Kensington Oval early in 1955. In those marches in three innings Gibbs took only one wicket, conceding 131 runs in 44 overs.

It was not until the following year, 1956, that Gibbs's bowling began to make an impact. It was a major contribution to British Guiana's victory in the first regional quadrangular tournament as a result of first-innings lead in drawn matches against both Jamaica and Barbados. He took four wickets for 113 runs in 80 overs against Jamaica and four for 68 in 34 overs against Barbados. These performances proved to be turning point in his career.

Gibbs's rise to greatness was facilitated by a fortuitous event – namely, the death in a car crash in 1959 of the talented Jamaican all-rounder, O'Neil Gordon "Collie" Smith, at the age of 26. The presence of Smith, an accomplished off-spinner, and that of the Trinidadian right-arm spinner, Sonny Ramadhin, for several years prevented Gibbs from gaining a regular place in the West Indies team. Gibbs's development was also made possible or was accelerated by the relatively early decline of the team's spin twins, Ramadhin and the Jamaican left-hander, Alfred Valentine, and the astuteness of Frank Worrell. Worrell was the first captain of the West Indies to recognise fully and appreciate the tremendous potential of Gibbs and to make him a permanent member of the regional team. This occurred on the tour of Australia in 1960-1 when Gibbs replaced Ramadhin in the Test team and eclipsed Valentine, heading the team's Test bowling averages with 19 wickets for 395 runs in 192.2 overs and an average of 20.78.

Gibbs's success, however, was due to the considerable talent and ability which he possessed. Fundamental to this success were two other factors. The first one was the confident, indomitable, competitive spirit which he showed. His great confidence in his own ability often inspired him to persist until he dismissed his opponents, very few of whom he seemed to hold in high esteem. It was also his determination, courage and confidence which enabled him to survive and eventually overcome the frustration and disappointments which he suffered during the difficult period from 1969 to 1972 when it seemed that the end of his Test career was imminent. In nine Tests in that period against India, New Zealand and England he took only 17 wickets at a high cost of 59.47 runs each, before experiencing a remarkable resurgence against Australia in the Caribbean in 1973, when he headed the team's bowling averages, capturing 26 wickets at an average of 26.76 each.

The second fundamental factor which contributed to his success was the aggressive, competitive approach which he adopted to bowling. He was never satisfied merely with containing the opposing batsman by means of negative, defensive bowling with the hope that they would eventually become impatient and lose their wicket by attempting an injudicious stroke. Rather he preferred to resort to the more positive method of attack, putting pressure on the batsman until he managed to dismiss them.

His aggressive intent was reflected in his brisk short approach to the wicket, his lively action and the speed with which he returned to his bowling mark and completed his overs. His emphasis on attack distinguished him from many other West Indian off-spinners, such as his compatriot, Norman Wight, the Barbadian, Norman Marshall, and the Jamaican, Reginald Scarlett – essentially defensive bowlers who concentrated on containing the batsmen.

Yet Gibbs was as economical as any other spin bowler, presenting a rare combination of aggression and economy like the great English off-spinner, Jim Laker. Throughout his long Test career, he seldom conceded more than an average of 2-2 ½ per runs over, even when playing on very docile pitches against the greatest of batsmen.

This achievement was due partly to his consistent control of length and line and his ability to bowl to a well-set field. It was very uncharacteristic for him to bowl a full toss, a long hop or a badly directed delivery, and he rarely bowled even half volleys. In short, he was one of the few bowlers from whom batsmen could not expect to receive a really bad ball even during a marathon spell of bowling.

His persistent accuracy enabled him to contain the world's greatest batsmen and made it possible for the West Indies captain to use him as a stock bowler. Seldom, if ever, has a captain been forced to withdraw him from the attack because of the mastery of the opposing batsmen. In fact, the only time in his career when the opposition managed to some extent to dominate him was during one or two innings in the 1968-69 tour of Australia.

It was in one-day limited-over cricket matches that Gibbs best demonstrated his accuracy, as he would show repeatedly that he could bowl his quota of overs as economically as any other bowler. I remember seeing him bowl 12 overs for 26 runs for Warwickshire in a Gillette Cup final at Lord's against Sussex in 1968. In 1972, he returned an even more remarkable analysis of 12 overs for 15 runs for Warwickshire in a Gillette Cup semi-final game against Worcestershire. In fact, his performances helped to dispel the assumption and belief widely held in English cricketing circles that there was no place for spin bowlers in one-day cricket.

The respect which Gibbs's bowling commanded was due not only to his accuracy, but also to his clever variations of flight. His deceptive, tantalizing flight was responsible for the downfall of many batsmen. These victims were usually bowled or caught in the outfield. Gibbs's reputation as a master of deceptive flight made batsmen so ultra – cautious that very few of them were confident and bold enough to advance down the pitch regularly when he was bowling. Most players, with the notable exception of a few Australian batsmen, preferred to play his bowling from the crease.

This marked reluctance of batsmen "to use their feet" to him helps to explain why so few of his victims in Tests were stumped (only eight out of 309). Gibbs at times appeared frustrated by the lack of enterprise of batsmen who consistently refused to respond to his inducements to them to leave the crease but instead concentrated on dour defence, making full use of the forward defensive prod.

Such an approach, however, was often not safe, particularly on turning wickets. This was because one of Gibbs's assets was his ability to impart a prodigious amount of spin to the ball, enabling him to secure many victims from catches, especially by Garfield Sobers, at short leg off the inside edge of the defensive bat. Towards the end of Gibbs's career his ability to produce devastating spin, except on very helpful wickets, seemed to have declined. As a result very few of his victims were secured through catches at short leg.

Gibbs often gave the impression that he welcomed a real challenge and so reserved his best performances for the most important occasions, namely, Test matches. His record in Test cricket is certainly far more impressive than his achievements in Caribbean Shell Shield or English county cricket, where his performances were often somewhat mediocre. Moreover, in Test matches he tended to bowl better against the more accomplished batsmen in the team than against the "tail-enders". It is significant that a remarkably high proportion of his victims consisted of numbers one to six in the batting order.

In fact, Gibbs's main value to the West Indies team was his ability to break the backbone of the opposing team's batting by dismissing the openers, if necessary, and the middle-order batsmen. After performing this invaluable function, he was often withdrawn from the attack to allow the fast bowlers to demolish the "tail-enders". The adoption of this policy, especially during the era of Wesley Hall and Charles Griffith, and Gibbs's somewhat mediocre performance against lower-order batsmen, help to explain why he was never able to secure a larger haul of wickets than twenty six in any Test series during his long career. He had 26 victims in only two of the 19 Test series in which he participated, namely, in England in 1963 and against Australia in the Caribbean in 1973.

Gibbs's bowling also suffered to some extent because he never seemed to have completely mastered the ability to bowl effectively from around the wicket. This weakness generally enabled left-handed batsmen to play his bowling with less difficulty than many of their more gifted right-handed team-mates. It was also a handicap to him on turning pitches, where right-handed batsmen were often able to survive for longer periods than expected by skilfully using their pads against the turning ball bowled over the wicket, knowing that the umpire was likely to give them the benefit of the doubt when lbw appeals were made.

Nevertheless, Gibbs was an effective bowler on all types of wickets and against all batsmen. His greatness lay largely in his exceptional ability to coordinate his wide range of skills to produce the variety that was the most distinctive trait of his bowling without losing his persistent accuracy. No two successive balls that he bowled seemed exactly alike. Rather they were usually at least slightly different in pace, flight, length, line and spin. It was this variety which made even the world's greatest batsmen cautious, uncertain, and at times even confused, when playing against him. To make matters worse for the opposing batsmen, Gibbs was a very thoughtful bowler who sought successfully to spot and exploit their weaknesses.

Gibbs's greatness is enhanced by the fact that much of his success was achieved on hard unresponsive wickets which were excellent for batting. He was able to contain and worry the best of batsmen even on docile pitches, while he was always dangerous and often devastating on wickets which favoured spin. Nothing more could be expected or required of a spin bowler. Indeed he was a very reliable bowler who rarely let the West Indies team down. Except during the period from 1969 to 1972, he could be depended on to secure at least eighteen to twenty wickets in any full Test series.

Gibbs's crowning achievement was that he broke the Englishman, Fred Trueman's record (307 wickets) for the largest number wickets taken by any bowler in the history of Test cricket. He achieved this feat on the first day of the final Test of his career against Australia at the Melbourne Cricket Ground in January 1976, when he had the opener, Ian Redpath, caught by Michael Holding for 101. Gibbs ended his career with 309 wickets in 79 Tests with an average of 29.09 and a best innings bowling performance of eight wickets for 38 runs in 53.3 overs against India at Kensington Oval in 1962, enabling the West Indies to win the game by an innings and 30 runs. He held the world record for the largest number of Test victims for nearly five years, that is, until December 1981 when it was broken by the great Australian fast bowler, Dennis Lillee. Gibbs was the first, and for a long time the only, spin bowler to capture 300 wickets in Tests. He has taken nearly twice as many wickets in Tests as any other West Indian spin bowler, easily eclipsing Ramadhin (158 wickets) and Valentine (139).

Gibbs's outstanding attributes and invaluable contribution to West Indies cricket are aptly summed up by his cousin, team-mate and eventually captain, Clive Lloyd, thus:

> There was never a more whole-hearted cricketer for the West Indies, nor an off-spinner in anything like his class. He was by no means a mechanical spinner, instead always thinking about the game, working an opponent out, assessing his strengths and weaknesses and laying the trap for him. A fierce competitor, he would be giving total effort, no matter if the total was 300 for two and the sun

scorching, no matter if his finger had been rubbed raw.[180]

☙

Lance Gibbs will long be remembered and honoured for the nineteen years of very distinguished service that he gave to West Indies cricket. It was this sustained effectiveness over a remarkably long period which has distinguished his achievements from those of almost all the other great spin bowlers the world has seen, and has placed him in a category virtually by himself.

For Further Reading

Jonas, Pryor (ed.)	**Sportrait Lance Gibbs** (Georgetown: Office of the Prime Minister, 1976).
Lawrence, Bridgette with Scarlett, Reg	**100 Great West Indian Test Cricketers** (London: Hansib Publishing Ltd, 1988).
Lawrence, Bridgette & Goble, Ray	**The Complete Record of West Indian Test Cricketers** (Leicester: ACL & POLAR Publishing, 1991).
Lister, Simon	**Supercat the authorised biography of Clive Lloyd** (Fairfield Park: Fairfield Books, 2007).
Goble, Ray &, Sandiford, Keith	**75 Years of West Indies Cricket 1928 – 2003** (London: Hansib Publications, Ltd., 2004).
Sambhudat (known as Shako), Ramnarine	**WI in Test Matches Facts and Feats, 1938 – 2013** (2014).

Chapter 48

FAMOUS INDO-GUYANESE CRICKETERS

The origin of cricket in Guyana is not definitely known. It is believed that the game was introduced in the country by British residents in the middle decades of the eighteenth century. From then the game spread gradually to other inhabitants, including East Indians from India, who first arrived in 1838.

By the end of the nineteenth century a growing number of East Indians in British Guiana had begun to play cricket. This development was given a great fillip in the early decades of the twentieth century by three important events.

Early Critcal Events

The earliest of these three events was unprecedented, namely, the selection of an East Indian for the first time in a Guyanese national cricket team. This occurred in January 1910 when J. A. Veerasawmy, a left-arm bowler, was chosen to play in a game against Trinidad at the Queen's Park Oval in Port-of Spain. In this game, which Trinidad won by an innings and 180 runs, Veerasammy's contribution was negligible. Batting at Number 11, he had scores of 0 and 1 not out and failed to take a wicket, conceding 37 runs in eight overs.

Owing to his departure for England to pursue legal studies and the disruption to regional intercolonial cricket caused by the First World War, Veerasammy did not represent British Guiana again until more than eleven years later in September 1921, again against Trinidad in Trinidad. In that match, which the Trinidadians won by an innings and 80 runs, Veerasawmy was his team's most successful bowler, capturing five wickets for 67 runs in 37 overs, of which 13 were maidens.

Veerasawmy played only one other first-class game for his country. That game was against Trinidad at Bourda in September 1922, when he had scores of 12 and two not out and analyses of one for 33 in seven overs and 0 for 9 in two overs with the ball.

Veerasawmy's selection for British Guiana fired other Indian cricketers with a desire to represent their country. The second Indian to have that honour was C. Pooran, a middle-order batsman who played in a game against Trinidad in January and February 1929 at the Queen's Park Oval, but suffered the ignominy of being dismissed for a duck in both innings in a match which Trinidad won by 223 runs. Not surprisingly, he was never selected to represent British Guiana again.

Veerasawmy was also largely responsible for the second event which gave a substantial impetus to Indian cricket in British Guiana. Owing mainly to his initiative, in 1914 the British Guiana East Indian Cricket Club (B.G.E.I.C.C.) was formed in Georgetown. This club soon became the best and most influential Indian cricket club in the colony, producing most of the early accomplished cricketers.

The third development which boosted Indian cricket considerably in the early twentieth century was the beginning of two competitions for Indian players. One competition was virtually annual between Indians in the three counties of Demerara, Essequibo and Berbice for the Flood Challenge Cup, presented by Thomas Flood, a leading Indian businessman and politician. The other competition, which was inaugurated by Veerasawmy, was a periodic one for the Kawall Cup between Indians in British Guiana, Trinidad and Suriname, with the first contests taking place in 1919 and 1924. These two competitions helped to bring to prominence the Indians who represented British Guiana in the 1930s and 1940s.

THE 1930S AND 1940S

In the 1930s two Indians were selected for the national team in intercolonial matches. The first was R. B. Rohoman, a slow bowler who played two games in 1934 against Barbados and Trinidad. In the first of these two matches against Barbados in January at the Queen's Park Oval. Rohoman was his team's best bowler, capturing 11 wickets for 194 runs, four for 64 from 18 overs in the first innings and seven for 130 from 38.4 overs in the second. Nevertheless, Barbados won the game by 143 runs.

The second Indian to play for British Guiana in the 1930s was Chatterpaul Persaud, an all-rounder who was the first accomplished Indo-Guyanese batsman. In his international debut against Barbados at Bourda in September 1937, Persaud scored a century (174), sharing a mammoth record partnership of 381 runs for the fourth wicket with Peter Bayley (268), enabling British Guiana to make a total of 629 runs and to secure a rare easy victory by an innings and 229 runs. Persaud, again batting at No. 5, missed a century by four runs in his next first-class innings a week later at Bourda against Trinidad when he scored 96. He was involved in two century stands of 100 and 179 respectively with opener Celso De Freitas (153) and his skipper, Vibart Wight (127), enabling his team to make another massive score of 627 runs. His bowling was also valuable as he took six wickets in the match, two for 36 in 10 overs in the first innings and four for 90 in the second. His good all-round performance enabled his team to win a closely contested game by two wickets. Persaud's contribution, especially his brilliant batting, was a major factor in British Guiana's winning of this 1937 regional intercolonial tournament.

In spite of the selection of Veerasawmy, Pooran, Rohoman and Persaud in the 1920s and 1930s and J. Bahadur, J. Naipaul and Sonny Bajnauth in the 1940s, until the 1950s very few Indians represented the country in cricket. Most national cricket teams did not have a single member of Indian descent. This was due partly to the discrimination suffered by players from Berbice in team selection, where marked preference was given to cricketers from Demerara, especially Georgetown. In these circumstances the only Indian who appeared regularly in the Guianese national team before the mid 1950s was Ganesh Persaud. Persaud, a Georgetown- based player who was a middle-order batsman and a brilliant fieldsman especially in the covers, participated in eight intercolonial games in 1950, 1951 and 1952, scoring 419 runs in 14 innings with a highest score of 96 and a modest average of 29.92 runs an innings.

THE MID 1950S: A WATERSHED

This situation began to change markedly in the 1950s owing largely to the initiative of the West Indian batsman and Guianese skipper, the Barbadian Clyde Walcott, who in 1954 was appointed Cricket Organiser and Coach on the estates of the British Guiana Sugar Producers' Association. His influence was partly responsible for the selection of several Berbicians in the national team, including three Indians, the middle-order batsmen, Rohan Kanhai and Joe Solomon, and the wrist spinner, Ivan Madray.

The invaluable contribution of these three players played a major role in enabling British Guiana to win the first regional quadrangular tournament staged at Bourda in 1956. Both Kanhai (129 and 195) and Solomon

(114 not out and 108) scored two centuries, while Madray was the team's leading wicket-taker. These games against Barbados and Jamaica were also unprecedented in Guianese cricket history by the inclusion of as many as four Indians in the national team- Kanhai, Solomon and Madray being joined by the all-rounder Wilfred Edun in one game and by the medium pacer Bajnauth in the other. Thereafter Indians were almost invariably regular members of the national team.

The 1950s were also a watershed in another way. The decade witnessed the selection for the first time of Indo- Guianese for the West Indies team, following the precedent set in 1950 when the Trinidadian spin bowler, Sonny Ramadhin, became the first Indian to represent the region. Wilfred Edun, a medium- fast bowler who was also a useful lower- order batsman, was a member of the West Indies touring side to New Zealand in 1956, but was not selected for any of the four Tests. The country had to wait until the following year, 1957, for its first Indian Test player. Rohan Kanhai, who represented the West Indies in all five games in a Test series in England not only as a batsman, but also as a wicket-keeper in three of them.

ROHAN KANHAI

Rohan Kanhai is the finest batsman produced by Guyana and the most outstanding West Indian player of Indian extraction. He had a long and distinguished career both for Guyana and the West Indies. He is arguably the finest, certainly the most audacious and inventive, strokeplayer in the long history of West Indies cricket. The zenith of his career was probably in the early 1960s when he was the West Indies most productive batsman with excellent aggregates of 503, 495, 497 and 462 runs in four successive Test series against Australia, India, England and Australia respectively. In his entire career of 79 Tests he scored 6227 runs including 15 hundreds and 28 half-centuries with a very good average of 47.53 runs an innings. In the last thirteen of these Tests he served as captain, the first Indian to lead the regional Test team.

Apart from this accomplishment, Kanhai's achievements as a Guyanese in Tests are numerous and unique. He was the first Guyanese to score a Test hundred at Bourda (150 against England in 1968), a double hundred in a Test (256 against India in 1959), two centuries in the same Test (117 and 115 against Australia in 1961) and to lead the West Indies for an extended period.

Kanhai is also the only Guyanese whose first two Test centuries were double hundreds and the fastest Guyanese to achieve 4000, 5000 and 6000 runs in Tests. Furthermore, he has the highest score by a Guyanese at the famous Lord's cricket ground, 157 in 1973. His other achievements include being the first Guyanese to be named among the prestigious Wisden Alamanac's Cricketers of the Year (in 1964), the most consecutive Test appearances (61) by a Guyanese and scoring more runs in Tests (1212 runs including four centuries and four fifties) than any other West Indian at the Queen's Park Oval in Trinidad.

Kanhai proved to be the first of an increasing number of Indo-Guyanese to have represented the West Indies in Test cricket. The list includes in chronological order Ivan Madray, Joe Solomon, Alvin Kallicharran, Leonard Baichan, Sewdatt Shivnarine, Faoud Bacchus, Shivnarine Chanderpaul, Ramnaresh Sarwan, Mahendra Nagamootoo, Narsingh Deonarine, Ryan Ramdass, Sewnarine Chattergoon, Devendra Bishoo, Assad Fudadin, Veerasammy Permaul, Rajendra Chandrika and Vishaul Singh.

Kanhai, Madray and Solomon may be regarded as the first generation of Indo-Guyanese Test players, Kallicharran, Baichan, Shivnarine and Bacchus as the next and the others who represented the West Indies in Tests since the 1990s as the latest generation. The most successful of these players in Tests apart from Kanhai were Solomon, Kallicharran, Baichan, Chanderpaul, Sarwan and Bishoo.

JOE SOLOMON

Joe Solomon, a contemporary of Kanhai, was a reliable right-handed middle-order batsman, who had an excellent defence. The finest achievement of his career of 27 Tests was in his first Test series in India in 1958-59 when he became the first Indian and Guyanese to head a series batting average. Solomon scored 351 runs with a phenomenal average of 117 runs an innings. His modest Test record of 1326 runs in 27 Tests with an average of 34.00 with one century and nine fifties was surpassed greatly by his career for Guyana in first-class cricket which eclipsed that of any other Guyanese- 1905 runs (including nine hundreds and four fifties) in 23 matches with an average of 68.03. He, however, is best remembered for effecting the run out that produced the first tied Test in cricket history against Australia at Brisbane in December 1960.

ALVIN KALLICHARRAN

Apart from Rohan Kanhai and Shivnarine Chanderpaul, Alvin

Kallicharran, an aggressive left-handed middle-order batsman, is arguably the most outstanding Indo-West Indian cricketer. Among his achievements were a century in his first Test innings against New Zealand at Bourda in April 1972, the only Guyanese debutant to make a first- appearance hundred at home. He followed this knock with another century in his next Test innings in Trinidad two weeks later, thus becoming the first and still the only West Indian to score back-to-back centuries in consecutive Tests on debut. These two hundreds enabled him to lead his team's batting averages for the series, emulating the precedent set by Joe Solomon thirteen years before in India.

Kallicharran proceeded to become the fastest Guyanese to make both 1000 Test runs (in 21 innings) and 2000 Test runs (in 40 innings). He was also one of the Wisden Cricketers of the Year in 1983, the year after his Test career, like that of Faoud Bacchus later, came to a sudden end when he was banned from the West Indies team for playing cricket in apartheid South Africa. By then he had played 66 Tests, scored 4399 runs, including 12 centuries and 21 fifties, at a commendable average of 44.43 runs an innings. He led the regional team in nine Tests in 1978 and 1979 during the Kerry Packer World Series Cricket crisis, the second Indian and the fourth Guyanese after Marius Fernandes, Kanhai and Clive Lloyd to be accorded that honour.

In his long and successful first-class career which ended in 1990, Kallicharran played more matches and scored more runs and centuries than any other Guyanese in the history of the game. In 505 such matches, he made 32, 650 runs, including 87 centuries, with a highest score of 243 not out and an average of 43.64 runs an innings.

Leonard Baichan

A contemporary of Kallicharran was another Berbician left-hander, Leonard Baichan. Baichan, a solid, stolid determined opening batsman, was one of the most successful Indo-Guyanese cricketers, though he had only a short Test cricket career of three matches. Like Kallicharran, he had the distinction of scoring a hundred in his first Test, 105 not out against Pakistan at Lahore in February 1975. His Test career batting average of 46.00 is better than that of any other Guyanese except Chanderpaul, Kanhai and Lloyd. His performance for Guyana in first-class cricket is also commendable. In 34 matches he scored 2136 runs, including five centuries and 12 fifties with an average of 41.88 runs an innings. The presence of world-class openers, Roy

Fredericks, Gordon Greenidge and Desmond Haynes, prevented Baichan from having more Test appearances.

Shivnarine Chanderpaul and Ramnaresh Sarwan

Since the end of the Test careers of Alvin Kallicharran and Leonard Baichan, there have been only two Indo-Guyanese who have occupied a prominent and regular place in the West Indies Test team- Shivnarine Chanderpaul and Ramnaresh Sarwan. For several years they were the only two Guyanese in the regional Test team. Both of them made an impressive entry into Test cricket at the age of nineteen, Chanderpaul scoring 62 against England at Bourda in April 1992 and Sarwan 84 not out against Pakistan at Kensington Oval in May 2000. Apart from Brian Lara they were frequently the team's most productive batsmen, especially in Test cricket.

Sarwan played 87 Tests in which he scored 5842 runs, including 15 centuries and 31 fifties with an average of 40.01. One of his most significant accomplishments is that he made the two highest scores by a Guyanese in Tests- 261 not out against Bangladesh at Kingston in June 2004 and 291 against England at Bridgetown in February 2009. This second double century in addition was the longest innings (in minutes- 698 minutes) by a Guyanese in Test cricket and contributed to his achieving the largest aggregate (626 runs) by a Guyanese in a Test series in the Caribbean. Sarwan also had the honour of being captain of the regional team in four Tests, the seventh Guyanese and the fourth Indian after Kanhai, Kallicharran and Chanderpaul.

Even more impressive than Sarwan's attainments were those of his contemporary, Shivnarine Chanderpaul, the first teenager to represent the West Indies in Test cricket since Alvin Kallicharran in 1972. Chanderpaul, in striking contrast to Sarwan, was an essentially defensive left-handed middle-order batsman. Yet ironically, he managed one of the fastest Test centuries against Australia at Bourda in April 2003 off only 69 deliveries.

Most of Chanderpaul's numerous other achievements reflect several of his better- known virtues such as his deep concentration, the high value which he attached to his wicket, his careful shot selection and his physical fitness. For example, he is the only batsman in Test cricket history to face 1000 deliveries without being dismissed. Moreover, apart from the great Australian, Don Bradman, Chanderpaul is the only player to achieve a Test average of more than 100.00 in two consecutive calendar years- 111.60 in 2007 and 101.00 in 2008. He has also scored more Test runs in a calendar year (1065 runs, including four hundreds and six fifties in 2002) than any other Guyanese. Furthermore, he has been involved in more century partnerships in Tests than any other West Indian cricketer. One of them was his famous run chase with Sarwan in the fourth innings of a Test against Australia in Antigua in a game in 2003 which the West Indies won by three wickets.

Chanderpaul is highly respected in Barbados where he scored more Test runs (1412 runs, including four hundreds and nine fifties) than any other West Indian. He has also made more Test hundreds and fifties in the Caribbean than any other cricketer.

At the end of his long and productive career Chanderpaul had more Test appearances (164) than any other West Indian cricketer. In the process he became the first East Indian to play 100 Tests for the West Indies and only one of three Guyanese, the others being Clive Lloyd (110 Tests) and Carl Hooper (102 Tests). His Test aggregate has been surpassed only by Brian Lara (11953 runs at an average of 52.88) whom he replaced as the pillar of his team's batting after Lara retired in 2006.

In his Test career Chanderpaul, the second West Indian to reach 10,000 runs, scored 11,867 runs (including 30 centuries and 66 fifties with a highest score of 203 not out and an excellent average of 51.37). In the process he became the oldest Guyanese (38 years and 39 days) to score a Test double century, surpassed only by the Barbadian, Gordon Greenidge.

Chanderpaul had the honour to lead the regional team in 14 Tests- the sixth Guyanese skipper and the third Indo-Guyanese after Kanhai and Kallicharran. He, however, was not successful, winning only one of these matches. Eventually he resigned from the position in 2006 to concentrate on his batting. He will go down in history as the Guyanese with the best statistical Test record in terms of the number of runs, centuries, fifties and average. Not surprisingly, he has received several accolades, including being one of the Wisden Cricketers of this Year in 2008 and the ICC Player of the Year that same year.

Conclusion

Since the 1950s Indo-Guyanese cricketers have been making a substantial contribution to Guyanese cricket and a very useful one to West Indies Test cricket. Eighteen of the fifty Guyanese who have played Test cricket are Indians. Their contribution has been mainly in the area of batting, for only five of them, namely, Ivan Madray, Sewdatt Sewnarine, Mahendra

Nagamootoo, Devendra Bishoo and Veerasammy Permaul, were selected primarily for their bowling. None of these bowlers, however, have been sufficiently successful with the ball in Test cricket to command a regular place in the regional team for an extended period.

For Further Reading

Birbalsingh, Frank & Shiwcharan, Clem	**Indo-West Indian Cricket** (London: Hansib Publishing Ltd, 1988).
Birbalsingh, Frank	**Indian- Caribbean Test Cricketers and the Quest for Identity** (Hertford: Hansib Publications, 2014).
Kanhai, Rohan	**Blasting for Runs** (London: Souvenir Press, 1966).
Seecharran, Clem	**From Ranji to Rohan** (Hertford: Hansib Publications, 2009).
Sambhudat (known as Shako), Ramnarine	**WI in Test Matches, Facts and Feats, 1938 – 2013** (2014).

Chapter 49

Shivnarine Chanderpaul: From Unity to The Top of The World

This is an apt description of the career of Guyana's and the Caribbean's most renowned current cricketer, Shivnarine Chanderpaul. Born in August 1974 in the little-known village of Unity on the East Coast of Demerara about twenty miles from Guyana's capital, Georgetown, Chanderpaul during the year 2008, reached unprecedented heights in his very successful career as an international cricketer.

This diminutive left-handed, middle-order batsman who loves to bat at Number 5, had two major achievements in 2008. Firstly, in July Chanderpaul attained the top position in the International Cricket Council's (ICC's) Test batting ratings, ahead of his closest rivals, Kumar Sangakarra of Sri Lanka and the Australians, Mike Hussey and Ricky Ponting. This achievement was largely as a result of his outstanding performance in a series in the Caribbean against the world champions, Australia. Although the Aussies won the rubber 2-0, Chanderpaul was voted Man-of-the-Series for his splendid batting. In six innings he scored 442 runs, including two centuries and three fifties, with a phenomenal average of 147.33.

Chanderpaul's second achievement in 2008 was even more prestigious. In September, the ICC in its fifth annual awards named Chanderpaul its Cricketer of the Year, an improvement on his performance in the previous year, 2007, when he made the short list. In 2008 he eclipsed the other nominees, Mahela Jayawardene of Sri Lanka and the South Africans, Graeme Smith and Dale Steyn, to take the top award. He thus joined the illustrious company of India's Rahul Dravid (2004), England's Andrew Flintoff (2005) and Australia's Ricky Ponting (2006 and 2007), the previous winners of this top prize.

Chanderpaul was also included in the ICC's World Test Team for 2008. The other members of this imaginary side were Graeme Smith (South Africa, captain), Virender Sehwag (India), Mahela Jayawardene (Sri Lanka), Kevin

Pietersen (England), Jacques Kallis (South Africa), Kumar Sangakkara (Sri Lanka, wicket-keeper), Brett Lee (Australia), Ryan Sidebottom (England), Dale Steyn (South Africa) and Muttiah Muralitharan (Sri Lanka).

The ICC in its press release announcing Chanderpaul's award stated that he "had an outstanding year with the bat becoming one of the world's most consistent and determined players."[181] In the twelve-month period under consideration, Chanderpaul played eight Tests, scoring 819 runs, including three hundreds and six fifties, all against the top seven teams in the world, with an excellent average of 91.00. He made 247 runs in three Tests in South Africa late in 2007, 130 runs in two matches against Sri Lanka in April 2008 and 442 runs against Australia in the following May and June. He also played 13 One-Day International matches, scoring 598 runs, including one century and five fifties with an impressive average of 74.75.

Chanderpaul's achievements in 2008 were unique in several ways. Firstly, he topped the world's batting average in both versions (the longer and the shorter) of the game. Secondly, he became the first Guyanese or West Indian to be ranked the ICC Number One batsman in the world. Thirdly, he was the only West Indian batsman or bowler in the top ten positions in the ICC ratings. Fourthly, he is the first West Indian player to win a major prize at the ICC Awards. Finally, he was the only West Indian on the ICC's 2008 World Test team.

Chanderpaul has exerted immense influence on the fortunes of West Indies cricket especially in recent years. In particular, he made a substantial contribution to two rare Test victories of the regional team. At Port Elizabeth in December 2007, when the West Indies secured its first ever Test win in South Africa, Chanderpaul scored a century (104) in the first innings. Four months later in April 2008, when the team defeated Sri Lanka at the Queen's Park Oval in Port of Spain, Trinidad, to level the Test series, it was he with an unbeaten innings of 86 and his fellow Guyanese, Ramnaresh Sarwan (102) who enabled the West Indies to reach a challenging winning target of 254 with an impressive fourth-wicket partnership of 157.

During the period 2007-2009 Chanderpaul reached two important landmarks. Firstly, in December 2007 he became only the third West Indian to pass 7000 runs in One Day International matches during an undefeated innings of 127 against Zimbabwe at Harare, his 209th ODI innings. He thus joined Brian Lara (10405 runs in 289 innings) and Desmond Haynes (8648 runs in 237 innings). Secondly, in 2009 he became the first Guyanese and only the fourth West Indian, after the Barbadian, Garfield Sobers, the

Antiguan, Vivian Richards, and the Trinidadian, Brian Lara, to pass 8000 runs in Test cricket.

Chanderpaul's success has been achieved at a time when cricket has been serving increasingly to make the Anglophone Caribbean a tourist attraction. The region's most popular game is diversifying its tourism product, formerly restricted largely to its seas and beaches. The staging of the ICC's 2007 limited-over World Cup in the Caribbean in particular has given a fillip to the development of sports tourism. Tourist agencies in Caribbean Test- and ODI-playing territories are now exploring seriously how they can capitalize on the love for cricket to attract visitors especially from the United Kingdom and North America.

Tourists who have seen Chanderpaul bat have not been impressed by his awkward-looking, square-on stance, his crab-like movement across the stumps or his strokeplay which is seldom spectacular. Rather they admire his technique, superb defence, immense powers of concentration, good footwork, insatiable appetite for runs, his reliability and productivity especially in challenging circumstances, the high value he attaches to his wicket and his prolonged occupation of the crease. They are also struck by his character, especially his unassuming manner, his courage, calmness, confidence, single-minded determination, dedication and his tremendous fighting spirit.

These are the virtues that are responsible for Chanderpaul's phenomenal success in the last seven years, the zenith of his impressive career. Now 39 years old, he has fulfilled the great expectations he created in his maiden Test series against England in the Caribbean in 1994 nineteen years ago when he scored four fifties in six innings and achieved an average of 57.60. He was then only nineteen years of age, the first teenager to represent the West Indies in cricket in over twenty years.

Chanderpaul, who has played more than 150 Test matches and scored over 11,000 runs in Tests, has now become the Guyanese with the most Test appearances. These impressive national records, however, are surpassed in prestige by the recognition given to him in 2008 by the ICC. Guyanese and other Caribbean cricket fans hope that the little man from Unity, known as Tiger, will continue to maintain his excellent performances and remain at or near the top of the cricketing world. They expect that by the end of his international career he will surpass Brian Lara by becoming the West Indian with the most runs in Test cricket.[182]

For Further Reading

Birbalsingh, Frank	**Indian-Caribbean Test Cricketers and the Quest for Identity** (Hertford: Hansib Publications, 2014).
Mc Gowan, Winston	**West Indian Cricket Triple Centurions (From Tarilton to Chanderpaul)** (Georgetown: The Author, 1998).
Sambhudat (known as Shako), Ramnarine	**WI in Test Matches Facts and Feats, 1938-2013** (2014).

Chapter 50

More Truth About Carl Hooper

Early in 2001, about a year ago, an article appeared in the **Stabroek News** daily newspaper entitled "The Truth about Carl Hooper", one of Guyana's best-known cricketers. It was published partly in response to the savage criticism made by certain prominent Caribbean commentators and analysts at the time of his appointment as captain of the West Indies team for the Test series against the visiting South Africans. That article sought to present an objective analysis and appraisal of Hooper's career in the three important areas of one-day international (ODI), first-class and Test cricket. This sequel is designed to focus on some of Hooper's achievements during the past year.

In this period Hooper has reached three major landmarks in limited-over international cricket (i.e. ODI matches), namely, 200 games, 5000 runs and 100 catches. His career record in such cricket is as follows: 205 games, 187 innings, 38 times not out, 5310 runs (including seven hundreds and 28 fifties), with a highest score of 113 not out against India at Gwalior in 1988 and an average of 35.63 runs an innings. In bowling, where he has demonstrated the twin virtues of economy and effectiveness, he has captured 180 wickets in 1446 overs at an average cost of 34.79 runs each, conceding 4.32 runs an over. Furthermore, he has taken 100 catches in ODI matches.

Only three other West Indians presently have at least 200 ODI appearances, namely, the batsmen, Desmond Haynes (238) and Richie Richardson (224) and the fast bowler, Courtney Walsh (205). Hooper has also recently joined the group of five Caribbean batsmen who have scored over 5000 runs in such games- Haynes 8648 runs (average 41.37), Brian Lara 7257 (av. 42.43), Vivian Richards 6721 (av. 47.00), Richardson 6248 (av. 33.41) and Gordon Greenidge 5134 (av. 45.03). Hooper's tally of wickets in ODI games (180) has been surpassed by only two West Indians. Curtly Ambrose (225) and Walsh (227). He is now approaching Richards' record of 101 catches in such cricket, having already eclipsed Lara (82) and Richardson (75). These achievements attest to both his ability and durability. He continues to be "a colossus in the one-day game",[183] as the famous **Wisden Cricketers' Almanack** described him in 1996.

Where Test cricket is concerned, Hooper has passed four significant milestones in the past year, April 2001- April 2002- 5000 runs, 10 centuries, 100 wickets and 100 catches. Before his magnificent double century (233) last week at Bourda against India, he had scored 5020 runs in Tests with 10 hundreds, including a top score of 178 not out against Pakistan in Antigua in1993, and a moderate but improving average of 35.10 runs an innings. He is the ninth West Indian to score 5000 runs in Tests, joining Richards (8540), Garfield Sobers (8032), Greenidge (7558), Clive Lloyd (7515), Haynes (7487), Lara (7257), Rohan Kanhai (6227) and Richardson (5949). He has joined these players as well as George Headley (10), Clyde Walcott (15), Everton Weekes (15) and Alvin Kallicharran (12) as the only West Indians who have scored at least 10 Test hundreds. Hooper is thus the thirteenth West Indian to achieve this distinction.

In bowling in Tests Hooper has taken 103 wickets at an average of just over 50 runs a wickets. He is the fifteenth West Indian to capture 100 Test wickets, the last being Ian Bishop, and only the third Guyanese, following the example set by Lance Gibbs (309 wickets) and Colin Croft (125) who, unlike Hooper, were specialist bowlers. Hooper continues to be one of his team's best fieldsmen, especially at slip and at short extra cover and short midwicket. He has taken 106 catches in Tests, joining three West Indians who have passed the landmarks of 100 catches in such matches- Richards (122), Sobers (109) and Lara (107).

All these achievements are palpable evidence of Hooper's considerable value to West Indies cricket as an all-rounder or utility player. His crowning distinction for which he was honoured earlier this week, the third week of April 2002, by the Guyana Cricket Board is phenomenal and deserves greater recognition. Hooper is the first and so far the only cricketer in history to achieve the treble of 5000 runs, 100 wickets and 100 catches in both forms of the international game, namely, limited-over and Test cricket. Garfield Sobers aceived this "golden treble" in Test cricket and Vivian Richards in one-day international matches. No other West Indian, however, is even remotely close to either achievement.

Nevertheless, no other West Indian player has been as consistently and severely maligned as Carl Hooper. It is also significant and instructive to note that Hooper is the only Guyanese to have performed most of the feats outlined above. Partly for this reason Hooper occupies a very special place in the history of Guyanese and world cricket.

For Further Reading

Goble, Ray & Sandiford, Keith	**75 Years of West Indies Cricket 1928-2003** (London: Hansib Publications Ltd., 2004).
Lawrence, Bridgette & Goble, Ray	**The Complete Record of West Indian Test Cricketers** (Leicester: ACL & Polar Publishing, 1991).
Warne, Shane	**Shane Warne's Century – My Top 100 Test Cricketers** (Edinburgh: Mainstream Publishing Company, 2009).
Sambhudat (Known as Shako), Ramnarine	**WI in Test Matches Facts and Feats, 1938-2013** (2014).

Chapter 51

History at Bourda, 2005

The year 2005 was a significant year in the history of cricket at the famous Bourda ground. At the end of March and the beginning of April the ground was the venue for the first Test of a series between the West Indies and South Africa. The game was only the sixteenth Test and the beginning of only the fourth series between the two teams.

The West Indies have had fewer clashes with South Africa than against any other long-established team in international cricket. Although South Africa began playing Test cricket in 1889 and the West Indies in 1928, for more than sixty years the two teams could not and did not play against each other because of the South Africans' abominable racist apartheid policy. It was not until April 1992 in the post-apartheid era, when South Africa was readmitted to Test cricket after the apartheid ban which had lasted 22 years, that the inaugural Test between the two sides took place, the first game between South Africa and a non-white team.

That historic match, a one-off Test, was played at Kensington Oval in Barbados, where the West Indies, under the captaincy of the Antiguan, Richie Richardson, gained an exciting come-from-behind victory by 52 runs. After that success the West Indies lost three consecutive Test series to South Africa, two in South Africa (in 1998-99 and 2003-4) and one at home (in 2000-01). The regional team was keen to atone for these defeats by winning the 2005 Test series in the Caribbean.

The first match of this series at Bourda was historic in many ways. For example, it was the first occasion that Guyana's captain, Shivnarine Chanderpaul, was asked to lead the regional team in a Test match. He was the sixth Guyanese to be accorded that honour. Like two of his Guyanese predecessors, namely Marius Fernandes in 1930 and Alvin Kallicharran in 1978, Chanderpaul was thrust into the position unexpectedly in circumstances which may be described as an emergency or crisis, namely, a dispute over players' contracts.

Chanderpaul responded by scoring an impressive double century. His innings was a very significant achievement from several perspectives. It was the highest score by a West Indian in his debut as skipper of the Test team. He surpassed the scores of his previous Guyanese predecessors on a similar occasion- 22 and 19 by Fernandes, 84 by Rohan Kanhai in 1973, 30 and 163 by Clive Lloyd in 1974, 0 and 22 by Kallicharran in 1978 and 69 and 35 by Carl Hooper in 2001. In short, Chanderpaul, following Lloyd's example, is the second Guyanese to score a century in his first Test as captain. Furthermore, he became only the second captain in the long history of Test cricket dating back to 1877, to score a double century on his captaincy debut, emulating the New Zealander, Graham Dowling, who made 239 against India at Christchurch in February 1968.

It was Chanderpaul's maiden Test double hundred, eclipsing by far his previous highest Test score of 140 against India at Bourda and at Eden Gardens in 2002. It was his fourth Test hundred at Bourda, more than any other Guyanese batsman in Tests there. It was also the second highest Test score by a Guyanese at the ground, thirty runs less than the 233 made by Hooper against India in 2002 when they shared a fourth-wicket partnership of 293. Chanderpaul's double century was his twelfth Test hundred, making him equal with Kallicharran on the list of Guyanese with the greatest number of Test centuries. He was then below Lloyd (19 centuries), Kanhai (15) and Hooper (13).

Chanderpaul and his fellow double centurion, the Jamaican, Wavell Hinds (213), became only the second pair of West Indian batsmen to score double hundreds in the same innings of a Test match. This enviable feat was first achieved by West Indians almost forty seven years earlier at Sabina Park in Jamaica in 1958 against Pakistan by the Barbadians, Garfield Sobers (365 not out, then the world's highest Test score) and Conrad Hunte (260). Sobers and Hunte shared a second-wicket partnership of 446. Their brilliant batting enabled the West Indies to amass a mammoth score of 790 for three wickets declared, still the region's highest Test innings total.

In contrast, at Bourda in 2005 the West Indies made 543 for five declared, their highest score in a Test innings against South Africa, surpassing the 427 made at Capetown in 2004 . In short, the game at Bourda in 2005 was the first occasion that the West Indies scored over 500 runs in an innings in sixteen Tests against South Africa. This was sweet revenge for in the first innings of the previous four Tests between the two teams South Africa had scored over 500 runs. Before that, however, neither team had achieved a total of 500 runs in an innings in eleven Tests.

The Test at Bourda in 2005 was one of the rare occasions that the West Indies led South Africa on first innings. In fact, it was the only occasion that the regional team seemed well-placed to gain an innings victory over South Africa in a Test. The innings by Hinds and Chanderpaul were the highest ever by the West Indies against South Africa, surpassing the previous best score of 202 by the Trinidadian, Brian Lara, at Johannesburg in 2003. No South African has yet scored a Test double century against the West Indies. Their most productive innings against the West Indies is 192 by Herschelle Gibbs at Centurion in 2004.

The partnership of 284 runs which Hinds and Chanderpaul shared is the highest by the West Indies for any wicket against South Africa, exceeding the 174 made for Chris Gayle and Ramnaresh Sarwan at Centurion in 2004. It was also a record for the fourth wicket in Tests between the two teams, surpassing the 249- run stand by Jacques Kallis and Gary Kirsten at Durban in 2003. Furthermore, it was the second highest partnership in Tests between the two sides for any wicket, falling 17 runs short of the 301 runs made by Graeme Smith and Herschelle Gibbs at Centurion in 2004.

The stand by Hinds and Chanderpaul was also the second highest partnership for the West Indies in Tests for the fourth wicket. It eclipsed the 283 made by Frank Worrell (261) and Everton Weekes (129) against England at Trent Bridge in 1950. It was, however, well short of the 399 runs put on by Sobers (226) and Worrell (197 not out) against England at Kensington Oval in Barbados in 1960. At the conclusion of the Test between the West Indies and South Africa at Bourda in 2005, Chanderpaul was given the Man-of-the-Match award. This game turned out to be the last Test to have been played at Bourda, for in 2007 this famous ground was replaced as the local venue for Test cricket by the new stadium at Providence built for the 2007 ICC World Cup. This fact has made the 2005 Test even more historic than it would otherwise have been.

CHAPTER 52

REMEMBERING THE GLORY DAYS OF WEST INDIES CRICKET

Cricket is the most popular sport of the overwhelming majority of Guyanese. Many Guyanese follow the performance of the West Indies in international cricket more closely than that of their national team in regional competitions. They continue to be disappointed and saddened by the limited success in Test cricket by the West Indies since the mid 1990s. They are embarrassed and ashamed that in this current period the West Indies almost invariably has been ranked a lowly seventh or eighth among the ten Test-playing teams.

This painful reality often evokes memories of the phenomenal results of the West Indies in Tests in the 1980s and early half of the 1990 which have been described in Guyana and elsewhere in the Caribbean as "the glory days of West Indies cricket." In this remarkable period between 1980 and 1995 the West Indies under the leadership of the Guyanese Clive Lloyd, followed by the Antiguans Vivian Richards and Richie Richardson, were undefeated in 27 consecutive Test series and two one-off Tests against South Africa in 1992 and Sri Lanka in 1993. This era was glorious for at least three main reasons.

Firstly, it was the period when the West Indies, undisputed world champions, enjoyed its greatest success in its long history of Test cricket which dates back to 1928, over 80 years ago. It surpassed by far the region's performance in the mid 1960s when under the captaincy of Barbadian, Garfield Sobers, the West Indies became world cricket champions for the first time. This first period of ascendancy from 1965 to 1968 was short-lived, in striking contrast to the prolonged period of dominance from 1980 to 1995.

Secondly, these fifteen years were an unprecedented achievement of unbroken dominance in the long history of international Test cricket dating back to its inception in 1877. The game's closest comparison was Australia's sequence of 12 series without defeat (10 wins and two draws) in 19 years between 1934 and 1953, including six years from 1939 to 1945 when Test cricket was completely interrupted by the Second World War. Between 1980 and 1995 the West Indies won 19 and drew eight series and played 115 Tests, winning 59, losing only 15 and drawing 41. Their dominance was reflected in the fact that the composition of the regional team in a Test series was seldom changed except for injury and many of its members had the rare experience of never participating in a rubber that was lost.

Thirdly, the period of supremacy from 1980 to 1995 was glorious because of the numerous specific outstanding achievements by the team. One of them was a sequence of 27 consecutive Tests without a loss between January 1982 and December 1984, surpassing the record of 26 games without defeat set by England between 1968 and 1971. Furthermore, at one stage the West Indies had the impressive accomplishment of suffering only two defeats in 38 Tests and three in 54 Tests. For seven years between 1981 and 1988 no visiting team won even a single Test in the Caribbean, even though as many as 19 games were played. The regional team was so strong that it usually defeated its opponents abroad, even though they enjoyed home advantage.

1984 in particular was a year of phenomenal achievement for the West Indies. It included eleven Test wins in succession, surpassing the previous record of eight successive victories by Australia sixty-four years before in 1920-1. The first three of these eleven victories were against Australia, enabling the West Indies to defeat the Aussies 3-0 in a five-match rubber in the Caribbean. This was not only the largest margin of victory achieved by the West Indies in a series against Australia, but also, more remarkably, the first occasion in Test cricket that a team did not lose a single second-innings wicket in a five-match series.

Furthermore, in their next five Tests between June and August 1984, the West Indies became the first team to win every match in a five-game series against England in England. All five wins were by massive margins, namely, an innings and 180 runs, nine wickets, eight wickets, an innings and 64 runs, and 172 runs. This impressive achievement was repeated in the Caribbean two years later in 1986, again with convincing victories-by 10 wickets, seven wickets, an innings and 30 runs, 10 wickets, and 240 runs.

The remarkable success which the West Indies enjoyed in this golden era between 1980 and 1995 was due to many factors. Some of them may be considered general and others specific. Two of the general factors and four of the specific ones will be highlighted.

The basic underlying reason for the success was the fact that almost the entire team consisted of quality players. Most of them, in addition to the natural talent with which they were endowed, were partly indebted to their experience in English county cricket for their development into world-class players. The high quality of the team was reflected in the following eleven players who played almost unchanged in a series against India in the Caribbean in 1983: Gordon Greenidge, Desmond Haynes, Vivian Richards, Larry Gomes, Gus Logie, Clive Lloyd, Jeffrey Dujon, Malcolm Marshall, Andy Roberts, Michael Holding and Joel Garner. Of these it was only Gomes and Logie who, though very able, were not truly top-class players by the highest international standards.

The second general factor which contributed immensely to the West Indies success was that the team benefited from the availability of an abundant supply of talent. This asset gave the region the extraordinary ability to replenish its team with quality players to replace those who became unavailable through injury, retirement or any other reason.

Particularly impressive was the amazing succession of fast bowlers which enabled the team to maintain a quality three or more often four- pronged pace attack. These bowlers included Andy Roberts, Michael Holding, Wayne Daniel, Colin Croft, Joel Garner, Sylvester Clarke, Malcolm Marshall, Winston Davis, Eldine Baptiste, Courtney Walsh, Patrick Patterson, Curtly Ambrose, Ian Bishop, Anthony Gray and Winston and Kenneth Benjamin. The sustained effectiveness of the pace attack was one of four major specific factors responsible for the West Indies ascendancy between 1980 and 1995. The other three factors were the team's strong batting line-up, good leadership and excellent fielding, including wicket- keeping.

Apart from speed, the pace attack was usually distinguished by three qualities, namely, hostility, penetration and good control of line and length which exerted considerable pressure on the opposing batsmen. The best of the pacemen were very outstanding bowlers who had excellent strike and economy rates and an excellent Test career bowling average. For example, Malcolm Marshall, arguably the most effective of them, in 81 Tests took 376 wickets, with an average of 20.94, a strike rate of one wicket every 46 balls and an economy rate of 2.68 runs an over. Joel Garner's figures were equally impressive. In 58 Tests he captured 259 wickets at an average of 20.97, with a strike rate of a wicket every 50 ball and an economy rate of 2.47 runs an over.

The effectiveness of the fast bowlers meant that there was no regular place in the team for a spinner. This explains why the Guyanese, Roger Harper, the most successful of the spinners, had only 25 appearances in a Test career lasting 10 years, from 1983-1993, even though he was also a brilliant fieldsman and a useful lower-order batsman. In these Test appearances Harper, an economical off-break bowler, captured 46 wickers at a very satisfactory average for a spinner of 28.06 runs each with a best innings performance of six for 57 in 28.4 overs against England at Old Trafford. This performance enabled the West Indies to win the Test by an innings and 64 runs.

The foundation of the team's strong batting line-up was Gordon Greenidge and Desmond Haynes, the longest and best opening pair in the history of West Indies Test cricket. In Tests these two Barbadian openers shared 16 hundred partnerships, 26 over fifty and an average opening stand of 47.32, with a best of 298 against England in Antigua in 1990. Their productivity was also reflected in their commendable Test career batting average of 44.72 and 42.49 respectively.

The foundation set by Greenidge and Haynes was built on by a formidable middle-order whose ability and success were reflected in their Test career statistics- Alvin Kallicharran (average 44.43- 12 centuries, 21 fifties in 66 Tests); Clive Lloyd (46.67- 19 centuries, 39 fifties in 110 Tests); Vivian Richards (50.23, 24 centuries, 45 fifties in 121 Tests); Larry Gomes (39.63- 9 centuries, 13 fifties in 60 Tests); Richie Richardson (44.49- 16 centuries, 27 fifties in 86 Tests); and Gus Logie (35.79, 2 centuries, 16 fifties in 52 Tests).

All these specialist batsmen not only were technically very sound but also, with the exception of Gomes, were aggressive stroke makers who could dominate most bowling attacks. Their productivity was supplemented by the significant contribution of wicket-keeper Jeffrey Dujon. Although Dujon usually batted as low as Number 7, in his Test career of 81 appearances he scored 3322 runs, including five centuries and 16 fifties, with an average of 31.94. The team total also frequently received some support from the bowlers, most of whom had sufficient ability with the bat to ensure that the tail often wagged. This ability was reflected in the Test career batting average of several of them, notably Malcolm Marshall (18.92), Winston Benjamin (18.80), Roger Harper (18.44) and Andy Roberts (14.94). Marshall scored eight fifties in Tests with a highest score of 92, while Harper and Roberts both had three Test fifties including a top score of 74 and 68 respectively and Benjamin two fifties with a best of 85.

During the period of supremacy the West Indies team profited from very able leadership provided initially by Clive Lloyd, the longest serving and most successful West Indies captain. Lloyd led the West Indies in 74 Tests, winning 36 and losing only twelve. He was the skipper when the West Indies won eleven consecutive Tests in 1984, including the unique 5-0 thrashing of England in England. It was also he who introduced the use of the much-feared four-pronged pace attack.

Lloyd, a "father figure", had the respect and loyalty of the team whom he welded into a strong harmonious unit with a very professional approach, a determination to win, a pride in success and a disappointment in defeat. In short, the team had an excellent attitude. As Lloyd himself observed, "it was professionalism and togetherness, players realizing the importance of what they had to do and their commitment. These guys were totally West Indian in everything they did."[184]

Lloyd placed a high premium on mental toughness and physical fitness. His team prepared for success by a strenuous work regime at practice. This emphasis helped to make the West Indies the best fielding side in the world. The fielding was distinguished by very safe catching in the slips, especially by Lloyd, Richardson and Greenidge, athleticism in the outfield and strong accurate throwing, exemplified particularly in Richards, Holding and Harper.

The team also had an outstanding wicket-keeper in Dujon, who had sharp reflexes and was very athletic. On three occasions he achieved 20 or more dismissals in a five-match Test series and in his entire career effected 267 catches and five stumpings in 81 Tests. His fitness and the stamina of the fast bowlers were benefits of the demanding work regime.

The factors which were responsible for the dominance of the West Indies in the "glory days" of the 1980s and early 1990s are clearly not present in the current team. The current deficiencies especially in batting, bowling and attitude largely explain why Darren Sammy's team has usually been ranked an embarrassing eighth in the International Cricket Council's Test ratings instead of the undisputed first place occupied in the "glory days." This unwelcome situation is due partly to the marked decline in Guyanese cricket with the result that only one Guyanese, namely, Shivnarine Chanderpaul, commands a regular place in the regional Test team. This is a marked change from the beginning of the "glory days" when there were usually four Guyanese in the team, Faoud Bacchus, Colin Croft, Alvin Kallicharran and Clive Lloyd, the last three making an invaluable contribution to the side's dominance. Guyanese, like other Caribbean cricket fans, long for a return to such success, but this seems to be a very distant prospect.

For Further Reading

Manley, Michael with Symmonds, Donna	**A History of West Indies Cricket – revised edition** (London: Andre Deutsch Ltd., 2002).
King, Tony and Laurie, Peter	**The Glory Days – 25 Great West Indian Cricketers** (Oxford: Macmillian, 2004).
Goble, Ray & Sandiford, Keith	**75 Years of West Indies Cricket 1928-2003** (London: Hansib Publications, Ltd; 2004).

Part Eight

Labour and Trade Unionism

Monument in memory of
Hubert Nathaniel Critchlow

CHAPTER 53

HUBERT NATHANIEL CRITCHLOW AND THE BEGINNING OF TRADE UNIONISM IN BRITISH GUIANA

One of the main developments in the history of Guyana in the twentieth century was the birth and development of labour organisation. This development was crucial to the alleviation of many of the problems which adversely affected the life of the working class. Professional historians are extremely wary of explanations of events and developments which attribute too much importance to any single individual. It is difficult, however, to escape acknowledging the remarkable contribution of one man, Hubert Nathaniel Critchlow, to the origins and early history of the organised labour movement in Guyana. It was due largely to his vision, initiative, industry, determination and endurance that the first enduring trade union in the country, the British Guiana Labour Union (B.G.L.U.), was formed in January 1919. For this reason Critchlow is appropriately called "the father of trade unionism in Guyana".

The beginning of the trade union movement was a major development in the long history of intense struggle and conflict between capital and labour. This confrontation, first evident during the era of slavery, entered a new phase in 1838 when the former slaves, or "apprentices" as they were then euphemistically called, became fully free legally. They were then entitled to wages for their labour and had for the first time an ample opportunity to shape their own destiny. Their white ex-masters, on the other hand, were fearful that freedom and the resultant obligation to pay wages for labour would undermine their social status and erode the source of their wealth.

Two of the most salient elements in the conflict between the freed men and their former masters after 1838 were the related questions of employment and wage rates. The white planters believed strongly that it was in their best interest to have a cheap, immobile, easily controllable labour force. To achieve this end they imported thousands of Portuguese, Indian, African and Chinese indentured or contracted workers. The presence of these immigrants in increasing numbers enabled the planters by 1848, ten years after Emancipation, to control the labour market and to be in a position to depress wages paid to free workers, mostly the former apprentices.

As time elapsed, the situation facing free workers became worse. By 1870 wages in British Guiana had become extremely low as a result of the planters' exploitation of a labour surplus. Wages were lowered further after 1884, when the sugar industry began to experience a prolonged crisis owing to competition which Guianese and Caribbean sugar faced in the British market from government-subsided beet sugar produced by continental European countries.

By 1900 the lot of both urban and rural workers in British Guiana was unenviable. The most distressing feature was that wages were extremely low and stationary in circumstances where the cost of living was high and steadily increasing. Rents for housing and the prices of consumer goods in particular were subject to regular increases.

There were also other disturbing elements in the workers' plight. For example, the working day was very long, normally 10 – 10 ½ hours in Georgetown. There was also a high level of unemployment and underemployment both in the towns and the sugar belt which dominated the coastal rural districts.

These circumstances, especially disputes over wages, provoked sporadic protests both by urban, mainly black, and rural, mostly Indian, workers. These periodic, often spontaneous outbursts produced few positive gains for the workers in their struggle with employers who were often oppressive, arrogant and intransigent. There were no trade unions or any other organisation to represent the workers in their struggle. The fact that the workers were not organised and that their protests were often unrelated and lacking in good leadership, planning and execution rendered their cause more difficult and unsuccessful.

Two other important considerations made the situation of the workers even more bleak. Firstly, the workers had little political representation, for the property and income criteria which made citizens eligible to vote and to sit in the local legislature were far beyond the reach of the poorly paid workers. Consequently, at best the workers could only hope that one of the minority of black middle-class members of the legislature would support their cause.

Secondly, the government, which theoretically had a special responsibility under British colonial policy to protect the interests of unrepresented groups, was largely indifferent to the terrible plight of the workers. Thus it failed to introduce any legislation to regulate wages and hours of work. Rather it supported the plantocracy, the merchants and other employers in their use of political and financial power to exploit workers, periodically using the military forces under its jurisdiction to suppress workers' protests. Its attitude was clearly demonstrated in its reaction to a major strike for increased wages initiated in November 1905 by waterfront workers in Georgetown led by Hubert Nathaniel Critchlow. Governor Hodgson told a meeting of the strikers

> If you break the law in connection with your grievances, it is my duty as Governor of the Colony, and as the person who has to protect the property and interests of the mercantile community to protect them.[185]

The support which he gave to the employers was a major cause of the failure of the protest.

This November-December 1905 Protest, initially of waterfront workers in Georgetown, is a very historic event, especially in relation to working-class struggle and the origins of an organised labour movement in Guyana. It was significant from the standpoint of the wide range and large numbers of urban residents involved – various categories of workers apart from dock-workers, women, and the unemployed, especially residents of South Georgetown. It also witnessed the participation of East Indian workers from rural sugar estates, particularly on the East Bank of Demerara, the earliest significant example of working-class unity across the racial divide normally skilfully manipulated and exploited by the white plantocracy. Finally, it was this 1905 Protest which brought to visible prominence for the first time, Hubert Nathaniel Critchlow, hitherto a largely unknown, young waterfront worker.

The causes, course and eventual failure of the Protest had a major and enduring impact on Critchlow. It was this experience which made him extremely conscious of the arrogance and recalcitrance of the employer class, the organisational weakness of the workers, the lack of support of the government for workers, and the crucial need to organise workers into a trade union. Many years later, in an address which he delivered to the World Trade Union Conference in 1945, Critchlow stated that the genesis of the trade union movement in British Guiana could be traced back to this abortive Protest of 1905.

In this address, which he entitled "History of the Trade Union Movement in British Guiana", Critchlow observed

> Our working hours were 10 ½. The system of quarter day existed. There was no overtime for night work. We asked the employers to change these conditions. The reply was that we must take them or go. I organised a strike on the waterfront in December 1905. Our claims were for an increase of pay, which was very low. There was no trade union and the employers refused. So I got the working men, boys together, and they agreed that when there were six boats in the harbour they must strike. A great thing and at that time I did not know that all the estates in the country followed us and struck on account of low wages.[186]

The defeat of this 1905 Protest was due largely to the opposition of the government who supported the employers and dispatched the police to suppress it. It was also a result of the organisational weakness of the workers who did not have anybody to plan and guide their struggle and to equip them to conduct a sustained battle to obtain redress for the many abuses and injustices to which they were subject.

Critchlow was no doubt encouraged in his thinking about the need for a workers' organisation by an identical suggestion made at the same time by Dr. Rohlehr. Rohlehr, a black medical doctor, was sympathetic towards the workers and was one of their spokesmen during the 1905 Protest. In January 1906, one month after the collapse of the protest, at a meeting at the Town Hall in Georgetown, he urged workers to form a trade union. Later in that year a meeting was held in Georgetown to form a labour union, but this objective was not achieved. Twelve more years were to elapse before this goal became a reality.

British Guiana was in fact lagging behind some of the other major British West Indian territories, notably Jamaica and Trinidad, where labour organisation was concerned. Labour unions had been formed in Jamaica and Trinidad in the 1890s, although they were not legal entities. In Jamaica some workers were organised in small unions according to their craft, whereas Trinidad had one general union, the Trinidad Workingmen's Association, representing all categories of workers. It is not known whether Critchlow's desire and intention to establish a workers' organisation in British Guiana were influenced in any way by these developments in Jamaica and Trinidad.

For many years after 1906, however, no significant progress was made in British Guiana in the direction of labour organisation. One major obstacle which Critchlow and other labour leaders throughout the Caribbean faced was the fact that as yet there was no legal provision for the formation and operation of trade unions in British Guiana and elsewhere in the British West Indies.

The failure of the 1905 Protest and of another strike by waterfront workers in Georgetown in 1906 seems to have discouraged Critchlow. What is certain is that he did not take any significant public action to promote the cause of workers during the following seven years. While he, his fellow waterfront workers and other workers in Georgetown were relatively quiet during this period from 1907 to 1913, there were several significant protests by predominantly East Indian sugar workers in Berbice, particularly one in Rose Hall in 1913.

Critchlow only came into prominent public focus again after the outbreak of the First World War in 1914. The severe difficulties which the working class in particular experienced as a result of the war seem to have galvanised him into a new phase of militant action and reemphasised the need for a labour organisation. The war resulted in greatly increased cost of living and many other hardships for workers whose already unenviable economic position grew worse. In response to the deterioration of their situation, workers in Georgetown as well as on the rural sugar estates staged numerous strikes and work stoppages in the early years of the war. There was a high incidence of such action in 1916. Although these protests drove some employers to grant modest wage increases to their workers, on the whole they were largely unsuccessful.

The worsening economic situation drove workers in Berbice to try to form a trade union in 1917. Much of the inspiration and initiative for this move is attributed to a clergyman, Rev. R.T. Frank, who had just returned from England where he was impressed with the impact of the trade union movement. Frank is said to have organised a meeting in the Congregational Church in New Amsterdam, as a result of which a trade union was founded. Very little is known of this union which is believed to have collapsed within a few months, owing to a lack of financial support, the hostility of employers who dismissed members of the union and opposition from government authorities, who are said to have harassed the leaders of the union.

While the workers in Berbice were experiencing these setbacks, their counterparts in Georgetown were gaining a measure of success. The first major success achieved by protesting workers was in the capital in January 1917 and was due largely to the influence of Critchlow. Critchlow led waterfront workers there in a 13-day strike which triggered off strikes among other urban workers and forced employers to make two significant concessions – a wage increase of 10 per cent and a reduction of the normal working day from 10 ½ to 9 hours. Workers were thus able to secure a measure of relief in two of their main areas of dissatisfaction. In December of the same year, 1917, militant action led by Critchlow enabled some workers in Georgetown to secure a second wage increase of 10 per cent.

These successes were due largely to the influence of Critchlow who had emerged as the undisputed leader of the waterfront workers. However, they did not satisfy Critchlow, much to the annoyance of employers. Critchlow continued to lead the workers in pressing employers to make further concessions. He emphasised that the modest wage increases were being negatived by the continuous rise in the cost of living in war-time conditions, especially the growing cost of consumer goods.

Early in 1918 Critchlow presented a petition to the Georgetown Chamber of Commerce requesting an 8-hour working day. His employers put pressure on him to withdraw the petition, but, unlike its other signatories, he refused and was dismissed. This display of courage earned Critchlow the respect of many workers and made him feared by employers who refused to employ him for fear that he would cause their workers to become more militant and dissident. Critchlow, unable to secure employment anywhere in Georgetown, eventually took a momentous decision which had a great influence on the subsequent history of the country. He resolved to devote his time and energies to organising workers. The decision was largely responsible for his ability in January 1919 to form the British Guiana Labour Union (B.G.L.U.), the first enduring trade union in the colony, which he served initially as its full-time Secretary-Treasurer.

Critchlow's success in forming the union was also due to several other factors. Firstly, he was able to exploit the growing solidarity especially among workers in Georgetown particularly since the protests of 1917. Secondly, he profited from his enhanced reputation among these workers in the wake of these successful protests, and in particular from the strong support of his former colleagues on the waterfront.

Thirdly, Critchlow benefited from support from the rising Labour Party in Britain and from Governor Wilfred Collet who had assumed responsibility for the administration of the colony of British Guiana in April 1917. Critchlow, probably much to his surprise, discovered that Collet, in striking contrast to his predecessors, was in favour of the formation of a trade union. He made this discovery during a discussion with the governor in December 1918 when he led a workers' demonstration to government house as a result of which Collet agreed to meet a small delegation of demonstrators, including Critchlow. Collet, recognising the difficulties which the unrepresented workers faced, advised Critchlow to establish a genuine trade union and to seek the assistance of unions in Britain. Shortly after this meeting with the governor, Critchlow held a public meeting in Georgetown and proposed to the disaffected workers that they form a union. The workers agreed and many of them paid their entrance fee on the spot and the B.G.L.U. (now the Guyana Labour Union) was born.

Clearly, its formation was a result of the initiative and drive of Critchlow and the harsh socio-economic conditions faced by the working class in the colony. The union, of course, was not a legal entity, as there was still no legislation permitting the legal recognition of trade unions anywhere in the British Caribbean. Apart from the short-lived effort in Berbice in 1917, the B.G.L.U. was the first trade union to be established in the country and proved to be enduring. Partly for this reason Hubert Nathaniel Critchlow, in whose honour a monument stands on the grounds of Parliament Buildings in Georgetown, will always be remembered in Guyana.

For Further Reading

Alert, C.V.	**The Life and Work of Hubert Nathaniel Critchlow** (Georgetown: The Daily Chronicle Ltd., 1949).
Chase, Ashton	**A History of Trade Unionism in Guyana, 1900-1961** (Georgetown, 1964).
Harry, Carlyle	**Hubert Nathaniel Critchlow – His Main Tasks and Achievements** – revised edition (Georgetown, 1977).

Rodney, Walter	**A History of the Guyanese Working People, 1881-1905** (Baltimore: The John Hopkins University Press, (1981).
Drakes, Francis (Now Nehusi, Kimani)	"The Causes of the Protest of 1905", **History Gazette,** No.22, July 1990.
Drakes, Francis (Now Nehusi, Kimani)	"The Reaction of Sir Frederick Hodgson to the Protest of 1905", **History Gazette,** No. 37, October 1991.
Woolford, Hazel	"Hubert Nathaniel Critchlow: The Crusader", **History Gazette**, No.43, April 1992.

Chapter 54

Obstacles To the Early Trade Union Movement in British Guiana, 1919 – 1930

The establishment in January 1919 of the British Guiana Labour Union (B.G.L.U.), due mainly to the vision and initiative of Hubert Nathaniel Critchlow, was an important development in the history of the country. The union was active from its formation, but encountered numerous obstacles which limited its success in its struggle especially against the two main evils which workers faced, namely, low wages and a high level of unemployment and underemployment. It faced some of its most formidable obstacles in the initial phase of its existence between 1919 and 1930 when it was the only labour organisation in the country.

One of the major problems which the union faced at the outset was the fact that it was not, and could not be, registered because of the absence of legislation in the colony giving legal recognition to labour organisations. Owing, however, to pressure from the B.G.L.U. and the Colonial Office in London, which was harassed by the British Labour Party, whom Critchlow had approached for support, in June 1921 the legislature of British Guiana passed a Trade Union Ordinance entitled "An Ordinance to provide for the Regulation and Registration of Trade Unions". Under the provisions of this ordinance, in July 1922 the B.G.L.U. was registered, thus becoming a legal entity. It was the first registered trade union in the dependent British Empire.

The union profited considerably from the nature of the British Guiana Trade Union Ordinance which, unlike the initial ordinances in many other countries in the British West Indies, protected labour organisations from damages and other forms of discrimination in the event of strike action. In fact, as late as 1930 British Guiana was the only British colony in the Caribbean where the Trade Union Ordinance protected labour organisations from legal action as a result of strikes.

Apart from the problem of gaining legal recognition, the most serious obstacle which the B.G.L.U. faced initially was that of internal strife and disunity. This difficulty stemmed essentially from ultimately abortive efforts by ambitious middle-class black and coloured professionals and politicians, such as the educator/journalist A.A. Thorne, Dr. T.T. Nichols and the lawyers, A. McLean Ogle and J.S. Johnson, to seize the leadership of the union from Critchlow, whom they considered too uneducated to lead the organisation. This was a reference to the undistinguished academic record of Critchlow who had been forced to leave primary school early at the age of fourteen at the death of his father to work to provide financially for his family. The professionals also questioned the integrity of Critchlow and his ability to administer properly the union's funds which initially were in his name because the banks refused to accept deposits in the name of a union which was not a legal entity. Their motion, however, to undermine Critchlow was overruled by the union and a vote of confidence in Critchlow was passed. Thereafter the middle-class elements tended to dissociate themselves from the B.G.L.U., depriving it of valuable support and respect. The rift was so pronounced that eventually A.A. Thorne established his own union, the British Guiana's Workers League, the country's second trade union in 1931.

Throughout the initial phase of its existence, the B.G.L.U. encountered stiff opposition from employers, especially planters and merchants. Many employers viewed the union with great mistrust, believing that it would promote industrial unrest and, by demanding higher wages, shorter working hours and other material benefits for workers, cause the financial ruin of their businesses. They therefore did everything possible to ruin the union. In particular, they used their political, economic and social influence to try to ensure that the governor, the local legislature and the civil authorities did not support the cause of the union.

Critchlow often complained about the lack of collaboration and responsiveness of the government and of police surveillance of the union's public meetings. In May 1928 a senior police officer reported to the Colonial Secretary that Critchlow had made the following remarks at a public meeting

☙

> He don't want no man to get themselves in no trouble for the government don't like him and they will do anything to put him in prison but he is a free English subject and can speak as he likes. He don't mind how many spies is sent out to listen

to him and to report him.[187]

☙

The opposition of the employers, government and police was a particularly formidable obstacle when the B.G.L.U. staged public protests. This was very evident in 1924 when the union staged its largest protest in the initial phase of its existence. On March 31 of that year the waterfront workers in Georgetown went on strike in response to a call by the union. This strike was followed by a workers' demonstration through the streets of the capital. On April 3 the protest expanded when a large group of workers from sugar estates on the East Bank of Demerara embarked on a march to Georgetown to demonstrate solidarity with the striking dock workers. They were stopped, however, at Ruimveldt and eventually dispersed when a combined force of the police and militia opened fire on the crowd, killing thirteen workers and wounding twenty-four of them.

The failure of such protests was also due to other factors besides the use of political and military power against the working class. Prominent among the other factors was the financial weakness of the B.G.L.U. which rendered it incapable of rendering strike relief to workers and thus made it difficult for workers to sustain and endure long strikes. This financial weakness stemmed basically from the fact that many members of the union could not afford to pay even its low dues and so they either resigned from the union or their membership lapsed. The alienation of many of the middle-class professionals from the union was another financial blow. By the late 1920s the union was in such desperate financial straits that it was forced to sell some of its assets in order to survive. In the absence of adequate funding, it found it not only difficult to maintain some of its rural branches, but also necessary to curtail its urban activities. This helps to explain why the union's achievements were less impressive in the late 1920s than in the earlier half of the decade.

By the late 1920s it had become increasingly clear to the union that one of the main obstacles to the success of its efforts to promote the welfare of the working class was its lack of political power. This disability was a result of the fact that the income and property qualifications for both the franchise and a seat in the legislature had been deliberately placed beyond the reach of the poorly paid workers. The union sought to secure constitutional reforms to remove this disability, but without any immediate success. In fact, the plight facing the union and workers in this regard became more bleak in 1928 when

Crown Colony government was imposed on the colony, strengthening the position of the predominantly white planter and mercantile interests. Nearly two more decades were to elapse before the workers secured a representative in the local legislature.

However, in spite of the variety and potency of the obstacles which the B.G.L.U. faced, the union survived, contrary to the expectation of many of its critics and opponents. Furthermore, it was able by struggle to achieve some significant benefits for workers in the 1920s, including increased wages, a shorter working day, restrictions in house rents and workers' compensation for industrial accidents and injuries. The benefits gained, however, did not satisfy workers who were not fully conscious of the formidable obstacles which the union faced in its struggle to improve their lot.

For Further Reading

Chase, Ashton	**A History of Trade Unionism in Guyana, 1900-1961** (Georgetown: 1964).
Spackman, Ann	"Official Attitudes and Official Violence: The Ruimveldt Massacre, Guyana, 1924", **Social and Economic Studies**, Vol.22, No.3, 1973.
Wilson, Silvius	"The Background to the Ruimveldt Incident of 1924", **History Gazette,** No. 67, April 1994.
Wilson, Silvius	"The Causes of the Ruimveldt Incident of 1924", **History Gazette,** No. 68, May 1994.

Part Nine

BIOGRAPHY

Mary Noel Menezes

Gordon Rohlehr

Pryor Jonas

Chapter 55

U.W.I. Honours Sister Mary Noel Menezes

In October 2005 one of Guyana's most distinguished scholars and most noble citizens was honoured by the University of the West Indies at its graduation ceremony at the St Augustine campus in Trinidad. Sister Mary Noel Menezes, respectfully and affectionately called "Sister" or "Sister Noel" by those who know her, was awarded an honorary degree of Doctor of Laws (LL.D). She was the only female among a small select group of four eminent Caribbean nationals who were awarded honorary doctoral degrees by the region's premier educational institution.

Whereas the other three awardees, namely, Professor Raymond Gosling, a scientist, Justice Joseph Archibald and Mr Tajmool Hosein, a legal luminary, were honoured for their academic/professional achievements, Sister Menezes' award was in recognition of both her academic accomplishments as a professional historian and her altruism. At a special luncheon in honour of the four Honorary Graduants, the host, Dr. Bhoendradatt, the Pro Vice Chancellor and Campus Principal, commended her for being a rarity in today's increasingly materialistic world by being a scholar who was a genuine philanthropist. At the same function she and the other awardees were described by the university's Guyanese Vice-Chancellor, Professor Nigel Harris, as "persons of substance and stature."

Most of Sister Menezes' life as an academic was spent at the University of Guyana. After teaching for two years at colleges in the United States of America in the mid 1960s, she joined the U.G. staff in September 1967 and served there until her retirement 23 years later in 1990. During this lengthy period she had numerous academic achievements. Among them was the enviable reputation that she gained, as being one of the institution's most stimulating and engrossing teachers. Moreover, Sister, an efficient, creative, fearless administrator, served as head of the Department of History for nine years (1977-1986), transforming this hitherto humdrum department into one of the finest departments in the entire university.

Furthermore, in 1973 she initiated the university's first Master's Degree Programme – a M.A. in Guyanese and West Indian History. She served as the Chief Co-ordinator of this programme for 17 years, from its inception to her retirement in 1990. In that capacity she trained a new generation of professional Guyanese historians. Some of them, notably Dr. James Rose and Dr. David Chanderbali, respectively the Vice-Chancellor and Registrar, Mr. Tota Mangar, the Dean of the School of Education and Humanities, and Ms. Cecelia Mc Almont, the Head of the Department of Social Studies, were still serving the university in 2005 at the time of Sister's award. Others, including Dr. Basdeo Mangru, the university's first Master's graduate, Dr. Marguerite Chase-Garvey and Dr. Kimani Nehusi, were pursuing successful academic careers overseas.

Sister Menezes was one of U.G.'s leading researchers and most prolific writers. Her research greatly enhanced knowledge especially of two areas in Guyanese history in which she became the recognised authority. These areas are the history of the Amerindians, the subject of her doctoral dissertation at the University of London in England from 1970 to 1973, and the history of the Portuguese. She produced four books on these two subjects, namely, **British Policy Towards the Amerindians in British Guiana, 1803-1873** (Oxford: Clarendon Press, 1977); **The Amerindians in Guyana 1803-1873. A Documentary History** (London: Frank Cass and Co. Ltd, 1979); **Scenes from the History of the Portuguese in Guyana** (London: The Author, 1986); and **The Portuguese of Guyana: A Study in Culture and Conflict** (Gujarat: The Anand Press, 1992).

Two other of her numerous publications are particularly cherished by students. Her book, **The Amerindians and the Europeans**, is one of the most informative sources of knowledge for this popular theme in the Caribbean Examinations Council's (CXC) Caribbean History syllabus. Secondly, her **Guide to Historical Research**, later revised with a new title, **How To Do Better Research**, continues to be an invaluable guide especially to university students in all disciplines on research methodology.

Sister Menezes' growing stature as a professional historian received special recognition on at least three occasions in the late 1970s and early 1980s. The first occasion was in 1978 when she became the first female president of the Association of Caribbean Historians, founded ten years before in 1968. She served in that capacity for two years. Secondly, in 1980 she was promoted to the position of Professor of History at U.G., the first holder of this post.

Finally, in 1981, she was appointed a member of the Drafting Committee of UNESCO's **General History of the Caribbean**.

At her retirement from U.G. in 1990 Sister Menezes was honoured in a touching public ceremony on campus, the first of its kind for a member of the teaching staff in the university's long history dating back to 1963. This was clear evidence of the very high esteem in which she was held by the university community.

While recording achievement after achievement as a teacher, administrator, researcher and writer, Sister Menezes remarkably found time to be involved in a number of philanthropic activities. As the U.W.I. public orator, Professor Barbara Lalla, stated in the citation for Sister before presenting her to Chancellor Sir George Alleyne to receive her honorary degree in Trinidad in 2005, she is "a selfless and effective humanitarian… who has rendered phenomenal humanitarian service."

Sister's most demanding and amazing philanthropic work was her 35 years of service (1968-2003) at the St John Bosco Orphanage in Plaisance, where she lived and was in charge for most of this period. Furthermore, since 1970 she has been visiting the Mahaica Hospital for patients suffering from Hansen's Disease regularly and also served at the Cheshire Home in Mahaica for twenty years from 1981 to 2001. Moreover, in 2000 she started a Mercy Boys' Home in Prashad Nagar in Georgetown for boys leaving the St John Bosco Orphanage at the age of 16 who have no one and nowhere to go. She presently manages this new home.

Among Sister's many other acts of public service are the following: a member of the Council of Management of the St. Joseph Mercy Hospital from 1985 to 2002; a member of the Heritage Society from 1985 to the present; a member of the Advisory Committee of the Canadian Organisation for Development through Education (CODE) from 1989 to the present; and a member of the Advisory Council of Guyana's Ministry of Foreign Affairs since 2002.

Sister Menezes has been the recipient of numerous awards over the years. Among them were several prestigious fellowships from institutions in the United Kingdom, the United States, Canada and Portugal and from the government of India. She has also received national recognition when she was awarded the Golden Arrow of Achievement by the government of Guyana in 1982 and the Outstanding Guyanese Women Award in 1989.

Sister Menezes' academic work and public service are partly an expression of her religious vocation. Since 1947, when she was admitted into the Sisters of Mercy in Dallas, Pennsylvania, in the United States, she has been an active member of that Roman Catholic community. From 1990 to 1998 she served as the Regional Supervisor of these sisters in Guyana. During those years, in 1994, she wrote a **History of the Sisters of Mercy** to commemorate the 100th anniversary of their work in Guyana. More recently, in 2004, she was invited to become one of the six members of the Mercy International Research Commission, a body designed to encourage scholarly use of the archival and other resources of the Sisters of Mercy worldwide.

Sister Menezes' award of an honorary doctorate degree by UWI in 2005 was the second occasion that she has been the recipient of such an honour. The first occasion was in 1983 when her *Alma Mater*, The College Misericordia in Dallas, Pennsylvania, where she completed a B.A. Degree in History in 1964, conferred on her a Doctorate of Humane Letters. The award from UWI 22 years later was evidence of her substantial and sustained contribution as both an academic and philanthropist. It is clearly well deserved.

Chapter 56

Pryor Jonas: Mentor, Educator, Sportsman and Sports Commentator

Ronald Murphy Jonas, named after his father, a police constable, but better known as Pryor Jonas, was born on June 21, 1929. In spite of his humble origins, he rose to national prominence in Guyana. He often said that he had knowledge especially of three subjects, namely, Mathematics, Religion, and Sport. This statement truly reflects three major priorities and emphases of his life.

The first significant development in Jonas' rise from obscurity to prominence occurred in 1940 when he won a much-coveted Government County Scholarship and entered Queen's College, the country's most prestigious secondary school. He attended Queen's until 1948, serving finally there as a prefect, captain of Pilgrim House and Vice-Captain of the college's cricket team. He was a leading member of a class which is said by some commentators to have had the most gifted students in the 170-year history of the school, dating back to 1844.

At Queen's Jonas excelled in Mathematics, winning the Sixth Form Prize in the subject in his final year there. Later, in 1971, he completed a Bachelor's Degree in Mathematics and English at the Cave Hill Campus of the University of the West Indies in Barbados. By then he had embarked on his long and very distinguished career as an educator, especially as a teacher of Mathematics.

This career began in 1953 when, after being employed for five years as a surveyor in his country's Lands and Mines Department, he joined the staff of Queen's College as an Assistant non-Graduate Master. In subsequent years he taught Mathematics not only at his *alma mater*, but also at several other secondary institutions, including Bishop's High, St. Rose's High, St. Joseph's High, Central High, Christ Church Secondary and North Ruimveldt Multilateral Schools. In addition, for many years he prepared students for the regional Caribbean Examinations Council examination in the subject by means of a radio broadcast and a weekly page in the **Stabroek News** daily newspaper. In 2003, he was honoured by Queen's College for 50 years of teaching.

His dedication and excellence as a teacher were a reflection of his religious faith which was a very important element in his life. A deeply committed Christian, known to many as Brother J. or Brother Jonas, he sought consistently to witness for his Saviour, Jesus Christ, by word and by deed. He was a spiritual mentor to many people, especially young men.

His faith was reflected in the virtues which he sought to instil in his students in the classroom, especially honesty, discipline, conscientiousness, justice, industry and excellence. In short, he taught his students more than Mathematics. As one of them observed, "Mr. Jonas valued character in equal measure as he did academic excellence. By his own example, and his words of guidance and advice, it is clear, in retrospect, that he was moulding us to be honourable and successful – and in that order."[188]

Although Pryor Jonas influenced many people as an educator and Christian, it was through his involvement in sport that he became known to most Guyanese. His role in sport was diverse – player, administrator, coach, analyst and historian. He first demonstrated his immense interest in sport during his secondary school career when he not only played table tennis and chess and was a versatile athlete, specialising in the 100 and 200 yards sprints and the High and Long Jumps, but also was, above all an accomplished footballer and cricketer. He represented Queen's with distinction in football and cricket, being awarded the school's colours in both games, and continued after he left school by playing for the Young Men's Christian Association (Y.M.C.A).

In football he played as a forward at inside right in the old, now abandoned 5-3-2-1 formation. A stylish player, he used his ability to "dribble" to penetrate defences and to score many goals through placement rather than power. After he ceased playing, he maintained his involvement in the sport by coaching at Queen's and refereeing local matches. He became a qualified referee with the London Football Association in the United Kingdom in 1959 and was also recognised by his national Football Referees Association as a "First Grade" Referee.

Pryor's involvement in cricket was even more active, impressive and lengthy than that in football, lasting until his death in 2005. At Queen's College he was described by his captain, Fred Wills, as "a very good bowler with admirable control of length."[189] His effective right-arm medium pace bowling enabled him, along with two of his Queen's team-mates, to gain selection in a British Guiana Colts XI in October 1947 in a historic match against a visiting Leeward-Windward Islands team, the first encounter between these islands and one of the four major cricketing territories in the Caribbean, namely, British Guiana, Barbados, Jamaica and Trinidad and Tobago. According to a contemporary report, "this trio acquitted themselves well. Favourable comment was made of the bowling of Jonas."[190]

At the end of his playing career several years later, Jonas succeeded in gaining accreditation from the United Kingdom-based Association of Cricket Umpires as a qualified umpire, one of the first Guyanese to achieve this success. He encouraged other Guyanese umpires to seek this certification and was highly esteemed for the training sessions which he conducted to prepare them for the examination. Furthermore, he umpired local matches and served for many years as the President of the Guyana Cricket Umpires Council.

Even more widely known than his role as a player, administrator, umpire, coach, advisor and trainer was his work for several decades as a sports commentator, both on radio and in the print media. His commentary was varied, focusing on many games, including chess and bridge which he played competitively especially in his later years. It also addressed table tennis, boxing, football and, above all, cricket, particularly West Indies cricket, his special passion.

His great love for cricket was partly reflected in the fact that in 1985 he had his name changed by deed poll to Pryor Ronald Jonas, after the former Trinidadian and West Indies cricketer, Prior Jones. He normally made and kept hand-written notes about cricket matches and compiled his own statistics. His knowledge of the game was so profound that at times he successfully challenged the accuracy of the famous, **Wisden Cricketers' Almanack**, which is generally accepted as the world's authority on cricket. His sterling contribution as a sports commentator was acknowledged by the Guyana Cricket Board who in 2002 gave him a well-deserved honour.

Pryor Jonas' death on May 8th, 2005 at the age of 75 was a tragic loss to all lovers of sport, especially cricket. The nation misses his informed, perceptive and often thought-provoking contributions. It will be difficult to replace him. As Chetram Singh, the President of the Guyana Cricket Board, remarked in a tribute to him at the time of his death, Pryor Jonas was "one of the greatest enthusiasts of cricket."[191] Regrettably, he died before the realisation of one of his major passions and hopes, namely, the return of the West Indies to world cricket ascendancy enjoyed in the 1980s and early 1990s, "the glory days of West Indies cricket."

FOR FURTHER READING

Jonas, Joyce (ed.)   **Sportsmen & Sportsmanship. Selected Articles by Pryor Jonas** (Georgetown, 2007).

Chapter 57

U.W.I. Honours Outstanding Guyanese Academic – Gordon Rohlehr

Early in October 2007 the St Augustine, Trinidad, campus of the University of the West Indies (U.W.I.), the Caribbean's premier tertiary educational institution, accorded a very special honour to an outstanding Guyanese academic, Daniel Frederick Gordon Rohlehr. Rohlehr, Professor of West Indies Literature there, retired from the institution about a month before at the end of the previous academic year after forty years of service there. He now bears the title of Emeritus Professor of Literature in the Department of Liberal Arts of the Faculty of Humanities and Education at St Augustine. His retirement was marked by three days of special celebration which was unprecedented in the long history of the campus for its duration, scale, diversity and grandeur. It was truly a unique remarkable occasion.

Gordon Rohlehr was born in what was then the colony of British Guiana in 1942 in the middle of the Second World War. His very distinguished academic career may be said to have really begun in 1953 when at the age of eleven he won a Government County Scholarship and entered Queen's College, the country's leading secondary school. Throughout his eight years at Queen's Rohlehr was a very successful student, excelling especially in English Language and English Literature. In the middle years of his career there, Rohlehr was a prominent member of a class which in the view of some analysts is the most outstanding group of students in the long history of the school. Among the top students of that very distinguished class were the late historian/politician, Walter Rodney, Vic Insanally, the owner of the advertising agency, Guyenterprise, Victor Boodhoo, an eminent U.W.I.-trained medical practitioner and Ewart Thomas, a renowned professor and the first black Dean of the prestigious Stanford University in the United States of America.

In 1961, the final year of Rohlehr's career at Queen's, he won one of the six or seven very competitive and highly coveted undergraduate Open

Scholarships which U.W.I. (then U.C.W.I., University College of the West Indies, a college of London University in England) offered each year to Caribbean students based on a special entrance examination. Three years later he graduated from the university with a First-Class Bachelor of Arts Degree in English Literature, a rare achievement in a very challenging field of study. This achievement enabled him to win one of the university's external postgraduate scholarships entitling the recipients to pursue graduate studies overseas. He enrolled in Birmingham University in England which three years later in 1967 awarded him a Doctorate Degree in English Literature for a thesis entitled "Alienation and Commitment in the Works of Joseph Conrad".

Regrettably, the University of Guyana then missed a golden opportunity to recruit Rohlehr to its staff. As a result, he took up a teaching position in the Department of English at St Augustine in 1968 as a lecturer. There he developed an awesome reputation as a teacher, researcher, thinker, mentor, consultant and expert in Caribbean culture. His very productive work, both in quantity and quality, resulted in his promotion to Professor in 1985.

One of Rohlehr's outstanding virtues is that he is a meticulous researcher and a prolific writer. During his career at St Augustine he wrote more than 100 essays on a variety of subjects, especially West Indian literature, oral poetry, the calypso and popular culture in the Caribbean. Some of these essays are readily available in four of the six major books which he has authored, including two published by Longman in 1992, namely, **My Strangled City and Other Essays** and **The Shape of That Hurt and Other Essays**. His first book had appeared eleven years earlier in 1981. It was a penetrating analysis of the trilogy of the Barbadian writer, Edward Braithwaite, and was entitled **Pathfinder: Black Awakening in the Arrivants of Edward Kamau Braithwaite.**

Rohlehr's most celebrated work, however, is his monumental study of Trinidadian calypso which he published in 1990 under the title, **Calypso and Society in Pre-Independence Trinidad**, and described as "a sort of social/cultural history of Trinidad through the lens of a popular oral and performed poetic and musical art-form".[192] This book has played a major role in creating respect, appreciation and understanding for calypso not only as folk entertainment but as fine art and poetry. It has located calypso in its social, political and historical context, examining its contribution to Trinidadian culture and the construction of Trinidad nationalism. It has been supplemented by a series of important additional essays which Rohlehr wrote on calypso between 1997 and 2003. These essays appeared in 2004 in a book entitled **A Scuffling of Islands: Essays on Calypso**.

Rohlehr was also co-editor of **Voiceprint**, an anthology of oral and related poetry from the Caribbean which Longman published in 1988. All his publications reflect industry, a spirit of enquiry, thinking and rethinking, meticulous analysis, and, though profound in thought, are presented in what one scholar has described as "elegant delightful and readable prose."[193]

These publications served to establish and enhance his reputation as an outstanding scholar and to result in numerous invitations to lecture in the Caribbean, the United States, Canada and the United Kingdom. Rohlehr has served as Visiting Professor at several prestigious universities, including Harvard, Johns Hopkins and Tulane University in the United States and York University in Canada.

The very high esteem with which he is held in Trinidad and elsewhere was clearly evident in the retirement celebrations that were organized in his honour by the Faculty of Humanities and Education of the U.W.I. St Augustine campus form October 4-6, 2007 under the title, "From Apocalypse to Awakenings". These were three days of varied activities, well-attended by university staff and students, the public, representatives of the government of Trinidad and Tobago, members of Rohlehr's family and some of his former school-mates at Queen's College.

The celebrations began with a session organised by the Dean of the Faculty, Dr. Ian Robertson, a Guyanese who was a contemporary with Rohlehr as a student at Queen's College. This session was entitled "The Memory of Burnt Out Days", which was the title of the last of several short stories which Rohlehr wrote for the Queen's College Annual School Magazine during his career there between 1953 and 1961.

In this session three of Rohlehr's former schoolmates at Queen's, namely, Alvin Thompson, who had just retired as Professor of History at the Cave Hill Campus of U.W.I., Arlington Chesney, the Director of CARDI and this writer, presented reminiscences of Rohlehr at secondary school. We spoke not only of his academic achievements, but also of his extracurricular activities as a debater, cricketer and writer. A tribute from Terry Holder, another of Rohlehr's classmates, was read as well as a tape recording by Ewart Thomas. The session ended with the presentation to Rohlehr of a gift of memorabilia related to Queen's College from Vic Insanally. It set the stage for the remainder of the three days' proceedings.

The heart of the celebrations was in the form of a conference in which a number of academic papers were presented by university staff and graduate students, many of whom had been taught by Rohlehr. All the papers dealt with some aspect of Caribbean Literature, History or Culture. Many of them examined, analysed and evaluated Rohlehr's contribution to scholarship in these fields. Among the titles of the papers presented were the following; "UWI, St Augustine, Rohlehr and the Rehumanisation of History"; "Exorcising 'History as-Duppy': Rohlehr's Perspectives on Trauma and Caribbean Society"; "Caribbean Intellectual Praxis: The Art of Gordon Rohlehr"; and "Ah never Get Weary Yet: Rohlehr's Forty Years in Calypso." The papers were almost invariably informative and stimulating.

The celebrations included the launching of Rohlehr's most recent work which was specially prepared to mark the closure of his forty years of teaching at UWI. The book, entitled **Transgression, Transition, Transformation. Essays in Caribbean Culture**, consists of twelve essays and three addresses on ethnicity, racial and cultural hybridity, history, colonial education, carnival and cricket. It explores texts which appeared between 1997 and 2007 about the shaping of Caribbean identity.

The celebrations also included lunch-time invited readings of short stories, a calypso night, a jazz evening and two receptions. For some participants the highlight was the "Award Ceremony & Film Tribute" on the first evening. The film was put together by students who travelled to Guyana to interview Rohlehr's family and to visit the areas where he grew up. He was presented with gifts by his Faculty, the Ministry of Community Development, Culture and Gender Affairs, and a secondary school.

Rohlehr was visibly moved by the celebrations which were phenomenal and reflected deep appreciation for his immense contribution as a scholar especially to West Indian literature, culture and education. This writer's only regret was that the University of Guyana and the Guyanese nation as a whole have profited in only a very limited measure from the work of this outstanding Guyanese scholar. Guyana's loss has clearly been Trinidad and Tobago's gain.

Part Ten

Nationalism and the Movement Towards Independence

The P.P.P. Cabinet in 1953

Dr. Jung Bahadur Singh

Forbes Burnham, Governor Alfred Savage and Cheddi Jagan

CHAPTER 58

THE ORIGINS AND GROWTH OF NATIONALISM IN BRITISH GUIANA, 1880-1961

The term "nationalism" or "nationalist movement" has several meanings. When professional historians use it in the context of colonialism, they usually mean the struggle against colonialism by a section or most of the subject people in a colony. Initially this anti- colonial struggle almost invariably took the form of an attempt by the nationalists to secure a greater say in the government of the colony from the colonial power or regime. Eventually, however, the struggle, if successful, resulted in the end of colonialism by the attainment of self-government or political independence.

It is difficult to say when nationalism, as just defined, originated in British Guiana, the product of the unification in 1831 of the two former separate colonies of Demerara- Essequibo and Berbice. Nationalism may arguably be said to have emerged in British Guiana at least as early as the 1880s when black and coloured middle-class professionals, especially lawyers, doctors, teachers and journalists, with the collaboration of Portuguese businessmen, initiated and led a movement designed to secure a change in the colony's archaic constitution which gave a virtual monopoly of power to the small white British sugar plantocracy. The efforts of these early nationalists were successful, resulting in significant changes of the constitution in 1891.

The constitutional reforms of 1891 resulted in a gradual but progressive displacement of the white British planters in the country's two main government bodies, the Court of Policy and the Combined Court, by black, coloured, Portuguese and, later, East Indian and Chinese politicians, who were elected by a predominantly black electorate. By 1927 this major change in the composition of the colony's legislature had become so pronounced that there was only one planter among the fourteen elected members of the Court of Policy and Combined Court.

This displacement of the white planter oligarchy disturbed the British government so much that it intervened in 1928 to arrest the trend and turn the constitutional clock back. Certain problems which the country was facing were used as a reason, excuse or opportunity to abolish the 1891 constitution and to introduce in its place a system of virtually full Crown Colony government, in which almost all political power was taken away from the elected representatives and invested in the governor, the non-elected element and the Colonial Office in London.

This important development, which was the first occasion of the suspension of the constitution in the colony's history, angered the nationalists. It drove them not only to seek to recover the ground lost, but also to secure political concessions from the colonial regime which were in advance of those which they enjoyed at the time of what some scholars describe as "the rape of the constitution" in 1928. In short, the year 1928 ushered in a new phase in the nationalist thrust in British Guiana. At the time of the outbreak of the Second World War in 1939, eleven years later, this sense of nationalism was growing slowly and was distinguished by at least five major characteristics.

Firstly, in 1939 nationalism in British Guiana was narrowly based, especially from the two perspectives of class and geographical location. It was largely restricted to the urban black and coloured middle class, resident mostly in Georgetown and to a lesser extent New Amsterdam. It did not seriously involve the masses of the people, the working class in the towns and countryside.

Secondly, from the perspective of ethnicity, the nationalist thrust in 1939 was dominated by Africans, with comparatively little involvement by East Indians, especially relative to the numerical strength of East Indians in the colony's population. This limited involvement of East Indians in nationalist politics in 1939 was to a large extent a legacy of their minimal interest for a variety of reasons in Guianese politics in the late nineteenth century and the first decades of the twentieth century. One reason was that they were concentrating more on building a strong economic base than on politics. Furthermore, many of them, hoping to return to India, regarded their stay in British Guiana as temporary and so did not get involved in local politics. Others, who clearly had no plans to return to India, remained aloof from Guianese politics because of a nostalgic attachment to the land of their birth and a resultant reluctance to accept British Guiana as their real home.

A third major feature of nationalism in British Guiana on the eve of the Second World War was that it was led and promoted mainly by individuals and organisations that had what could be described as special or sectional interests, that is, a concern above all with the welfare of one group or area in the colony rather than with the welfare of the entire country. In fact, in 1939 both the Guianese middle class and working class, for example, were closely associated with an international black cultural organisation, the League of Coloured Peoples, while the Indian middle class was linked with the British Guiana East Indian Association, a body founded in 1917. This ethnic division was reinforced somewhat by developments in the trade union movement. Black workers tended to be members of the British Guiana Labour Union and the British Guiana Workers' League, while Indian workers tended to belong to the Man Power Citizens' Association. While the two cultural groups mainly influenced the middle class in Georgetown, the trade unions influenced workers in the countryside as well.

The fourth striking trait of Guianese nationalism in 1939 was that it was not well-organised. There were no modern political parties in the country, that is, stable political entities with full-time staff, nor any national political parties. At best the colony had what could be described as mostly short-lived political clubs or political associations. Often these bodies were formed suddenly to fight for a particular cause and once their objective was realized or the issue lost importance they became defunct. Sometimes they also collapsed or became divided as a result of internal dissension or jealous rivalry, especially among the leaders. Even more enduring and more influential quasi-political associations such as the predominantly black People's Association or the British Guiana East Indian Association had no mass following and no bureaucratic organisation with paid full-time staff. Admittedly, especially after 1928, the constitution did not provide political groups with much incentive for stability and modern organisation, for it afforded only limited power and influence to the elected members of the legislature.

Perhaps the most significant feature of Guianese nationalism in 1939 was that it was reformist rather than revolutionary, that is to say, the nationalist leaders were not seeking political independence from Britain but rather to modify the colonial system in ways which would give them greater participation and responsibility in the government of the colony. In short, they were seeking to reform colonialism, not to bring an end to colonial rule.

Nationalism in British Guiana, as in many other colonies in the British Empire, underwent major changes as a consequence of the Second World War. In general, for various reasons and in several ways the War gave a great impetus to nationalism. The war was promoted by Britain and her allies as a struggle for democracy in the face of the threat of Hitler's Nazi German imperialism. At the end of the war some Guianese, including ex-servicemen who had supported the mother country's war effort, began to ask whether democracy and anti-imperialism would be extended to the colony or whether these benefits were only to be enjoyed by Europe and the United States.

The war also witnessed the issuing of the famous Atlantic Charter, a statement of war aims and fundamental principles for the post-war world issued jointly by the United States President, Franklin Roosevelt, and the British Prime Minister, Winston Churchill, in August 1941. Among the principles was one calling for self-determination, that is, the right for peoples to choose their own government. This principle of self-determination was also emphasized later in the United Nations Declaration of Human Rights.

Anti- colonialism also got a boost from another consequence of the War, namely, a significant change in the international balance of power with the U.S.A. and the U.S.S.R. emerging as the leading world powers. For different reasons these two influential states were in favour of political independence for colonies.

It was these global developments related to the Second World War which helped to make the British government think seriously of granting independence ultimately to all British colonies. As Gordon Lewis states in his excellent study entitled **The Growth of the Modern West Indies**

> In Colonial Office theory West Indians were at school, gradually being groomed for self-government, when they were 'ready'. But both the pace and the terms of the 'advance' were set by the imperial power.[194]

This was to be British Guiana's experience. It was in keeping with one of the main recommendations of the famous Moyne Commission which was sent by the British government in 1939 to the British West Indies to investigate the causes of the popular disturbances which had occurred all over the region. The Commission envisaged a slow process of political evolution in which the official element in the Legislative Council would be progressively reduced, while the number of elected members would increase and the franchise extended to greater numbers.

In the first phase of its policy of evolution towards independence for British Guiana after the War, the British government for at least two reasons did not have to address the question of independence seriously. Firstly, although there were a few Guianese voices who were demanding self-government, there was no modern political party in the colony promoting nationalism and substantial political advance as had emerged in the three other main British Caribbean colonies, Jamaica, Trinidad and Barbados.

Admittedly, the holding in 1947 of the first national elections in British Guiana since 1935 did prompt the formation of a few new parties, of which the most important was the British Guiana Labour Party, led by Dr. Jean Bahadur Singh. This party was founded in June 1946 and the first article of its constitution listed among its goals, "Immediate change of the Constitution of British Guiana to provide 24 elected members based on universal adult suffrage" and, more significantly, "the attainment of complete independence within 5 years."[195] Although some members of the party called for self-government for British Guiana, they do not seem to have evoked any response in London. In any event, the party, which was an unsuccessful attempt to form a coalition of different interest groups, collapsed shortly after the 1947 elections were over.

The importance of the establishment of solid political parties to significant political advance was noted by Governor Charles Woolley in a letter to the British Secretary of State, Arthur Creech-Jones, in January 1948 just before the dissolution of the British Guiana Labour Party. Woolley remarked

> There can be no real progress towards a cabinet system until the party system has developed further. The British Guiana Labour Party is the only party in existence at present, and this only came into being shortly before the elections. It at present claims the allegiance of seven of the elected fourteen seats, but it can hardly be regarded as a homogeneous association and it remains to be seen how long its unity will survive.[196]

Apart from the absence of vibrant nationalist political parties, the other factor which hindered any visible advance towards independence in the years immediately after 1945 was a proposal for the formation of a political federation of the British West Indies. This proposal tended to divert some focus from the question of advance towards independence in the individual territories such as British Guiana.

The most significant development in Guianese politics in the years immediately following World War II was the formation in 1946 of the Political Affairs Committee (P.A.C.) by Cheddi and Janet Jagan and two trade unionists, Ashton Chase and Jocelyn Hubbard. The P.A.C. was not a political party, but rather a body formed largely for the purpose of political education, especially informing interested persons about Marxism and relating Marxist principles to conditions and problems in British Guiana. The main aim of the P.A.C. was to lay the foundation of a "strong disciplined and enlightened Party equipped with the theory of Scientific Socialism."[197]

More important to the growth of nationalism in the immediate post-war years than the formation of the P.A.C. was the entry into the legislature in 1947 of Cheddi Jagan, who won a seat on the East Coast of Demerara. Jagan, a dentist, had returned home in 1943 with his American wife, Janet, after studying for seven years in the United States. Dr. Jagan had a Marxist view of the situation in British Guiana, seeing the problems and needs of the colony as reflecting an international problem of capitalist exploitation and colonialism. In the legislature he championed working-class interests, addressing issues such as a minimal wage and rent control. He seldom raised there the question of independence for the colony. Partly for this reason the British government did not address the matter.

The question of the independence of British Guiana was also discussed occasionally in the local press, but did not evoke much overt interest then. For example, in January and February 1949 the **Argosy** newspaper carried a long series of articles about the prospect of the colony becoming self-governing. There was, however, little visible response in terms of letters to the editor, prompting him to remark after the publication of the ninth article, "if there has been verbal discussion we have heard little of it."[198]

This situation of relatively little focus locally or in London on independence for the colony began to change in 1950 when the Political Affairs Committee gave way to the People's Progressive Party (P.P.P.). The P.P.P., which was formed out of the P.A.C. and a part of the remnants of the defunct British Guiana Labour Party, was the first modern political party in the country's history. At the outset it announced that it had three major aims. One of them was "to win a free and independent Guiana",[199] one of the earliest clearcut calls for the independence of the country.

The new party's two other principal goals were economic development by radical alteration of the economy and the creation in British Guiana of a socialist society. These three aims, which implied a complete political, economic and social revolution, were not really compatible with the declared British policy of gradual advance to self-government after a period of tutelage under the guidance and supervision of the mother country.

This approach of the British government, which made independence a distant goal, was reflected in the somewhat vague terms of reference of a commission under the chairmanship of E.J. Waddington which the Colonial Office sent to British Guiana in December 1950. The commission was instructed "to review the franchise, the composition of the Legislature and of the Executive Council, and any other matters, in the light of the economic and political development of the Colony, and to make recommendations."[200]

Though the commission recommended a more advanced constitution, providing, for example, universal adult suffrage and a system of ministerial responsibility, its proposals, which were largely adopted by the British government, fell far short of independence and, understandably, did not satisfy many nationalists. For example, John Carter, a member of the Legislative Council and a leading figure in the L.C.P., in his comments on the commission's report recommended that a definite period should be set after which British Guiana would attain independence, as had been done in Libya. Cheddi Jagan was also critical of the commission's proposals, demanding "real independence" for the colony in an article which appeared in the January 1952 issue of the **Bulletin of the World Federation of Free Trade Unions**.

Notwithstanding such responses, the attitude and approach of the British government to the question of political independence for British Guiana were not seriously affected until the 1953 general election. This was the first election in the country's history to be conducted on the basis of universal adult suffrage, an advance introduced earlier in the other main British colonial possessions in the Caribbean, in 1944 in Jamaica, 1946 in Trinidad and 1951 in Barbados. In its election brochure the P.P.P. stated that it stood for independence for British Guiana and urged Guianese "to fight for independence, striking blow after blow at the Imperialist stronghold."[201]

Contrary to the expectations of the British government, the P.P.P. gained a decisive victory in the elections, winning 51 per cent of the votes cast and 18 of the 24 seats in the Legislative Council. The party's success was due to a variety of factors, including its dynamic charismatic leadership provided by Cheddi Jagan and Forbes Burnham, hard work, the support of the trade union movement, the strength of its organisation with branches or cells all over the country and the attractiveness of its electoral manifesto, which emphasized economic development, improved social services and political independence. The P.P.P. also profited from the weakness and fragmentation of the opposition which consisted of four political parties and 79 independent candidates. Finally, its success was also due to its appeal to the country's two main races, East Indians and Africans, as well as to the newly enfranchised and largely working-class electorate.

The P.P.P. victory, which came as a surprise to the Colonial Office, was a major blow to British ideas about the political evolution of British Guiana. The British government had hoped and expected that the new Guianese electorate would return to power the politicians whom it had earmarked as trustworthy to be trained to hand over power to eventually at the time of independence. The new electorate, however, voted for a fundamental change in the old political order. Very few of the favoured politicians who had held positions of importance in the previous governmental bodies were elected to the new legislature. This meant that the British government's aim to ensure continuity and the eventual transfer of power into "safe hands" was defeated. Instead Britain was now faced with the prospect of a Marxist government in power in the colony, a particularly unwelcome development in the midst of the international Cold War. Political figures, whom the British viewed as "radicals and communists", had now replaced individuals whose moderate or conservative politics was more acceptable to the Colonial Office and who were considered better qualified to govern by virtue of experience and social status and were being trained for an eventual smooth transition of power. These misgivings were a fundamental reason why the British government removed the P.P.P. from office in October 1953, a few months later.[202]

From the outset the P.P.P. made it clear that one of its principal objectives was to gain independence for British Guiana. A few days after the electoral victory, Janet Jagan is purported to have remarked

༄

> We mean to break away from the British Empire. We're sick and tired of being tied to Britain and hampered at every turn by England's selfish economic policies. Everything we do is determined

by England. British Guiana is nothing but a subservient satellite. We must achieve equality and then independence.²⁰³

☙

A few months later, in August 1953, Forbes Burnham, the Minister of Education and chairman of the party, observed

☙

The Governor and the State Council are reactionary forces which must be expurged by 1957 [i.e. the scheduled date for the next election]… We must sweep away imperialism and foreign power from our midst.²⁰⁴

☙

These demands for independence, however, were not addressed by the British government. In fact, in October 1953, after the P.P.P. was only 133 days in office, the Colonial Office suspended the colony's constitution and removed the P.P.P. from power on the alleged ground that the party had subverted the constitution and was in the process of establishing a communist dictatorship in the colony. Instead, it introduced into the colony for the first time in its history a pure Crown Colony system of government, with completely nominated Legislative and Executive Councils and nominated ministers. This interim arrangement, which was to last indefinitely, remained in place until 1957, when a new constitution was introduced.

This period of interim government from October 1953 to August 1957 was conceived and described by the British government as "a period of marking time" in the advance towards independence.²⁰⁵ In fact, it was a period of repression with the government detaining in prison some of the P.P.P. leaders, including Dr. Jagan, under Emergency Orders or restricting their movements to certain specified areas. In short, not only was there no advance towards independence in these years, but rather the colony's political clock had been turned back.

Although the period of the interim government did not see any progress towards independence, it proved critical for the nationalist movement, for it witnessed the emergence of new political alignments. In 1955 ideological, ethnic and personal factors resulted in a split in the P.P.P. into two competing factions, one led by Cheddi Jagan and the other led by Forbes Burnham, both calling themselves the P.P.P.-P.P.P. Jaganites and P.P.P. Burnhamites. Though ethnicity played an important part, the split was not completely racial, for some prominent black and coloured members, including Sidney King, Rory Westmaas and Martin Carter, continued to support Jagan, while some notable Indian members, such as Dr. J.P. Lachmansingh and Jai Narine Singh, joined Burnham.

In the following year, 1956, a significant split occurred in Dr. Jagan's faction of the P.P.P., making it more ethnic in character. Westmaas, Carter and King left the party, with the first two retiring from active politics and King initially declaring himself an independent, but subsequently in 1958 joining forces with Burnham in opposition to Jagan.

In addition to these significant developments within the original P.P.P., this period of the interim government witnessed the emergence of three new parties- the United Democratic Party (U.D.P.), the National Labour Front (N.L.F.) and the Guiana National Party, led respectively by John Carter, Lionel Luckhoo, and Cecil Gray. The most substantial of these three groups was the U.D.P which represented a reorganization of the National Democratic Party that had contested the 1953 election, joined by several independents and some members of weaker parties which had disappeared after that election.

The subservience of the interim government to the British made both factions of the P.P.P. acknowledge the need and call for political independence. These calls, however, went unheeded by the British government, though, ironically, in February 1956 the British Prime Minister, Anthony Eden, and the US. President, Dwight Eisenhower, signed the Washington Declaration endorsing the rights of peoples to governments of their own choice.

In 1957 Britain resumed its policy of political advance for British Guiana towards independence by reforming the colony's constitution. The new constitution, which restored the elective principle, was very similar to that of 1953, with provision for universal adult suffrage and a measure of ministerial responsibility for the winning party at elections.

The new elections were held in August 1957 and were rightly perceived as a test of the strength of the new political groupings. The contest was between the two factions of the P.P.P. Jagan and his supporters won 48 per cent of the votes and nine of the 14 elected seats, the Burnhamites 26 per cent of the votes and three seats and the U.D.P. and N.L.F. one seat each. The successful N.L.F. candidate was Stephen Campbell, the first Amerindian to enter the country's legislature.

Not long after the 1957 elections, the political situation in the country changed significantly. The split in the P.P.P. was finalized when Burnham changed the name of his party to the People's National Congress (P.N.C.) Furthermore, political alignments became more racial. In 1958 Burnham lost two of his main East Indian supporters. Lachmansingh died and Jai Narine Singh, allegedly annoyed by Burnham's acceptance of Sidney King whom he considered an African racist, resigned and formed his own party, the Guianese Independence Movement. Moreover, in 1959 the U.D.P. dissolved and most of its African members, including its leader, John Carter, joined the P.N.C.

Thus by 1960 Guianese politics, including its nationalist movement, was being dominated by two mass parties- the P.P.P., led by Cheddi Jagan, with a predominantly East Indian membership and the P.N.C., led by Forbes Burnham, with its membership largely African. In short, by 1960 the process of disintegration of what initially in 1950 had been a comprehensive united multiracial nationalist movement was complete, with the existence of two mass-based parties on essentially ethnic lines.

This important development weakened both the P.P.P. and the Guianese nationalist movement, but did not destroy either of them. In fact, it occurred at a time when some nationalists were beginning to give greater priority and urgency to the question of independence for British Guiana and were requesting the British government to do likewise. In June 1958, for example, a resolution, originally proposed by Jai Narine Singh but amended by Cheddi Jagan, was unanimously adopted by the Legislative Council to ask the Secretary of State for the Colonies in London to receive a representative delegation from the colony "to discuss constitutional reform with a view to the granting to British Guiana of the status of a fully self-governing territory within the Commonwealth."[206]

This approach to the British government was fuelled partly by the realization by Guianese nationalists of the significant political progress being made by other territories in the British Empire, especially Singapore, the Gold Coast which attained independence in March 1957, Nigeria and the three British Caribbean colonies of Jamaica, Trinidad and Barbados which had been accorded a large degree of internal self-government. Some nationalists, notably Cheddi Jagan, believed that British Guiana had already satisfied all the criteria normally required by the British government for the grant of political independence to a colonial possession.

After discussions in London in September 1958 with Guianese ministers, the Secretary of State for the Colonies instructed the governor to appoint a committee to canvass opinions in the colony about constitutional advance before he convened the requested conference. The committee, appointed in November 1958, submitted its report the following August, but because of the transfer of the governor to Kenya the promised conference, which was originally scheduled for the last quarter of 1959, was not held until March 1960.

During the period between June 1958 and March 1960 the British government was able to concretise its policy towards the independence of British Guiana. It came to the position that the colony could proceed to independence and was likely to do so under the leadership of the electorally successful P.P.P., although it had serious misgivings about the party because of its Marxist proclivities.

The British government's new commitment and approach to independence for British Guiana was evident on two occasions in 1959. Firstly, in August of that year it rejected a recommendation from Jai Narine Singh, the leader of the Guianese Independence Movement and a member of the Legislative Council, that British Guiana should be placed provisionally under the trusteeship of the United Nations and after a suitable period of development should become independent.

Secondly, the British government decided to allow British Guiana to remain outside the West Indies Federation and to seek independence as an individual territory as the P.P.P. government desired, although the Colonial Office's own preference was for the colony to join the federation. It accepted, admittedly with some reluctance, the P.P.P.'s position that the question of joining the federation should be determined definitely by the Guianese people later after the federation achieved dominion status and British Guiana self- government. It felt that the P.P.P.'s position was "an understandable attitude"[207] in view of the party's aspirations to achieve independence for the colony at the earliest opportunity and sensibility to the fact that British Guiana with its large East Indian population was demographically very different from the federation with its African preponderance. British Guiana, in fact, never joined the short-lived West Indies Federation and both the Guianese nationalists and the British government continued to give independence for the colony priority in terms of its future political development. This was a source of satisfaction especially to the P.P.P. for the party was fearful that both the colony and the metropolitan government might be seriously deflected from the question of independence by the federation issue.

1960 was an important year for the Guianese nationalist movement for it witnessed two significant developments. One was the declaration by the British government for the first time of a time-table, admittedly somewhat vague, for the colony's independence. This declaration was made in London in March 1960 at the conclusion of the historic first British Guiana Constitutional Conference.

The initial proceedings of the conference showed the British Guianese participants had three different views about the colony's independence. The P.P.P. delegates, Dr. Jagan, the Minister of Trade and Industry, Brindley Benn, Minister of Natural Resources and Balram Singh Rai, Minister of Community Development and Education, requested immediate independence within the Commonwealth at least by August 1961, when the life of the existing Legislative Council was scheduled to expire. The P.N.C. delegates, led by Forbes Burnham, urged that progress to independence should be "by stages and not one step."[208] They advocated the immediate or early grant of internal self-government to the colony as a step in the direction of independence. Thirdly, one delegate, namely, Jai Narine Singh, requested immediate independence outside the Commonwealth.

The second of these views was endorsed by the British Secretary of State, Iain Mc Leod, who successfully "stressed the need for orderly transfer of responsibility and power"[209] to British Guiana. The principle of independence for the colony was accepted, but no precise time-table was formulated. It was decided that by August 1961 another election would be held in the colony under a new constitution agreed to at the conference providing for full internal self-government and that at least two years after that election the British government, if requested by the colony's legislature, would convene another constitutional conference to set a precise date for independence. This decision meant that the earliest possible date for independence would be late in 1963. The conference concluded that "the constitutional changes that had been worked out to take effect in 1961 provided a workable pattern for the constitutional advance of British Guiana."[210]

This decision to defer the colony's independence was a great disappointment to the P.P.P. delegation and Jai Narine Singh who, after opposing it without success, expressed their objections in writing, emphasising that the conclusions and compromises reached at the conference were imposed by the British government. In its statement the P.P.P. delegates asserted

☙

We are far from satisfied with the result of this Conference. We came here with a mandate for independence. We are going back still as Colonials with a Crown Colony status. The result of this Conference is clearly imposition by discussion. We have compromised
(i) In an attempt to reach accord and to advance the progress of British Guiana toward independence.
(ii) Under threats that if the Conference broke down the points already negotiated might not be implemented.
(iii) Under protest that they do not measure up to the aspirations and democratic rights of the Guianese people.
We hold ourselves free at all times to take all constitutional measures to achieve independence as quickly as possible.[211]

☙

In his statement Jai Narine Singh observed

☙

I agree with the Statement made by Dr. Jagan and further say that in my view the Conference has failed, and Her Majesty's Government has failed to appreciate the wishes and demands of the Guianese people.
I am dissatisfied with the results of the Conference in view of the categorical demand by the Guianese Independence Movement for independence outside the Commonwealth now. The conclusions and compromises reached were impositions by her Majesty's Government on the delegation and are not in accordance with equity and justice under a democratic system.
The Guianese Independence Movement shall in the circumstances continue the struggle for

independence of British Guiana."[212]

☙

The conclusions of the conference were questioned in the British House of Commons where a least one M.P., Mr. Brockway, expressed the view that the new constitutional arrangements were "being imposed by the Government upon British Guiana" and asked "why should not British Guiana have as advanced a constitution as other territories in the West Indies?"[213] Another M.P., Mr. Fisher, who had just returned from a visit to British Guiana, expressed his concern about the implied commitment to grant complete independence to the colony by 1963. He asked the British government to reconsider this pledge "because she is certainly not ready for complete independence... and may well not be ready for it in three years' time." Furthermore, he suggested the "quickest, surest and best way" for British Guiana to achieve independence "might be by joining the West Indies Federation."[214]

The promise of independence at the conference may have helped to prompt an important development which further complicated the nationalist movement. In November 1960, Peter D' Aguiar, a prominent Portuguese businessman, announced the formation of a new party, the United Force (U.F.). D' Aguiar had begun visible involvement in national politics in the 1953 election when he stood unsuccessfully as an independent candidate in a Georgetown constituency. He did not stand in 1957, but early in 1960 he began to seek a group that he might lead.

D' Aguiar declared that the United Force had three main intentions. Firstly, it was to oppose socialism and communism. Secondly, it was to oppose what it described as the "racialism" of the P.P.P. and P.NC. Finally, it was to offer the country an economic programme financed largely by American and British capital as the basis for economic development. In short, the announced objectives of the new party made it clear that it was opposed to much of what both the P.P.P. and P.N.C. represented, though even before its formation and shortly afterwards it is said to have made unsuccessful overtures to both these parties for some form of alliance.

D'Aguiar hoped the U.F. would receive substantial support from at least three groups, namely, the Portuguese minority, the coloured middle class and the Amerindians, among whom he believed he had advantages which neither the P.P.P. nor the P.N.C. possessed. Obviously, because he was Portuguese he could reasonably expect support from the Portuguese minority who felt somewhat threatened in the increasingly ethnic local political environment and were therefore likely to vote race. Furthermore, he felt that the U.F. could attract the coloured middle class, who were largely urban, mainly conservative ideologically, and occupied mostly in business or the civil service, by offering free economic enterprise and a more acceptable ideology than that of the P.P.P. or P.N.C. Finally, he hoped that his adherence to Roman Catholicism would appeal to the Amerindians in the interior, who had a long and deep indebtedness to Roman Catholic and other Christian missions. He also reckoned that finances and even some leaders for his party could be secured from wealthy East Indians who had fallen out with the P.P.P. or who recognized that a Marxist party was not in their best economic and financial interest.

The formation of the United Force strengthened and intensified the growing trend of Guianese politics being drawn progressively around sectional groups, although, like the P.P.P. and P.N.C., the new party claimed that it was representing all Guianese. The core of the party's leadership consisted largely of businessmen and from the outset the party was perceived by many Guianese, especially nationalists, as "a white man's party" formed to defend the status quo, reinforcing capitalism and colonialism.

In August 1961 the U.F. contested its first election where the key issue was which party would eventually lead the country into independence. The P.P.P. emerged victorious, winning 20 seats in the Legislative Council, while the P.N.C. gained 11 seats and the U.F. four seats in a contest in which few voters seemed to have crossed racial lines. The percentages of votes gained by the P.P.P. and P.N.C., 42. 6 per cent and 41 per cent respectively, were almost identical to the ratio of East Indians and Africans in the population when the coloureds are counted with Africans, while the share of votes, 16. 4 per cent, secured by the U.F. closely approximated the combined size of the Portuguese, other European, Amerindian and Chinese populations. In short, the elections results clearly reflected the deep racial divisions which increasingly were dominating national politics.

As a result of the election the P.P.P. continued in power, but with greater responsibility than before, for the new constitutional changes had removed many of the vestiges of the Crown Colony system and introduced a large measure of internal self-government. The P.P.P. ministers were given responsibility for all internal matters except the audit of public accounts, criminal proceedings and the public service. External affairs (except foreign trade) and defence also remained under the control of the British

Government. In short, after the August 1961 election, a large measure of responsibility was conferred on the majority party. The constitution, however, was still far short of full self-government, for the governor still retained wide powers.

The P.P.P. government assumed its new responsibilities with the expectation that Britain would keep her promise to grant British Guiana independence within a few years. The British government, in fact, still intended to fulfil this promise. Admittedly, however, it was very concerned about one issue, namely, the Marxist orientation of the P.P.P., though Cheddi Jagan almost invariably was careful not to give a positive or definitive answer to the question frequently posed to him as to whether or not his party and he were communists.

Nevertheless, the British government felt that in view of the fact that the P.P.P. had won both elections since the restoration in 1957 of the policy of advance towards independence, it had no alternative but to allow Cheddi Jagan and his party to lead the country to independence. Furthermore, as a United States official noted in May 1961, the British government also believed that "the Jagans provide the most responsible leadership in the county and would be difficult to supplant."[215] Its policy by late 1961, however, was to try to detach or deflect the P.P.P. from its seeming orientation towards the Soviet block and to attract or guide it to the Western bloc. As a telegram from the British Foreign Office to its ambassador in Bonn on 9th November 1961 stated, "the West must get ahead of the East in British Guiana."[216]

In the view of the British government, the best means of achieving this end was to provide the P.P.P. government with the economic developmental aid which the party considered its top priority, partly to finance a $110 million Development Plan. Because of Britain's economic difficulties, it regretted that it was unable to provide additional aid to British Guiana and its other colonies or to guarantee any loans. It hoped, however, that the P.P.P. government could obtain the necessary aid from other countries in the West. It was therefore happy to encourage and facilitate the P.P.P.'s attempts to obtain aid from the governments of Germany, France and Italy, where in November 1961 the P.P.P. government sent a mission led by Brindley Benn, the Deputy Prime Minister and Minister of Natural Resources. The British government's main hope, however, was that the needed aid would be provided by the United States, where Prime Minister Cheddi Jagan went on a mission in October 1961.

These circumstances provided an opportunity for the U.S. government to get more involved in the affairs of British Guiana. Washington exerted pressure on the British government to abandon its intention to allow British Guiana to proceed to independence under the leadership of Cheddi Jagan, in the process delaying the independence of the colony.

For Further Reading

Despres, Leo Rand	**Cultural Pluralism and Nationalist Politics in British Guiana** (Chicago: Mc Nally, 1967).
Lewis, Gordon	**The Growth of the Modern West Indies** (New York & London: Monthly Review Press, 1969).
Lutchman, Harold	**From Colonialism to Co-operative Republic, Aspects of Political Development in Guyana** (Puerto Rico, 1974).
Lutchman, Harold	"The British Guiana Constitutional Change of 1891", **History Gazette**, No. 40, January 1992.
Drakes, Francis (now Nehusi, Kimani)	"The Development of Guyanese Political Organisation up to 1953", **History Gazette,** No.27, December 1990.
Rose, James	"The Coming of Crown Colony Government to British Guiana in 1928.", **Guyana Historical Journal**, Volume II, Georgetown: 1990.
Ramnarine, Tyran	"East Indian Political Representation in British Guiana, During the Latter Part of Indenture, 1890-1917"in **Ibid.**
Walker-Kilkenny, Roberta	"Women in Social and Political Struggle in British Guiana 1946-1953", **History Gazette**, No. 49, October 1992.
Rose, James & Williams, John	"International Perceptions of the People's Progressive Party by 1953", **History Gazette**, No.72, September 1994.
Jagan, Cheddi	**The West on Trial** with a new epilogue (St.John's: Hansib Caribbean, 1997).
St. Pierre, Maurice	**Anatomy of Resistance. Anti-Colonialism in Guyana 1823-1966** (London: Macmillan, 1999).
Palmer, Colin	**Cheddi Jagan and the Politics of Power: British Guiana's Struggle for Independence** (Chapel Hill: University of North Carolina Press, 2010).

CHAPTER 59

BRITISH PERCEPTIONS OF GUYANESE POLITICIANS IN 1953: CHEDDI JAGAN

1953 was one of the most momentous years in the history of Guyana. It witnessed two striking but contrasting events. Firstly, in April the country had a general election under a new constitution which resulted in a convincing victory for the People's Progressive Party (P.P.P.) led by Cheddi Jagan, a dentist, with Forbes Burnham, an attorney of law, as its chairman. Secondly, in October the British government suspended the new constitution and removed the P.P.P. from power.[217]

By early 1953 the British government had developed views of the leading political figures in British Guiana. These views were shaped by several forces, especially reports of British officials and business interests in the colony and personal interviews in London with some of the Guianese politicians and trade unionists. Some of the strongest views were held about Cheddi Jagan.

In 1953 Cheddi Jagan was regarded in London as by far the most important Guianese political figure. This opinion was due not only to his leadership of the P.P.P. and its precursor, the Political Affairs Committee, but also to the militant role he had played in the Legislative Council since 1947 when he elected to represent an East Coast Demerara constituency. In 1953 there were at least five major components which combined to produce the overall perception which the British imperial government had of Jagan.

Firstly, Cheddi Jagan was viewed as a threat to British capital in British Guiana, especially British investment in the sugar industry. He was seen as a champion of the sugar estate workers, whom he not only represented in the legislature, but also mobilized at public meetings at which he delivered speeches which helped to promote strikes and other forms of industrial action. He was feared especially by the Sugar Producers' Association (S.P.A), the body which represented the owners of the sugar plantations in the colony. The S.P.A. was disturbed not only by the impact which Jagan's speeches were having on sugar estate workers, but also by his advocacy of nationalization of the sugar and bauxite industries.

The S.P.A. made regular representation to the governor of the colony and the metropolitan authorities, complaining of Jagan's activities and even transmitting reports of his speeches to workers. Typical of such speeches was one which he made in April 1951 at a meeting on the railway line at Plantation Uitvlugt on the West Coast of Demerara. He is reported by the S.P.A. to have told the workers

> The Sugar Producers are ruling everything in this country even the government… They are holding you like an Octopus, you can't get away, and they are sucking your blood, the suckers! You are all suffering from malnutrition… The Venn Commission recommended a pension scheme to be run by the estates for the workers, and the Sugar Producers shouted they got no money to run the scheme. The Sugar Producers never got money to do anything for the workers, and you all must ask yourselves where Bookers is getting the money from to build big and modern houses at Bel Air for Mr. Seaford and all the big chiefs coming from England. You the workers have to work for this money for them to live happy and you get nothing. You all ask for land to plant rice and ground provisions and they said they got no land… They bring out white men from England as overseers with big salaries and the East Indian drivers have to teach them the work.[218]

Some plantation proprietors, who believed Jagan's activities were causing ill feeling and unrest among workers, took legal action to deny him access to their estates by means either of trespass notices or injunctions in the Supreme Court. Such measures were taken, for example, by the owners of Plantations Ogle and Schoon Ord, prompting Jagan eventually to appeal to the British government for access to the sugar estates for political purposes.

The British authorities considered the issue a delicate matter. On the one hand, they regarded Jagan's speeches as "inflammatory" and his activities on the estates as "Subversive of the S.P.A.". Nevertheless, they felt that it would be "difficult to deny Dr. Jagan the right to speak to his constituents on political matters". Moreover, some of them were conscious that one of British Guiana's main problems was widespread poverty among the working class due to poor wages paid by employers, especially the owners of sugar plantations.[219]

In the circumstances Jagan was able ultimately to have access to the sugar estates and to mobilise the support of the workers there for the P.P.P. in the 1953 elections. He was, however, still regarded by the British government as a threat to British business interests in the colony. After all, he was advocating radical economic reforms in keeping with the stated aim of the P.P.P. "to build a just socialist society in which the industries of the country shall be socially and democratically owned and managed for the common good."[220]

The second main element in the British government's perception of Cheddi Jagan early in 1953 was that he was regarded in London as "one of the leading labour politicians"[221] in British Guiana, as Dr. Rita Hinden, the secretary of the Fabian Colonial Bureau, described him in a letter to the Secretary of State for the Colonies. This reputation was derrived partly from his strong championing of the interests of workers in the Legislative Council since 1947 as well as during workers' protests, such as the one at Enmore in 1948.

Thirdly, in 1953 Cheddi Jagan was also viewed in London as a strong opponent of the British government's plans for decolonisation in British Guiana. In particular, it was known that he did not approve of the British government's policy of gradual political and constitutional evolution towards independence. Instead, he was demanding "immediate independence and self-government".[222]

Jagan and the British government were at loggerheads especially over the new Waddington constitution, which was hailed in London as a major constitutional development with its innovations of universal adult suffrage and the grant of a measure of ministerial responsibility to the winning political party. For Jagan, however, the constitution was unacceptable for it fell short of self – government.

He was particularly critical of the checks and balances embodied in the new constitution. He felt that these features were "studiedly put in at various stages to perpetuate the old order" and "will not permit any solution of the pressing social and economic problems of the people"[223]. As Minister of State Lennox Boyd noted after an interview with Jagan in London in November 1951, Jagan believed that the constitution's checks and balances "would involve the continuance of that degree of interest and vested influence in governmental affairs of which he complained the country had suffered so much in the past."[224] Jagan contended that there was no need for such checks and balances and that the elected members of the proposed new House of Assembly were capable of running the country "efficiently and prosperously"[224]

Jagan's views, however, were not shared by the British government, who felt that the elected members would need first to prove themselves able before they could be granted greater or full responsibility. The Colonial Office maintained that until the elected members were able to demonstrate that they could handle a measure of ministerial responsibility competently, they would not inspire the confidence needed to attract foreign capital which was regarded as vital for the country's development. In short, one objection which the British government had to Jagan's views was that it was not clear what the grounds were for thinking that the territory would be more prosperous under self-government.

The British government in 1953 saw Cheddi Jagan not only as being at variance with its approach to decolonisation in British Guiana, but also, fourthly, as opposed to its vision of what British Guiana should be after it gained political independence. It was very conscious that he was the leader of the political party which was strongly opposed to capitalism and had announced aims and a programme "to build a just socialist society in which the industries of the country shall be socially and democratically owned and managed for the common good."[225] It found Jagan's advocacy of nationalisation of the sugar, bauxite, gold and timber industries very unwelcome

Jagan's economic vision for British Guiana was a reflection of his Marxist ideas. The allegation that he was a "communist" was, in fact, fifthly, the aspect of his political make-up and activities that the British found most disturbing. Jagan recognised that in the existing Cold War environment that it would be prejudicial to his political prospects if he acknowledged that he was a "communist" and so he sought to avoid a clear declaration of his commitment to Marxism. This was evident, for example, in the interview which he had in Georgetown with N.L. Mayle, a visiting official from the Colonial Office, in March 1952. According to Mayle

> I asked him point blank whether he thought British Guiana would be better off as a satellite of Russia. He said no and denied he was a communist. He complained that he was being called a communist by his local political opponents for their own purposes. I said I thought he acted very much like a communist.[226]

The British government not only recognised that Jagan's economic ideas were Marxist. It also took note that he made visits to countries behind the Iron Curtain and that he and his wife, Janet, were presented in Political Intelligence Reports from Georgetown to be "actively and openly engaged in the distribution of propaganda material of Communist origin."[227] So, in spite of Jagan's denials and evasion, by 1953 many of the officials in the Colonial office had come to the conclusion that he was a "communist". However, he and the P.P.P. were not thought to be communist in the sense of being controlled by any communist organisation outside the colony.

By 1953 the British had begun to classify Cheddi Jagan and two other leaders of the P.P.P., namely, Janet Jagan and Sidney King, as "communists" or "extremists", while others, notably Forbes Burnham, Ashton Chase and Jainarine Singh, were deemed "moderates". In short, as early as 1953, two years before the split of the original P.P.P. in 1955, the British government had begun to view Cheddi Jagan as a greater danger or evil than Forbes Burnham. This was the earliest manifestation of a British policy, which would increasingly become more clear-cut, of preferring and eventually ensuring that British Guiana would gain political independence from Britain under Burnham's leadership rather than under that of Cheddi Jagan.

FOR FURTHER READING

| Rose, James & Williams, John | "International Perceptions of the People's Progressive Party by 1953", **History Gazette**, No.72, September 1994. |

Chapter 60

Turning Back the Clock: The Suspension of The British Guiana Constitution In 1953

1953 was one of the most important years in Guyanese history. It witnessed two major developments. One of them was the country's first essentially democratic election, held on April 27 in accordance with the provisions of a new and comparatively advanced constitution recommended by the British government's Waddington Commission of 1950.

This constitution introduced several new features into Guyanese political life, including universal adult suffrage at the age of 21 and a ministerial system. It provided for a two–chamber legislature, comprising a House of Assembly of three official and 24 elected members and an Executive Council. This Executive Council had 10 members, namely, four officials and six of the elected members of the House of Assembly who were granted ministerial powers and responsibilities. In short, the elected ministers had a majority on the Executive Council which was the main instrument of policy.

In the general election held under this constitution the People's Progressive Party (P.P.P.), led by Cheddi Jagan and chaired by Forbes Burnham, secured a decisive victory, winning 51 per cent of the votes cast and 18 of the 24 elected seats. Leading members of the party as a result were elected to all six ministerial posts filled from the House of Assembly. The ministers and their portfolios were as follows:

> Cheddi Jagan – Agriculture, Forests, Lands and Mines.
> Forbes Burnham – Education
> Ashton Chase – Labour Industry and Commerce
> Sidney King (later Eusi Kwayana) – Communications and Works
> Joseph Latchmansingh – Health and Housing
> Jai Narine Singh – Local Government and Social

Welfare

A few months later in October, after the ministers had spent only 133 days in office, the second major development of the year occurred. The British government suspended the new constitution, dismissed the ministers and sent troops to the colony to deal with any popular protest that might occur because of the deposing of the freely elected representatives of the people. It entrusted the administration of the colony to an interim government of approved individuals until a new constitution was devised and another general election held. This interim body administrated the colony until 1957.

This was the second occasion that the British Government had turned back the political clock of British Guiana because of its disapproval of developments which occurred in the wake of the introduction of a new constitution for the colony. The first occasion was twenty-five years before in 1928 when it scrapped a constitution introduced in 1891. This 1891 constitution led unexpectedly to a gradual erosion of the political power of the favoured white plantocracy and mercantile class and a transfer of much of this power increasingly into the hands of the rising black and brown middle class.

The decision of the British authorities in London to suspend the colony's constitution again in 1953 stemmed essentially from two somewhat related factors, namely, their dissatisfaction with, and their fear of, the P.P.P. – led government of British Guiana. Their thinking was influenced considerably by three sources – the regular reports of the governor of the colony, Alfred Savage, a letter from a visiting British official, Stephen Luke, and correspondence and meetings with the officials of Booker Brothers, the leading British capitalist firm in the colony.

The series of reports from Savage in July, August and September 1953 indicated to the British Colonial Office "quite clearly that the situation was progressively and rapidly deteriorating"[228] and required firm intervention to check and reverse the apparent decay. In his political report for July Savage noted that "it would clearly be politic to avoid a crisis for as long as possible".[229] Then in a letter dated August 27 to Sir Thomas Lloyd, a senior official in the Colonial Office, he observed that the "P.P.P. members are using their position to undermine the government".[230] Furthermore, in his political report for August, the governor stated that "extremist views prevail… probably a deliberate intention to wreck the constitution".[231]

Finally, even more disturbing to the Colonial Office were the sentiments that he expressed to Lloyd in a letter written on September 13 in which he observed: "I am rapidly coming to the conclusion that unless the opposition elements rouse themselves quickly… we shall have to go back on the new Constitution which would mean use of force".[232] He reiterated this opinion in a telegram four days later in which he stated: "I consider a breakdown in the Constitution is probable in any case within a few weeks… it would almost certainly be accompanied by disorder… forces must be acquired".[233]

The governor's increasingly gloomy picture of the situation in British Guiana was confirmed in a pessimistic report by Stephen Luke, Comptroller of Development and Welfare for the West Indies, who paid an official visit to the colony early in September 1953. Luke in a lengthy letter of September 12 to Philip Rogers, a senior Colonial Office functionary, stated:

> The situation is unquestionably most disquieting… I formed the opinion that the senior officials are completely disheartened and pessimistic; that the public service is approaching demoralization; that the business and commercial community are embittered and frightened; and that there is grave anxiety among responsible and fair – minded people like the Anglican Archbishop. I was told that all private investment has ceased; there is, for instance, unemployment in the building industry because virtually all private building has stopped. As you no doubt know, a run has started on the Government Saving Bank.[234]

These disturbing reports from Savage and Luke were influential in causing the Secretary of State for the Colonies to decide on September 23, 1953 to suspend the constitution of British Guiana. The decision was communicated by telegram to Governor Savage in Georgetown on the following day and was announced publicly by the Colonial Office about two weeks later. This drastic unexpected action was taken because the British authorities in both London and Georgetown were extremely displeased with, and fearful of, the P.P.P.

The friction between the two parties stemmed partly from the fact that the governor and the other British officials in the colony wrongly assumed and expected that the inexperienced P.P.P. ministers would be subservient to them, soliciting and following their advice. The P.P.P. government often ignored or rejected their advice on the ground that it was designed to promote white local and metropolitan interests rather than the welfare of the common people of the colony who had returned the party to power in the recent April general election. Cheddi Jagan and the other five P.P.P. ministers, guided by their own independent thinking, devised policies which the British government often regarded as "blunders" resulting from their lack of experience in governance and their attempt to honour "a host of irresponsible election promises".[235] In addition, all the P.P.P. ministers were believed by the British government to possess, as Governor Savage put it, "a deep bitterness of feeling against Britain, the past administration and against society generally".[236]

The British government was also annoyed and disappointed because it believed that the P.P.P. was not making a serious effort to work the new and relatively advanced constitution which had granted British Guiana a fair measure of self – government. As Governor Savage complained to the Colonial Office in a dispatch of September 13, 1953

> In spite of the growing difficulties I persisted in a policy of tolerance, goodwill and cooperation, but it became evident that there was little intention on their part to cooperate with me or the other members of the Executive Council, or, in some cases, with Heads of Departments. As a general rule, they face us in Executive Council with their minds made up as the result of previous discussion… and it is practically impossible to induce them to accept any reasonable compromise.[237]

The governor was particularly disturbed by the attitude of the P.P.P. ministers to the white British expatriate officials who occupied most of the senior positions in the civil service. The ministers contended that these officials should be replaced by capable qualified Guianese to whom priority should be given in all appointments. Their stand caused the governor to accuse the P.P.P. of seeking to undermine and get control of the civil service and of conducting a campaign which made the positon of the expatriate officials "virtually impossible."[238]

The government's view was endorsed by Sir Stephen Luke. Luke after his official visit early in September 1953 reported that the "Ministers clearly aim of getting rid of them [the white expatriate officials and civil servants] as quickly as possible and there are signs that they will turn their attention to purging the civil service of those who are not politically acceptable to them".[239]

These allegations against the P.P.P. were partly a reflection and result of the strong opposition which the party had to the 1953 constitution under which it achieved office. From the outset the party had made an unsuccessful attempt to have the British government amend the constitutional proposals. Among these amendments which it had demanded in vain were the abolition of the largely nominated Upper House or State Council, voting at the age of 18 instead of 21 and the removal of the three most senior British officials (the Chief Secretary, the Attorney General and the Financial Secretary and Treasurer) from the House of Assembly and the Executive Council. Governor Savage was very disturbed by the views which the P.P.P. leaders expressed about the constitution, especially outside the legislature. In his opinion their views were "quite irresponsible… and have verged on the seditious".[240]

Savage came slowly to a conclusion that the P.P.P. contained an extremist element, led by Janet Jagan and Sidney King, which had a sinister secret plan or agenda. That plan, he believed, was to force the British government to concede full self-government at an early date "by creating disorder and economic chaos"[241] in the country.

The British metropolitan government received similar disturbing allegations about the P.P.P. from officials of Bookers in the colony. In a September 1953 letter Henry Seaford, a Bookers Shipping executive, expressed deep fears for the future of the company and the colony. He stated that

> ഇ
> What the majority of the Ministers are trying to do is to cause chaos in the Colony then go to the Colonial Office and say that it is because

they have not complete control, that these things are happening. The aim is to get rid of all white officials and make life so unpleasant for other Whites that they will get out. Schools are to be taught communism and those Masters that don't agree will be fired. Can you imagine what this Colony will be like in 5 years' time if this sort of thing continues? Unless something drastic is done, Bookers will cease to exist as a large firm in 5 years. I consider that the future of Bookers is at stake.[242]

൙

Seaford, Savage and the British metropolitan authorities were also disturbed by a general strike in the sugar industry which started on August 30, 1953. This protest was called by the P.P.P. – dominated (still unrecognized) Guiana Industrial Workers Union (G.I.W.U.) to secure increased wages and improved working conditions for all sugar workers and to enforce its demand for recognition as the bargaining agent for sugar workers in place of the less militant Man Power Citizens' Association (M.P.C.A.), the union favoured by the Sugar Producers Association.

The British government was annoyed and concerned that some of the P.P.P. ministers were "publicly fomenting this strike", viewing their support as irresponsible behavior that was causing a depression in the colony's economy. It became alarmed by the receipt of news of an attempt to start a general sympathy strike in the colony on September 22 in support of the sugar workers. It was this news which was the final or immediate cause of the decision which the Colonial Office made on the following day to suspend the colony's constitution.

Although the sugar strike ended on September 24, this decision was not reversed. This was because the British government believed that the suspension of the constitution was necessary above all to forestall what it believed was a plan of the P.P.P. to set up a communist state in British Guiana.

Understandably, in this Cold War era the British government was paranoid about communism. The P.P.P. was known as the only Marxist party to win an election in the British Caribbean. It was also known that its leaders imported and distributed Marxist literature in the colony and had visited Eastern European countries to attend conferences. Furthermore, since it won the April 1953 election, it had repealed legislation banning the importation into British Guiana of left-wing literature and had removed the prohibition against certain West Indian labour leaders visiting the country.

Such action helped to convince the governor that the P.P.P. had "communistic aims and intentions" and Sir Stephen Luke that the party was committed to "thorough going and communist totalitarianism".[244] The governor also reported that the P.P.P. was contemplating a coup early in October and secession of the colony from the British empire.

Although these ideas influenced the British authorities, they failed to provide then or subsequently any concrete evidence that the P.P.P. was plotting to subvert the constitution and convert the colony into a communist state. They, however, could easily believe that there was communist subversion because they perceived that the P.P.P. was being increasingly dominated by a group of "communist extremists"[245] led in their opinion, by Janet Jagan and Sidney King. They reckoned that most of the eighteen P.P.P. members in the House of Assembly were supporters of the "extremists" rather than of the "moderate" leaders, among whom they classified Forbes Burnham, Ashton Chase and Jainarine Singh.

In its official public declaration early in October 1953 explaining its reasons for its drastic intervention in the colony, the Colonial Office stated that "Her Majesty's Government has decided that the Constitution of British Guiana must be suspended to prevent Communist subversion of the government and a dangerous crisis both in public order and in economic affairs… The faction in power has shown by their acts and their speeches that they are prepared to go to any lengths, including violence, to turn British Guiana into a Communist state". [246]This declaration was obviously deliberately contrived to rationalise and justify the drastic unexpected action taken by the British government.

For Further Reading

Jagan, Cheddi	**Forbidden Freedom** (People's Books Co-operative Society Ltd., 1954).
Rose, James	"The Suspension of the British Guiana Constitution, 1953", **History Gazette**, No.25, October 1990.
Payne, Hugh	"The Expulsion of the People's Progressive Party from the government", **Ibid**., No.51, December, 1992.

Chapter 61

The United States of America and The Beginning of The Delayed Political Independence of British Guiana

Each year the Guyanese nation commemorates the anniversary of its political independence from Great Britain. The grant of independence status on 26th May 1966, however, occurred later than had been expected. At a Constitutional Conference in London in March 1960, the British Government had committed itself to the principle of political independence for British Guiana "at any time not later than two years after the 1961 general election".[247] In short, the country was expected to become independent by 1963 at the latest.

The August 1961 election was won by the People's Progressive Party (P.P.P.), led by Cheddi Jagan, which gained 42.6 per cent of the votes cast and 20 seats in the Legislative Council. The People's National Congress (P.N.C.), led by Forbes Burnham, received 41 per cent of the votes and 11 seats and the United Force (U.F.), led by Peter D' Aguiar, obtained 16.4 per cent of the votes and the remaining four seats.

In November 1961 the legislature passed a resolution calling on the British government in the United Kingdom to grant political independence to British Guiana as promised. In response to this resolution the British government announced its willingness to hold a conference of British Guiana's political leaders to determine the form of the independence constitution and to fix a date for independence. This response was much to the satisfaction of the P.P.P. which hoped to lead the country to independence within the promised time, that is, by 1963.

Eventually, however, the British government reneged on this promise and the date of independence was deferred until May 1966. This delay of about three years was due to several factors. Among them was the inability of the three main Guianese political parties to agree on an independence constitution and a date for independence and the political and civil strife in the country in 1962, 1963 and 1964. The main reason for the delay, however, was probably a somewhat invisible factor, namely, the influence of the government of the United States of America, which is the special focus of this essay.

The United States had demonstrated a special interest in the Caribbean at least from the famous declaration of 1823 of the so-called Monroe Doctrine in which its government claimed exclusive right to the American hemisphere. This interest was shown initially and for a long time in periodic American intervention especially in three countries, namely, Cuba, Puerto Rico and the Dominican Republic. No similar intervention or even significant interest was witnessed in the affairs of the British Caribbean apart from the exigencies of the Second World War which prompted Washington to secure air and/or naval bases in British Guiana and elsewhere in the Anglophone Caribbean.

The United States government only began to show obvious interest in the politics of British Guiana after the formation in 1950 of the P.P.P., a Marxist – oriented party in the era of the Cold War, marked by intense fear in the U.S. of communism. This interest became more serious when the P.P.P., led by Cheddi Jagan with Forbes Burnham as its chairman, won the 1953 general election decisively, securing 51 per cent of the votes cast and 18 of the 24 seats in the legislature.

One of the main expressed objectives of the P.P.P. from its inception was the early independence of British Guiana. The U.S. government, however, was completely opposed to the idea of British Guiana proceeding to independence under a P.P.P. government. It was therefore very pleased when the British government suspended the Guianese constitution and put the P.P.P. out of office in October 1953 after only 133 days in power. This gratification was because, as Secretary of State, John Dulles observed in October 1953, "the U.S. government would be gravely concerned at the threat to the security of the hemisphere which would arise if British Guiana fell victim to international communist conspiracy".[248] This satisfaction in Washington, however, was replaced by dismay, concern and anger when the P.P.P. returned to office in 1957 after four years of an interim government and the party's victory in the 1957 general election.

American concern about British Guiana grew significantly after Fidel Castro's successful revolution in Cuba in 1959 and Cuba's subsequent emergence as a Marxist state, the first in the hemisphere. The U.S. authorities were determined that another independent Marxist state would not emerge in the Caribbean in British Guiana. They were particularly fearful that British Guiana might not only become "a second Cuba"[249] but also a base for the spread of communism into the entire continent of South America. They became more disturbed after the Marxist P.P.P. won the 1961 general election, strengthening the prospect that British Guiana might proceed to independence under its government. They therefore began to exert pressure on the British government to persuade it to abandon this intention. They were particularly disturbed when late in 1961 the British representative at the United Nations reiterated Britain's commitment to independence for British Guiana.

Initially U.S. pressure failed to achieve its intention. The British government continued to declare its intention to grant independence to British Guiana under the P.P.P. government, although the U.S. authorities made it clear to London that such a step would be considered "an unfriendly act".[250] By the beginning of 1962 Dean Rusk, the American Secretary of State, acknowledged that the question of the independence of British Guiana was beginning to place strain on the Anglo – American alliance along with other issues such as Britain's refusal to sever ties with Cuba and her reluctance to take the U.S. into confidence about her plans for Rhodesia. He felt that a British decision to defer the independence of British Guiana was a small price for Britain to pay to maintain the health and intimacy of the alliance.

The U.S. authorities also felt peeved for several reasons. One of them was the fact that they had to depend on the British to achieve their objective in relation to British Guiana. As John Hemmings, a leading officer in the British embassy in Washington, observed in February 1962

൦ൟ

> The most difficult thing for Americans who are worried about British Guiana is to accept that theirs is not the prime responsibility… Agitated Americans, including Congressmen, who write to the State Department urging that America do something about British Guiana, are told that this is primarily a British responsibility. Back comes the rejoinder, why don't you make the British do something.[251]

൦ൟ

The U.S. government was also peeved that the British government had not kept them directly informed about details about its plans in relation to British Guiana. As Hemmings also stated in February 1962,

> I think the State Department feels strongly that we have not kept them fully consulted about British Guiana on a Government – to – Government basis; I have been asked why we did not tell them that our plans were laid to move troops and ships to Georgetown.[252]

The British government, however, continued for at least three reasons to resist American pressure for a change in its policy towards British Guiana. Firstly, it felt that British Guiana was as ready for political independence as many of her other colonies who were proceeding to or had been granted that status. Secondly, it believed that the P.P.P. had a right to govern British Guiana in view of its victory in three successive general elections in 1953, 1957 and 1961. Thirdly, it feared that failure to proceed as planned would bring Britain criticism in the United Nations and cause its empire and the rest of the world to question the sincerity of its declared general policy of decolonisation.

In 1962 the U.S. State Department suggested to Britain several alternatives to granting independence to British Guiana under the leadership of the Marxist, Cheddi Jagan. One alternative suggested was to hold another general election in the colony to see if there would be a change of government, though the State Department was not very optimistic about this approach. Washington also suggested that if Britain delayed the grant of independence, the allegedly "more moderate" element in the P.P.P., led possibly by Balram Singh Rai, might be persuaded to secede from the party and join the P.N.C. and U.F. to form a multiracial coalition.

Thirdly, the State Department suggested that the British government should suspend the constitution of British Guiana again, as it had done in 1953, put the P.P.P. out of office and reimpose direct British rule. Washington, in fact, preferred this suggestion to others, including one in favour of independence under a P.N.C./U.F. coalition. The British government, however, found this suggestion of the reintroduction of direct

British rule totally unacceptable for several reasons, especially because it "would arouse the strongest opposition inside and outside British Guiana … a territory in which she [Britain] had no profound interest".[253] In any event such a step would have "very considerable long-term political, military and financial implications".

Thus initially, at least until the early months of 1962, Britain rejected the overtures of the United States to persuade her to abandon her willingness to allow British Guiana its proceed to independence under the Jagan – led P.P.P. or at least to defer the grant of independence. The British government, however, eventually succumbed to the American pressure.

The U.S. resorted to a variety of tactics in its effort to get the British government to modify its plans for the independence of British Guiana. One of the tactics was to try to persuade the British government to re-examine the apparent premise of its policy that there was no reasonable alternative to working with the P.P.P. At least as late as March 1962, for example, the British authorities did not regard Forbes Burnham and the People's National Congress as a viable alternative, even in the unlikely event that the P.N.C. defeated the P.P.P. in an election which the U.S. government was advocating.

The thinking of the Colonial Office on this issue was clearly outlined in a "Top Secret Note", dated March 5, 1962 on a letter sent by Dean Rusk to the British Foreign Secretary, Lord Home. The "Note" stated

> If new elections are held … it is by no means certain that Dr. Jagan would be defeated… If, however, Dr. Jagan's party were defeated, it is likely that Mr. Burnham would become Premier and few who know him can imagine that a Government led by him would be any better. Certainly, the new Ministries would be less experienced than Dr. Jagan's Ministers, and it should be remembered that quite apart from their share of responsibility for the recent demonstrations and disorders, it is the Burnham party which has been mainly responsible for fanning racial enmities.[255]

The U.S. administration welcomed the 1962 disturbances in the colony which grew largely out of a strike by civil servants over conditions of service and a trade union strike over the controversial Kaldor budget of January 1962. These disturbances were exploited not only by the local opposition political parties, the P.N.C. and the United Force, but also by the United States. The U.S. authorities believed that the disturbances would make Britain decide to defer the independence of British Guiana as they desired. They also hoped that the disturbances would give Britain an excuse to hold fresh elections in the colony which would result in the defeat of the P.P.P..

The disturbances, in fact, did make the British government review the wisdom of its plans for British Guiana and give greater consideration to American advice to seek to remove the P.P.P. from power. These developments were reflected in a Colonial Office memorandum of February 1962, in which it was stated that

> Unless Dr. Jagan's Government can in the near future show that it can govern, it may in the interest of British Guiana become necessary to remove it. This is a matter which is being closely studied. But whatever administration were to succeed the present one, it would have to demonstrate real and substantial economic progress if it were to have any chance of success. This is impossible without substantial US aid. Before any steps are taken to replace Dr. Jagan's government by another, we should seek a prior US commitment to underwrite a large part of British Guiana's development plan.[256]

The British government was particularly concerned about the fact that the disturbances required the dispatch of British troops to the colony. Some British officials, however, also saw possible benefits which could be derived from the disturbances there and the deferral of the colony's independence. In their view this not only would remove some of the strains on the Anglo – American alliance but also might enable Britain as compensation to claim U.S. support for some of its policies elsewhere in its empire, such as financial aid for the West Indies Federation.

These were some of earliest signs of the willingness of the British government, in response to U.S. pressure and developments in British Guiana, to modify its declared policy in relation to the colony's independence. Washington seized every opportunity to thrust its views about the colony on the British authorities, expressing its fear about what it called "the British Guiana situation".257

The U.S. administration received encouragement and pressure from some of its nationals. In March 1962, for example, A.G.E. Vander Tuuk, an American businessman who had recently visited British Guiana on a business trip, sent a letter and a memorandum to the U.S. President, John Kennedy, about political developments in the colony. In this correspondence he warned against "independence in the near future" because "it can only lead to complete communist control" which "will create an explosive basis for spreading communism to Suriname, Brazil, Venezuela and throughout South America".258

This communication took place at a time when the U.S. government was reviewing its policy towards British Guiana and President Kennedy was becoming more interested and involved in the situation in the colony. The considerations preoccupying the President were clearly stated in an instructive document which Kennedy sent to Dean Rusk in March 1962 and copied to other leading American officials, including the Attorney General, the Secretary of Defence and the Director of the Central Intelligence Agency.

In this document, entitled "National Security Action Memorandum No 135", Kennedy stated

> No final decision will be taken on our policy toward British Guiana and the Jagan government until (a) the Secretary of State has a chance to discuss the matter with Lord Home (the British Foreign Secretary) in Geneva and (b) Hugh Fraser (a British Colonial Office official) completes his on – the – spot survey in British Guiana for the Colonial Office .
> The questions which we must answer before we reach our decision include the following;
> 1. Can Great Britain be persuaded to delay independence for a year?

2. If Britain refused to delay the independence, would a new election be possible? If so, would Jagan win or lose? If he lost what are the alternatives?
3. What are the possibilities and limitations of United States action in the situation?"[259]

೧೦

This proved to be the prelude to important new developments in the U.S. policy towards British Guiana which had significant influence on the colony's movement to independence, including a further delay in the achievement of this status.

For Further Reading

Fraser, Cary	**Ambivalent Anti-Colonialism: The United States and the Genesis of West Indian Independence** (Westport: Greenwood Press, 1994).
Rose, James & Williams, John	"International Perceptions of the People's Progressive Party by 1953", **History Gazette**, No.73, September 1994.
Jagan, Cheddi	**The West on Trial** with a new epilogue (St. John's: Hansib Caribbean, 1997).
Rabe, Stephen	**U.S. Intervention in British Guiana: A Cold War Story** (Chapel Hill: The University of North Carolina Press, 2005).
Palmer, Colin	**Cheddi Jagan and the Politics of Power: British Guiana's Struggle for Independence** (Chapel Hill: University of North Carolina Press, 2010).

Part Eleven

Miscellany

Front page of Daily Argosy, 10 October 1953, announcing the suspension of the colony's constitution

Peter D' Aguiar

Stephen Campbell, the first Amerindian legislator

CHAPTER 62

THE BRITISH OCCUPATION OF GUYANA IN 1796

One of the unique features of Guyana is that it is the only English-speaking country in South America, a continent which is dominated by Spanish-speaking republics. This distinctive feature is a result of the fact that for about one hundred and seventy years Guyana was a British colony until it obtained political independence in May 1966. The beginning of this long period of almost uninterrupted British rule, with the exception of several months in 1802-3, dates back to April 1796 when British forces occupied the Dutch colonies of Berbice and Demerara-Essequibo.

This occupation in 1796 was the third of four occasions that the British took possession of at least a part of the territory which today constitutes the Republic of Guyana. One feature was common to all four occasions, namely, the British were adopting a practice normally employed by the principal European powers of capturing each other's colonial possessions during a period of international warfare.

The first occasion that the British occupied Guyana was during what historians term the Second Anglo-Dutch War of 1665-67. In 1665 an English expedition sent to Guyana under one Major John Scott captured the Dutch colonies in the Pomeroon and Essequibo, but was repulsed when it attacked Berbice. This first period of British rule of Guyana proved to be short-lived, for within about a year the British garrison in Essequibo surrendered to a force comprising European soldiers, Amerindian auxiliaries and African slaves dispatched by the Dutch authorities in Berbice and the colony in the Pomeroon was destroyed by a French force.

The second period of British rule of Guyana occurred one hundred and fifteen years later during the American War of Independence (1776-83) and, like the first occasion, did not last long. In 1780 during this conflict, Britain declared war on the Netherlands largely because the Dutch colony of St. Eustatius was being used by Americans as a privateering base against

British territories and shipping, under the protection of the Dutch flag. In the following year, 1781, the British sent an expedition to Guyana which captured the three separate Dutch colonies of Demerara, Essequibo and Berbice easily. In 1782, however, the small British garrisons which were left in these colonies succumbed to French forces. The French remained in control of Demerara, Essequibo and Berbice until 1784, shortly after the end of the American War, when they restored them to their Dutch allies.

The third period of British occupation of Guyana which began in 1796 was longer and far more significant than the two previous occasions of British rule. It occurred during a time of intensive international warfare stemming from the repercussions of the famous revolution which began in France in 1789. In February 1793 France declared war on Britain and the Netherlands and both France and Britain sent fleets to the West Indies.

By then British interest in Guyana was considerable and growing steadily. This development was a result of a major change in Dutch colonial policy in the early 1740s when the Dutch West India Company, in an effort to promote the development of Essequibo, abandoned its hitherto restrictive approach and instead opened Essequibo to the settlement of all nationalities. The Company also applied this novel policy to Demerara where it began to pioneer a new Dutch colony in 1746.

As a result of this change of Dutch policy, from the 1740s a growing number of British settlers began to establish themselves in Essequibo and Demerara. Many of the early British settlers were planters from the older British West Indian colonies, especially Barbados and Antigua, where the soil was becoming exhausted and therefore more difficult and more costly to cultivate. They were attracted to Essequibo and increasingly to Demerara by the fertility of the soil there, the cheapness of land and the ease with which it could be secured, and the Dutch government's offer of exemption from taxes for a period of ten years. The success of some of these pioneers, like the Clarkes of Barbados, encouraged other British subjects to settle in Essequibo and Demerara.

British settlers were also attracted to Essequibo and Demerara by other advantages which these two Dutch colonies possessed. Foremost among these considerations were the mild climate, the complete or virtual absence of hurricanes, earthquakes and severe droughts, the availability of cheap internal water transport for produce and the abundance of the harvests of sugar, coffee and cotton, the staples of the colonies' diversified export economy.

The influx of British settlers into Essequibo and Demerara, which were merged by the Dutch government in 1789 to constitute a single entity, the "United Colony of Demerara and Essequibo", was so steady and substantial that by 1796 it was estimated that they comprised a majority of the white population there. The strength of their presence and their representations played an important part in the coming of British rule to Guyana for the third time in 1796.

British occupation of Demerara-Essequibo and Berbice in April 1796 was not due primarily to the desire of the metropolitan government in London. Rather it was undertaken mainly in response to a written request from Antony Beaujon, the Dutch governor of Demerara-Essequibo, who early in 1796 appealed to the commander-in-chief of the British forces in the West Indies based in Barbados to take possession of this Dutch colony.

Beaujon's unexpected initiative was prompted by three main considerations. Firstly, it was the result of his growing dissatisfaction with developments in the Netherlands which late in 1794 had been successfully invaded and overrun by French armies with the assistance of Dutchmen who were sympathetic to the French Revolution. Their success was so resounding that eventually the British troops who were helping the Dutch government abandoned the country and the Dutch ruler, Prince William V of Orange, fled to England for refuge. In his absence William's Dutch opponents, with French support, abrogated the old Dutch constitution, abolished his office, and proclaimed the Netherlands to be a republic, the Batavian Republic, which from its foundation was closely linked to, and dependent on, France. Consequently, the Republic did not have the support of many officials in Dutch colonies overseas.

These developments were resented by Beaujon, who was a strong supporter of the old Dutch constitution, regretted its abrogation and had little or no sympathy for the principles and ideas of the French Revolution. He became more and more dissatisfied with the Batavian Republic because of its subservience to France and increasingly well-disposed towards Britain, whose political system he admired.

The second consideration which drove Beaujon to solicit British rule was his desire to bring an end to a critical situation facing the commerce of Demerara-Essequibo since early in 1795. This crisis stemmed largely from punitive action taken by Britain against Dutch trade because of her annoyance at the growing control exercised by her enemy, France, over the Netherlands, now the Batavian Republic. This increasing animosity eventually culminated in war. In February 1795 Britain declared a general embargo on Dutch shipping, resulting in the detention of Dutch vessels in British ports, and in the following September ordered the seizure of Dutch vessels on the high seas where she had mastery. This action virtually severed Demerara-Essequibo's vital connection with the Netherlands.

In these circumstances planters in Demerara-Essequibo found it virtually impossible to export their produce to their normal market, and to secure supplies from their customary source, in the Netherlands. Hardly a Dutch vessel dared cross the Atlantic. Only seven ships left Demerara-Essequibo for the Netherlands in 1795 and none in 1796, whereas normally 25 vessels sailed each year from the colony to the metropolis. Admittedly, a substantial increase of trade with the United States helped the colonists, but it did not bring an end to the crisis. According to an English resident, by the beginning of 1796 many of the colony's white inhabitants, especially English and Dutch colonists, no longer were seeing any benefit to be derived from "belonging to a country [the Netherlands or Batavian Republic] which could neither protect them or their trade" from the British.[260] They had come to the conclusion that "something was necessary to be done to enable them to open their ports, and ship from the Colony the produce which had been accumulating for several years."[261] One answer to their predicament, as they and Beaujon recognised, was to accept British rule, thus permitting export of their produce in British vessels to Britain.

The third and most important factor prompting Beaujon to request British intervention was an acute fear that the French were planning to take over Demerara-Essequibo. He believed that he had discovered evidence of a plot among some French residents to overthrow the government, surrender the colony to France and use it as a base for future attacks on the British West Indies.

Motivated by these considerations, early in 1796 Beaujon sent a confidential messenger on a secret mission to Barbados with a written appeal to General Knox, the commander of the British forces, to send an expedition to take possession of the Dutch colony of Demerara-Essequibo. To induce a favourable response from the General, he not only emphasised that French possession of the colony would spell doom for the British West Indies, but also promised to help raise a black corps of 500 men to assist in the defence of the colony after its capture.

In response to Beaujon's request, an expedition of eight warships and 1300 soldiers was sent to Demerara-Essequibo in April 1796. The governor and the legislature of the colony soon surrendered on very generous terms. The latter included a guarantee of security for the person and property of residents (except Frenchmen), the grant of equal trading rights and privileges as enjoyed by other British subjects in the West Indies, and the maintenance of existing laws and institutions. The governor and other Dutch officials were also to be allowed to retain their jobs provided they were not known to be favourably disposed to France. Berbice, which also capitulated, received similar concessions. Not surprisingly, Beaujon was retained as governor of what was now the new British colony of Demerara-Essequibo, but the supreme military command was given to Lieutenant Hislop, a British officer who had accompanied the expedition.

The British capture of Demerara-Essequibo and Berbice was welcomed by many of the inhabitants. The only public dissent was manifested by a few residents who were strongly disposed towards France. Demerara-Essequibo and Berbice remained British possessions until December 1802, when they were restored to the Netherlands in accordance with the provisions of the Treaty of Amiens which brought a temporary truce among European Powers.

They were reoccupied, however, by Britain for the fourth and final time when hostilities broke out again in Europe in 1803. Although the Dutch did not realise it then, they would never regain control of Demerara-Essequibo and Berbice, which they finally ceded to Britain in 1814 when definitive peace was made among the European Powers. Britain was eager to retain the two colonies largely because of the tremendous economic growth which they had experienced under British rule since 1796 and the considerable increase of British settlers there. She continued to rule these colonies, which in 1831 were unified into a single entity, called British Guiana, until May 1966 when the country gained political independence.

For Further Reading

Thompson, Alvin	**Colonialism and Underdevelopment in Guyana, 1580-1803** (Bridgetown: Carib Research and Publications, Inc. 1987).
Mc Gowan, Winston	"The French Revolutionary Period in Demerara-Essequibo, 1793-1802", **History Gazette**, No 55, April 1993.

CHAPTER 63

CHRISTMAS IN GUYANA 200 YEARS AGO

This essay will focus on some of the salient features of the Christmas season in Guyana in the late 1790s, comparing and contrasting them with the principal traits of Christmas in modern Guyana. Much of the knowledge of Christmas in Guyana 200 years ago has been obtained from the informative but comparatively little-known writings of George Pinckard. Pinckard was an English medical doctor who spent thirteen months in Demerara, Essequibo and Berbice in 1796 and 1797 as a physician to the resident British garrison. His experiences there are recorded in his valuable book, **Letters from Guiana 1796-97**.

Two hundred years ago the population of Guyana consisted of three racial groups- Amerindians, Europeans and Africans. Whereas today Christmas is celebrated by all Guyanese, in the 1790s it was observed mainly by the Europeans and Africans with little participation by the Amerindians.

One of the most striking differences between the Christmas season then and that today was the absence then of any significant religious emphasis. Today most churches in Guyana hold special Christmas Eve or Christmas morning services to commemorate and celebrate the birth of Christ. In marked contrast in 1799, although Christmas was recognised as a major Christian festival, there was very little religious observance in Demerara-Essequibo for several reasons.

Firstly, the white population there was notorious for its irreligiosity and love for worldly pleasure. Furthermore, the colony had very limited facilities for organised Christian religious practice. As yet it did not have any building especially constructed for Christian worship and it had only two ministers of religion – an Anglican clergyman and a minister attached to the Dutch Reformed Church. These ministers each conducted a service on Sundays in a room in the Court House in the colony's capital, Stabroek, which was renamed Georgetown in 1812. These services were attended by a small exclusively white congregation, consisting predominantly of residents of Stabroek and its environs. Whites in the more distant countryside had no such opportunity. For example, one Dutch planter on the East Coast of Demerara in 1799 stated that he had never heard a single sermon in his twenty four years of residence in the colony.

Pinckard captured the limited facilities for, and interest in, Christian worship in the late 1790s in Demerara-Essequibo in the following description

> All the ceremonies of the Sabbath are utterly disregarded. No church or temple is to be found in the settlements; nor have the inhabitants ever appropriated any house, or other building for the performance of divine service – Sunday, it is true, has been set apart as a day of rest, but no solemn ceremony marks it as the Sabbath. Idleness and merriment alone distinguish it from the other days of the week.[262]

The white population of the colony, almost all of whom were supposed to be at least nominal Christians, did not demonstrate any greater religious interest at Christmas than in the remainder of the year. Nor did the Blacks, the numerically dominant group in the colony, show any religious devotion at Christmas. This was not surprising for the overwhelming majority of Blacks in Demerara-Essequibo, who were mostly slaves, were not Christianised. This was the result of a deliberate long-standing policy of the white authorities and slave owners of denying slaves access to Christianity for fear that instruction in the Christian faith would make them more discontented and rebellious.

This marked absence of significant religious observances at Christmas which was evident in Demerara- Essequibo in the late 1790s among both Whites and Blacks continued until 1808 when an important development took place. In that year the London Missionary Society (L.M.S.) sent a missionary named John Wray to Demerara in response to a request from Hilbertus Hermanus Post, the Dutch proprietor of Plantation Le Resouvenir on the East Coast of Demerara. Wray inaugurated a mission, especially for slaves, at Le Resouvenir, where by November 1808 he had erected a commodious church building which he named Bethel Chapel.

Thereafter, that is to say from Christmas 1808, one of the highlights of the Christmas season in Demerara-Essequibo was the holding, initially at Le Resouvenir, of well-attended Christian religious services on Christmas Day and on the following day, now called Boxing Day. Apart from an understandable focus on the birth of Christ, these religious meetings at Christmas were distinguished by two special events, namely, the baptism and marriage of slave converts. This development is reflected, for example, in the following entry for 26 December 1822 in the private journal of Rev. John Smith, Wray's famous successor as the minister in charge of Bethel Chapel.

> A great many people came from various parts with a view of attending chapel today. Till past 9 o'clock I was engaged in finally examining the candidates for baptism, and again this morning till near 12. The congregation would have filled the chapel had the latter been twice as large…Today I married five couples and baptised 74 individuals including about 20 children. A comfortable Xmas to me. [263]

Where the minority white population (consisting mainly of government officials, merchants and plantation proprietors and senior staff) was concerned, Christmas Day in the late 1790s, a public holiday, was marked by numerous parties and special dinners. As Pinckard remarked in a letter, "On the subject of Christmas, I should tell you that it is not less a period of festivity here, than in England. The planters make parties, and the merry feasting of the season goes round."[264]

Similar merriment also took place among the numerically dominant black population. A small minority of the slaves and almost all the free Blacks lived in Stabroek and New Amsterdam, the capitals of the colonies of Demerara-Essequibo and Berbice. Most of the slaves, however, lived and worked as field and factory hands on the sugar, coffee and cotton plantations in the countryside.

The main festivity among slaves in the 1790s centred around dances which were held on the plantations in the evening of Christmas Day. It was facilitated by a relaxation of the normal security regulations. Slaves were allowed to leave the plantations where they resided without white supervision or passes from their owners to attend dances on other estates. There they had the joy of meeting their relatives, friends, lovers and shipmates with whom they had endured the traumatic Atlantic crossing from Africa to Demerara-Essequibo and Berbice. As Pinckard remarked in his description of Christmas Day 1796

&

> In the evening, their loved African dance crowned the holyday. Parties of them go from the different plantations to spend the mirthful hours with their more particular friends or acquaintances of the neighbouring estates, and it is a happy meeting of relatives, lovers, and fellow-passengers, who made the voyage together from their native land. The whole country exhibits one moving scene of dancing gaiety. Cheerful crowds are met in every quarter.[265]

&

The jollification was not merely tolerated or permitted by the white slave-masters, but deliberately encouraged by them to provide what they regarded as a much-needed salutary outlet for the pent-up anger of the slaves engendered by the cruelty of the slave system. In fact, the existing slave laws recognised the value of the provision of merriment as a means of controlling the slaves and reducing the incidence of flight, rebellion and other forms of slave resistance. Thus a clause of the 1784 slave code of Demerara, which was still in force in 1799, stipulated that "everyone shall be allowed to give his Negroes leave to dance once a month, the regular holidays not included, but never later than two o'clock in the morning under the penalty of one hundred and fifty guilders."[266]

The masters encouraged such merriment especially at Christmas by providing the slaves with a lavish supply of rum which was welcomed by the slaves. This practice later became the cause of dissension among slaves on the East Coast of Demerara, when those who were converted to Christianity as a result of the work of John Wray and other clergymen from the London

Missionary Society refused on spiritual and moral grounds to continue to participate in the dances and in the consumption of alcohol.

In addition to the emphasis on merriment, Christmas in the 1790s was a special occasion for slaves in other respects. For example, it was an occasion when they dressed most attractively and decorated their heads in peculiar ways. As Pinckard observed about Christmas Day 1796

> cheerful crowds are met in every quarter, dressed out in all the gaudy trappings they can collect, with their hair cut and fashioned into multitudes of whimsical shapes, representing various figures of helmets, wigs, crowns and the like; and decorated with a profusion of beads, bits of riband, and other tinsel ornaments.[267]

The slaves also welcomed Christmas as an occasion when they received some special additional allowances of food, drink and clothing from their masters. In addition to alcohol, many masters gave their slaves meat for consumption at lunch-time or dinner-time on Christmas Day. According to Pinckard

> Christmas…is a holyday to the slaves who usually receive some indulgences of food, and some present of clothing to augment the happiness of the festival. We have seen new hats distributed among the men of a whole gang, and a bit of coarse canvass for a petticoat given to each of the women; and never were children more delighted with toys, than these poor beings were on the joyous occasion of receiving these humble, but to them splendid offerings. Some fresh meat was also served out to them as a high feast for dinner.[268]

The slaves' happy response to the grant of these modest allowances, reflected their terrible plight under slavery, a system of extreme deprivation. Meat was particularly welcome because it was not a normal component of the slaves' rather monotonous diet of salted fish and plantains in some form. Although some animals were maintained by each plantation and slaves were required each evening at the completion of their work in the field to proceed to the "backdam" to cut and fetch a bundle of grass for the estate's cattle and horses, animals on the whole were in short supply. Consequently, there was often a great scarcity of meat, which was normally reserved for the white population. Lunch or dinner on Christmas Day which included meat was therefore a welcome rarity to the slaves.

Soon, however, the festivity and mirth of Christmas Day ended and the slaves returned to the rigour and drudgery of work under the slave system. The slave masters hoped that the relief provided by the merriment and allowances of Christmas Day would serve to make the slaves submit, however reluctantly, to the terrible injustice of slavery.

For Further Reading

Pinckard, George	**Letters from Guiana, 1795-97** (extracted from **Notes on the West Indies** (Georgetown: Daily Chronicle Ltd, 1942).
Bolingbroke, Henry	**A Voyage to Demerary, Containing a Statistical Account of the Settlements There and Those of the Essequibo, the Berbice, and other Contiguous Rivers of Guiana** (orig. pub. 1808). Reprint Georgetown: Daily Chronicle Ltd, 1941).

CHAPTER 64

THE EFFECTS OF THE HAITIAN REVOLUTION ON GUYANA

The Haitian Revolution (1791-1804) is one of the most momentous events in the history of the Americas. It is unique for it is the only occasion in the history of this hemisphere, which witnessed hundreds of slave rebellions, that slaves succeeded in overthrowing the system of slavery and establishing an independent state, the first black republic in the Americas. The long duration of the revolution and the magnitude of its significance ensured that it would have considerable impact on the wider world. Its impact affected even the apparently remote Dutch colonies of Demerara-Essequibo and Berbice on the distant mainland of South America.

The most important effect of the Haitian Revolution on the area that today constitutes the Republic of Guyana is that it was a major contributory factor to the coming of British rule there in 1796.[269] At that time, a period of international warfare known as the French Revolutionary Wars, France had been weakened by the loss of St Lucia, Louisiana, Mauritius, territory in India and by the threatened loss of Saint-Domingue, by far its most valuable colonial possession. It was believed in Demerara-Essequibo and Berbice that France wished to compensate for those losses partly by taking possession of Dutch Caribbean colonies, especially Demerara-Essequibo and Berbice, where the majority of white residents consisted of Dutch and British planters with a minority of Frenchmen.

News which reached these two Dutch colonies about the massive slave uprising in Saint-Domingue, the excesses of the great revolution in France and the French government's decision to abolish slavery in the French empire, made the British and Dutch residents of Demerara-Essequibo and Berbice fear that violent political and social upheaval would follow there if the French gained possession of these colonies. This fear resulted in intense anti-French feeling and a decision to solicit British occupation and rule to forestall the realisation of the objective of an alleged conspiracy of French residents to enable France to take possession of the two colonies. These were among the major circumstances which prompted the Dutch governor early in 1796 to invite the commander of the regional British forces in Barbados to occupy the colony. In response to this request, Demerara-Essequibo and Berbice were occupied by British troops in April 1796 and remained under British rule until May 1966 except for a brief intermission of about nine months in 1802-1803 when they were restored to the Netherlands.

The heavy French military commitments in Saint-Domingue in an ultimately unsuccessful effort to suppress the slave uprising may have prevented the French from attacking these two Dutch colonies and thus pre-empting the British. What is certain is that the British felt secure initially in their possession of Demerara-Essequibo and Berbice because of France's preoccupation with Saint-Domingue.

The rebellion also had important repercussions on the economy of Demerara-Essequibo and Berbice. Initially, it was a severe blow to planters and merchants in these colonies who also owned plantations in Saint-Domingue or had extended credit to planters there. These planters and merchants were saddened by the loss of their assets in Saint-Domingue and by their inability to recover their debts and other investments there.

On the other hand, the revolution in Saint-Domingue within a few years led to a significant increase in British capital investments in Demerara-Essequibo and Berbice. Merchants and absentee planters especially in London who had business interests in both these colonies and Saint-Domingue petitioned the British government in September 1795 to take possession of Demerara-Essequibo and Berbice. They regarded their investments in these two Dutch colonies as critical to their survival in business for they had incurred substantial losses in Saint-Domingue. Their business in Demerara-Essequibo and Berbice was now their only hope of gaining a livelihood, repaying their debts and obtaining credit. They were very fearful that French capture of these two colonies would be detrimental to their business. Although their request to the British government was not granted, they were delighted that other circumstances soon resulted in British possession of Demerara-Essequibo and Berbice. These colonies profited immensely after April 1796 from their investment because they could no longer invest in Saint-Domingue.

The Saint-Domingue Revolution also gave a boost to the economy of Demerara-Essequibo and Berbice in other ways. For example, it enabled these colonies partially to replace Saint-Domingue as a supplier of coffee especially to British markets. Coffee production in, and exports from, Demerara-Essequibo and Berbice increased considerably, rising by 65 per cent between 1796 and 1800 compared to the previous four years. By 1802 these two colonies had become the greatest producer of coffee in the British Empire.

The Haitian Revolution also had effects on slaves and slaveholders in Demerara-Essequibo and Berbice. The receipt of news of the uprising in Saint-Domingue made slaves there conclude that they too might be able to rebel effectively. They became more restless and more emboldened to revolt. On the other hand, the events in Saint-Domingue made slaveowners in Demerara-Essequibo and Berbice more deeply fearful of slave rebellions and drove them to resort to every possible mechanism to forestall or suppress them.

Finally, the Haitian Revolution played a part in bringing an end to slavery, especially in the British and French Caribbean. The tremendous loss of life and damage to property occasioned by this uprising as well as subsequent slave rebellions eventually helped to convince the metropolitan governments of the wisdom of abolishing an institution which would continue to provoke costly violent resistance.

CHAPTER 65

VILLAGE PROBLEMS AT THE END OF THE NINETEENTH CENTURY

The focus here will be on conditions in eighteen villages of British Guiana which in 1900 were under the control of the Central Board of Health. These villages were for the most part inhabited mainly by Africans. They included Sparendaam, Plaisance, Beterverwagting, Buxton and Friendship, Golden Grove and Nabaclis, Victoria, and Ann's Grove and Two Friends on the East Coast of Demerara. Also in Demerara were Agricola, Mocha and Craig on the East Bank, Bagotville, Goed Intent and Sisters, and Stanleytown on the West Bank and Den Amstel and Fellowship and De Kinderen on the West Coast. Finally, among them were Queenstown and Danielstown in Essequibo and Cumberland in Berbice.

In 1900 these villages were experiencing serious problems which made life for the residents very challenging. Perhaps their most fundamental and most disturbing problem was geophysical, namely, their inability for the most part to cope effectively with the formidable challenges of sea and river defence, drainage and irrigation. These difficulties stemmed from the fact that the coast was below sea level, the rivers often overflowed their banks and the country frequently suffered from seasons of heavy rainfall.

In these circumstances the principal annual works undertaken by most villages were the digging and clearing of drainage trenches and the construction or repair of sluices. In several villages, however, the main drainage could not be kept in order owing to a lack of funds. Furthermore, exceptionally heavy rainy seasons caused a considerable increase in expenditure for drainage, especially in large mechanically-drained villages such as Plaisance and Buxton, for the operation of such steam-driven machinery was very costly.

Ultimately the question of drainage everywhere was a matter of funds which tended to be short in all villages. Villages often had no option but to seek loans from the government to cope with the problem of drainage. In 1902, for example, the Golden Grove and Nabaclis Village Council borrowed $2000.00 to cover the cost of renewing the Nabaclis Sea Sluice. In that same year the Beterverwagting Village Council borrowed $950.00 to meet its share of the cost of replacing one of the boilers of the Triumph Draining Engine, which was the joint property of the villagers and the government.

The heavy rainfall which caused village problems also adversely affected the villages in other ways. In particular, it resulted in the erosion of village streets, thus increasing the cost of their upkeep. Many Village Councils discovered that after seeking to address the principal problem of drainage, they had no funds left to use to maintain and repair village roads. As Thomas Daly, the Inspector of Villages, reported about Plaisance in 1897,

> In consequence of the heavy expenditure for drainage because of a very heavy and long rainy season we have had, the works of making up the streets and digging trenches could not be carried out.[270]

The major financial difficulties which villages in British Guiana were encountering in the 1890s were a result of several factors. Prominent among them was the fact that the government, dominated by the White sugar plantocracy, was unwilling to use revenue in the national treasury to develop Black villages, apart from the grant of small loans repayable with interest. Furthermore, each year a significant part of village rates, by far the main source of funds available to Village Councils, was not collected, owing to the inability or unwillingness of villagers to pay them. The Inspector of Villages tended to blame the Chairmen of the Village Councils for this state of affairs, accusing them of dereliction of duty and criticising them for their reluctance to resort to legal proceedings to enforce rate payments. Occasionally, as was the case of Agricola in 1898, villages also suffered because of the misappropriation of rates by dishonest Village Overseers.

The truth, however, was that in the absence of a subvention from the government, even if all the rates were collected, the Village Councils would still have been short of funds to maintain and develop the villages properly. The uncollected rates, however, made the situation worse, preventing the Councils from being able to undertake budgeted works in relation to drainage, roads and sanitation.

The condition of the villages was obviously partly a result of the quality of their administration, especially the sense of responsibility and enterprise of the Village Chairman and the efficiency and integrity of the Village Overseer. The Overseer, a full-time salaried employee of the Village Council, played a crucial role in the collection of rates and the execution of village projects.

Determined Village Chairmen were sometimes able to ensure the collection of a high proportion of rates by putting an effective system in place and, if necessary, by exerting pressure on the villagers to pay their rates by taking legal action against them. For example, the success of the Council of Den Amstel and Fellowship in 1902-3 in securing the highest proportion (97 per cent) of collected rates was attributed to "firmness on the part of the Chairman in insisting on regular payments at stated times."[271]

Problems arose in village administration as a result of poor judgement in the choice of Village Overseers and the lack of effective supervision by the Chairman of the Overseer who sometimes used the opportunity to misappropriate village funds. The realisation of the importance of having an efficient Overseer prompted the Council of Ann's Grove and Two Friends to dismiss the Overseer in 1898 "on account of inattention to his work"[272] and to appoint a successor on probation. However, the overall view of the Inspector of Villages in relation to Village Overseers seems valid. He remarked

> I think that, as a whole the Councils have been fortunate in their selections, but I am sorry to say, there have been, exceptions, which have caused considerable loss to some of the villages.[273]

The administration of villages was sometimes adversely affected by a number of other factors, including the unwieldly size of the Council, a lack of harmony among the councillors, friction between the Chairman and other members of the Council and hostility between the Council and villagers. In 1898, for example, Mr. Hinds, the Chairman of the Plaisance Village Council, tendered his resignation in response to complaints by some councillors and other villagers, much to the regret of the Inspector of Villages, who regarded the complaints as "frivolous and vexatious".[274] However, one of his successors, W.J. Johnson, refused to resign although, according to the Inspector of Villages, "his office has not been a bed of roses," as a result of "uncalled for opposition and annoyance on the part of some of the Villagers."[275]

In 1900 many coastal and riverain villages were also facing economic problems, especially in the key area of agriculture, which was the main source of subsistence and income for many villagers. With the exception of rice, which was beginning to be grown in small quantities in some villages, most of the crops cultivated were perishable. Paramount among them were ground provisions, especially cassava, yams, tannias and sweet potatoes, but some fruits, vegetables, plantains, coffee and cocoa were also cultivated.

In a few villages there were scattered patches of sugarcane, with only Beterverwagting, with no more than 30 acres, having any significant area in canes. Cane farming on village lands was not making much progress for two main reasons. Firstly, most villagers did not see any benefit in giving up growing food crops in order to cultivate sugarcane. Secondly, village farmland was split up into lots which were too small to permit the cultivation of cane on a large and remunerative scale.

Agriculture in most coastal villages was in a precarious state. It was adversely affected by the vagaries of the weather (especially severe drought and very heavy rainfall), inadequate drainage, breaches in sea and riverain defence and the high cost of steam-driven drainage machinery. It suffered also from pests, disease, the inadequate knowledge of farmers and the small profit gained from the sale of ground provisions. Although these individually and collectively were formidable obstacles, the major problem which village farmers faced was what the Inspector of Villages rightly described in his 1903 Report as "the crushing weight of Praedial Larceny."[276]

Because of praedial larceny and other disincentives, peasant agriculture in African villages around 1900 was in a state of severe depression. Large areas of land were completely uncultivated and much of the rest was cultivated in only a perfunctory manner, some beds being tilled and others untilled. According to the Inspector of Villages in his 1899 Report, "nearly all the coffee and fruit trees in most of the villages have been allowed to die for want of attention."[277]

This apparent or relative neglect of agriculture was due partly to the fact that many adult African males left the coast for several months each year to seek their financial fortunes in gold mining in the interior. This temporary migration created labour problems in the villages, forcing some African villages to have to hire free East Indians to undertake necessary works in drainage and road maintenance.

Villages in 1900 also had problems in the area of sanitation and health. Their two most urgent needs in sanitation were an adequate pure water supply for drinking purposes and an efficient method for the disposal of faecal matter. Poor sanitation was the cause of many diseases and sicknesses found in villages, especially those conveyed by impure water such as dysentery, diarrhoea and enteric fever and those transmitted by insects, notably malaria and yellow fever.

This situation was partly a result of the attitude of the Central Board of Health which, influenced by the inadequate collection of rates in many villages, did little or no work there. Thus, although in the towns malaria was being tackled through the use of quinine, there were very few anti-malaria measures being undertaken in the villages.

Lack of funds made it difficult for villages to address the problems of sanitation adequately. Some of them, however, were making some progress. For example, in 1898 the Village Council of Bagotville applied for and secured a loan of $410.00 to perform certain sanitary works with the result that the situation was "much improved."[278] Furthermore, according to the Inspector of Villages, it "made a reservoir by which the villagers are now supplied with good drinking water."[279] Not surprisingly, the Chairman, Councillors and Overseer of the village were lauded by the Inspector for keeping the village "in good order".[280]

In short, at the end of the nineteenth century coastal and riverain villages in British Guiana were grappling with a diversity of serious problems, some geophysical and others administrative, financial, economic and medical. Owing to these problems, most of these villages were in a depressed state and their inhabitants were experiencing a disturbing deterioration in their quality of life.

For Further Reading

Ashmore, A.M.	**Memorandum on Village Administration from 1838-1902** (Georgetown, 1903).
Young, Alan	**Approaches to Local Self-Government in British Guiana** (London, 1958).
Adamson, Alan	"Monoculture and Village Decay in British Guiana, 1854-1872", **Journal of Social History**, September 1970.

Chapter 66

Milestones: Significant Dates and Developments in Guyanese History, 1498-2016

1498-99 Spanish explorers sailing along the northern coast of South America discovered the coast and rivers of Guyana, occupied then exclusively by Amerindians.

1530 A Spaniard, Pedro de Costa, driven off by Amerindians, made an unsuccessful attempt to establish a settlement in the Barima River.

1596 A major naval battle between Arawaks and Caribs in the Waini River.

1598 A visit by a Dutch expedition, including A. Cabeliau, to the rivers of Guyana, stimulated Dutch interest in the area.

1613 A tobacco plantation set up the previous year by the Dutch on the Corentyne River was destroyed by Spaniards.

1619 A Spanish expedition from the Orinoco was repulsed by the Arawaks of Essequibo.

1621 The formation in the Netherlands of the Dutch West India Company (WIC) which played an important role in Dutch colonisation of Guyana.

1624 The WIC established its first settlement in Guyana in Essequibo under Jan Van-der-Goes.

1627 The foundation of a private Dutch settlement in Berbice by the Van Pere family of Zeeland in the Netherlands.

1630 Arawaks and other Amerindians supported the Dutch in the Essequibo in an attack on San Thome, the Spanish capital in Venezuela.

MILESTONES: SIGNIFICANT DATES AND DEVELOPMENTS IN GUYANESE HISTORY, 1498-2016

1637	The first export of sugar, a small shipment from Essequibo to Zeeland.
1644	The union of the two Dutch settlements in Essequibo, with Kyk-over-al as the seat of government and the main centre of Dutch-Amerindian trade.
1650-51	The beginning of a Dutch settlement, later called Nova Zeelandia, in the Pomeroon River by Dutch migrants from Tobago and Brazil.
1659	The arrival of the first Christian clergyman, Johannes Urselius of the Dutch Reformed Church, who settled at Nova Zeelandia.
1664	The establishment of the first sugar mill in Essequibo.
1665	An English expedition, led by Major John Scott, captured and plundered the Dutch settlements in the Essequibo and Pomeroon for a year before being repulsed by a force from Berbice.
1671	An agreement between the Dutch authorities in Berbice and Essequibo delimited the boundary of the two colonies at the Abary River.
1673	A mutiny was staged by Dutch soldiers at Fort Nassau in Berbice.
1684	Fort Nassau was rebuilt, a larger brick structure replacing the earlier wooden one.
1686	Commander Abraham Beckman of Essequibo introduced legislation limiting the purchase and sale of Amerindian slaves.
1687	A major revolt was staged against the Dutch by Amerindians in Berbice, supported by African slaves.
1689	An attack by French privateers on the Dutch settlements in Berbice and Pomeroon resulted in the cessation of Dutch colonisation in the Pomeroon until the late 18th century.
1690	Samuel Beckman, one of the more able and energetic of the early Dutch administrators, was appointed Commandeur of Essequibo, retaining the position until 1707.
1708-9	Two destructive raids were conducted on the Dutch colony in Essequibo by French privateers.

1712	The Dutch colony in Berbice was ravaged by a French squadron.
1713	Berbice, unable or unwilling to pay a substantial ransom demanded, was ceded to France, but was restored to Dutch rule the following year.
1718	The seat of Dutch government in Essequibo was shifted to Cartabo, near Kyk-over-al.
1720	The government of the colony of Berbice was taken over by a new body, the Berbice Association.
1721	Laurens de Heere, the new Commandeur of Essequibo, initiated a gradual movement of Dutch settlers and plantations from the upper river to the coast.
1731	The first serious slave rebellion in Essequibo on Plantation Poelwyk on Caria Island.
1732	The promulgation of a new constitution for Berbice.
1738	The beginning of a Christian mission among Amerindians in Berbice by Moravians, forbidden by Dutch planters to evangelise Black slaves.
1739	The seat of government in Essequibo was removed from Cartabo Point to Flag (Fort) Island at the mouth of the river.
1740	The opening of Essequibo to all nationalities resulted in an influx of English planters, especially from the British Caribbean.
1741	The Dutch authorities in Essequibo made a peace treaty with a group of runaway slaves in the Cuyuni.
1742	Laurens Storm van's Gravesande, arguably the most outstanding Dutch administrator in colonial Guyana, was appointed Commandeur of Essequibo.
1744	The completion of the construction of Fort Zeelandia on Flag (Fort) Island.
1746	The beginning of the Dutch colony of Demerara.
1748	A prolonged war between the Caribs and Warraus in the Cuyuni.

Milestones: Significant Dates and Developments in Guyanese History, 1498-2016

1750   The appointment of Gravesande as Director-General of Essequibo and Demerara and his son, Jonathan, as Commander of Demerara.

1753   Borselen, an island about 32 kilometres up the Demerara River, was made the capital of Demerara.

1755-56   The occurrence in the Mazaruni of one of the worst conflicts between the Dutch and the Amerindians largely as a result of slave raiding by a Dutch planter.

1763   The outbreak in Berbice of the most formidable slave rebellion in Guyanese history.

1766   The government of Essequibo sent an envoy to the Spanish authorities in the Orinoco in an unsuccessful attempt to persuade them to extradite runaway slaves from Essequibo.

1769   The arrival in Demerara of James Chamberlain, an English Jesuit, one of the first Roman Catholic priests to serve in Guyana.

1772   The occurrence of the most serious slave rebellion in Essequibo's history.

1773   Demerara was granted its own Court of Policy and Court of Justice.

1774   A Spanish attack on the Dutch post at Moruka, causing extensive dislocation of Amerindian residents.

1775   The digging of the No. 1 Canal to link the Demerara River to the Essequibo.

1781   The British attacked and captured Demerara, Essequibo and Berbice.

1782   A French squadron captured the three colonies from the British.

1783   The French established a post office and the first regular ferry boat to cross the Demerara River.

1784   Demerara, Essequibo and Berbice were restored to the Netherlands by France.

1789   Demerara and Essequibo were joined into one entity called "The United

	Colony of Demerara-Essequibo" with a single Court of Policy.
1790	The importation of the first printing press by J.C. De la Coste of Demerara.
1791	The conclusion of a treaty between Spain and the Netherlands at Aranguez in relation to the flight of slaves from Essequibo to the Orinoco.
1792	The dissolution of the Dutch West India Company and the assumption by the States General of control over Demerara-Essequibo.
1793	The publication in Demerara of Guyana's first newspaper.
1795	The outbreak of a major rebellion by Maroon slaves on the West Coast of Demerara.
1796	British capture and occupation of Demerara-Essequibo and Berbice.
1800	The opening of a small private boarding school for boys and girls in Stabroek, the capital of Demerara-Essequibo.
1802	The return of Demerara-Essequibo and Berbice by Britain to the Netherlands in accordance with the terms of the Treaty of Amiens.
1803	Britain's capture and reoccupation of Demerara-Essequibo and Berbice.
1805	The introduction of steam engines in the sugar industry.
1807	The abolition by the British government of the slave trade from Africa.
1808	The beginning of the Christianisation of the slaves with the arrival in Demerara of Rev. John Wray.
1810	The opening of St George's Chapel, Stabroek's first church building.
1812	Stabroek was renamed Georgetown.
1813	The first of a number of destructive fires in Georgetown.
1814	Demerara-Essequibo and Berbice were ceded to Britain by the Netherlands.

Milestones: Significant Dates and Developments in Guyanese History, 1498-2016

1815   The arrival in Demerara of Josiah Booker whose brothers joined him in 1833 in establishing the influential firm, Booker Bros. & Co.

1816   The beginning of the political career of Peter Rose, the most influential local politician in the following four decades.

1817   Ordinances were passed for the annual registration of slaves in Demerara-Essequibo and Berbice.

1818   The opening for public worship of St Andrew's Kirk, one of Georgetown's oldest churches.

1823   The outbreak of a massive but unsuccessful slave rebellion on the East Coast of Demerara.

1826   The beginning of the implementation in Berbice and Demerara-Essequibo of the British government's policy of slave amelioration.

1828   The operation of the first steamer on the Demerara River and the establishment of the first bank, a savings bank for slaves in Demerara-Essequibo.

1829   The opening in Georgetown of the Durban Park race course, named after the governor, Sir Benjamin D'Urban.

1831   The unification of the colonies of Berbice and Demerara-Essequibo into a new entity, British Guiana.

1832   The introduction into the local sugar industry of the vacuum pan, resulting in the production of a greater quantity and better quality of sugar.

1833   The passage in the British Parliament of the Abolition Act outlawing slavery in British Guiana and the rest of the British Empire with effect from 1st August 1834.

1834   In August slaves, now called apprentices, on the Essequibo Coast led by Damon staged a protest on learning that they were required to serve their masters for four or six more years before they would become free.

1835   The arrival in British Guiana of a batch of forty (40) Portuguese immigrants from Madeira, the first of about 30,000 Portuguese to come between 1835 and 1880.

1837　The establishment of a Mayor and Town Council for Georgetown.

1838　The arrival in British Guiana of the first batch of 396 East Indian immigrants from India, eleven weeks before the former African slaves became completely free legally on August 1, 1838 with the termination of apprenticeship.

1839　Eighty-three (83) former apprentices purchased Plantation Northbrook, later renamed Victoria, on the East Coast of Demerara, the first free village.

1841　The beginning of Liberated African immigration to British Guiana, mostly from Sierra Leone, and continuing until at least 1852.

1842　The occurrence of the first general strike in Guyanese history in Demerara and Essequibo, ending in victory for the workers.

1843　The establishment of the Georgetown Hand in Hand Fire Insurance Company resulted in fire insurance becoming the first kind of insurance offered to Guyanese.

1844　The foundation of Queen's College and the Royal Agricultural and Commercial Society.

1845　The resumption of East Indian immigration from India after a temporary suspension.

1847　The arrival of the first batch of Ursuline nuns and the opening of St Rose's High School for girls.

1848　The opening of the Demerara Railway for traffic from Georgetown to Plaisance.

1850　The establishment of the first Council of Education.

1852　The occurrence of a serious yellow fever epidemic.

1853　The arrival of the first batch of Chinese indentured immigrants from China.

1854　Guyanese and other British Caribbean sugar producers lost their preferential tariff in the British market.

1856 A violent protest by Blacks against the Portuguese known as the "The Angel Gabriel Riot".

1858 The foundation of the Georgetown Cricket Club, the oldest surviving cricket club in the Caribbean.

1865 British Guiana and Barbados contested the initial first-class cricket matches in the Caribbean, the first in Barbados with a return game in Georgetown.

1866 The foundation of the Catholic Grammar school, later renamed St Stanislaus College.

1868 The opening of the first official museum, sited in Company Path in Georgetown.

1869 The occurrence at Plantation Leonora of the first major uprising of East Indian indentured workers.

1870 The appointment of a Royal Commission to inquire into the conditions faced by East Indian immigrants.

1871 The opening of telegraph communication.

1872 The uprising by East Indian indentured immigrants at Devonshire Castle on the Essequibo Coast.

1873 The beginning of the illumination of the streets of Georgetown with gas lights.

1876 The introduction of legislation to enforce compulsory elementary education.
Queen's College became a government institution.

1881 The opening of Stabroek market in Georgetown.

1882 British Guiana's captain, Edward Wright, became the first batsman to score a century in first-class cricket in the Caribbean.

1883 The formation of the Constitutional Reform Association that led a movement for the reform of the colony's constitution, which gave Whites a virtual monopoly of political power.

1885   The beginning of the systematic mining and export of gold.

1887   The opening of the Victoria Law Court in Georgetown.

1889   The opening of the Town Hall in Georgetown.

1890   The discovery of diamonds in the Mazaruni District.

1891   The colony's constitution was modified, undermining the political dominance of the white planter class.

1893   The opening of St George's Cathedral.

1895   British Guiana won the inter-territorial regional cricket tournament, introduced in 1891, for the first time.

1896   The introduction of secret ballot at elections for the legislature.

1897   The opening of the Demerara-Essequibo railway from Vreed-en-Hoop to Tuschen.

1899   The Paris International Tribunal settled the boundary between British Guiana and Venezuela.

1900   The extension of the Georgetown Railway to Rosignol.

1903   The beginning of the export of rice.

1905   The occurrence of a major working-class protest in Demerara initiated by the waterfront workers in Georgetown.

1909   The opening to the public of the Georgetown Public Library.

1913   The beginning of air transport with the first aeroplanes flying in the country.

1914   The beginning of the Infant Welfare and Maternity League, inaugurated as the "Baby Saving League".

Milestones: Significant Dates and Developments in Guyanese History, 1498-2016

1916   The formation of the British Guiana East Indian Association and the beginning of significant East Indian participation in formal national politics.

1917   The end of East Indian indentured immigration from India and the beginning of bauxite production in British Guiana.

1918   The occurrence of a major influenza epidemic, resulting in thousands of deaths.

1919   The formation of the British Guiana Labour Union, the country's first trade union, founded by Hubert Nathaniel Critchlow.

1920   The establishment of the Chinese Association of British Guiana.

1922   The beginning of a permanent Girl Guides Movement with the establishment of two companies in New Amsterdam.

1924   The occurrence of a major disturbance, in which black waterfront workers in Georgetown received support from East Indian sugar workers on the East Bank of Demerara.

1926   The holding in Georgetown of the first British Guiana and West Indian Labour Conference.

1928   A major constitutional change resulting in the introduction of Crown Colony government.

1929   The introduction of Income Tax.

1930   The inauguration of May Day Celebrations by the British Guiana Labour Union.

1931   The formation of the country's second trade union, the British Guiana Workers' League, founded by Alfred Thorne.

1935   The opening of the first local privately-owned commercial radio station.

1936   The formation of the Man Power Citizens' Association, the country's third trade union, by Ayube Edun and C.R. Jacob.

1939   The occurrence of a strike by workers at Plantation Leonora, culminating in a fatal clash between the strikers and the police.

1941   The registration of the British Guiana Trades Union Council.

1942   Bishop's High School, founded in 1870, became a Government institution.

1946   The formation of the Women's Political and Economic Organisation, the first women's political group, and the Political Affairs Committee.

1947   General Elections which resulted in the initial entry into the legislature of Cheddi Jagan, Guyana's longest serving parliamentarian.

1948   A clash between striking sugar estate workers at Enmore and the police resulted in the death of five workers, remembered as "The Enmore Martyrs".

1949   The formation of the first Credit Union, the British Guiana Teachers' Association Women's Auxiliary Co-operative Credit Union Ltd.

1950   The formation of the People's Progressive Party (P.P.P.), the first mass-based political organisation in Guyanese history.

1952   The opening to the public of the present zoo in the Botanical Gardens.

1953   After a decisive electoral victory, the P.P.P. is removed from office by the British government after 133 days in power and an interim government is installed.

1955   A split occurred in the P.P.P., which became divided into two factions, one led by Cheddi Jagan and the other by Forbes Burnham.

1957   After an election which resulted in a victory for the Jaganite faction of the P.P.P. and in Stephen Campbell, a candidate of the National Labour Front, becoming the first Amerindian legislator in Guyanese history, the Burnhamite faction of the P.P.P. changed its name to the People's National Congress (P.N.C.).

1959   British Guiana won the third West Indies Athletics Championship held at the Georgetown Cricket Club ground.

1960   The formation of a third major political party, the United Force (U.F.),

Milestones: Significant Dates and Developments in Guyanese History, 1498-2016

led by Peter D'Aguiar.

1961   The introduction of a new constitution granting internal self-government was followed by the last elections held under the First Past The Post System, resulting in victory by the P.P.P. and Cheddi Jagan becoming the country's first premier.

1962   The introduction in the House of Assembly of the "Kaldor Budget", which met with stiff opposition.

1963   The establishment of the University of Guyana with an initial batch of 164 students utilising the facilities of Queen's College until the Turkeyen Campus was opened in 1969.

1964   In the wake of the first general election under the system of Proportional Representation, a P.N.C. - U.F. coalition came to power, with Forbes Burnham as Prime Minister.

1965   The establishment of the Bank of Guyana.

1966   After 163 years of uninterrupted British rule dating back to 1803, British Guiana became politically independent on May 26 under the new name, Guyana, with Forbes Burnham its first Prime Minister.
Guyana was admitted to the United Nations and became a member of the World Bank.
Venezuela seized Guyana's half of the island of Ankoko in the Cuyuni River.

1967   The Critchlow Labour College, the educational arm of the trade union movement, was established.
Suriname hydropower workers were evicted by the police from Guyana's New River Triangle.

1968   The People's National Congress (P.N.C.) became the ruling party, when it secured an overall majority in the questionable December general election.
The Soesdyke-Linden highway was completed.
President Raul Leoni declared Venezuelan sovereignty over a nine-mile strip off the Essequibo coast.

1969   A rebellion against the central government by some prominent cattle ranchers in the Rupununi was staged in an unsuccessful attempt at

secession from Guyana.
A National Insurance Scheme (NIS) was introduced by the government.
The Guyana Defence Force (GDF) retook a camp – now Camp Jaguar – from Suriname which had established it in Guyana's New River Triangle.

1970 Guyana became a republic in February, severing all remaining official links with the British monarchy. Arthur Chung became president.
Linden, Corriverton and Rose Hall were established as towns.
The government introduced local national awards – the Medal of Service, the Arrow of Achievement, the Cacique Crown of Honour, the Order of Roraima and the Order of Excellence – replacing British honours.

1971 The Canadian-owned Demerara Bauxite Company (DEMBA) was nationalised.

1972 Guyana hosted the first Caribbean Festival of Creative Arts (CARIFESTA) and a meeting of the Non-Aligned Foreign Ministers.

1973 Guyana became one of the original four members of the newly formed Caribbean Community (CARICOM), together with Barbados, Jamaica and Trinidad and Tobago, a successor to the Caribbean Free Trade Association (CARIFTA), established in 1968.
The P.N.C. emerged victorious at controversial national elections.

1974 The refusal to appoint eminent Guyanese historian Dr. Walter Rodney to a teaching position at the University of Guyana evoked protests within the institution and in the wider society, events associated with the formation of the Working People's Alliance (W.P.A.), initially a pressure group which became a political party formally in 1979.
Guyana's batting star Rohan Kanhai, and Englishman John Jameson set a world record of 465 runs for the highest second-wicket partnership in first-class cricket, playing for Warwickshire against Gloucestershire in the English county championship.
Commercial railways in Guyana came to an end with the closure of both the Vreed-en-Hoop – Parika and the Georgetown-Rosignol railways.

1975 The E.R. Burrowes School of Art was established.
There were State visits to Guyana by General Yakubu Gowon, Nigeria's head of state, Sir Seretse Khama, President of Botswana, and President Luis Echeverria of Mexico, the first visit by a Latin American head of state.
The West Indies cricket team, led by Guyanese Clive Lloyd and containing four other Guyanese – Roy Fredericks, Lance Gibbs, Alvin

Kallicharran and Rohan Kanhai – won the first limited-over World Cup tournament in England.
The government introduced a policy of co-education at Queen's College and Bishop's High School.

1976   The holdings of the sugar magnate, Bookers, were nationalised, and the Guyana Agricultural Workers Union (GAWU) was recognised, instead of the Man Power Citizens' Association (MPCA), as the bargaining agent for sugar workers after thirty years of struggle.
The National Cultural Centre in Georgetown was opened.
The government extended its authority over church and private primary and secondary schools and introduced a policy of free education from nursery to university.

1977   Guyana established diplomatic relations with China and Cuba and severed relations with Israel.

1978   Guyana attracted considerable unwelcome international attention as a result of the famous tragedy at Jonestown in the North West District where 914 members, mostly Americans, of a religious cult, The People's Temple, including the leader, Jim Jones, died of murder/suicide.
The Canje River Bridge and the Demerara Harbour Bridge were opened to vehicular traffic.
A national referendum was held on the Constitutional Amendment Bill, with the political opposition boycotting the poll.

1979   The Caribbean Examinations Council (CXC) offered its first Caribbean Secondary Examination Certificate (CSEC) examinations to its member countries, including Guyana.
Radio Demerara and the Guyana Broadcasting Service (GBS) were merged to form a new entity, the Guyana Broadcasting Corporation (GBC).
A number of W.P.A. leaders were charged with arson of the Ministry of National Development. In a demonstration outside the court Father Darke, a photographer for the **Catholic Standard**, was stabbed by a member of the House of Israel and later died.

1980   Michael Parris, a featherweight boxer, became the first and so far the only Guyanese to win a medal at the Olympic Games, when he secured a bronze medal in Moscow.
Dr. Walter Rodney, historian and political activist, co-leader of the Working People's Alliance (W.P.A.), was assassinated.

1981 The inaugural ceremony of Guyana's first executive President, Forbes Burnham, was held, in keeping with the provisions of a new constitution of 1980 and following the P.N.C. victory in the General Elections of December 15, 1980, which were not deemed free and fair.

1982 The ruling P.N.C. government banned wheaten flour and prohibited the importation of wheat and some other basic food items. These items were reintroduced in 1985-86 by President Hugh Desmond Hoyte.
The Guyana Gold Board was established.
The Protocol of Port-of Spain of 1970 which placed a moratorium on territorial claims in the boundary controversy between Guyana and Venezuela expired, and Venezuela refused to renew it.

1983 The West Demerara Hospital Complex at Vreed-en-Hoop was opened. Guyana achieved a unique double, winning the 4-day Shell Shield and the limited-over Geddes-Grant/ Harrison Line tournaments, the two major cricket competitions held annually in the Caribbean.

1984 Guyanese Clive Lloyd was publicly honoured by the West Indies Cricket Board during the fifth Test against the visiting Australians in Jamaica for becoming the first West Indian cricketer to play 100 Test matches.

1985 Forbes Burnham died and was succeeded as President by Hugh Desmond Hoyte.

1986 The **Stabroek News** newspaper began publication.
After the fraudulent 1985 national elections five political parties formed the Patriotic Coalition for Democracy (PCD) to agitate for electoral reform and to seek international pressure on the P.N.C. to hold free, fair elections.

1987 The Guyana Prize for Literature was introduced with an initial Awards Ceremony. The Prize was to provide encouragement for the development of good creative writing by Guyanese.

1988 The Economic Recovery Programme (ERP) was launched by the government.

1989 Arthur James Seymour, poet and man of letters and one of the most distinguished personalities in Guyanese culture, died.

Milestones: Significant Dates and Developments in Guyanese History, 1498-2016

1990   Cambios began to operate under the Dealer in Foreign Currency (Licensing) Bill of November 1989.

1991   The former Minister of Foreign Affairs, Rasleigh Jackson, was awarded the Order of Roraima for his distinguished service in the field of foreign affairs.

1992   After 28 years in power, the P.N.C. was voted out of office in the first essentially fair national elections since 1964 and the People's Progressive Party (P.P.P.) led by Cheddi Jagan came to power.

1993   The National Art Gallery was established at Castellani House in Georgetown.
David Granger's **Guyana Review,** a monthly news magazine, was launched.
In November the country suffered its worst floods since the Great Flood of 1933.

1994   The Test career of Guyana's newest cricket star, Shivnarine Chanderpaul, began. His 62 against England at Bourda was the highest score ever made by a West Indian teenager on his Test debut.

1995   The alarming spilling of cyanide waste from Omai Gold Mines Ltd. into the Essequibo River caused a major environmental disaster.

1996   Shivnarine Chanderpaul became the first and so far the only Guyanese to score a triple century in first-class cricket, 303 not out for Guyana against Jamaica at Sabina Park.
The initial publication of the **Kaieteur News** newspaper appeared.

1997   Guyana's national poet, Martin Carter, died.
Guyanese Lance Gibbs, Rohan Kanhai and Clive Lloyd were among 13 West Indians included in the International Cricket Council's (ICC) Hall of Fame set up to honour past legends of the game as part of the ICC's Centenary Year Celebrations.
After four years and five months in office Cheddi Jagan died. He was succeeded as President by Samuel Hinds briefly, then by his wife, Janet Jagan, Guyana's first female head of state.

1998   The year began with serious political unrest in the wake of the General Elections of December 1997, prompting the intervention of Caricom in an attempt to reconcile the two main political parties through the

Herdmanston Accord.
The Guyana-Suriname Ferry Service began operations.
The Caribbean Examinations Council introduced the Caribbean Advanced Proficiency Examination (CAPE) to replace the British General Certificate Education (GCE) 'A' Level Examination in its member countries, including Guyana.

1999　Following the resignation on medical grounds of President Janet Jagan, she was replaced by the then young Minister of Finance, Bharrat Jagdeo.

2000　The University of Guyana opened its second campus at Tain, Port Mourant in Berbice, 31 years after the opening of its first campus at Turkeyen on the East Coast of Demerara in 1969.
Suriname gunboats evicted Guyana's CGX oil rig from waters off the Corentyne.

2001　Justice Desiree Bernard became the first female Chancellor of the Judiciary not only in Guyana and the Caribbean but also in the entire Commonwealth.
Andrew 'Sixhead' Lewis became the first Guyanese to win a world championship in professional boxing, the World Boxing Association (WBA) welterweight title.

2002　Carl Hooper became the first Guyanese to score a double century in Test cricket on home soil. His career-best 233 against India at Bourda is still the highest score by a Guyanese in a Test in Guyana.
The Mash Day Jailbreak, when five prisoners escaped from the Camp Street Prison in Georgetown, led to an unprecedented spate of crimes in the country.

2003　The University of Guyana had special virtually year-long celebrations for the 40th anniversary of its foundation in 1963.

2004　The Georgetown Broadcasting Corporation and the Guyana Television Broadcasting Company merged to form the National Communication Network (NCN).

2005　Serious flooding was experienced in Georgetown and other areas of the coastland.
A new political party, the Alliance For Change (AFC), was launched. It was headed by sitting parliamentarians Raphael Trotman and Khemraj Ramjattan from the P.N.C. /R and the P.P.P. /C respectively.

Milestones: Significant Dates and Developments in Guyanese History, 1498-2016

2006   The P.P.P. /C won General Elections for the fourth consecutive time, following victories in 1992, 1997 and 2001.
The Caribbean Single Market and Economy (CSME) was launched with Guyana and five other states taking part.
Two new technical institutes, the Upper Corentyne Technical Institute and the Essequibo Technical Institute, were opened.

2007   The Cricket Stadium at Providence on the East Bank of Demerara was opened, replacing the famous Bourda ground as the venue for international cricket, beginning with this year's World Cup matches.
The United Nations Arbitral Tribunal on the Convention on the Law of the Sea found the CGX rig had been operating in Guyana waters when it was evicted by Suriname in 2000. The Tribunal fixed the maritime boundary between Guyana and Suriname.

2008   Heavily-armed bandits invaded the East Coast Demerara village of Lusignan killing 11 persons, including five children. Weeks later, similarly armed bandits attacked the mining community of Bartica killing 12, including three police officers.
Guyana's best cricketer, Shivnarine Chanderpaul, became the first Guyanese or West Indian to be named the International Cricket Council's Cricketer of the Year.
Guyana hosted Carifesta X after the government of the original hosts, Bahamas, opted out of its commitment to host the region's premier arts festival.

2009   Berbician middle-order batsman Narsingh Deonarine became the first batsman to score over 1000 runs (1068) in a Caribbean regional first-class cricket season, breaking the record of 974 runs made by the former Leeward Islands batsman Stuart Williams in 2002.

2010   There were two notable achievements in sports. Firstly, Guyana won the inaugural West Indies Cricket Board T20 tournament, thus qualifying to participate in the Champions League tournament in South Africa. Secondly, Aliann Pompey won a silver medal in the women's 400 metres at the Commonwealth Games in India, complementing the gold medal she had won in the same event at the Games in 2002, thus becoming the first Guyanese representative to win two medals at these Games.

2011   There was significant expansion of sport infrastructure with the completion of an Olympic-size swimming pool at Liliendaal on the

East Coast of Demerara, the construction of an all-weather tarmac at the Guyana National Stadium at Providence on the East Bank of Demerara, the resurfacing of the National Park Cycling Track in Georgetown and the commencement of the all-weather synthetic track at Leonora on the West Coast of Demerara.

In the November General and Regional Elections the P.P.P. /C was returned to office for a fifth consecutive term with Donald Ramotar replacing Bharrat Jagdeo as president. The opposition, A Partnership for National Unity (APNU) and the Alliance for Change (AFC), collectively gained a majority of seats in the National Assembly, an unprecedented development in the post-independence history of Guyana.

2012   The joint opposition, A Partnership for National Unity (APNU) and the Alliance for Change (AFC), used its one-seat majority in the National Assembly to reduce the P.P.P. /C's initial budget of $192.8 billion by $20.8 billion. These "cuts" to the budget were the first of their kind and were challenged legally by the P.P.P. /C administration.

2013   Several personalities who had made a substantial contribution to Guyana died. These included Harold Davis, a former Chairman of the Guyana Sugar Corporation (GUYSUCO) and former Pro-Chancellor of the University of Guyana, Harry Sarran Ramsaroop, the director of the Dharm Shala; Aubrey Bishop, former Chancellor of the Judiciary and head of the Faculty of Law of the University of Guyana; Dale Bisnauth, a Guyana Presbyterian minister and former Minister of Education; and Pandit Reepu Daman Persaud, the founder of the Guyana Hindu Dharmic Sabha, the main visionary behind the annual Deepavali motorcade and longstanding P.P.P. member of Parliament.
Venezuela evicted the oil exploration vessel, **The Teknik Perdana**, from Guyana waters.

2014   In May a Commission of Inquiry into the death of Walter Rodney opened. In November Parliament was prorogued by President Ramotar in order to avoid a no-confidence vote by the opposition which was expected to bring down the government and trigger fresh general elections.

2015   The APNU + AFC coalition won the May national general elections, bringing an end to P.P.P. /C rule since 1992 and ushering into office David Arthur Granger, the coalition's leader, as president.
Exxon Mobil drilled a well offshore Demerara and in 2016 announced a major oil find.
Venezuela issued a decree claiming sovereignty over Guyana's territorial

waters off Essequibo.

2016　The long-awaited local government elections, not conducted since 1994, were finally held.
Bartica, Mabaruma and Lethem were officially named towns.

For Further Reading

Balkaran, Lal　**Timelines of Guyanese History, 1498-2006** (Scarborough: LBA Publications, 2007).

Notes

These notes for the most part provide references to quotations in the text. Some of them, however, provide cross references to other relevant chapters in the book.

1. See Chapter 62 below.
2. Pinckard, George **Letters From Guiana.** Extracted from **Notes on The West Indies…And The Coast Of Guiana** (Georgetown: The "Daily Chronicle" Ltd., 1942), 236-37.
3. Pierronet, Thomas "Remarks Made during a residence at Stabroek Rio Demerary (Lat. 6.10N) in the latter part of the year 1798" in **Collections of the Massachusetts Historical Society for the year 1799**, 1st series, Vol.vi, Boston, 1800, 13-14.
4. Pinckard, 84.
5. **Ibid.**, 202.
6. See Chapter 62 below.
7. See below, especially Chapter 22.
8. For a more detailed examination of the gold mining and rice cultivation industries after 1884, see Chapters 23 and 24 below.
9. On fishing, see Chapters 25 and 26 below.
10. On labour problems and the birth of trade unionism in British Guiana, see Chapter 53 below.
11. **British Guiana, Report of the Inspector of Villages for the Year 1898-99** (Georgetown,1899).
12. **Abstract of the Census of the Population of the Colony of British Guiana, As taken on the 31st of March, 1851** (Georgetown, 1851).
13. **Ibid.**

14. British Library, London, U.K., Egerton Papers 1720, Douglas to Bentinck, 12 July 1763, Clarke to Bentinck, 16 July 1762, encl. Memorandum Concerning Rio Demerary – by Gedney Clarke, 17 July 1762.

15. Cited in Harris, C.A. and de Villiers, J.A.J., **Storm Van's Gravesande. The Rise of British Guiana** (London: Hakluyt Society, 1911), 594 – 95.

16. For the causes and consequences of this economic crisis in Suriname, see Chapter 27 below.

17. On British capture and occupation, see Chapter 62 below.

18. For the reasons for this growth, see Chapter 27 below.

19. On the Prohibitory Order of 1805 and the British Abolition of the Atlantic slave trade and their consequences, see Chapter 17 below.

20. For more information on African immigrants into British Guiana in the nineteenth century, see Chapter 4 above.

21. Dalzel, Archibald **The History of Dahomy. An Inland Kingdom of Africa** (London, 1793), 61.

22. Edwards, P. (ed.) **Equiano's Travels: The Interesting Narrative of the Life of Olaudah Equiano or Gustavus Vassa the African** (London, 1967),9.

23. **Ibid.**, 8-9.

24. Dalzel,61.

25. 'Journal of Captain Phillips', published in Churchill, A. and I, **Collection of Voyages and Travels**, 3rd edn. (London, 1744-6), Vol.6,235.

26. Atkins, John **A Voyage to Guinea, Brasil and the West Indies** (London,1735),72.

27. 'Journal of Adam Starr: Seaman:20th August to 6th September, 1781, in Plimmer, Charlotte and Denis, **The Damn'd Master** (London, 1971), entry for 21 August 1781.

28. Phillips, 235.

29. Slatees were African slave merchants who supplied the visiting European traders with captives.

30. Park, Mungo **Travels in the Interior Districts of Africa performed under the Direction and Patronage of the African Association in the Years 1795, 1796 and 1797** (London: Everyman's Library, 1969), 244-45.

31. Moore, Francis **Travels into the Inland Parts of Africa** (London,1738), cited in Curtin, Philip (ed.), **Africa Remembered; Narratives by West Africans from the Era of the Slave Trade** (Madison: The University of Wisconsin Press), 57.

32. Martin, Bernard and Spurrell, Mark, eds., **The Journal of a Slave Trader** (London: Epworth Press, 1962), 103.

33. Atkins,175.

34. Newport Historical Society, Rhode Island, U.S.A., Peleg Clarke Letter Book, John Fletcher to Peleg Clarke, October 19, 1775.

35. Snelgrave, William **A New Account of Some Parts of Guinea and the Slave Trade** (London: James, John and Paul Knapton, 1734), 173.

36. Cited in Benezet, Anthony **Notes on the Slave Trade** (Philadelphia: Joseph Crukshank, 1781), 4.

37. Falconbridge, Alexander **An Account of the Slave Trade on the Coast of Africa** (London: J.Phillips,1788), 30.

38. **Ibid.**

39. **Report of the Lords of Trade of the Committee of Council Appointed for the Consideration of All Matters Relating to Trade and Foreign Plantations…Concerning the Present State of the Trade to Africa and Particularly the Trade in Slaves** (London,1789).

40. Evidence of James Towne, February 8, 1791 in **Minutes of the Evidence Taken Before a Committee of the House of Commons Being a Select Committee, Appointed on the 23rd day of April 1790, to take the Examination of the Several Witnesses Ordered by the House Respecting the African Slave Trade** (London,1791).

41. 'Journal of Adam Starr', **op.cit.**, entry for 21 August, 1781.

42. Evidence of Thomas King, June 19, 1789 in **Abridgement of the Minutes of the Evidence, Taken Before a Committee of the House of Commons, Being a Committee of the Whole House, to whom it was referred to consider of the Circumstances of the Slave Trade…1789** (Chicago: Afro Am. Press 1969).

43. Labat, Jean **Voyage du Chevalier des Marchais en Guinée, Iles Voisines, et à Cayenne Fait en 1725, 1726 & 1727** (Paris: Guillaume Saugrain, 1730), II, 144-45.

44. Moore, in Curtin, 57.

45. Snelgrave, 162-64.

46. JOURNAL of W.J. Van HOOGENHEIM kept since the revolution of the Negro Slaves in Rio Berbice, begun the 28th of February, 1763. Transcribed and translated by Barbara L.Blair- entry for March 6, 1763.

47. **Ibid.**, entry for February 28, 1763.

NOTES

48. **Ibid.**, entry for March 6, 1763.
49. Rev. John Smith to Burder, 21 August 1823, printed in London Missionary Society, **Report of the Proceedings against the late Rev.J.Smith of Demerara** (London, 1824), 183-84.
50. **Ibid.**
51. **Report of the Trials of the Insurgent Negroes before A General Court Martial, held at Georgetown, Demerara, on the 25th August 1823, and continued by adjournment, until the 11th of October following** (Georgetown, 1824), 175.
52. WRA, ABI/28, Minutes of the Court of Policy of the Colony and Dependent Districts of Demerary and Essequebo, 5 May 1823.
53. C.O. 111/39, Murray to Bathurst, 24 August, 1823.
54. **Ibid.**
55. L.M.S. Archives, Smith's Journal, March 1819.
56. **Ibid.**, July 1823.
57. The Bible, Exodus, Chapter 20, Verse 8.
58. C.O. 111/39, Murray to Bathhurst, 14 February, 1824.
59. L.M.S. Archives, B.G. Demerara/Box 1/ Folder 1/ Jacket C, Wray to L.M.S. Directors, 14 February,1809.
60. Quammina to L.M.S. Directors, 8 February, 1809, enclosed in **Ibid.**
61. L.M.S. Archives, Smith's Journal, entry for 22nd October, 1822.
62. Cited in Wallbridge, Edwin **The Demerara Martyr: Memoirs of the Rev. John Smith, Missionary to Demerara** (London: Charles Gilpin, 1848), 90.
63. **Ibid.**, 146.
64. **Ibid.**, 107.
65. **Ibid.**, 105.
66. **Ibid.**, 119.
67. L.M.S. Archives, Cheveley's Journal, 20.
68. Wallbridge, 120.
69. **Ibid.**, 131-32.
70. **Ibid.**, 156.
71. WRA, Minutes of the Court of Policy, Demerara-Essequibo, 17th September, 1823.

72. **Ibid.**
73. WRA, Proclamation by Governor Murray, 22 April 1824, encl. Bathurst to Murray, 18 March 1824.
74. **Ibid.**
75. See Chapter 5 above.
76. Williams, Eric **History of the People of Trinidad and Tobag**o (Port-of-Spain, P.N.M. Publishing Houise, 1962), 95.
77. Cited in Thompson, **Colonialism**, 32, 253.
78. C.O. 111/103, Managers of Wolfert Katz's Estates to Lieutenant Governor Henry Beard, 14 February, 1826, reproduced in Thompson, Alvin. **A Documentary History of Slavery in Berbice, 1796-1834** (Georgetown: Free Press 2002), 203.
79. Cited in Thompson, **Ibid.**, 78.
80. WRA, Charles Edmonstone to Lieutenant-Governor Bentinck, encl. in Minutes of the Court of Policy of Demerara and Essequibo, 18 January1810, cited in Thompson, **Ibid.**, 132-33.
81. See Colvin's correspondence as U.S. Consul in the U.S. National Archives in Washington, D.C.
82. See Chapter 22 above.
83. Cited in **British Guiana Adminstrative Report 1905**.
84. **British Guiana Administrative Report 1922.**
85. See Chapter 22 above.
86. Van Berkel, Adriann **Travels in South America between the Berbice and Essequibo Rivers and in Surinam 1670-1689** translated and edited by Walter Edmond Roth (Georgetown: Daily Chronicle Ltd., 1948), 69.
87. Cited in Thompson, **Colonialism**, 230-231.
88. WRA, AF 3/3C, **British Guiana Blue Book, 1838.**
89. WRA, AF 3/21, **British Guiana Blue Book, 1868**.
90. WRA, AF 3/5C and 8B, **British Guiana Blue Book, 1854 and 1860.**
91. See WRA, **British Guiana Blue Books** for the late 1880s and early1890s.
92. Rodway, James and Stark, James **Guide-Book and History of British Guiana** (London: Sampson Low, Marston & Company, 1893).
93. WRA, AF 3/40, **British Guiana Blue Book, 1894-1895**.
94. WRA, AF 3/48, **British Guiana Blue Book, 1902-1903**.

95. WRA, AF3/49, **British Guiana Blue Book, 1903-1904**.
96. WRA, AF3/55 to 65, **British Guiana Blue Books, 1910-1911 to 1919**.
97. Cited in **British Guiana Administrative Report 1927**.
98. WRA, AF3/74, **British Guiana Blue Book, 1928**.
99. **Report of the Director of Agriculture, 1951**.
100. For the beginning and early growth of sugar cane cultivation, see Chapter 21 above.
101. See Chapter 17 above.
102. For a more detailed examination of this crisis, see Chapter 22 above.
103. For a more extensive treatment of the beginning of the gold mining industry, see Chapter 24 above.
104. For more informative treatment of the expansion of rice cultivation, see Chapter 23 above.
105. L.M.S. Archives, B.G. Demerara /Box1/Folder1/Jacket A/, Post to Forbes, 5 April 1807.
106. **Ibid.**
107. **Ibid.**
108. L.M.S. Archives, B.G. Demerara /Box1/Folder1/Jacket A/, Report relating to a Mission to Demerara, etc. Read 14 September 1807.
109. **Ibid.**
110. L.M.S. Archives, B.G. – Demerara /Box1/Folder1/Jacket A/, Extract of a Letter from Hy van Cooten to J. Forbes, 31 August 1807.
111. L.M.S. Archives, West Indies/British Guiana, Extracts from the Journal of Rev. John Wray, at Demerara, 1807-1809, entry for 13 February, 1808.
112. **Ibid.**
113. L.M.S. Archives, B.G. Demerara /Box1/Folder1/Jacket A/, Report relating to a Mission to Demerara, etc. Read 14 September 1807.
114. C.O. 111/13, Burder to Liverpool, 29 January 1812, encl. Extract from Instructions given by the Missionary Society to their Missionaries in the West Indies. A true copy of the Instructions given to the Rev. Mr. Wray, Nov. 23, 1807, and to several other missionaries since.
115. Cited in Wallbridge, 34.
116. C.O. 111/13, Extract of a letter from Demerary, 26 December 1811.
117. Cited in "Demerara", **The Evangelical Magazine,** Vol.xx (London,

1812),401.

118. L.M.S. Archives, B.G. Demerara /Box1/Folder1/Jacket C/, Wray to Directors L.M.S., 6 March 1809.

119. Wray to Burder, no date [1810], printed in "Demerara", **The Evangelical Magazine**, Vol. xviii (London, 1810), 369.

120. L.M.S. Archives, B.G. Demerara /Box1/Folder 3/Jacket C/, Wray to Bogue, 16 December 1812.

121. C.O. 111/11, Case of the Reverend Mr. Wray of Demerara, no date [1811].

122. See Chapter 28 above.

123. C.O. 111/8, Bentinck to Castlereagh, 4 November 1808 and enclosures.

124. For a copy of the new proclamation, see Lovett, Volume II, 323-24.

125. L.M.S. Archives, B.G.-Demerara /Box1/Folder3/Jacket B/, Davies to Directors L.M.S., 13 October 1812 enclosed, Instructions for the Burgher-Captains from H.L. Carmichael.

126. See Chapter 28 above.

127. Cited in Cruickshank, J.Graham **Notes on the History of St. Andrew's Kirk** (Georgetown, 1930),3.

128. Cited in Lord, Wellesley **A History of St Andrew's Kirk, 1818-1968** (Georgetown:The Daily Chronicle, 1968), 6.

129. **Ibid.**,7.

130. **Ibid.**,8.

131. **Ibid.**,9.

132. Cited in Hobbs, Doreen **Jewels of the Caribbean. The History of the Salvation Army in the Caribbean Territory** (St. Albans, U.K.: The Campfield Press,1986),42.

133. **The Salvation Army 1895-1995 A Century of Service. The Guyana Division Centenary Congress June 21-26, 1995.** (Georgetown,1995), back cover.

134. **Ibid.**,29.

135. Interview with Major Mc Kenzie, May 1995.

136. See **The Constitution and By-Laws of the Full Gospel Fellowship in Guyana.** Revised, Approved and Promulgated at Biennial Business Conference, 1st July 2006.

137. Mohabir, Philip **Hands of Jesus** (Thyparken II, Denmark: Powerhouse Publishing,2003), the front inside cover.

NOTES

138. Mohabir, Philip **Building Bridges** (London: Hodder and Stoughton, 1988),150.

139. Cited in McGowan, Winston, "Evangelical Youth Camps in Guyana", **Arise,** July-September 1978,22.

140. L.M.S. Archives B.G. – Demerara /Box 2/Folder2/Jacket A/, Smith to Burder, 4,21 March 1817.

141. "Annual report of the Commissioner of Education of British Guiana, 1925", partly printed in Gordon, Shirley **Reports and repercussions in West Indian education 1835-1933** (London:Ginn and Co Ltd.,1968), 152.

142. H.A. Matthews, Education District Officer to the Inspector of Schools, 1 July 1902.

143. **Argosy,** August 1881.

144. Swettenham to Stipendiary Magistrates, January 2, 1902.

145. H.A. Matthews, Education District Officer to the Inspector of Schools, 1 July 1902.

146. **Ibid.**

147. **Ibid.**

148. **Report of West India Royal Commission (The Moyne Commission)** (St. Michael: Government of Barbados, 2000 – reprint of 1945 work).

149. **Ibid.**

150. "Annual Report of the Commissioner of Education of British Guiana, 1925", printed in Gordon, **Reports and Repercussions**,151.

151. **Ibid.**

152. Cited in McGowan, Winston **A Concise History of Queen's College 1844-2009** (Georgetown: The Queen's College of Guyana, 2009), 1.

153. Cited in **Ibid.**,3.

154. **British Guiana – Report of the Principal of Queen's College for the year 1880** (Georgetown, 1881).

155. **British Guiana – Report of the Principal of Queen's College for the year 1886** (Georgetown, 1887).

156. Cited in Cameron, Norman **A History of the Queen's College of British Guiana** (Georgetown: F.H. Persick,1951),64.

157. **British Guiana – Report of the Principal of the Queen's College for the year 1898-1899** (Georgetown,1899).

158. Cited in **British Guiana – Report of the Principal of Queen's College, for**

449

the year 1900-1901 (Georgetown,1902).

159. Cited in Mary Noel Menezes' work on the history of the University of Guyana.
160. See the minutes of the University of Guyana Board of Governors.
161. See the Handbook of the University of Guyana.
162. Thomas, Clive OPEN LETTER to Vice-Chancellor, Staff and Students, University of Guyana, August 1, 1974.
163. See the pronouncements of the University's Board of Governors during this period.
164. **Ibid.**
165. Rodney, Walter **The Groundings with my brothers** (London: Bogle L' Overture Publications),5.
166. Rodney, Walter **How Europe Underdeveloped Africa** (Washington, D.C.: Howard University Press,1981),vii.
167. **Ibid.**
168. **Ibid.**
169. **Ibid.**,205.
170. Cited in "Proceedings of a Commemorative Symposium In Honour of Professors Elsa Gouveia and Walter Rodney", **History Gazette**, No.66, March 1994,18.
171. See **Guyana Historical Journal**, Volume 1, 1989, viii.
172. **Ibid.**, vii.
173. See the list of titles of the **Gazettes** published later in this chapter.
174. Kirke, Henry **Twenty-five Years in British Guiana** (London: Sampson Low, Marston & Company Limited, 1898), 65.
175. In earlier writings, I in error gave King's first name as Hampden. His right name is Clement Hampton King.
176. **The Daily Chronicl**e, 18 September 1887.
177. **The Demerara Daily Chronicle**, 30 August 1882.
178. **The Daily Argosy**, 12 November 1948.
179. **The Wisden Cricketers' Almanack** 2004 (Alton, Hampshire: John Wisden & Co. Ltd.,2004), 1183.
180. Cited in Lawrence and Goble, **The Complete Record**,57.

181. Cited in "Chanderpaul gets Cricketer of the Year award" in **Stabroek News**, 11 September, 2008, 27.
182. Note that Chanderpaul eventually did not become the most prolific West Indian Test batsman, his Test aggregate being 86 runs less than that of the Trinidadian, Brian Lara, when their Test careers ended.
183. **The Wisden Cricketers' Almanack, 1996.**
184. Cited in King, Tony and Laurie, Peter T**he Glory Days. 25 Great West Indian Cricketers** (Oxford: Macmillan, 2004),104.
185. **The Daily Chronicle**, 2 December 1905.
186. Critchlow, Hubert N. "History of the Trade Union Movement in British Guiana", text of an address given at the World Trade Union Conference of 1945.
187. WRA, Inspector General of Police to Colonial Secretary, 2 May 1928.
188. This is one example of several tributes from his former students which appeared in the daily newspapers at the time of Jonas' death, commending him for his contribution to both their academic expertise and their character.
189. **The Queen's College of British Guiana School Magazine**, 1946-1947, 26.
190. **The Queen's College Magazine**, 1948-49, 22.
191. Cited in **Stabroek News**, 10 May 2005.
192. See the cover of the book.
193. See the comments made about Rohlehr's work during the conferebnce in his honour at the St. Augustine campus in October 2007.
194. Lewis, Gordon **The Growth of the Modern West Indies** (New York and London: Monthly Review Press, 1969), 107.
195. Located in documents at the Cheddi Jagan Research Centre.
196. C.O. 1031, Woolley to Creech Jones, January 1948.
197. CJRC, PAC Bulletin, No 1, 6th November, 1946.
198. See **Argosy**, January. February 1949.
199. C.O. 1031/778, Supplement to Guiana Diary No 49, 1951. Political Parties of British Guiana and their Stated Aims.
200. Cited in Shahabuddeen, Mohamed **Constitutional Development In Guyana 1621-1978** (Georgetown, 1978), 499.
201. CJRC, CJ 052, People's Progressive Party Manifesto, 1953.
202. See Chapter 60 below.

203. Located in documents at the Cheddi Jagan Research Centre.
204. C.O. 1031/1169, Appendix dated 1st October 1953 to a letter from the Secretary of State for the Colonies entitled "Political Situation In British Guiana-Appendix Biographies of Leading Members of People's Progressive Party. The Ministers…L.F.S. Burnham."
205. Cited in Colonial Office, **Report of the British Guiana Constitutional Conference Held in London in March, 1960** (London: Her Majesty's Stationery Office, 1960), 4.
206. Singh, Jai Narine **Guyana: Democracy Betrayed** (Kingston: Kingston Publishers Ltd, 1996),84.
207. For the P.P.P.'s view on joining the West Indies Federation, see especially documents in the Cheddi Jagan Research Centre.
208. Cited in **Colonial Office, Report**…(1960),5.
209. Cited in **Ibid.**,5.
210. **Colonial Office, Report**…(1960),13.
211. Cited in **Ibid.**, 16, Annex B.
212. Cited in **Ibid.**,16, Annex D.
213. -216. See documents in series C.O. 1031 and F.O. 371 in PRO.
217. See Chapters 58 and 60 for a more detailed account of these two events in 1953.
218. C.O. 111/809/2/, British Guiana Sugar Producers Association to D.J. Parkinson, Acting Colonial Secretary, Public Buildings, Georgetown, 5th June 1951.
219. C.O. 111/809/2/, Comment by James Vernon, 10th Novemeber, 1951 on **Ibid.**
220. C.O. 1031/778, Supplement to Guiana Diary No.49, 1951 – Political Parties of British Guiana and their Stated Aims
221. C.O.111/809/2/, Rita Hinden to Tom Cook, 20 March 1951.
222. C.O.1031/776, Press Statement by Hon. Dr. Cheddi Jagan, M.L.C., British Guiana, 1 November 1951.
223. **Ibid.**
224. C.O.1031/776, N.L. Mayle to Sir Charles Woolley, 10 November 1951.
225. CJRC, CJ052, AIMS and PROGRAMME OF PEOPLE'S PROGRESSIVE PARTY
226. C.O. 1031/776, Extract from "Notes on British Guiana", Mr. Mayle's visit

NOTES

to the West Indies.1952.

227. C.O.111/809/2/, The Officer Administering the Government of British Guiana to the Secretary of State for the Colonies, 17 July 1951.

228. -231. See the series C.O.1031 in the PRO.

232. C.O.1031/12/, Savage to Lloyd, 13 September 1953.

233. C.O. 1031/12/, Savage to Colonial Office, 17 September 1953.

234. C.O.1031/12/, Luke to Rogers,12 September 1953.

235. **Ibid.**

236. C.O.1031/12/, Note by Governor, no date [September 1953].

237. C.O.1031/12/, Savage to Lloyd, 13 September1953.

238. C.O. 1031/12/, Luke to Rogers, 12 September 1953.

239. **Ibid.**

240. C.O. 1031/12/, Savage to Lloyd, 13 September 1953.

241. C.O. 1031/12/, Savage to Lloyd, 13 September 1953.

242. C.O. 1031/12/, Seaford to Jock Campbell, 8 September 1953.

243 C.O. 1031/12/, Lyttelton to Rogers, 16th September, 1953.

244. C.O. 1031/12/, Luke to Rogers, 12 September 1953.

245. C.O. 1031/12/, Note by the Governor, no date [September, 1953]; Savage to Lloyd, 13 September.1953.

246. Cited in Jagan, Cheddi **The West on Trial** (New York: International Publishers, 1967), 125.

247. See Colonial Office, **Report of the British Guiana Constitutional Conference…March,1960** (London,1960),5.

248. For a rare book-length study of U.S. policy towards Guyana see Rabe, Stephen **US Intervention in British Guiana. A Cold War Story** (Chapel Hill: The University of North Carolina Press, 2005). For John Dulles' views see 45-46.

249. -261. For the quotations in these notes see series C.O. 1031 and F.O. 371. in the PRO. For a more detailed study of US attitude to and relations with British Guiana in the colony's pre-independence era, see Fraser, Cary **Ambivalent Anti-Colonialism: The United States and the Genesis of West Indian Independence, 1940-1964** (Westport:Greenwood Press, 1994), Rabe, Stephen, **op**.**cit**.

262. Pinckard, 236-237.

263. L.M.S. Archives, Smith's Journal, entry for 26 December 1822.
264. Pinckard, 242.
265. **Ibid.**
266. See the 1784 slave code of Demerara.
267. Pinckard, 242-43.
268. **Ibid.**, 242.
269. See Chapter 62 above.
270. **British Guiana – Report of the Inspector of Villages for the Year 1897-98** (Georgetown, 1898).
271. **British Guiana – Report of the Inspector of Villages for the Year 1902-1903** (Georgetown, 1903).
272. **British Guiana – Report of the Inspector of Villages for the Year 1898-99** (Georgetown, 1899).
273. **British Guaian – Report of the Inspector of Villages for the Year 1899-1900** (Georgetown, 1901).
274. **British Guiana – Report of the Inspector of Villages for the Year 1897-98** (Georgetown, 1898).
275. **British Guina – Report of the Inspector of Villages for the year 1902-1903** (Georgetown, 1903).
276. **Ibid.**
277. **British Guiana – Report of the Inspector of Villages for the Year 1898-99** (Georgetown, 1899).
278. **Ibid.**
279. **Ibid.**
280. **Ibid.**

A Select Bibliography of Guyanese History

This is a selection of major works on the history of Guyana. Some of these books and articles, a minority, are included in the list For Further Reading, which is presented at the end of most chapters in the book.

ADAMSON, Alan	**Sugar Without Slaves: The Political Economy of British Guiana, 1838-1904** (New Haven: York University Press, 1972).
BALKARAN, Lal	**Bibliography of Guyana and Guyanese Writers 1596-2004** (LBA Publicatrions,2004).
BISNAUTH, Dale	**The Settlement of Indians in Guyana 1890-1930** (Leeds:Peepal Tree Press,2000).
BRAVEBOY-WAGNER, Jacqueline	**The Venezuela-Guyana Border Dispute: Britain's Colonial Legacy in Latin America** (Boulder: West view Press, 1984).
BURROWES, Reginald	**The Wild Coast: An Account of Politics in Guyana** (Schenkman, 1984).
CAMERON, A.J. McR.	**The Berbice Uprising 1763** (Caribbean Press, 2011).
CAMERON, Norman	**150 Years of Education in Guyana 1808-1957** (Georgetown: The Author,1968).
CHASE, Ashton	**A History of Trade Unionism in Guyana, 1900 to 1961** (Georgetown: New Guyana Co. Ltd., 1964).
CHASE, Ashton	**Guyana: A Nation in Transit Burnham's Role** (Georgetown, 1994).
CLEMENTI, Cecil	**The Chinese in British Guiana** (Georgetown, 1915).
CLEMENTI, Cecil	**A Constitutional History of British Guiana** (London: Macmillan and Co. Ltd. (1937).

DALTON, Henry	**History of British Guiana**, 2 vols. (London: Longman, 1855).
DALY, Vere	**A Short History of the Guyanese People** (London: Macmillan, 1975).
DE BARROS, Juanita	**Order and Place in a Colonial City. Patterns of Struggle and Resistance in Georgetown, British Guiana, 1880-1924** (Montreal: McGill-Queen's University Press, 2000).
DESPRES, Leo	**Cultural Pluralism and Nationalist Politics in British Guiana** (Chicago: Rand McNally and Company, 1967).
EUROPEAN UNION, NATIONAL TRUST OF GUYANA & GUYANA HERITAGE SOCIETY	**Aspects of European Guyanese Heritage** (Georgetown: Guyanese Heritage Society, 2017).
FARLEY, Rawle	"The Rise of the Peasantry in British Guiana", **Social and Economic Studies**, Vol II, No.4, March 1954.
FARLEY, Rawle	"The Rise of the Peasantry in British Guiana", **Caribbean Quarterly**, Vol.x, No.1, March 1964
FERGUSON, Tyrone	**To Survive Sensibly or to Court Heroic Death: Management of Guyana's Political Economy 1965-85** (Georgetown: Public Affairs Consulting Enterprise, 1999).
FRASER, Cary	**Ambivalent Anti-Colonialism: The United States and the Genesis of West Indian Independence, 1940-1964** (Westport: Greenwood Press,1994).
GLASGOW, Roy	**Race and Politics Among Africans and East Indians** (The Hague: Martinus Nijhoff, 1970).
GOPAUL, Nanda	**Resistance and Change. The Struggles of the Guyanese Workers (1964 to 1994) with emphasis on the sugar industry** (New York: Inside News Publications, Inc.,1997).
GOSLINGA, Cornelis	**The Dutch in the Caribbean and on the Wild Coast 1580-1680** (Gainesville: University of Florida Press, 1971).
GOSLINGA, Cornelis	**The Dutch in the Caribbean and the Guianas, 1680-1791** (Assen: Van Gorcum & Comp., 1985).

GRANGER, David	**National Defence. A Brief History of the Guyana Defence Force 1965-2005** (Georgetown: Free Press, 2005).
GRAVESANDE, Laurens	**The Rise of Bitish Guiana,** compiled from his despatches by Harris, C.A. and De Villiers, J.A.J. 2 Vols. (London: Hakluyt Society, 1911).
GREEN, Hamilton	**The Rocky but Righteous Road to Guyana's Independence** (Eccles: Corbin Media Group, 2016).
GREEN, William	"The Apprenticeship in British Guiana, 1834-38", **Caribbean Studies**, No.9, July 1969.
GREEN, William	**British Slave Emancipation, The Sugar Colonies and the Great Experiment, 1830-1865** (Oxford: Clarendon Press, 1976).
GREENIDGE, Carl	**Empowering A Peasantry in a Caribbean Context. The Case of Land Settlement Schemes in Guyana, 1865 to 1985** (Kingston: The University of the West Indies Press, 2001).
HARTSINCK, J.	"The Story of the Slave Rebellion in Berbice", translated by W. Roth, **Journal of the British Guiana Museum and Zoo**, December 1958-December 1960.
HIGMAN, Barry	**Slave Populations of the British Caribbean 1807-1834** (Baltimore: The John Hopkins University Press,1984).
ISHMAEL, Odeen	**The Guyana Story from Earliest Times to Independence** (Bloomington: The Author,2013).
JAGAN, Cheddi	**Forbidden Freedom. The Story of British Guiana** (London: Lawerence & Wishart, 1954).
JAGAN, Cheddi	**The West on Trial** with a new epilogue (St. John s: Hansib Publications, 1997).
JOSEPH, Cedric	"The Venezuela-Guyana Boundary Arbitration of 1899: An Appraisal" **Caribbean Studies**, Vol.10, No.2, July 1970.
JOSEPH, Cedric	**Anglo-American Diplomacy and The Re-opening of the Guyana- Venezuela Boundary Controversy, 1961-1966** (Trafford Publishing, 2008).
KWOK-CRAWFORD, Marlene	**Scenes From The History of the Chinese in Guyana** (Georgetown: The Author,1989).

LAURENCE, Keith	**A Question of Labour: Indentured Immigration into Trinidad and British Guiana 1875-1917** (Kingstron: Ian Randle Publishers, 1994).
LEWIS, Gordon	**The Growth of the Modern West Indies** (New York: Modern Reader Paperbacks, 1968).
LOOK LAI, Walton	**Indentured Labour. Caribbean Sugar: Chinese and Indian Migrants to the British West Indies, 1838-1918** (Baltimore: The Johns Hopkins University Press, 1993).
LUTCHMAN, Harold	**From Colonialism to Cooperative Republic. Aspects of Political Development in Guyana** (Rio Piedras: Institute of Caribbean Studies University of Puerto Rico, 1974).
MANDLE, Jay	**The Plantation Economy: Polpulation and Economic Change in Guyana, 1838-1960** (Philadelphia: Temple University Press, 1973).
MANGRU, Basdeo	**Indians In Guyana** (Chicago: Adams Press, 2000).
MCGOWAN, Winston	"The French Revolutionary Period in Demerara-Essequibo, 1793-1802", **History Gazette**, No.55, April 1993.
MCGOWAN, Winston	**The Atlantic Slave Trade, Slavery and the Demographic History of Guyana** (Turkeyen: Department of Social Studies, University of Guyana, 2006).
MCGOWAN, Winston	**The Origins and Development of Guyanese Cricket** (Turkeyen: Department of Social Studies, University of Guyana, 2006).
MCGOWAN, Winston, ROSE, James and GRANGER, David (eds.)	**Themes in African-Guyanese History** (Georgetown: Free Press, 1998).
MENEZES, Mary	**British Policy towards the Amerindians in British Guiana 1803-1873** (Oxford: Clarendon Press, 1977).
MENEZES, Mary	**The Amerindians in Guyana 1803-1873. A Documentary History** (London: Frank Cass and Co. Ltd, 1979).
MENEZES, Mary	**The Portuguese of Guyana: A Study in Culture and Conflict** (Gujarat: Anand Press, 1992).

MENEZES, Mary	**Scenes from the History of the Portuguese in Guyana** (London: The Author, 1986).
MENEZES, Mary	"The Backgorund to the Venezuela-Guyana Boundary Dispute", **History Gazette**, No 21, June 1990.
MENEZES, Mary	**Guyana and the Wider World** (Georgetown: Guyenterprise, 2017).
MOOHR, Michael	"The Economic Impact of Slave Emancipation in British Guiana, 1832-1852", **The Economic History Review**, 2nd series, Vol.xxv,No.4,1972.
MOOHR, Michael	"The Discovery of Gold and the Development of Peasant Industries in Guyana, 1884-1917: A Study in the Political Economy of Change", **Caribbean Studies**, Vol.15, No.2, July 1975.
MOORE, Brian	**Race, Power and Social Segmentation in Colonial Society: Guyana after Slavery, 1838-1891** (New York: Gordon and Breach, 1987).
MOORE, Brian	**Cultural Power, Resistance and Pluralism. Colonial Guyana, 1838-1900** (Kingston: The University of the West Indies Press, 1995).
NATH, Dwarka	**A History of Indians in Guiana** (London: The Author, 1970).
NATH, Dwarka	**A History of Guiana**, 3 vols. (London: The Author, 1975).
NETSCHER, Peter	**History of the Colonies Essequibo, Demerary and Berbice** translated from the Dutch by W.E. Roth (Georgetown, 1929 originally published in 1888).
NEWMAN, Peter	**British Guiana. Problems of Cohesion in an Immigrant Society** (Oxford: Oxford University Press, 1964).
PALMER, Colin	**Cheddi Jagan and the Politics of Power: British Guianas Struggle for Independence** (Chapel Hill: University of North Carolina Press, 2010).
PAYNE, Hugh	**10 Days In August 1834-10 Days that Changed the World** (New York: Caribbean Diaspora Press Inc., 2001).
RODNEY, Walter	**A History of the Guyanese Working Peopke, 1881-1905** (Baltimore: The Johns Hopkins University Press,

	1981).
RODWAY, James	**A History of British Guiana from the year 1688 to the Present Time,** 3 vols. (Georgetown: J. Thompson, 1891-4).
RODWAY, James	**The Story of Georgetown** (Georgetown: The Argosy Co. Ltd, 1920).
RUHOMAN, Peter	**Centenary History of the East Indians in British Guiana 1838-1938** (Georgetown, 1949)
SALLAHUDDIN	**Guyana: The Struggle for Liberation (1945-1992)** (Georgetown, 1994).
SAMBHUDAT (Known as SHAKO), Ramnarine	**WI in Test Matches Facts and Feats 1928-2013 (2014).**
SANDERS, A.	"Amerindians in Guyana: A Minority Group in a multiethnic Society", **Caribbean Studies,** Vol XII, No.2, July 1972.
SEECHARRAN, Clem	**'Tiger in the Stars'. The Anatomy of Indian Achievement in British Guiana 1919-29** (London: Macmillan Education,1997).
SEECHARRAN, Clem	**Sweetening Bitter Sugar . Jack Campbell The Booker Reformer In British Guiana 1934-1966** (Kingston: Ian Randle Publishers,2005).
SEECHARRAN, Clem	**Hand-In-Hand History of Cricket in Guyana 1865-1897** (Hertford: Hansib Publications Limited, 2016).
SHAHABUDDEEN, Mohamed	**The Legal System of Guyana** (Georgetown, 1973).
SHAHABUDDEEN, Mohamed	**Constitutional Development in Guyana, 1621-1978** (Georgetown,1978).
SHAHABUDDEEN, Mohamed	**From Plantocracy to Nationalization: A Profile of Sugar in Guyana** (Georgetown, 1983).
SINGH, Jai Narine	**Guyana: Democracy Betrayed. A political history, 1948-1993** (Kingston: Kingston Publishers Ltd, 1996).
SMITH, Raymond	**British Guiana** (London: Oxford University Press, 1962).
SPINNER, Thomas	**A Political & Social History of Guyana, 1945-1983** (Westview,1984).

ST PIERRE, Maurice	**Anatomy of Resistance. Anti-Colonialism in Guyana, 1823-1966** (London: Macmillan Education Ltd, 1998).
THOMPSON, Alvin	**Colonialism and Underdevelopment in Guyana, 1580-1803** (Bridgetown; Carib Research & Publications, 1987).
THOMPSON, Alvin	"Dutch Society in Guyana in the Eighteenth Century", **The Journal of Caribbean History,** Vol.20,2, 1985-6
WEBBER, A	**Centenary History and Handbook of British Guiana** (Georgetown, 1931).
WILL, H.A.	**Constitutional Change in the British West Indies, 1880-1903** (Oxford: Clarendon Press, 1970).
WILLIAMS, Denis	**Prehistoric Guyana** (Kingston: Ian Randle Publishers, 2003).
WILLIAMS, Eric	"The Historical Background of British Guiana's Problems", **Journal of Negro History**, Vol. xxx, No.4, 1945.
WOOLFORD, Hazel (Compiler and Editor)	**An Introductory Reader for Women's Studies in Guyana** (Georgetown: Caribbean Association for Feminist Research and Action, 2000).
YOUNG, Alan	**Approaches to Local Self Government in British Guiana** (London, 1958).

INDEX

A

Africa (mostly West Africa),
23, 28-31, 37-38, 42-45, 48-50, 52-54, 56-61, 69, 72, 98, 106, 114-115, 117, 122-123, 169, 172, 174, 180, 189, 247-250, 252, 255-256, 258-259, 267

African (black),
3, 7, 9, 11-14, 20, 23-25, 28, 30-34, 37, 45, 50-52, 54, 56, 67, 86, 97, 107, 115, 121, 127, 132-135, 137, 139, 141, 150, 154, 171, 173, 177, 179, 184, 186, 188, 194-195, 200, 213, 220-222, 226, 248, 250, 256-258, 268, 277-279, 338-339, 364-365, 371, 373-375, 379, 388, 406, 408-410, 417, 418, 420-421, 423-424

Agostini, Edgar,
283

Agriculture,
9, 23-24, 39, 142, 151, 159, 420

Akara,
68, 70

Akawaios,
25

Albion,
285

Alexander, Alexander (Ghurib Das),
199-201

Ambrose, Curtly,
325, 333

American (See also United States of America),
3, 31, 135

Americas,
22, 37, 39, 46, 50, 52, 54, 56-57, 61, 67, 69, 97, 99, 101-102, 172, 197, 207-208, 258, 395, 414

Amerindians (See also Akawaios, Arawaks, Arekuna, Caribs, Macusi, Patemonas, Wai Wai, Wapisianas, Warraus),
3-4, 7, 12, 14, 22-23, 25-26, 28, 32-34, 39, 65-66, 69-70, 84, 88, 91, 110, 125-127, 141, 147-150, 154, 161, 175, 213, 220, 222, 226, 259, 267, 278, 352, 379, 408, 422-425, 432

INDEX

Amiens (Treaty of),
407, 426

Ancestral worship,
23, 173

Angel Gabriel Riot,
429

Anglican (Church of England),
3, 14, 171-175, 182, 184, 187-189, 193-195, 214, 219, 221-222, 224, 230-231, 238, 263, 334, 339, 408

Animism,
23, 173

Anna Catherina,
210

Anna Regina,
135, 244

Annatto,
126, 161-162

Antigua,
4, 39, 110, 291, 299, 319, 323, 326, 328, 404

Apprentices (Apprenticeship, Apprenticed labourers),
30, 115-121, 262, 268, 338-339, 427-429

Arawaks,
25, 422

Arekuna,
25

Asia,
22, 169, 172, 199

Asiatic Cricket Club,
280

Association of Caribbean Historians,
352

Atlantic Ocean,
48, 50, 52, 54, 56-57, 60, 62, 98, 117, 120, 123, 150, 406, 411

Atkinson Field,
156

Austin, William Piercy,
219, 229, 238

Australia (n),
198-199, 285-286, 296-300, 302-303, 307-310, 315, 318-319, 321-322

Austria,
8, 128

B

Bacchus, Faoud,
291, 304, 316-317, 335

Baga,
49, 53

Bahadur, J.,
314

Baichan, Leonard,
286, 289, 316-318

Bajnauth, Sonny,
314-315

Balata,
10, 145

Bangladesh,
318

Barbados/ Barbadian,
4, 9, 12, 20, 30, 37-39, 42-43, 46, 49, 56, 65, 86, 95, 99, 106, 110, 114, 125-126, 157, 164, 173, 199, 207, 252, 280-285, 288-291, 293-295, 334, 360, 368, 370, 374, 404-406, 415, 434

Barracoons,
48, 52-53

Bartica,
205, 210, 217

Batavian Republic,
405-406

Bauxite,
20, 131, 167, 383, 385, 431

Bayley, Peter,
295, 313-314

Beaujon, Antony,
187, 405-407, 415

Beckman, Abraham,
423

Beete, Joseph,
187

Beet Sugar,
8-9, 128-131, 143, 165-167, 339

Belfield,
20, 204

Belfield School for Girls,
204

Benin,
48

Benjamin, Winston,
334

Benn, Brindley,
380

Bentinck, Henry,
188-192

Berbice (Colony),
1-4, 23, 28-29, 37-42, 45, 48, 54, 56, 62-67, 76, 88, 94, 97, 101-106, 114, 125-127, 133, 141, 147-149, 161-162, 175, 180, 194, 213, 221, 267, 364, 403-404, 407, 410, 414-415, 422-423

Berbice (County),
17-18, 20, 33, 132, 134, 137-138, 201, 222, 244, 279, 285-286, 293, 296, 301, 313-314, 342-344, 417

Berbice (River),
68, 70, 102-103, 148, 213

INDEX

Berbice Association,
68, 424

Berbice Cricket Club,
279

Berbice High School,
233, 239

Berkel, Adriann Van,
148

Bermuda,
280

Berring Strait,
22

Bethel Chapel,
73, 75-78, 81-82, 87, 91-94, 99, 179, 186, 192-194, 410

Better Success,
135

Birth Rate,
13, 29, 107

Bishop, Ian,
326

Bishop's High School,
231, 233, 432, 435

Bissoo, Devendra,
302, 316

Blairmont,
16

Blue Book,
142, 150-152, 154-155

Bondu,
52, 61

Booker Brothers (Mc Connell and Company),
131, 383, 388, 391-392, 427

Booker, Josiah,
427

Booth, William and Catherine,
198-199

Borselen Island,
425

Boundary Disputes,

   (a) With Suriname,
   159

   (b) With Venezuela,
   6, 262, 269

Bourda Cricket Ground,
20, 284-285, 289, 293-300, 304, 306, 312-315, 317-318, 326, 328-330

Brady, Lieutenant,
87

Brazil,
38, 43, 97-98, 125, 165, 400, 423

Bristol,
163

Britain,
6, 23, 38, 78, 95-97, 105-106, 108,

114-115, 117, 128, 165, 182, 249, 344, 366-367, 371, 380, 397, 400-401, 403-407, 426

British Commonwealth,
6, 376

British Empire,
5, 29, 106, 116, 346, 371, 374, 393

British (Metropolitan) Government,
9, 28, 31, 73-74, 76, 95, 102, 106, 110, 116-118, 130, 367, 370-371, 379-380, 382

British Guiana,
1, 6-8, 23, 280-286, 289, 293-294, 299, 301-303, 306, 312-314, 317, 342, 364

   (a) *Unification in 1831,*
      1, 23, 105, 141, 149-150, 161, 364, 407, 427

   (b) *Independence in 1966,*
      1, 6, 23, 25, 296, 366

British Guiana Cricket Club,
279

British Guiana East Indian Association,
138, 366, 431

British Guiana East Indian Cricket Club/Everest Cricket Club,
280, 285, 313

British Guiana/Guyana Cricket Board,
279, 326, 357

British Guiana Labour Party,
368-369

British Guiana/Guyana Labour Union,
16, 338, 343-344, 346-349, 366, 431

British Guiana Sugar Producers' Association,
314

British Guiana Trades Union Council,
432

British Guiana Workers' League,
347, 366, 431

British Labour Party,
344, 346

British Market,
8, 72, 106, 108, 111, 128, 136, 163-166, 339, 429

British Parliament,
95-96, 104, 114-115, 242

British Settlers,
1, 11-12, 14, 23, 28, 31-32, 39, 94, 108, 163, 195, 277, 279, 312, 404-405, 424

Brown, Herbert,
155-158

Browne, Archibald,
194, 197

Browne, Cyril Rutherford,
294-295

Burnham, Forbes,
239, 248, 251, 363, 371-374, 376, 382, 386-387, 393, 395, 397-398, 432-433, 436

Bush Expeditions,
109, 133-134

Bush Lot,
13

Butcher, Basil,
286, 296-297, 302

Butts, Clyde,
298

C

Cabelieu, Abraham,
422

Campbell, Stephen,
263, 269, 373-374, 402, 432

Canada/Canadian,
9, 25, 129, 201, 247, 353, 361

Cape Coast Castle,
53

Caria Island,
424

Caribbean/West Indies (mostly British),
4-5, 7, 10, 12, 22, 30, 37, 39-40, 42, 56-57, 60, 62-63, 68, 73-74, 80, 85, 98, 106, 109-110, 114-117, 125, 129-130, 138, 140, 151, 157, 164, 169, 171-173, 180, 183, 199, 207-209, 214, 221-222, 230, 242, 246-247, 249, 253, 255-258, 278-279, 282-283, 289-291, 293, 304-307, 309, 318-319, 321, 323, 325, 332, 339, 342, 344, 352, 356-358, 360-362, 367, 370, 392-393, 395-396, 405-406, 424, 428-429

Caribbean Community,
424

Caribbean Examinations Council,
67, 352, 355, 435

Caribbean Festival of Creative Arts,
435

Caribbean Free Trade Association,
434

Caribbean Secondary Examination Certificate,
435

Caribs,
23, 25, 422, 424

Carmichael, Hugh Lyle,
189-192

Cartabo,
424

Carter, John,
370, 373-374

Carter, Martin,
373

Cassava,
10, 26, 70, 125

Castlereagh, Lord,
106

Catholic Grammar School/St. Stanislaus College,
429

Cattle Rearing,
18, 24, 140, 145

Cent Bread Riots,
14

Central Board of Health,
16, 417, 421

Centre of Evangelism,
210

Ceylon/Sri Lanka,
111, 141, 164, 297, 321-322, 331

Chamberlain, James,
425

Chamber of Commerce,
343

Chanderpaul, Shivnarine,
273, 280, 286, 295, 299-300, 304, 316-319, 321-324, 328-330, 335, 437, 439, 451

Chandrika, Rajendra,
316

Charcoal,
10, 145

Charlestown,
193

Chase, Ashton,
369, 386-387

Chatham High School,
303

Chattergoon, Sewnarine,
316

China,
24, 30, 120, 435

Chinese,
7, 11-12, 14-15, 24-25, 30, 32, 137, 139, 201-202, 226, 268, 277, 279-280, 338, 364, 379, 428

Chinese Association of British Guiana,
43

Chinese/Cosmos Sports Club,
279-280

Christiani, Robert,
276, 285, 288-291, 295-296

INDEX

Christianity,
3, 23-24, 65, 73-74, 76, 80, 92, 94, 102, 117-118, 169-174, 176, 179-180, 182, 192-194, 201, 211, 213, 215, 220-221, 225, 409, 411

Christmas,
92, 97, 408-413

Chung, Mrs.,
201-202

Churches (See also Missions),
17, 18, 408

    (a) *Adventist,*
        217

    (b) *Anglican (See Above)*

    (c) *Assemblies of God,*
        214-215, 217

    (d) *Baptist,*
        202, 214, 217

    (e) *Canadian Presbyterian,*
        201, 224

    (f) *Christian Bretheren,*
        202, 214

    (g) *Christian Catholic,*
        214

    (h) *Christian Mission,*
        202, 214

    (i) *Church of Christ,*
        214

    (j) *Church of God,*
        214

    (k) *Church of God of Prophecy,*
        214

    (l) *Church of the Nazarene,*
        214, 216-218

    (m) *Church of Scotland,*
        222

    (n) *Congregational,*
        76, 93, 169-178, 224, 343

    (o) *Covenant Church,*
        215

    (p) *Dutch Reformed,*
        3, 173-175, 194-196, 213, 408, 423

    (q) *Elim Mission,*
        214

    (r) *Full Gospel Fellowship,*
        209-212, 214-215, 217

    (s) *Kitty Bible/Baptist,*
        216

    (t) *Love and Faith World Outreach,*
        215

    (u) *Lutheran,*
        2, 3, 20, 201, 213, 224

    (v) *Methodist,*
        95, 224

    (w) *Moravian,*
        213, 224

    (x) *New Testament Church of God,*
        214-215

    (y) *Pilgrim Holiness/Wesleyan,*
        214, 217

    (z) *Presbyterian,*
        193-197

    (aa) *Roman Catholic,*
        224

    (bb) *Salvation Army,*
        198-208, 214

Clarke, Gedney,
40, 404

Clarkson, Thomas,
113

Claxton, William,
173

Coburn, Brother,
199-200

Coffee Cultivation/Production,
5, 10, 19, 23, 28, 32, 39-40, 63, 72, 106, 108, 111, 133, 141, 148, 162-165, 404, 415-416, 420

Collet, Wilfred,
344

Colonial Office,
144, 155, 189, 191, 346, 365, 370-371, 388-390, 392-393, 399

Colonial Secretary/Secretary of State for the Colonies,
189-190, 347, 369, 374-375, 389

Coloureds,
6-7, 11, 184-185, 277, 279, 364-365, 373, 379,

Colvin, A.V.,
134-135

Combined Court,
7-8, 11, 364

Compulsory Educational Ordinance (1876),
225-226, 429

Congo,
46

Constantine, Learie,
295

Constitutional Changes,
  (a) *1891:*
  6-8, 146, 268, 364-365, 388, 430
  (b) *1928:*
  348-349, 364-365, 388

Constitutional Reform Association,
429-430

Corentyne,
13, 20, 244, 285, 301

Cotton,
5, 23, 28, 32, 40, 63, 72-73, 104, 108, 111, 115, 126, 133, 141, 148, 162-165, 179, 404

Court/Council of Policy,
1-2, 7-8, 11, 70, 73-74, 91, 94-95, 108-109, 187-189, 191, 196-197, 364, 425-426

Creoles,
33, 88-89, 107, 133

Cricket,
19-20, 24, 277-336, 430, 434-437, 439

INDEX

Crime,
17

Critchlow, Hubert,
16, 269, 347-349

Croft, Colin,
286, 302, 326, 335

Crowe, Martin,
297

Crown Colony Government,
274, 348-349, 364-365, 379

Crown Lands,
142, 144-145

Cuba,
37, 43, 165, 395-396, 435

Curtis Campbell and Company,
131

D

D'Aguiar, Peter,
378-379, 394, 402, 433

Dahomey/Dahomeans,
46

Dalrymple, Samuel,
188

Damon (1834),
427

Damon, Cleo,
208

Das, Harry,
210

Davies, John,
178-180, 182-183, 186, 188, 190-191, 194

Davson and Company,
131

De Caires, Francis,
289

De Costa, Pedro,
422

Deficiency Laws,
94

Defreitas, Celso,
314

De la Coste, J.C.,
426

Demerara Colony (also Demerara-Essequibo),
23, 28-29, 37-38, 40-42, 45, 48, 54, 62-63, 65-67, 73, 76, 80, 93-95, 97, 101, 105-106, 114, 127, 133, 141, 148-149, 170, 173-178, 183, 186, 193-195, 213, 220-221, 267, 364, 403-407, 409-410, 414-415, 424-426

Demerara County,
17, 33, 137, 200, 214, 222, 228, 285, 293, 313, 428

Demerara Cricket Club,
279, 303

Demerara River,
134, 142, 179, 190, 214, 425, 427

Deonarine, Narsingh,
302, 316

Department of Agriculture,
137, 157

Department/Division of History, University of Guyana,
248-250, 261, 265-266

De Saffon Institute,
221

De Saffon, Pierre Louis,
221

Devonshire Castle,
429

Diamonds,
10, 20, 130-131, 145, 167, 430

Dias, Francis,
7, 239

Diseases,
11, 16, 107

Dowling, Graham,
329

Drainage,
11, 138, 417, 419-421

Drought,
10-11, 18, 70, 138, 420

Drum,
23

Drayton, Harold and Kathleen,
248, 251-252

Dujon, Jeffrey,
291, 333-335

Durban Park,
20, 427

Durban, Sir Benjamin,
239, 427

Dutch (Nationality),
2, 23, 31, 37, 194

Dutch (Language),
2, 126, 267

Dutch Creole,
175, 180

Dutch West India Company (WIC),
39-40, 127, 149, 161-162, 404, 422, 426

E

East Bank Demerara,
210, 285, 293, 340, 348, 417, 431

East Coast Demerara,
12, 20, 33, 36, 56, 71, 75-76, 80, 82-83, 87-89, 91-93, 96-99, 101-102, 109, 111, 145, 153, 155-156, 170, 174-176, 179, 189, 192-193, 204, 212, 214, 220, 243, 278-279, 321, 409, 411, 417, 428

East Indians,
1, 11-12, 14-15, 24, 25, 30-34, 43, 117, 120, 123, 129, 132, 134-135, 137-138, 140, 150, 154, 166-167, 200-201, 225-226, 234, 263, 268, 274, 277, 280, 312-320, 339-342, 364-365, 371, 374-375, 379, 383, 421, 428-429, 431

Edmonstone, Charles,
133

Education (See also Queen's College and University of Guyana)
11, 17-18, 23-24, 65, 117-118, 205, 220-228, 262, 268, 274, 428

Edun, Ayube,
431

Edun, Wilfred,
315

Edwards, David,
208

El Dorado,
23, 141

Elections,
- (a) *of 1947,*
  368, 432,
- (b) *of 1953,*
  370-371, 373, 382, 384, 387-388, 390, 395, 397
- (c) *of 1957,*
  373-374, 395, 397
- (d) *of 1961,*
  379-380, 394, 397, 433
- (e) *of 1964,*
  433
- (f) *of 1968,*
  433
- (g) *of 1973,*
  434
- (h) *of 1980,*
  436
- (i) *of 1985,*
  436
- (j) *of 1992,*
  437

Elliot, Richard,
180

Emancipation,
30, 33-34

England,
18, 76, 93, 104, 113, 179, 187, 199, 207-208, 220, 229, 247, 278, 290-291, 295, 297, 299, 301-303, 307-309, 315, 318, 321, 323, 330, 332, 334-335, 343, 352, 360, 371-372, 383, 405-410

English Language,
2-3, 24, 126, 175, 180, 403

Englishmen,
4, 11, 14, 18, 31, 48, 53, 58-60, 75-76, 126, 134, 172, 175, 199, 281, 295, 298, 307, 310

Enlightenment,
113

Enmore,
268, 384, 432

Essequibo Coast,
135, 211

Essequibo Colony, (See also Demerara-Essequibo),
2-3, 23, 28-29, 37, 38-42, 45, 48, 54, 62, 64, 66, 109, 125-127, 133, 147-149, 161, 167, 204, 267, 279, 403-404, 422-425

Essequibo County,
6, 17, 20, 33-34, 137, 222, 285, 293, 313, 417, 428

Essequibo River,
9, 127, 142

Europe/Europeans,
3, 8, 12, 14, 23, 25, 28, 32, 38-39, 48, 51, 54, 59-60, 67-68, 106, 125, 128, 133, 136, 141, 147-148, 161, 170, 195, 199, 220, 248-249, 252, 258, 339, 352, 367, 379, 403, 407-408

Evangelicals (see also Pentecostals),
98, 113, 169, 202-203, 213-218

Ewing Estates,
131

Executive Council,
7-8

F

Fernandes, Marius,
285, 295, 317, 328

Fiscal,
185, 187-188, 191

Fish/Saltfish,
148-150, 152-153, 180

Fish Glue,
10, 151

Fisheries,
148-152, 155-157

Fisheries Committee/Commission,
153-154

Fisheries Division,
157

Fishing,
10, 13, 147-160

Flag (Fort) Island,
424

Flood, Thomas/Flood Challenge Cup,
313

Flooding,
11, 18, 23, 32, 138

Fon,
53

Forts,
- (a) *Nassau*, 70, 423
- (b) *Zeelandia*, 424

France,
6, 8, 113, 127-128, 166, 210, 249, 404-407, 414-415, 425

Franchise Qualifications,
7, 11, 348

Francis, George,
295

Frank, R.T.,
342-343

Free Blacks/Coloureds,
29, 83, 93-94, 170-171, 179, 193, 220, 410

French Guiana,
151, 209

French Revolution (1789),
404-405, 414

France in Guiana,
127, 133, 403-404, 407, 414-415, 423, 425

Fudadin, Assad,
316

Fula,
52

Full Gospel Fellowship,
168, 209-212

G

Gambia,
51-52, 61

Garner, Joel,
333

Garnett Cup,
278

Gaskin, Berkeley,
289, 301

Gayle, Chris,
330

Georgetown,
4, 8, 10, 12-13, 18-19, 33-34, 36, 56, 67, 76, 86-89, 91, 93, 134, 144, 150, 153, 156-158, 170, 193, 195, 199-202, 205, 207, 209-212, 214-215, 221, 227-228, 244, 246, 266, 268-269, 275, 278-282, 284-285, 293, 303, 313-314, 321, 340-344, 348, 365-366, 378, 408, 426, 428-430

Georgetown Cricket Club,
20, 276, 279, 281, 284-285, 293, 388, 429, 432

Germans/Germany,
8, 31, 128, 156

Gibbs, Glendon,
295-296

Gibbs, Lance,
276, 286, 296, 298, 303, 306-311, 326, 434, 437

Gladstone, Jack,
75, 83-85, 91, 93

Goddard, John,
290

Gold (Mining, Exports),
9, 12, 20, 130-131, 141-146, 151, 167, 420, 430

Gold Coast,
50, 374

Gomes, Larry,
333-334

Gomez, Gerry,
290

Goveia, Elsa,
219, 255-256, 259, 269

Gravesande, Jonathan,
425

Gravesande, Laurens Storm Van's
40, 149, 424, 425

Gray, Bain,
224-225, 228

Gray, Cecil,
373

Greenidge, Geoffrey,
299

Greenidge, Gordon,
291, 318-319, 325-326, 333-335

Grenada,
199

Griffith, Charles,
309

Ground Provisions,
9, 18-19, 73, 134-135, 137, 139-140, 145, 383, 420

Guadeloupe,
110

Guiana Independence Movement,
374-375, 377-378

Guiana Industrial Workers Union,
392

Guiana National Party,
373

Guiana Coast,
53, 132, 258

H

Haiti (see also Saint Domingue),
67, 414-416

Hall, Wesley,
309

INDEX

Hamilton, John,
75

Hampton Court,
285

Hand-in-Hand Fire Insurance Company,
428

Harper, Roger,
298-299, 334-335

Harragin, Bertie,
294

Hawke, Neil,
298

Hauraruni,
211

Hawkshaw, John,
170, 175, 187

Haynes, Desmond,
291, 318, 322, 325-326, 333-334

Headley, George,
290-291, 295, 326,

Health,
16-17

Hinds, Wavell,
300, 329

Hindu/Hinduism,
24, 209-210, 226

History Gazette,
265-275

History Society,
265-275

Hodgson, Frederick,
340

Holding, Michael,
210, 333, 335

Holland,
41, 170, 194

Hoogenheim, Wolfert Simon Van,
68-69

Hooper, Carl,
276, 299-304, 319, 325-327, 329, 438

Horse-Racing,
19-20

Hubbard, Jocelyn,
369

Hunte, Conrad,
329

Hussey, Mike,
321

I

Ibo/Iboland,
46, 53

Immigration/Immigrants,
12, 14-15, 30-31, 268, 427-428

Indentureship/Indentured Servants or Workers,
120-123, 135-137, 268, 338

India,
10, 12, 24, 30-32, 43, 117, 120, 122, 134-137, 259, 268, 285-286, 291, 299-300, 302-304, 307, 310, 315-317, 321, 325-326, 329, 333, 365, 428

Indian Immigrants,
12-14, 32, 134, 338, 353, 414

Insanally, Mohamed,
251-252

Insanally, Vic,
359, 361

Institute of Distance and Continuing Education (IDCE),
244

International Cricket Council,
321-323, 335

Inter-School Christian Fellowship,
216

Irish,
31

Irrigation,
11, 138, 417

Islam,
23-24

J

Jacob, Charles Ramkissoon,
239, 431

Jagan, Cheddi,
363, 369-374, 376-377, 380-387, 395, 397-401, 432-433, 437, 438

Janet, Jagan,
363, 369, 371-372, 386, 391, 393, 437

Jakin,
46

Jamaica,
37-38, 42, 50, 56, 60, 96-97, 99, 106, 111, 114-115, 164, 173, 189, 199, 207-208, 210, 232, 239, 242, 247-248, 255-257, 281, 289-291, 294-296, 299-300, 302-303, 306-307, 329, 342, 356, 368, 370, 374, 434

Jarvis, Terrence,
297

Jews,
125

Johnson, Ian,
296

Johnson, Hines,
302

Jonas, Ronald, Pryor,
350, 355-358

Jones, Bryn and Edna,
210

478

Jones, Mortimer,
208

Jones, Prior,
357

Jonestown,
435

K

Kaldor, Budget,
399, 433

Kallicharran, Alvin,
286, 289, 296-298, 302, 316-319, 326, 328-329, 334-335, 434-435

Kanhai, Rohan,
276, 286, 296-297, 302, 304, 314-315, 317, 319, 326, 329, 434-435, 437

Katz, Wolfert,
132-133

Kawall Cup,
313

Kayuka,
217

Kennedy, John,
400-401

Kensington Oval,
20, 289, 299, 303, 306, 310, 318, 328, 330

Kentish, Esmond,
302

Khan, Imran,
298

Kijk over al/Kjk-overal,
423

King, Clement,
20, 282, 293-294

King, Reon,
280, 302

King, Sidney (later Eusi Kwayana),
262, 373-374, 386-387, 391, 393

King, Thomas,
60

Kingston,
205, 207

Kirke, Henry,
277-278

Knight Case,
113

Knox, General,
406

Kofi/Cuffy,
56, 67-68, 70

L

Lara, Brian,
318-319, 322-323, 325-326, 330, 451

Latchmansingh, Joseph P.,
373-374, 387

Leahy, Lt. Colonel John,
88-89, 91

League of Coloured Peoples,
366, 370

Liberated Africans,
30-31, 43-44, 428,

Linden,
205, 244

Lloyd, Clive,
276, 286, 291, 296, 298-299, 303-305, 310-311, 317, 319, 326, 329, 331, 334-335, 434, 436-437

Logie, (Gus),
333-334

London,
78, 102, 116, 163, 172, 176, 182, 189-190, 194, 198-200, 207-208, 210, 229, 247, 365, 368, 382, 384-385, 396, 415

Lord's,
308, 316

Louisiana,
133, 414

Luckhoo, Lionel,
373

Luke, Stephen,
388-389, 391, 393

M

Mabaruma,
210

Macusi,
25

Madeira,
14, 18, 24, 30-32, 117, 120, 427

Madras,
302

Madray, Ivan,
296, 314-316

Madewini,
216-218

Mahaica,
86-87, 97, 180, 184, 189-190, 194, 353

Mahaicony/Abary Area,
134-135

Malaria,
16-17, 138, 421

Malta/Maltese,
31

Man Power Citizens' Association (M.P.C.A.),
366, 392, 431, 435

Manumission,
3, 29, 63, 110, 123

Maria's Pleasure,
13

Marshall, Malcolm,
333-334

Marshall, Norman,
307

Marshall, Samuel,
199-200

Martinique,
110

Matthews, H.A.,
225, 227

Mc Connell, John and Company (See also under Booker Brothers),
131

Mc Turk, Michael,
84

Mc Watt, Clifford,
289

Menezes, Mary Noel,
261, 275, 350-354

Middle Passage/Atlantic Crossing,
48-50, 54, 56-62

Militia,
69, 84, 86-87, 89, 94-95, 133

Miscegenation/Mixed Race or Population,
13, 25, 28, 32-33

Missions (Christian),
- (a) *Church Missionary Society,*
  94, 169, 213-214, 222
- (b) *London Missionary Society,*
  74, 76, 78, 80-81, 93-94, 99, 169-170, 172-179, 193-194, 213, 220, 409-412
- (c) *Methodist Missionary Society,*
  95, 169-171, 173, 180, 187, 192-195, 197-199, 213
- (d) *Moravians,*
  170-171, 188, 213, 424

Mohabir, Philip and Muriel,
168, 209-212

Molasses,
9-11, 128, 130, 136, 141, 145, 164-165,

Monroe, Doctrine,
395

Moonsammy, Clement,
201, 207-208

Moore, Colin,
248

Moore, Robert,
255

Morawhanna,
16

Mortality Rate,
13, 29, 31-32, 34, 72, 107, 109

Moruka,
148, 210, 425

Moyne, Commission,
367

Murray, John,
73-74, 80, 85, 87, 89, 91, 93, 220

Muslims,
174, 226

N

Nagamootoo, Mahendra,
316

Naipaul, J.,
314

National Cultural Centre,
198, 211, 266, 435

National Democratic Party,
373

National Labour Front,
373, 432

Negro Education Grant,
222

Netherlands/States General,
1, 4, 23, 38-41, 68, 103, 125-127, 148, 161, 194, 196, 213, 275, 403, 405-407, 422, 425-426

Nevis,
170, 173

New Amsterdam,
1, 4, 8, 33, 150, 202, 205, 210, 221, 227, 244, 279, 343, 365, 410, 431,

New Colonial Company,
131

Newspapers,

    (a) *Argosy,*
    154, 226, 252, 269, 402

    (b) *Chronicle/Daily Chronicle,*
    284

    (c) *Essequibo and Berbice Gazette,*
    195-196

    (d) *Stabroek News,*
    255, 325, 356

Newton, John,
53-54

New Zealand,
199, 297, 299, 307, 317, 329

Nicholson, Robert,
187

Nigeria,
46, 374

North America,
22, 47, 133, 149-150, 205, 252, 257, 323

North Brook/Victoria,
428

North/West District,
22

Nova Zeelandia,
23

O

Obeah,
186

Orinoco,
64, 109

P

Pairaudeau, Bruce,
239, 286, 289, 296

Pakistan,
297-298, 304, 317, 326, 329

Parade Ground,
276, 284-285, 293-294

Parika,
210

Paris,
6, 430

Park, Mungo,
51

Parker Cup,
278

Parliament Buildings,
193, 337, 344

Parris, Michael,
435

Pass (Laws),
69, 103, 121

Pastimes/Recreation,
19-20

Patemonas,
25

Peasants/Small Farmers,
9, 11, 17, 25

Peggy,
82-83

Peking,
202

Pentecostals,
215

People's National Congress,
250-254, 374, 379, 393, 397, 399, 432-433, 437,

People's Progressive Party,
242, 269, 363, 369-380, 382, 390-395, 397-398, 432, 437

Persaud, Chatterpaul,
295, 313-314

Persaud, Ganesh,
314

Peter's Hall,
16, 214

Phillips, Thomas,
48

Pierre, Lance,
302

Pierronet, Thomas,
3, 278

Pinckard, George,
3-4, 408-412

Piwarri,
125

Plantains,
5, 133-134, 413, 420

Plantations,
23-24, 28, 36, 39, 65, 68-69, 73-74, 77-78, 83, 88, 94, 108, 146

   (a) *Alexandria,*
         70

   (b) *Bachelor's Adventure,*
         87-90, 103

   (c) *Better Hope,*
         86

   (d) *Chateau Margot,*
         84, 88, 91

   (e) *De Hague,*
         191

   (f) *Dochfour,*
         87

   (g) *Elizabeth,*
         70

   (h) *Hollandia,*
         70

   (i) *Juliana,*
         70

   (j) *Kitty,*
         189

   (k) *Lelienburg,*
         70

   (l) *Leonora,*
         135, 210, 268, 429, 431-432

   (m) *Le Resouvenir,*
         73, 80, 82-83, 94, 99, 170, 173, 179, 183-188, 193-194, 220, 409

   (n) *Liliendaal,*
         97

   (o) *Lusignan,*
         12

   (p) *Magdalenenburg,*
         70

   (q) *Montrose,*
         94

   (r) *Ogle,*
         383

   (s) *Schoonord,*
         383

   (t) *Success,*
         80, 83-86, 185

(u) *Vive La Force*,
134, 191

(v) *Zeelandia*,
70

Planters/Proprietors,
2, 5-7, 9, 11-30, 30-31, 39, 43

Political Affairs Committee (P.A.C.),
369, 382, 432

Pomeroon,
34, 110, 126-127, 403, 423,

Pooran, C.,
313

Ponting, Ricky,
321

Port of Spain,
283, 301, 303, 322

Portugal,
125, 353

Portuguese,
7, 11-12, 14, 18-19, 24-25, 30-32, 34, 37, 117, 120, 151, 153, 226, 248, 263, 268, 274, 277, 279, 338, 352, 364, 378-379, 427-428

Post, Hermanus,
82, 170-172, 175-176, 179, 181, 183, 188, 194, 220, 409

Poultry,
10, 184

Poverty,
18

Powell, William,
173

Praedial Larceny,
11, 17, 420

Prawns/Shrimps,
147, 154, 158-160

President's College,
235

Prohibitory Order of 1805,
28-29, 42, 105,

Protestants,
14, 32, 169

Providence Chapel,
179-180, 184, 291

Providence National Stadium,
285, 293, 330

Provision Grounds,
106

Purkis,
180

Q

Queen's College,
17, 219, 224, 229-243, 246, 255, 355-357, 359, 361, 428-429, 433, 435,

Queen's Park Oval,
20, 286, 291, 301, 312-313, 316, 322

Quamina,
75, 77, 78, 80-85, 88, 91-93

R

Race Relations,
- (a) *Black-Indian,*
  14, 21, 25-26
- (b) *Black-Portuguese,*
  19, 25
- (c) *Amerindians and other groups,*
  14

Racial Consciousness/Racism,
14, 269

Rae, Allan,
290

Rai, Balram Singh,
397

Raleigh, Walter,
238

Ramadhin, Sonny,
306, 310, 315

Ramdass, Ryan,
316

Ramring,
68

Rates,
16, 18, 418-419

Rawlings, Charles,
283

Recreation Ground,
291

Redpath, Ian,
310

Red Stripe Cup,
283

Rice,
5, 9-10, 12-13, 20, 24, 130-140, 142, 145, 150, 167, 420, 430

Richards, Vivian,
323, 325-326, 331, 333-335

Richardson, Richie,
299, 325-326, 328, 331, 334-335

Rivers,
- (a) *Abary,*
  423
- (b) *Barima,*
  148-149, 422
- (c) *Berbice,*
  68, 70, 102-103, 135, 148-149, 422
- (d) *Canje,*
  70, 103, 135, 149
- (e) *Corentyne,*
  17, 422
- (f) *Demerara,*
  134, 142, 179, 190,

214, 425, 427

(g) *Essequibo,*
9, 127, 142, 149, 424

(h) *Mazaruni,*
9-10, 142, 425, 430

(i) *Orinoco,*
149, 422, 425-426

(j) *Pomeroon,*
148

(k) *Puruni,*
142

(l) *Waini,*
149, 422

Roach, Clifford,
295

Roberts, Andy,
333-334

Rodney, Walter,
219, 246-260, 269, 276, 359, 434-435, 440

Rodway, James,
151

Rohlehr, Dr. John (Physician),
341

Rohlehr, Gordon,
350, 359-362

Rohoman, R.B.,
313

Roman Catholics (Catholicism),
14, 24, 32, 217, 230, 354, 379, 425

Rose, Peter,
263, 427

Rose Hall,
210, 285, 342

Ross, Andrew,
187

Royal Agricultural and Commercial Society,
18, 154, 428,

Rum,
9-11, 125, 128, 130, 136, 141, 145, 164-165, 411

Rusk, Dean,
396, 400

Ryk, Gabriel,
174, 194, 196

S

Sabina Park,
289, 291, 295, 302-303, 329

Saint Domingue, (see also Haiti),
37, 67, 97, 183, 253

Salvation Army,
198-208

Sandbach Parker,
131

Sanitation,
16, 18, 32, 419, 421,

San Thome,
422

Sarwan, Ramnaresh,
280, 304, 316, 318-319, 322, 330

Savage, Alfred,
363, 388-391

School of Oriental and African Studies,
247

Scotland/Scots,
31, 51, 113, 195-197, 200, 278

Scott, John,
126-127, 403

Secret Ballot,
7, 430

Secretary of State for the Colonies (See Colonial Secretary)

Seven Years War,
68-69

Sharp, Granville,
113

Sharpe, Sam,
56

Shell Shield,
283, 303-304, 309

Shivnarine, Sewdatt,
316, 319

Silver,
141-142

Simpson, William,
64-65

Singh, Jai Narine,
373-376, 386-388, 393

Singh, Jean Bahadur,
363, 368

Singh, Vishaul,
316

Skeldon,
201, 295

Slave Masters/Slave Owners/Slaveholders,
5, 23, 41, 43, 65, 73-74, 77-78, 92, 94, 98, 102-103, 106, 220

Slavery,
23, 26, 121-123, 172, 267, 338, 410-413

   (a)   *Amelioration,*
          73-75, 77, 95, 98, 111, 114, 221, 427

   (b)   *Manumission,*
          3, 29, 63, 110, 123

   (c)   *Resistance:*

   I. In the Guiana colonies-including

(aa) Runaways and Maroons,
64-65, 97, 180, 185, 267

INDEX

(bb) The 1763 Berbice Rebellion,
67-71, 88-97, 101-104, 162, 267, 425

(cc) The 1823 East Coast Demerara Rebellion,
72-104, 109, 111, 115, 192, 427

    (d) *Abolition,*
        23, 30, 34, 36, 42, 99, 111, 113-116, 221, 267-268, 427

Slaves,
3-5, 28-29, 41, 172

    (a) *Amerindians,*
        3, 110

    (b) *African-born,*
        23, 29, 98-99, 107

    (c) *Creoles,*
        29, 98-99, 107

    (d) *Females,*
        29-30, 64, 74, 107

    (e) *Males,*
        30

    (f) *Mulattoes/Coloureds,*
        64

    (g) *Old/Aged,*
        107

Slave Trade (Atlantic),
4, 23, 28, 30-31, 36-62, 67, 98, 102, 105-107, 110, 115, 122, 132, 161-163, 172, 249, 256, 258, 267

    (a) *Resistance in West Africa,*
        45-55

    (b) *Resistance at Sea,*
        56-62

    (c) *Abolition,*
        29, 30, 42, 46, 72, 104-115

Smith, O' Neil, "Collie",
306

Smith, Jane,
93

Smith, John,
36, 75-79, 82-84, 92-93, 96, 99, 194, 220, 410

Snow, John,
298

Sobers, Garfield,
297, 299, 308, 323, 326, 329-331

Social Stratification,
11-12

Society for the Propagation of the Gospel,
213

Solomon, Joe,
286, 291, 296-297, 302-303, 314, 316-317

South Carolina,
133

South Africa/South Africans,
299, 317, 321, 325, 328-331

South America,
4, 24, 37, 172, 199, 396, 400, 403, 414

Sovereign Cricket Club,
281

Spain/Spaniards/ Spanish,
23, 37-38, 109, 126, 149, 403, 422, 425-426

Springlands,
17

Square of the Revolution,
56, 67

Sri Lanka,
297, 321-322, 331

Stabroek,
1, 4, 170, 173-174, 179-180, 184, 188-190, 193, 195, 220-221, 408, 410, 426

St. Andrew's,
168, 193-195, 197, 242, 427

Stanleytown,
211, 217, 417

St. Augustine,
242, 246, 351, 359-362

Stayers, Sven,
302

St. Croix,
188

St. Eustatius,
403

Stewart, John,
84

St. George's Chapel, (Cathedral),
189, 193-195, 269, 426, 430

Stipendiary Magistrates,
118

St. Lucia,
95, 414

Straghan (Rev.),
174, 194

Strikes,
341-343, 428, 432

Strong, Leonard,
214

St. Rose's High School,
428

St. Stanislaus,
230, 233, 239, 429

Stuart, Colin,
302

St. Vincent,
207

Suddie,
20

Sugar/Sugar Cane,
5, 7, 8-12, 16, 18-19, 23-24, 32, 39-40, 63, 72-73, 106, 111, 114, 116, 125-131, 133, 135-136, 139, 141, 143-145, 148, 150, 160-167, 200, 252, 256, 339, 348, 382-383, 392, 395, 404, 420, 423, 426-429

INDEX

Sugar Producers' Association,
382-384, 392, 452

Swettenham Circular,
226

Suriname,
10, 37-39, 41, 64, 110, 127, 151, 159, 162-163, 171, 175, 183, 209, 313

T

Tain,
249

Talboys, Rev. Thomas,
194, 197

Taxation/Taxes,
8, 11

Teachers' Association,
15

Temnes,
134

Test Cricket,
285-286

Thomas, Clive,
251

Thomas, Ewart,
359, 361

Thompson, Alvin,
248, 255, 361

Thorne, Alfred,
347, 431

Timber,
10, 145, 385

Tinker, Hugh,
121

Tobacco,
126

Tobago,
180, 192

Tomba,
49, 53

Town Hall,
200-201

Trim, John,
285-286, 289-290, 301-303

Trinidad/Trinidadian,
20, 95, 148-149, 180, 207-208, 242, 246, 252, 276, 281-284, 286, 288-290, 294-295, 297, 301-302, 306, 312-313, 317, 323, 342, 351, 353, 356-357, 359-362, 368, 370, 374, 432, 434

Trueman, Fred,
310

Turkey,
164

Turkeyen,
243, 265

Turner, Glenn,
297

Tuschen,
430

U

Uitvlugt,
295, 383

Unemployment/Underemployment,
15, 339, 346

United Democratic Party,
373-374

United Force,
378-380, 394, 397, 399, 432-433

United Kingdom,
8, 151, 199, 201, 210, 259, 323, 356-357, 361

United States of America, (See also American),
43, 54, 58, 73, 98, 111, 129, 133-135, 141, 156, 164, 199, 252, 266, 274, 353-354, 359, 361, 367, 369, 378, 380-381, 394-401, 403-404, 406

Unity,
321, 323

Universal Adult Suffrage,
7, 370, 373

University (College) of the West Indies,
230, 232, 242, 246-248, 255-256, 351, 353-355, 359-361

University of Guyana,
219, 242-254, 261-275, 351-353, 360, 362, 433, 438

University of London,
247, 352, 360

Upper Guinea Coast,
53, 258

Ursuline Nuns,
428

Urselius, Johannes,
423

U.S.S.R,
367

V

Valentine, Alfred,
306-307, 310

Van Berckel, F.P.,
187, 191

Van Berkel, Adriann,
148

Van-der-Goes, Jan,
422

Van Pere Family,
422

INDEX

Veerasammy, J.A.,
312-314

Vegetables,
9, 139-140, 145

Venezuela/Venezuelan,
6, 64, 149, 400, 422, 430, 436

Venn Commission,
383

Vergenoegen,
205, 210

Villages,
16-19, 33, 118, 142, 145, 166, 268, 417-421

    (a)   *Agricola,*
           417-418

    (b)   *Ann's Grove,*
           419

    (c)   *Bagotville,*
           417, 421

    (d)   *Beterverwagting,*
           33, 153, 417-418, 420

    (e)   *Buxton,*
           73, 153, 210, 417

    (f)   *Clonbrook,*
           153

    (g)   *Craig,*
           417

    (h)   *Cumberland,*
           417

    (i)   *Danielstown,*
           417

    (j)   *De Kinderen,*
           417

    (k)   *Den Amstel,*
           417, 419

    (l)   *Fellowship,*
           417, 419

    (m)   *Friendship,*
           33, 417

    (n)   *Good Intent,*
           417

    (o)   *Golden Grove,*
           417

    (p)   *Greenfield,*
           153

    (q)   *Mocha,*
           417, 418

    (r)   *Nabaclis,*
           417

    (s)   *Plaisance,*
           33, 212, 353, 417-419, 428

    (t)   *Port Mourant,*
           301

    (u)   *Queenstown,*
           417

    (v)   *Sisters,*
           417

    (w)   *Sparendam,*
           417

    (x)   *Stanleytown,*
           417

    (y)   *Two Friends,*
           419

    (z)   *Victoria,*
           33

W

Waddington, E.J.,
370, 384-385, 387, 391

Wages,
12, 14-15, 17-18, 30, 42-43, 118, 129, 136, 144-145, 165, 338-341, 343, 346-347, 349, 369, 384, 391

Wai Wai,
25

Wakenaam,
13, 20

Walcott, Clyde,
289-290, 314, 326

Walker, George,
199

Wallbridge, Edwin,
89

Walsh, Courtney,
325

Wapisianas,
25

Warraus,
25, 148, 424

Wedgery, Edward (Mr. & Mrs.),
199

Weekes, Everton,
289-290, 326, 330

Wieting and Richter,
157

Wellington,
297

Wesley, John & Charles,
169

West Bank Demerara,
184, 190-191, 211, 217, 417

West Coast Berbice,
13, 65, 278-279

West Coast Demerara,
97, 135, 153, 184, 190-191, 285, 383, 417, 426

West Demerara,
89, 101

West Indian Agricultural Conference,
8-9

West Indies Cricket Tours to:

    (a) Australia,
    303, 306-308, 315

    (b) England,
    288, 309, 315-316, 332, 334-335

    (c) India,
    303-304, 329

    (d) New Zealand,
    315

    (e) Pakistan,
    317

INDEX

(f) *South Africa,*
 322, 328-330

West Indies Federation,
368-369, 375-376, 378, 399

Westmaas, Rory,
373

Whim,
13

Whites,
6-8, 12, 14, 19-20, 23, 29, 31-33, 45, 47-49, 51-54, 57-58, 60-61, 64, 67, 69, 73-74, 77, 86-89, 94-96, 99, 102-103, 135, 170-171, 173-175, 179, 181, 183-184, 186, 188, 192, 195, 201, 207, 213, 220, 229, 233, 338, 364, 408-411, 413, 418, 430

Wight, Leslie,
395-396

Wight, Norman,
307

Wight, Vibart,
314

Wilberforce, William,
96, 113

Williams, Denis,
267

Williams, Elsworth,
212

Williams, Eric,
117, 252

Williams, Stuart,
439

Windward Islands,
298, 356

Wisden Cricketers' Almanack,
326, 357

Wong, Sergeant,
202

Women,
8, 14-15, 206, 216, 269, 274

Women's Political and Economic Organization,
432

Woolley, Charles,
239, 368

Working People's Alliance,
253, 434-435

World War I,
137, 139-140, 263, 282, 294-295, 342

World War II,
155-156, 269, 282, 288, 295, 332, 359, 365-367, 369, 395

Worrell, Frank,
306-307, 330

Wray, (Rev. John),
76, 80-82, 169, 172-190, 194, 220, 409-411, 426

Wray (Mrs.),
180, 220

Wright, Edward,
20, 276, 281-283, 293-294, 429

Wyatt (Rev.),
94

Z

Zealand,
41, 125, 422, 423

Zimbabwe,
322

Printed in Great Britain
by Amazon